HOW TO MUTATE AND TAKE OVER THE WORLD

R·U· SIRIUS & ST· JUDE

BALLANTINE BOOKS
NEW YORK

All rights reserved under International and Pan-
American Copyright Conventions. Published in the
United States by Ballantine Books, a division of
Random House, Inc., New York, and simultaneously in
Canada by Random House of Canada Limited, Toronto.

Grateful acknowledgment is made to Simon & Schuster
and AP Watt Ltd. for permission to reprint an
excerpt from "Sailing to Byzantium" from *The Poems
of W. B. Yeats: A New Edition,* edited by Richard J.
Finneran. Copyright © 1928 by Macmillan Publishing
Company, renewed 1956 by Georgie Yeats.

Library of Congress Cataloging-in-Publication Data

Sirius, R. U., 1952–
    How to mutate and take over the world/
  R. U. Sirius & St. Jude.—1st ed.
      p.   cm.
    ISBN 0-345-39216-7
    I. St. Jude. II. Title.
  PS3569.I72H68 1996
  813'.54—dc20   95-26182
                                          CIP

Text Design by Alex Jay/Studio J

Manufactured in the United States of America

First Edition: February 1996

10 9 8 7 6 5 4 3 2 1

S-F
SIRIUS,
R.U.

TABLE OF CONTENTS

```
##############
#___/==$=\_     # <- From the High-Tech Fully Elec-
# /))-00(\      #    tronic Desk of R. U. Sirius
# ((( -)))      #
# )))\ /(((     # -> rusirius@well.com
##############
```

Date: Dec 21, 2000
From: rusirius
To: hyatt@ballantine.books.com

Trudy-0
this is Jude, signing onto R. U.'s account. He is not around, so I
thought I'd tidy up his .mailrc for him.

There's been a little problem. We've been set back a week. R.U.'s
run into yet another extreme situation. An extreme situation is
not that unusual for him, right, but this is . . . *more* extreme.

Got your enote. Yes, we all know we're over the latest deadline by 3 months, but after six years I think we have to face it: missed deadlines are NOT unusual. And this time, lovey, we're talking FINAL DELIVERY.

really: FINAL DELIVERY.

You see, R. U. was just getting ready to give the manuscript the last once-over. He had it with him, in fact, when the horrible thing happened. He'd gone to pick up his girlfriend Psycho Stār after work, at the Mitchell Brother Theater (legend has it that once there were *two* Brothers Mitchell . . .) R. U. and Psycho S were just inside the front doors, in the little lobby there, chatting with another dancer, Tiffany, getting ready to leave, when it happened.

    The doors bash open, there's a shout, and everybody turns to the doors just in time to see -- oh shit, it's Josephine, and she's got an automatic rifle cradled against her big baglady bosom, and she's screaming "TIME TO GO TO HELL, SIRIUS."

It's so unreal that nobody moves . . . no diving for the floor, no nothing: they just stand there and look, while Josephine, this nut who's been stalking R. U. since 1997, recites a poem. R. U. hates poetry, but he's just standing there while Josephine rants in blank verse, jogging the gun up and down with the fucking iambic, until she gets to the end . . . many many feet later, you bet. It's something about how she and he will be united forever in the Ether, or maybe it was in thee, either . . . something . . . She has a weird accent. Then she sort of nods her head, like "okay, that's that," raises the gun and blasts four shots point blank.

CONTRIBUTORS' TABLE OF CONTENTS

One shot nicked the top off R. U.'s right ear: he says it was like somebody slapping him on the side of the head. Two rounds hit nothing.

The fourth went straight into Psycho's mid-brain. Dead center forehead hit . . . right in her third-eye tattoo: heh: it was a 3rd *bulls*eye. heeheeheeeee

R. U. says it was such a perfect hit that Psycho's head just sort of opened up like a hatch, and her brain flopped onto the floor like a peeled cantaloupe. Josephine drops the rifle, looks at Sirius and says, "Jesus, you ARE a lucky sod."

Josephine sits down heavily on the floor, away from the little brooklet of blood now babbling down toward the doors, and starts going through her bags, muttering that she has something apropos to this whole thing that she'd like to read, she wrote it some time ago . . . it's right here somewhere . . . R. U. looks at Psycho twitching and sort of smiling on the floor, looks at

Josephine, looks up at the ceiling, and starts humming to him-self . . . THEN Tiffany flips -- begins to scream and scream, and people rush out from backstage, and it's complete bedlam.

In the chaos Sirius walks over to Josephine and tells her that he'd like to invite her out for a drink to talk things over, but she'll have to wait around for the police, and he's gotta finish the final reading of this book he's working on for Ballantine, so ciao.

Psycho died fairly soon -- sooner than you'd think, given her history -- smiling a sweet sweet smile the whole time. Funny thing. R. U.'s been trying to figure out how to ditch Psycho Stär for the last few months and several times he was muttering about finding a hitman. You might wonder why he didn't just break up with her. You don't know Psycho. She wouldn't go away.

Anyway, he went home that night and did the final proof on about half the book, didn't even call me. The following afternoon he called, and for ten minutes he just raved about how great the book was, before telling me, "something sorta weird happened last night." As he described the incident he couldn't stop laughing. R. U. always sees the humor in accidents . . . it's what I love about him. Anyway, he said that he was going to read the rest of the book (this was yesterday) and send it off to you the next day (Today!). "What the hell," I thought. Never cared much for Stãr. R. U. and his hysterical femmes. Sheesh. But then at midnight I got a call from his drinking buddy, Dave Vigliano. R. U. had had a few drinks and then broke out the Forget It! He said R. U. got this strange look on his face and popped six caps all at once. Then he looked even stranger and just tipped the whole bottle down his throat. Sluiced it all down with great glugs of scotch straight from the bottle. Goddess, that's disgusting: what a pig he can be. You know how I hate alcohol. Anyway, Vig wasn't too alarmed at that -- R. U.'s got such a monster tolerance for Forget It! that a usual dose won't even make him absent-minded . . . He can take six and still find his KEYS.

Anyway, he's sitting there in Vigliano's apartment looking (yes) bemused -- and then he starts picking up lamps and match-books and doilies and asking, "What's this? What's this here?" Vig is about to flip -- This is idiotic even for R. U., and he's thinking about Emergency Rooms, and suddenly R. U. lurches out of his chair, points out the door and shouts, "What's THAT?" And he was gone.

So he's around somewhere, having an out-of-brain experience. Vig says the last time he did a whole bottle of Forget It!, he snapped out of it in five days. That would be nice. But just in case, I've got his personality loaded into an expert system that I can crank up. It can finish reading the book and sign off on it *for* him. If the bastard doesn't get his brain up and running within the week, I'll run Cyb-RU for you, and you've got your final delivery, no problem. In fact, if he STAYS encrypted this time, we could strap him down and go for a total replacement. . . .

Hey. That means he'd become his image for real: R. U. SIRIUS!!! crazed Chairman-Mao King-Hip Poster Boy of the new an-archo-wanko-dada, doo-dah doo-dah . . . Starting out with a clean set of megalomemories, instead of the horrible lowlife past that must haunt his every thought as is (except when he's on Forget It!, of course). Hmmm, now that I think about it, maybe I'd be doing the poor bastard a favor. I could do it anyway. Just terminate the fucker -- replace him with his fantasy self, R. U. SIRIUSLY. What do you think? I'll leave it up to you. Save us a few days at the very least. And I sure could use the 17K!

OPERATING INSTRUCTIONS FOR AN EXPLODED POST-NOVEL

This is not a novel.
Don't think you can just hold your nose and jump into this.
You might get boiled . . . or vaporized. Anodized.
THIS IS NOT A NOVEL.

Before you start reading an exploded post-novel, you should think strategy.

First, since your attention span is going to be challenged, we advise you to buy several copies of this book and scatter them around in your life—certainly in your bedroom, bathroom, kitchen. When your eye falls upon a copy, you can fall upon it yourself. But delicately—someday it may be valuable.

While we do recommend reading this book from front to back—left to right—you can skip around as you please. It is disguised as a scrapbook. You can channelsurf it. Or graze through sections, munch munch munch. After you acquire the taste you'll feel strong enough to start at the beginning and read through to the end, in precisely that order. Don't take too much at one sitting. Do not overdose. It's dense, fast. Things get technical. There's a relentless quality to the first-person narrative that may exhaust you secondhand. Read only until the vertigo overwhelms you. When you find yourself crying out, "For god's sake, give it a break!!!" . . . well, exactly. Put the book down . . . gently. Rest. Watch TV. Read *Ben is Dead.* Go somewhere watery and lie in the hard radiation. Read a non-exploded novel. Take up crime. Then . . .

Read a little at a time. Swallow it slowly like crème brûlée. Or hold it in your cheek like Copenhagen Smokeless. But do not rush. If you go slowly enough, by the time you're done the made-for-TV movie will be out. Starring Steven Seagal as R. U. Sirius and Whoopi Goldberg as St. Jude.

Keep this book out of the reach of children. We're talking revolution. Don't try this at home. Well, maybe . . . but HEAR THIS. If you suddenly feel a violent apocalyptic act coming on, and you think we've inspired you . . . DON'T DO IT! We are revolutionists, yes, but we're talking about Dada revolution, *conceptual* revolution, VIRTUAL REVOLUTION. There's nothing revolutionary about killing yr

•¿¿¿•From the Electron-Chocked Desk of Jude Milhon•¿¿¿•
•¿¿¿¿¿¿¿¿¿¿¿¿•   •aka StJude•   •¿¿¿¿¿¿¿¿¿¿¿¿•
•¿¿¿¿¿¿¿¿¿¿¿¿•   •stjude@well.com•   •¿¿¿¿¿¿¿¿¿¿¿¿•
Date: 18 July 2001
Subject: ugh

Ken,
WHERE DID YOU GET THIS? WHY DON'T YOU PUT IT BACK?
This is one of the scungiest tricks we ever pulled on Ballantine. I don't think we should give this to Trudy for the book. Reminding them of . . . that . . . is not helpful. It's a sensitive topic, nimrod -- we gots another deadline crisis, right now, right right? Trudy's a saint, a fucking saint . . . as editors go . . . but she's got her limits.

fellow primates. Fragging them to tartare is absolutely standard. Old style. Passé. It's revolution-ary NOT to kill primates in your bloody revolution. Yes, we're talking to YOU. That's right, you with the microchip in your sphincter. No, not down there. We're up here in the black helicopter. Hahahah . . . *sucker*.

Heh, it's funny though -- killing off girlfriends was a good ploy. Did they ever believe it, or were they just nursing us along? You know, our best work has gone into moshing deadlines. We kill 'em . . . then they reve-nate -- RETURN OF THE UNDEADLINES! -- and we could make a book out of that shtick, but christ on a bike, we better not. hide it from trudy. deep-six the documentation.

btw, this is a weird edit -- I'm nancily crocheting your UNIX environment for you at the beginning, and at the end I'm grunting like a cornerback. You made me say sheesh, which is fucking ridiculous -- i've never said sheesh in my whole life, you moron, and the technology at the end is complete bullshit. Did it go to trudy in this form?

Yet Ballantine hasn't scrapped our scrapbook. Hard to believe.

gah.
>jude<

PART ONE
SEX &
DRUGS
& DATA
ENCRYPTION

PRELUDE: 1994
HOW, WHEN, WHERE AND WHY MUTATE?

January 2002:
R. U. Sirius' Diary
Introduction to the Scrapbook

We've made history . . . scratch that . . . We've made hirstory? Or . . . lessee. We've unmade his-tory. Hmmm, not bad . . . naaah. Whatever.

We've made a scrapbook. (That, at least, is certain.) Some of you may recall seeing your par-ents' or grandparents' scrapbooks. Well, ya know, we're kinda old ourselves. Old enough to be your . . . (lecherous grin) . . . Nevermind.

Listen heah young'un, if ya read this scrapbook (wheeze) you'll learn some secrets of techno-vampirism, maybe get a taste of some *real* immortality, with smelly, bodily sex even. (I know. I'm *such* a reactionary.) I mean, now that y'all got these slick, super-complex biologically-based hy-permedia databases, and the neural netheads and the nanotechies are hoping to give them an in-telligent consciousness any day now . . . now that you arrogant young fucks are about to put your experiences, memories and personal information onto infinitely replicable intelligent biologi-cal software and, in some sense, crack the mortality problem, well . . . you don't really give a fuck about the Old Species now do ya?

Take pity! Not on us, mind you. We've made *our* Faustian pacts. But think of your very own grandpappy and grandma, and quite possibly your mom and pop. They never even got to Netscape, never mind cracking the navigational language of the bio/hm/dbs. For them, immortal-ity is achieved only through *you* . . . and perhaps through their scrapbooks, where pictures and memoirs might be handed down through the ages.

Yeah, it's pathetic. I know. Obviously, if you solipsistic little bastards bother with their stuff at all, you'll just scan it and slot it in under Genetic Makeup, Personal. And let your electronics remember it.

Oh well. The old coots really weren't that interesting, were they? I mean . . . Eisenhower? Korea? Leave it to Beaver? American Bandstand? The Beatniks? Or maybe—Woodstock, the Beatles and the Stones, Kent State. You've heard quite enough of *their* story, haven't you? And didn't we just barely make it out the other end of their wimpout presidency?

In fact, take a look at *their* scrapbook, why dontcha. Whatta ya got? Sure, a few hairy mo-ments protesting. Then the shot from the seventies; dad looking like a fucking clown with his silk shirt open to the navel and a coke spoon around his neck. Mom in bell bottoms and a tube top looking 'luded up and fucked out. Cheesy, right? And then . . . they settled down *completely*. Af-ter that it's mostly vacation pictures. That's a quick study. They went to some places. They stood around in funny clothes. They took pictures of themselves to document that they were there. And *this* was the most important thing in their lives. Their scrapbooks tell us so.

So now, here *we* are with this silly archaic thing, this non-digital artifact of a slice of al-leged history just passed. What's *our* excuse? Fuck, man. What do you think? Somehow we've been declared the Leaders of the Revolution by the mainstream media. Hah hah . . . dontcha just *hate* us . . .

Ok. You and I know that Ballantine Books must have bribed a few people. *Quite* a few. And we know that the real Edge people will probably browse this puppy, scan a few of the better jokes, and restructure the molecules back into tree. That's fine. But you might as well check this overview of what lies ahead . . .

IN THIS SCRAPBOOK YOU WILL FIND:

Beginning in 1994, we've selected various hard newspaper and magazine clippings and text from online publications involving ourselves, people we worked with, members of MONDO VANILLI, etc. But we've also clipped stuff that just plain interested us, ranging from the political battles of our times to the technological developments—and most of all—the flat-out spectacle of human perversity. You will find diary notes from both St. Jude and myself (we both kept irregular diaries), email between ourselves and other people, our own published works, lyrics and product designs from my band, MONDO VANILLI, et cetera. *And* you will find all sorts of notes from the underground. Revolutionary tactics and hijinx brought to life. Since this revolution has no time to look back, we've scraped this together. We've picked what we can from the debris we've collected. This is as close to *Ten Days that Shook the World* [obscure reference . . . ? do name search] as it's gonna get.

Finally, do you mind if I wax a bit earnest on ya for a moment? Long ago, and far away, before the Nanotech faction of the Hassan I Sirius Revolutionary Brigade turned *Newt* Gingrich into a *toad* and smoked up all dem toxins, there was a (you'll forgive the term) serious situation that demanded a response. A gang—maybe even a majority—of stupid, fearful, American primates reacted to the inevitable chaos brought about by technologically assisted species mutation by attempting to impose authoritarian values and laws on the communications juggernaut. An even larger majority, having never been educated in future history, tried to impose a Calvinist work ethic and zero-sum economics on a cybernetic society. They succeeded only in snatching poverty out of the jaws of abundance. But we *kicked* they asses and we *tricked* they asses.

And now, here we are, on the threshold of a dream. Hmm, think I'll go celebrate with a nice slice of key lime pie. Toodles . . .

St. Jude's Introduction to the Scrapbook:
How to Mutate and Take Over the World!

How to Mutate and Take Over the World?
Okay, after I explain that, what do you want me to talk about?

All RIGHT: mutating and taking over the world . . . It's easy to figure out how and why, when you look at the history of our species: our own primate troop, the humans . . . <theme music comes up> We'll look at how we've been mutating so far . . .

Now, don't worry if my analysis is a little simplistic. That's the style nowadays: sound bites, synopses, very mechanistic. The times are like that—cause-effect, gene blueprints, engineering über alles, yeah yeah. OKAY, cut us some SLACK. Maybe we NEED a little simplicity. We've had a tough century here. So we just got through watching the sun set on the Age of Ideology, but keep your eyes on the ball: this is the dawning of the Age of Vulgar Empiricism, and let's get on with it. As I was saying:

Up to a point human evolution was physical: genes mutated and then got selected in or died out. Better bodies made the cut, and what worked better replaced the older stuff. No problem. But for the last fifty thousand years human bodies have changed only a little. Since then, any advances have come from the analogous process: cultural evolution. IDEAS mutated and then got selected in or out. Same as with the body: what works tends to remain, and what works better MAY supplant the older tech, the older ideas. But cultural selection is a tricky thing. It can be enforced—literally, by force. This newfangled stuff may work better for you, but it's against the Gods . . . so if you insist on doing it that way we'll have to kill you.

Today the gods are less vigilant, maybe, but the vigilantes are still on patrol. The political full spectrum, left, right, and moebius, are on full alert even as we speak, looking to stomp flat any new green shoots. No mutations allowed.

WHY MUTATE?
Do I really need to answer that?

HOW TO MUTATE?
Well, for us, cultural mutation should be easy: we got the channels, we got the megalomedia, we got the cross-fertilization. Ideas . . . happen. The more ideas the better. And by the evolution analogy, the wider all these ideas get spread around, the better. Nowadays we have to make an effort to STOP an idea from dispersing. But we still need more, better and cheaper ways to disperse them:

Multicast: the Net. Everybody talking to everybody. Instantly. Cheap.

Multitech: the reverse of mass production and standardization. Instead of being forced to buy item A, item ALT-A, or item A-COOL from the three biggest companies, you choose what you exactly want from among a thousand compatible flavors. A money-making operation could be one nerd online in half a garage. Think of it as the upside of Balkanization.

Multi-arts: like writing something and selling it online, direct to your readers. Instead of selling it to a big corporation which will rewrite it a dozen times, change the plot, the characters, the title, and make it into a movie starring Keanu Reeves.

Obstacle stomping: no censorship. None. Let the rotten stuff rot as it will. The only reason the straights are worried about bad influences is that there are no GOOD influences nowadays. (We could do something about that, too. Think about it.) And you ever think about what education COULD be? The mind just starts *quivering* . . .

HOW TO MUTATE . . . AND TAKE OVER THE WORLD?

And this idea—consciously mutating, and taking over the world—well, if you've got that idea, and you want to do it . . . then you just tell other people about it . . . and here we are. Aren't we?

Okay, on with the show. This book is supposed to seed the idea of conscious mutation. But it's more than that. This book is high art. It's the incarnation of a new form: you're holding here in your hands an exploded post-novel. We can tell you this candidly. If you're writing a review for this, that's what this is. We're also marketing it as a pre-deconstructed post-novel. We will do all the crit for you. You just lie there and try to enjoy it. We will help you because we NEED to be high-critted. We need to be argued over; we want to provoke duels, intradepartmental incidents, career assassinations. Wherever people are packin' syllabi, we want to be there. Ballantine is with us: we got backup.

These Ballantine people are nuts. They think that we are purée of Pynchon, Gibson, Mark Leyner and Douglas Adams???? Shit, they forgot Borges, Poe, and Hegel. These Ballantine guys have gotta be the idiot-saints of publishing. These Ballantine . . . Oh gods, let's try to make them happy: bring on the scrapbook. Onward into the past. Let's have some completely irrelevant flashbacks:

St. Jude's Diary, Spring 1994

Dig, this Spring the Zeitgeist is dealing with primate craziness in a retro flavor: The Rabble Rising. Yeah, that again. Robert Kaplan in the *Atlantic* quails at a Road-Warrior future rattling down on us in "The Coming Anarchy." The media are chewing on it. Only . . . when the Zeitgeist utters, the media never quite catch the words. Anarchy is a *system*. They mean ANOMIE, which is no systems allowed—one for one and all for none, and why not? Pretty scary, dudes: no ideologies, no ideals, no ideas, no future. (It works for me . . . I am your own worst Anomie.)

But it ain't so. I do stand for stuff. I believe in the future, the fictoidal Future. Millennium's coming, kiddies. And this time we know the Messiah will not blow us off. Because this time . . . He's . . . Technology.

It goes like this. Over most of the planet, life is not very rewarding, and it's certainly not very valuable. If we don't have anything else, we can have FUN. Hey, guns are fun. [Even *I* know this.] Getting crazy is fun too—swallow some chemicals, some alcohol, or just stir up your own internal mix: a little rage, some fear and lust, then let's see what we do. We know that messing with people who reputedly wanna mess with us is LOTS of fun. And hey, what CAN a person do? We're just people, and we need to have fun.

Kaplan says the well-educated, well-meaning people at the negotiating table may sign their agreements . . . but anything they reason or good-intention together will be blown away by the man in the street . . . the one with a grudge and a gun. And lots of buddies.

There are all kinds of negative trends coming on right now, on top of Kaplan's gloomy elitism. Got yer overpopulation, global warming and concomitant droughts, got effluents and lousy distribution and resource scarcity. Then you've got the *tribalism*. That's when very real subsets of bogus "nations" fuck with borders drawn on the map by colonial types. Add all THAT concomitant fun—and altogether the 3rd World, 4th and 5th Worlds and the rest of Steerage will sink with all hands aboard.

And it isn't only the Other Worlders who will snuff it. The American underclass sinks too. The great unemployed, *which includes your boho pals, n.b.* Slackers make a posture out of their position, but the fact is, we're all lucky to get paid for *anything*. If you're into breeding, you're pre-screwed: how you gonna feed your spawn? But of course the real agony is that we can't do much that has plain old nonmonetary VALUE. [Hmm; this is a protracted whine, innit?]

But wait: even in these value-debilitated times some people feel good about what they do. Serial killers seem to have a sense of vocation. Some whores do. Revolutionists too. (This may indicate that there's an intrinsic value to death, sex, and hope. We're simple people, primates.) But it's a hard decision—which of the three would I really wanta be if I grow up?

This has gotta be the low point on the 12-step graph. Fuck this: I'm going to bed.

April 1, 1994: Sun and I grunt at each other. Morning all. Enough sniveling. It's our day, fool! Wake up: time to make the revolution!!

Naah: I'm going back to sleep . . .

April 4, 1994: I've just read over these notes. I think it's PROZAC time . . . I've ripped my psyche with all kinds of chemical contraband. Why cavil at a prescription? Just gotta find a Dr Feelgood again . . .

April 19, 1994

1: The flyer for the talk starts like this:

WHEN CRYPTOGRAPHY IS OUTLAWED, ONLY

XUMWEER SNOEYKQ IJPQRGM PZIEBTCC

And the speaker (what a coincidence: it's my boyfiend, Eric Hughes!), is billed as "renowned cypherpunk . . ." Nya ha ha: this seems so . . . natural. As if the term Cypherpunk weren't something I made up ten minutes ago. Well, it was October 1992. Almost yesterday.

The past, present, and future have never been so moshed together. And since the future seems closer, it seems more malleable. The future is the ultimate plastic medium, for us sculptor wannabes. And we're going to hammer the hell out of it.

Hmm. Did I say that? I think the Zoloft must be cutting in. Prozac's sweet twin; psychic aspartame. (I feel rather GOOD.) At last, drug abuse pays off!

April 20, 1994: Yesterday I even cleaned my office some, and in a composting pilefile I found this, from 1992:

```
= = = = = = = = = = = = = = = = = = = = = = = = = = = = = = = = = = = = = = = = = = = = = = = = = = =
From: tcmay@netcom.com (Timothy C. May)
Subject: Crypto Anarchist Manifesto
Jude,
Here it is. If you introduce it (with a few words), all I ask is that
you indicate it was written in 1988, so people won't think I just
copied some of the stuff now beginning to seriously float around . . .
others have even begun to pick up on the term "crypto anarchy."
This is a historical document relating to the future. The Manifesto
was written in 1988, three years before a physical meeting in Oak-
land, California convened the Cypherpunk Movement.
```

The Crypto Anarchist Manifesto
```
Timothy C. May
tcmay@netcom.com

A spectre is haunting the modern world, the spectre of crypto anarchy.

Computer technology is on the verge of providing the ability for
individuals and groups to communicate and interact with each other
in a totally anonymous manner. Two persons may exchange messages,
conduct business, and negotiate electronic contracts without ever
knowing the True Name, or legal identity, of the other. Interac-
tions over networks will be untraceable, via extensive re-routing
of encrypted packets and tamper-proof boxes which implement crypto-
graphic protocols with nearly perfect assurance against any tamper-
ing. Reputations will be of central importance, far more important
in dealings than even the credit ratings of today. These develop-
ments will alter completely the nature of government regulation,
the ability to tax and control economic interactions, the ability
```

to keep information secret, and will even alter the nature of trust
and reputation.

The technology for this revolution -- and it surely will be both a
social and economic revolution -- has existed in theory for the
past decade. The methods are based upon public-key encryption,
zero-knowledge interactive proof systems, and various software protocols for interaction, authentication, and verification. The focus
has until now been on academic conferences in Europe and the U.S.,
conferences monitored closely by the National Security Agency.
But only recently have computer networks and personal computers
attained sufficient speed to make the ideas practically realiz-
able. And the next ten years will bring enough additional speed to
make the ideas economically feasible and essentially unstoppable.
High-speed networks, ISDN, tamper-proof boxes, smart cards, satellites, Ku-band transmitters, multi-MIPS personal computers, and
encryption chips now under development will be some of the enabling
technologies.

The State will of course try to slow or halt the spread of this
technology, citing national security concerns, use of the technology by drug dealers and tax evaders, and fears of societal disintegration. Many of these concerns will be valid; crypto anarchy will
allow national secrets to be traded freely and will allow illicit
and stolen materials to be traded. An anonymous computerized market
will even make possible abhorrent markets for assassinations and
extortion. Various criminal and foreign elements will be active
users of CryptoNet. But this will not halt the spread of crypto
anarchy.

Just as the technology of printing altered and reduced the power
of medieval guilds and the social power structure, so too will
cryptologic methods fundamentally alter the nature of corporations and of government interference in economic transactions.
Combined with emerging information markets, crypto anarchy will
create a liquid market for any and all material which can be put
into words and pictures. And just as a seemingly minor invention
like barbed wire made possible the fencing-off of vast ranches
and farms, thus altering forever the concepts of land and property rights in the frontier West, so too will the seemingly minor
discovery out of an arcane branch of mathematics come to be the
wire clippers which dismantle the barbed wire around intellectual
property.

Arise, you have nothing to lose but your barbed-wire fences!

....
Timothy C. May | Crypto Anarchy: encryption, digital money,
tcmay@netcom.com | anonymous networks, digital pseudonyms, zero
408-688-5409 | knowledge, reputations, information markets,
W.A.S.T.E.: Aptos, CA | black markets, collapse of governments.
Higher Power: 2^756839 | PGP Public Key: by arrangement.

——>8 cut here 8<——
Jeez, that brings it back. Our first meeting, all of us sitting around on the wall-to-wall in Eric's empty suburban house. The only furnishings were the flags that Tim brought: the ragged rasta freedom flag and the Jolly Roger, tacked up on opposite walls—to the discomfort or disgust of about a quarter of the meeters . . . ewwww, *outlaw stuff,*

I did my bit: I named us. The name hit me like a meteorite, one morning while I was washing my cat. At the second physical meeting I proposed it: we should be known as . . . Cypher-punks. With a Y. They picked up on it instantly. Laughing, cheers. Acclamation. Talk of instant T-shirts. Promises, promises . . .

. . . Makes me feel a right geezer to be dropping me own name like this . . . Nyih hih, sonny . . . Geeze on . . .

= =
Sept 12, 1994
From: StJude
To: rusirius
Subject: What's Left?

R.U.,
Articles in the SF Comicle on the resurgence of the Left in Europe. Holy Shit! What IS Left? Well, you can keep your good heart, but forget about the oldstyle handouts 'cause the Welfare State is gone, screw the poor, and while yr at it, screw the industrial working class. The industries have gone virtual -- we've noticed -- and any- way, we're PISSED OFF at the poor and the formerly-working class. They weren't there for us when we needed them for revolutionary purposes, so scroom. Scroom. No central planning in the old way, no gobliment taking over defaultwise, even. And that reminds me, you have to accept capitalism as your personal savior -- 'cause capital- ism is the best we can do in the enlightened-self-interest dept.

I love it. Don't you love it? You DON'T??

Well, I think it's cunning, how a thesis keeps on generating an anti-thesis in spite of its being unfashionable . . . How an extremities-amputating Centrism keeps on re-budding a Left limb.

And it would be nice if SOME tendency would pretend to be concerned about a human use for human beings. People DO like to do things occasionally, not just sit around. And it could make our lives nicer to DO stuff [Quality of Life is getting some Press now] -- life could be more interesting, more than just yr standard 1st-world diorama: family sitting around with curtains on the windows, with a modem, not dying of cholera. If we're underemployed [and I AM underemployed], is it because there's really nothing that NEEDS doing, just relax?

Well then, we've come to the point where human society is just a shape-up crew which the entrepreneurs draw upon for their occasional projects. The rest of the time we can watch sports or hang out on USENET? [Hey, I'M a 49ers fan, as you know.]

So there's finally an answer to the Left-ies' old question, What is to be done? And the answer is: Nothing right at the moment, check back next week?

grrr.

•¿¿¿•From the Electron-Chocked Desk of Jude Milhon•¿¿¿•
•¿¿¿¿¿¿¿¿¿¿•   •aka StJude•   •¿¿¿¿¿¿¿¿¿¿•
•¿¿¿¿¿¿¿¿¿¿•   •stjude@well.com•   •¿¿¿¿¿¿¿¿¿¿•
Date: 14 Aug 1994
To: rusirius
Subject: who is trudy, that all the Ballantine editors commend her?

well, trudy -- she's andover-brown, and since she said it just like that -- "andover-brown" -- i knew it was a code. andrew/drude (stpaul's-harvard) decoded it for me: it means her Mummy and Dadda are very Rich, for starts. (Andover.) And maybe Righter than Hitler. (Brown.)

She seems very nice. She'll help us make a book here. Relax. We'll subvert her.

We got us all this rebellious energy. We're all so forking clever, and we spend ourselves just sniping at the project managers. What a stupid waste. Underemployed? Join the revolution then, why not?

In fact . . .

how about we invent . . . the Dada Revolution? A fun sort of blood-less coup against all that is.

You and me, we grew up with the idea that humor is subversive. (So did everybody in Eastern Europe, now that I think about it.) Jeez, that means there was a secret force in the Cold war -- the same Fifth Column on both sides.

Squeaky voice: "Army InTELLigence? Gee, Bullwinkle, isn't that a contradiction in terms?"

Now that it's obvious that organized or chaotic brutality continues to be a factor in everyprimate's life . . . And now that the violence can't be stopped -- break it up, you kids! -- by the imaginary alpha-primates, God and the State, some kind of intervention is overdue . . . Let us suggest it's past time for . . . the 23rd International: The Dada Revolution!

If we can't have sanity, we can fake it with humor. Humor gives you the same distance from the situation, the same metaview, only laughing is easier than sanity and possibly more fun.

So let's embrace Dada, the only surviving ideology of the century that trained us to hate ideologies. Death to slogans! Long live Dada! I like it.

Wanta join?

[I'm not asking YOU. I know YOU.]

Let's write a manifesto, posthaste and forthwith!

cheer-O
>jude<

= =
Sept 14, 1994
From: StJude
To: rusirius
Subject: Marian the Libertarian

I just got into a fight with somebody and maybe I won, but I came up with this:

Cyber-Anarchists are always moaning about the disappearance of the commons -- the unfenced spaces in which free people can roam unfettered, imaginatively, as they may . . . but commons are more common now than ever in history. Just look at these lovely commons:

community vegetable gardens, like the old commons
public museums of all kinds (only since 1700s)
wilderness areas ... yeah i know, but nevertheless commons
public libraries that also lend tools, diskettes, videos.

Hey -- and the museums and libraries are now connecting to each
other, and we are connecting to everything, via the Internet. This
means the commons are all connecting into a HUGE commons ...
and it's called ... THE NET!!

World Wide Web is just a technological placeholder. Netting may start
out crude. But connectivity will get better and easier. And then
everybody will do it -- everyone will make use of the greatest of
commons, and take it completely for granted.

Are we sure? SURE!!
(At this point I ranted post-Malthusian assurances that as population
grows geometrically, electronic tech grows hypergeometrically, which
may be true. Think of the mythical Moore constant, which has computing power doubling and price halving every 18 months. It's pretty to
think so.)

And I loaded on the aphorisms:
We shall know the info, and the info shall make us free.
... But first the info will free itself, because it really really
wants to. ... etc)
= =
Sept 15, 1994
From: isataafl@never.never.lan
To: stjude
Subject: Free lunch wins!

————————BEGIN PGP SIGNED MESSAGE————————

Notes from Under The Solar Panels, Or
or, <how many other russian novels do i remember?>

Hey Jude,

I just went by my ex-girlfriend's to pick up my next-to-last, yea
indeed penultimate unemployment check. Doesn't matter to me yet,
'cause I've saved nearly every penny of every check to date. Except
for the Zoloft scrips I don't spend money. If I could scam the

scrips I'd be home free. Hmm: home-free. Sounds phuq of alot better than homeless.

Hey: but I got m' keys, got my passwords, got my chart of the guard's rounds, and I am now speaking excellent Spanish with the night cleanup crew. I sleep just fine on wall-to-wall carpet -- never the same office twice, no messing with leaving a pheromone trail -- and the GigaFirm has showers.

So during the day I'm just another anonymous sweatsuited consultant banging a laptop on a comfy couch in the vast wide-open-plan spaces of my ex-employer. No sweat about being recognized here. Everybody I worked with was downsized or outsourced. EVERYBODY got the chop, programmers, designers, muddle management. It was like a hostile nontakeover. Or an economic ethnic cleansing.

But I'm literally hanging in there. Nobody else did it, although everybody had their chance. I was bold and cunning, as us nerds are known to be. I duplicated keys, collected passwords, scoped out a few handy facts, and here I stay. I cannot otherwise. Too true.

I'm probably better nourished on the company's organic nerd-fodder than when I was opening a beer for dinner at noon after working all night . . . besides which, I don't have to work at all. Yes, I am successfully retired at twenty-two.

Frankly, that's not as great as you might think. If it weren't for the Net I'd be sunk. I'm living online, really; I'm living a virtually virtual life.

Oh well. Don't forget: I've occupied the workplace! I've seized control of the carpets of production!

```
########################################################
#########         • Trudy B. Hyatt •          #########
#########        • Editorial Assistant •       #########
#########     • Hyatt@Ballantine.Books.com •   #########
########################################################
```
Date: 8 Jan, 1995
From: hyatt@ballantine.books.com
To: StJude@well.com
Subject: Free lunch?

I don't understand this thing at all.

Trudy

```
love and revolutionary fervor from your buddy,
isataafl, aka free.lunch

ps: omega is the symbol of resistance to the end:
```

Ω Ω Ω Ω Ω Ω Ω Ω Ω Ω Ω Ω Ω Ω Ω Ω Ω Ω Ω Ω Ω Ω Ω Ω Ω Ω Ω Ω Ω Ω Ω Ω Ω

Ω LIVE FREE or DIE? Uh . . . could I get back to you on that one? Ω

Ω Ω Ω Ω Ω Ω Ω Ω Ω Ω Ω Ω Ω Ω Ω Ω Ω Ω Ω Ω Ω Ω Ω Ω Ω Ω Ω Ω Ω Ω Ω Ω Ω

```
—BEGIN PGP SIGNATURE—
Version: 3.8

iQCVAgUBLlpGQLf5jDqB
noEZAQGwfwP9GtsyIB7S+
zys/Y+8tTx5rCzRqKuNao
wiSPwfSLiz6t5RXnoClwt
Kaw9CFmTBynh1ZmLDgus5
tAqUhj1tVsYGVENulgZiO
AtOnpsBHmxStkhBgzKD3S
ABxEix1hh3CE29M8pWJNp
Aymlas9EY4wCbrMCGgUm4
hx1UIicB5xNLjC0==ZmHM
—END PGP SIGNATURE—
```

St. Jude's Diary
Dec. 12, 1994

Last night I was talking to a Patriot from Florida who assures me that people in the cities have NO idea what's really going on. All we hear is the managed news from the big corporations and the big govt. [I can believe that without really trying.] He says that Rush Limbaugh is just a stooge for the Powers That Be. He said if I want to know what's really happening I

•¿¿¿•**From the Electron-Chocked Desk of Jude Milhon**•¿¿¿•
•¿¿¿¿¿¿¿¿¿¿¿•   •**aka StJude**•   •¿¿¿¿¿¿¿¿¿¿¿•
•¿¿¿¿¿¿¿¿¿¿¿•   •**stjude@well.com**•   •¿¿¿¿¿¿¿¿¿¿¿•
Date: 9 Jan, 1995
From: stjude@well.com
To: hyatt@ballantine.books.com
Subject: Re: Free lunch?

It's easy, yet important. He's living in the corporate offices of his former employee, pretending to be a free-floating worker drone, and losing himself in the faceless mass.

He calls himself isataafl because Robert Heinlein -- libertarian toughguy that he was -- used the term tanstaafl in his future-world fiction. tanstaafl = there ain't no such thing as a free lunch.

See, Silicon Valley has been cleansing itself of full-time employees. The companies did massive firings -- called downsizing, and relied on part-time consulting -- called outsourcing, and phased out -- called obsolescing -- their fulltime employees who demanded health plans and paid vacations and all those other expensive things. This whole area of california became like a hightech shape-up crew -- which is an expression from longshoring i think . . . you hang around on the docks doing nothing until a boss comes up and says: you, you, and yeah, you over there with the muscles, follow me -- i got some bananas to unload. etc.

So Free Lunch made his own adjustments.

He's still around, still doing outrageous stuff . . .

need to get a shortwave radio and TUNE IN. He said the yeoman-farmer paradigm that founded this country is still alive, and all these ur-Patriots are broadcasting nationwide on shortwave. They're currently riled about the right of arms-bearing, because of the law to ban some assault rifles, which is a clear constitutional violation. And the Patriots spread the word on actions, like defending fellow-Patriot Red Beckman from the Feds who wanted to repossess his house for tax evasion, was it? So a rampant line of yeomen, including Bo Gritz—the guy that Rambo was modeled on—got together to patrol Beckman's house armed with soapy mops. They figured it was a good Everyman sort of yeoman image, the mops.

I'm gonna spread the word.

===
Date: Dec 13, 1994
From: StJude
To: SimCere, rusirius
Subject: you know those yeomen i told you about . . .

Well, last night in the small hours I had a nightmare. I dreamed I
was a Federal Marshal sent to repo Red Beckman's house, and out in
front I saw this picket line of rednecky middleaged dudes in para-
military gear, shouting something. The line kind of buckled, and
out burst Bo Gritz, trailing this comet-tail of suds. He came bar-
reling up toward me, only suddenly he was Sylvester himself,
stripped to the waist and sneering like he does, all shiny muscles
and scrolly lips, and he was bracing back to bat my brains out with
his soapy mop, a fairly clear violation of MY civil rights -- so I
shot him on full auto. Like 17, 18 times? Knocked him back about
30 feet, deader than shit. But then all his Patriot buddies dipped
THEIR soapy mops in his blood, and THEY came at me. So I just
smoked 'em all.

God, I woke up in a true cold sweat. What can it mean?

===
Date: Dec 13, 1994
From: simcere
To: StJude, rusirius
Subject: you know those yeomen i told you about . . .

Listen, you got all the symptoms of irony overdose.

Irony's everywhere nowadays, a major polluter. The Gen X-ers are outa
here, but we gotta make them clean up their conceptual toxic spills
when they leave. Pick up that scrap irony, you punks!

Pah.

I know a good 12-step for humor abusers.

love,
simcere

==
Date: Dec 14, 1994
From: stJude
To: rusirius, SimCere
Subject: that DREAM i told you about

Yeoman farmers, uh huh. The Libertarians keep hammering on America
being based on the virtue of the yeoman farmer -- who because he is
independent can afford to be virtuous and moral. For a healthy democracy, you need some healthy personnel . . . [Note nifty paradox: the
founders *decreed* a nation based on free association.]
. . . and if you're setting up a civilization, you need some personnel
you can depend upon. What did they have to recruit from, on this continent? Many farmers, a few nomadic trappers and hunters, and a piti-
ful few urbanites. Nomads don't figure as civilization. And urbanites
are corrupt -- this goes back to the Greeks' and Romans' prejudices --
because they are forced to compromise themselves. To live and work
amid such dense humanity, they're forced to <gasp> cooperate every
single day! All you got left to depend upon are farmers, virtuous and
free, who are free to ally themselves with other free beings as they
choose. Aha!

But regardless of this demographic rationale, most of the Libertarians I've met are not yeoman farmers. They're programmers.
Engineers. Yeoman technologists, maybe. And they don't want to
become yeoman farmers, no way -- having to live by their crops
and their religion? Is the Pope Amish? If the cities depress them,
they'd really rather head for the hills. In their Jeep Cherokees.
Back to Nomadism. (Libertarians secretly long to live by their wits
and their weapons.)
"A malcontent -- This is one of those old-style fighting men: he has
no love of civilisation, because he thinks the object of civilisation
is to make all the good things of life -- honors, plunder, beautiful
women -- accessible also to cowards."

Who said that? Oh, you know. It's Nietzsche, from DAYBREAK: Thoughts
on the Prejudices of Morality.

Guattari and Deleuze have picked up on nomadism. Intellectuals have always loved the wandering ronin as a metaphor. Wonder how good G&D's reflexes are. Can they shoot straight? Can you?
Do you want to NEED to?
I think civilization IS a good idea, myself.

Hmm. Let's start another one.
= =
Date: Dec 15, 1994
From: stjude
To: rusirius, simcere
Subject: let's have a civilization!

I should stop being so snotty about the Libertarians and Extrophians. They're trying to do the same thing: figure out what comes next. Nomad becomes farmer, farmer becomes urbanite. . . . then urbanite becomes. . . . strain strain . . . Er . . . exurbanite?

Exurbanite is the final stage according to the GrecoRomans: you do big-time merchantry in the city, not retail -- which is despicable because you lie to people to sell them things -- but large-scale import-export trade, which is noble because it makes you think strategically yea globally. And then you retire to the countryside to live independently.

This works for Greeks, Romans, Libertarians. And Extrophians -- telecomputing. The country house is a life-quality step upward from cities nowadays. But what about those stuck in hell city? There's not enough countryside to go around. The next step is not exurbanite. The next step is humane cities. Since this species invented cities we've wanted to swarm there, and forget the fucking farm . . . There are architects and designers who are working on what makes for inhabitable cities.

Yes, once again I can shrug this off -- other techno types are working on it. . . .
= =
Date: Dec 16, 1994
From: rusirius
To: StJude, SimCere
Subject: extrophians

I thought the extrophians wanted to get small and then disappear entirely, speaking entirely in terms of corporeal location mind you . . .

Topic: We ARE Mutating and Taking over the World!
Started by: Judith Milhon (stjude) on Thu, Dec 15 '94
48 responses so far

Consider that we are truly doing what we pretend we're doing: we're
making a scrapbook of our times. We should pack in whatever we want
to preserve, and
whatever we want to
spread around . . .   ##
                       #########   • Trudy B. Hyatt •   #########
The book is a time-   #########   • Editorial Assistant •   #########
capsule, yes -- but   #########   • Hyatt@Ballantine.Books.com •   #########
look out!   ##
it's a time-release   Date: 7 Dec 1995
PSYCHOACTIVE....   To: StJude:
And to get even more   Subject: Is this real?
grandiose: Dear Jude,
The book is a heat-
seeker aimed at the   About this next piece . . .
future.   Was this really online in 1994? Or did you just write it up after the fact?
it will explode high
up and seed the   It seems too perfect to be real, to say the least.
clouds with
self-replicating   Trudy
memes
and so we will take
over ...

TAKE OVER THE WORLD.

But you knew that.

48 responses total.
Topic: We ARE Mutating and Taking over the World!
Judith Milhon (stjude) Thu Dec 15 '94 (07:07)

Since the last several hundred thousand years, almost all the mutation going on around here, in this species, has been cultural. Every
new invention is a cultural mutation ... and so is every new idea.

We've hit a critical mass for information recently, and the cultural
mutation rate is going -- well, it's increasing. the 2nd differential

may be purty steep. With the bandwidth we have now (frustratingly
minuscule as it seems to frustrated techtypes) the idea synthesis is
purty brisk, even for a dull-witted species like ours ...

The idea is, we're mutating already.
Around here, we're mutating like crazy.

Nice.

•¿¿¿•From the Electron-Chocked Desk of Jude Milhon•¿¿¿•
•¿¿¿¿¿¿¿¿¿¿¿• •aka StJude• •¿¿¿¿¿¿¿¿¿¿¿•
•¿¿¿¿¿¿¿¿¿¿¿• •stjude@well.com• •¿¿¿¿¿¿¿¿¿¿¿•

Date: 7 Dec 1995
From: stjude@well.com
To: hyatt@ballantine.books.com
Subject: Too real?

Dear Trudy,

Yes yes, this is archived reality.
It was on the WELL back in 1994. It was the official coming-out of the
crucial meme -- yeah, that is, alteration and planet seizing.

Topic: We ARE Mutating
and Taking over the
World!
proliferating demons
like Lilith (lioness)
Thu Dec 15 '94 (07:16)

And convenient, too.
FOr the mutation-urge,
anyhow.

As long as it doesn't
kill the host organ-
isms, we ought to have
a fine party while it
lasts.

Topic: We ARE Mutating and Taking over the World!
HAIR all AFLUTTER in the Badlands! (scribe.waterfish) Thu Dec 15 '94 (08:29)

    WE don't need to mutate -- they do! And that means a lot of ex-
planations, or maybe it just means A real jolt from complacency,
which means a plan and/or a clear direction, not just for us but
for them ... simple people, primates, but you need to tell 'em
which channels to tune into, which ways to direct their intelligence, which clubs to belong to, what hats to wear, the high-brow
hate to hear this, but fuck it, it's the truth, isnm't that why
everybody and theirt dog hates clinton right now, because the
sonuvabitch actually expects something as arcane as *consensus*
from lower primates -- he needs to act Alpha even if he isn't, and
he won't and they're going to flush him down the toilet of history
because he won't shove an agenda down people's throats. Learn from
his fall -- learn to be extropian-fascists, dammit!

Topic: We ARE Mutating and Taking over the World!
Cranky bob (cb) Fri Dec 16 '94 (09:39)

    is there a disinction between 'mutation' and 'change,' except that
mutation sounds real cool?

Topic: We ARE Mutating and Taking over the World!
RUSirius (rusirius) Fri Dec 16 '94 (11:49)

    change is like what you do with your socks or what bill clinton tries
to accomplish. mutation is like growing a transgendered intelligent
third arm and watching it happen overamped on vasopressin. what it
looks like from the outside and what it feels like from the inside

Topic: We ARE Mutating and Taking over the World!
Judith Milhon (stjude) Fri Dec 16 '94 (13:52) 39 lines

    er ... <aaaak> yeah ... but one might also say that a mutation is a
significant change. qualitative, not just more of the same ... or
it's SO MUCH more of something that it becomes qualitative. There's
always been a flow of information among humans, yes. But through
most of human history it's been feedback: all I know is what my
neighbors and kin told me, and all they know is what theirs told
them ... and aint no use in talkin to me; it's the same as talkin to
YOU.

In this situation a new idea as mutation is easy to see. Of
course, in this situation a new idea, a mutation, will die out instantly, maybe along with its owner. If the idea or the invention
can sell itself, (to put it into the free-mkt capitalistic terms
folks find so congenial nowadays) ... if it makes life better for
people without disturbing their ideas of fitness too much, then it
will spread through the population. == A Successful Mutation.
Spread determines success, note.

Okay, that's qualitative change. Quantitative change becoming qualitative is like the increase in information flow with printing
presses, radio, tv, the internet. mere more becomes extreme difference. Even broadcast info with managed sources produced enormous
change in america. The level of idea-sophistication now compared
with 1900 is mind-boggling. (even though the level is still depress-
ingly low, maybe ...) and the Net! the Net! It may be more, but that
aint just the size of it ... The Net is a qualitative change in

species communication. (ok: i'll settle down.)
So ... mutation happens. Then maybe it spreads, changes everything.

Now the possibility for spread is instantaneous and planet-wide.

So the idea spreads ... and in the next moment, the next idea succeeds it, and the next and the next, and the barrage does not cease.
what will change everything must spread, yes, but it must stick. it
must persist, adhere, until it soaks into the everyday and becomes
(excuse the term) normal.

How does countercurrent become mainstream, and change the flow forever?

Topic: We ARE Mutating and Taking over the World!
Look what the cat dragged in! (scribe.waterfish) Sat Dec 17 '94 (00:53)

    And in the next moment, the next idea, the next thought ... becomes
the next fucking hairstyle, the next fucking computer game, the next
fucking rock band.... commodity culture have overtaken the market-
place of ideas -- unfortunately, everyone I know is either broke or
outta space. We're reaching a level of overload where the only thing
that makes sense is the most lower primate urge -- it's no accident
that Trent Reznor's "Closer" with the hook phrase, "I WANT TO FUCK YOU
LIKE AN *ANIMAL*" is the number one song in the Bay Area TODAY. Not
next year, not in the year 2000, but today, (according to LIVE 105)
and if that pissant excuse for an alternative radio station is spewing
this carnality, imagine what's going on on the lower levels of extrem-
ity ... ('scuse me while I masturbate ... ahhh, grunt, mmm)

Topic: We ARE Mutating and Taking over the World!
mag/tif(magdalen) Sat Dec 17 '94 (01:53)

    at least "mutating" is more potentially accurate than "evolving",
the latter being a far more overused term 'round these parts. we're
special, we're evolved. we're spiritual capitalists, we're rilly-
super-smart gys with (wow!) computers. we eat information for breakfast, and sprinkle new memes on top instead of raisins.
i know i've mutated since getting plugged in, but it's environmental
mutation. like when you live next to the uranium mines. i doubt
whether i or anyone else has "evolved" into the ultra-groovy
cryonically-regenerated SMI2LE new edger i once fantasized about.

mutation is addictive, though.

Topic: We ARE Mutating and Taking over the World!
Judith Milhon (stjude) Sun Dec 18 '94 (10:46)

>>how does countercurrent become mainstream, and change the flow
forever?

fads are maybe a hint ... some fads take right over, permeate the
culture, and take a while to die out. Then they're up for the peri-
odic retro revivals, the "quoting", the fuckin homage ... and the
damage is done, forever, if that fad involves a serious breakthrough
in what is permitted!

If sexual rebels and reproductive rebels and ... what other kinds,
think! ... if those who we ARE become limited role models as passing-
fad personae ... well, there we are forever -- dragging along with us
the previously forbidden ...

the question -- how to mutate and take over the world -- is entirely
serious. it's a real plot masquerading as a fake plot, a real
takeover, a real revolution ... masked as fiction.

Topic: We ARE Mutating and Taking over the World!
Bada Shanren (tbjn) Sun Dec 18 '94 (22:08)

Does the mutation happening here need to end with the mere publication of a book?

Topic: We ARE Mutating and Taking over the World!
Durga Doo (stjude) Mon Dec 19 '94 (14:42)

It bettah not. We need to think sequel, not to mention serializa-
tion, CD-ROM and comicbook rights ...

Topic: We ARE Mutating and Taking over the World!
stjude (stjude) Mon Dec 19 '94 (15:00)

in fact, this project could get realler real quick. If the project
is to make the fiction real, here's an easy first: welcome to the
virtual underground! We're it!

Topic: We ARE Mutating and Taking over the World!
Nolan Void (nvoid) Mon Dec 19 '94 (15:48)

>make the fiction real

Oh bummer, more reality to deal with. Why don't we make reality fictional instead?

Topic: We ARE Mutating and Taking over the World!
RUSirius (rusirius) Mon Dec 19 '94 (20:04)

mine is already.

Topic: We ARE Mutating and Taking over the World!
Boutros Boutros-Patrick (justpat) Mon Dec 19 '94 (21:38)

my life is a fucking cartoon

Topic: We ARE Mutating and Taking over the World!
Look what the cat dragged in! (scribe.waterfish) Sun Dec 25 '94 (15:33)

My life is exploded narrative ...

Topic: We ARE Mutating and Taking over the World!
jonl (jonl) Thu Dec 27 '94 (21:09)

ain't everybody's!?

SEGMENT ONE: 1995
WHEN RAD THINGS HAPPEN TO "BAD" PEOPLE

AN ALTERNATIVE FEVER-DREAM HISTORY OF THE HORRIBLE YEAR 1995, IN WHICH AN ORGANIZATION CALLING ITSELF THE HUMAN ANTI-DEGRADATION LEAGUE (THE HADL) FORMS TO BRING STANDARDS TO THE NET, OUR AUTHORS FLOG THE TIRED TROPE *RIOT GRRRRL*, AND MONDO VANILLI TOURS WITH A FUCKING ROBOT . . .

St. Jude's Diary
Jan. 1, 1995

Last night I had a nightmare:
It was the year 2002: I just knew this, although there was no way to tell. It was night, and moonlight was pouring across the carpet, but the moonlight looked green. Outside the window I knew that there was nothing but green, nothing at all. This was terrifying. I was very high up in some building, and people I know were with me in the room, but I don't remember who they were . . . And we all knew that we were doomed. We were just sitting there, looking at the green moonlight on the floor.

From another room we could hear what sounded like a party. Voices chanting rowdily, football-style, and then we heard what sounded like a hymn . . . lots of voices, mostly male, maybe drunk . . . I could make out some of the chorus: If it's the ennnnnd of the worrrrrld, then it's the ennnnnd of ENtropy! . . .

Then when the song ended there was a pause. And then a really loud chant: Extrophy! Extrophy! EXTROPHY!

What?

Jan. 2, 1995

I'm saving these three clippings. This is what the new year means to me . . . . :

S.F. Chronicle   Dec. 29, 1994
Brandy's Babes: Cyber-Brothel Spurs Cries for Net Restrictions

IBM to study limiting access

by Sandra Dayton

It's being touted as the first little whorehouse in Cyberspace, but Brandy's Babes, the latest in a rising tide of sex-related sites, has prompted a call for strict certification of software on the Internet. The service is accessible on the World Wide Web.

Brandy's Babes is the first sex site to offer video encounter sessions, which visitors can schedule with brothel employees. Members get special rates and privileges. Pages contain links to pictures of "Brandy," "Trish," "Christy," and

25

"Monika." Dancers will pose for customers in private virtual rooms.

IBM officials are exploring ways to restrict children's access to such services. Joe Peters, head of IBM's Internet services, says that the cyber-whorehouse is just one of many sex-related sites, "some so explicit that you wouldn't want your kids to even hear the names."

According to Bart Kertis, founder and chairman of the newly founded Internet Associated Trade Group, "The Internet's not built to allow for a centralized oversight group, and anyway, such a thing runs against the spirit of the Net."

Still, pornography on the Internet is prompting legal actions. Earlier this month a couple from Berkeley were convicted in Federal Court in Bunkerville Alabama on charges of transmitting obscenity through interstate telephone lines on a computer BBS.

AP 14 Dec 94 11:16 EST V0774
Copyright 1994. The Associated Journalists.

LOS ANGELES (Associated Journalists)—A leading Jewish organization is protesting what it sees as a rising tide of on-line hatred. The Simon Wiesenthal Center yesterday mailed a letter to the Prodigy on-line service, asking officials to stop hate groups from posting messages on their electronic bulletin boards.

The Center also suggested that the federal government police the Internet service in a similar way. "More and more of these groups are embracing and utilizing the information superhighway," said Rabbi Abraham Cooper, associate dean of the Center. "The slurs are the same but the venue is different."

The Wiesenthal center said it had monitored increased on-line activity by more than 50 hate groups in the last few months. The Internet offers discussion groups with titles like "Skinheads," "Revisionism" and "Vigilantes," all popular with white supremacists.

White supremacists and civil libertarians criticized the Wiesenthal Center's letter, saying it would stifle their ideas in the last forum where their communication isn't heavily censored. William Pierce, chairman of the National Alliance white supremacist group, stated, "On the Net it's possible for a dedicated individual to get his message out to thousands and thousands of people."

```
Topic 77[cpunk]: Zimmerman Defense Fund
Started by: richard Cadre (Cadre) on Fri, Dec 16, '94
    23 responses so far

    Phil Zimmermann Legal Defense Fund Appeal
    In November, 1976, Whitfield Diffie and Martin Hellman an-
nounced their discovery of public-key cryptography, beginning
their paper with "We stand today on the brink of a revolution in
cryptography."

    We stand today on the brink of a battle in that revolution. Philip
```

Zimmerman, programmer/designer of the free public-key program, Pretty
Good Privacy (PGP), is going to be indicted. Maybe. The government
has been playing with Zimmerman for nearly two years, in a case that
amounts to trial as ordeal.

If he's indicted, Phil will likely be charged with exporting munitions without a license. Strong cryptographic software such as PGP is
classed with munitions -- and he "exported" it when someone posted his
program on Usenet. Thus he's somehow in violation of statute 22 USC 2778,
and a criminal under ITAR, "International Traffic in Arms Regulations."

Already American industries are chafing against restrictions on
commercial cryptography. ITAR is targeted as a restraint to US software trade, a barrier to secure global communications -- and certainly a weapon against the political movement for privacy through
effective cryptography.

Phil Zimmerman has been a point man in that struggle. He continues
to work for "cryptography for the masses," largely at his own ex-
pense. He's now working on PGP Phone, which will make every personal
computer with a sound card and a modem into a secure telephone.

THIS IS REAL. The struggle continues. You can help!

You can make a donation to the Phil Zimmerman Defense Fund with
VISA or MasterCard via Internet mail. Worried about snoopers inter-
cepting your credit info? Don't worry -- use PGP.

In plain ASCII text write Amount Donated, Recipient: Philip L.
Dubois, Attorney Trust Account. Include bank, card number and date of
expiry, card name (yours, hopefully :-)), and your telephone number.
Use PGP and encrypt with the key below, ASCII-armor the output and
e-mail it to Phil Dubois (dubois@csm.org).
In the "Subject:" line put Phil Zimmerman Defense Fund.

Phil Dubois's public key:

————BEGIN PGP PUBLIC KEY BLOC————
Version: 27
    mQCNAiyaTboAAAEEAL3DOizygcxAe6OyfcuMZh2XnyfqmLKFDAoX0/FJ4+d2frw85T
uXc/k5qfDWi+AQCdJaNVT8jlg6bS0HD55gLoV+b6VZxzIpHWKqXncA9iudfZmRrtx4Es8
2n8pTBtxa7vcQPhCXfjfl+lOMrICkRuD/xB/9X1/XRbZ7C+AHeDONAAURtCFQaGlsaXAgT
C4gRHVib2lzlDxkdWJvaXNAY3NuLm9yZz6JAJUCBRAsw4TxZXmEuMepZt0BAT0OA/9IoC

```
BZLFpF91hV1+epBi49hykiHefRdQwbHmLa9KO0guepdkyFi8kqJLEqPEUIrRtiZVHiOLL
wkTRrFHV7q91AuETJMDIDifeV1O/TGVjMiIFGKOuNdzByyidjqdlPFtPZtFbzffi9BomTb
8O3xm2cBomxxqsV82U3HDdAXaY5Xw==
=5uit
```
—————END PGP PUBLIC KEY BLOCK—————

These exhibits A B and C sum it up—here's what we're heading into. In 1995 we're setting up to fight a war for cyberspace. At the moment, it looks like it's coming down to censorship vs. crypto.

In the last months the Press has been making a huge hoop-la about cyberspace—a new planet has swum beneath our ken, silent on a peak in Darien—yeah, yeah, but the reportage often carries the wrap-up hook that this new land is beyond the reach of law and decency, and what are we going to do about that? The few pioneers over there need to have their morals investigated immediately, and we gotta clean up the karma in Dodge. So the censors will march in to fight porn, racism and sexism . . . and crypto goes up against them to defend free speech. Unfortunately, crypto at this moment seems outgunned. Crypto right now is set up to defend mostly private free speech, individual email. And the big push from the censors is about free posting to the online bulletin boards, postings that can be read by everybody. Vicious, racist, sexist, porno stuff, there to be seen by even the most delicate of women, by the most tenderly underage kids . . . (That was the argument for the Hayes censorship of the movies . . . and so the cinema was THE escape from the last Depression—no ugliness, no poverty, no profanity, no unpunished crimes—family-safe, and guaranteed bogus.)

There's a book out now proposing that pornographers are walking point for free speech . . . if they get hit, it warns the rest of us we're in danger. Oh joy, I'm a pornograph myself. But as the ACLU has determined in real life, there are worse things than porn. Porn is easy to execrate, but racist speech is almost impossible to defend.

So, the Aryan Brotherhood is recruiting online? Racism is this country's hot button, so you can figure that black-white racism will be the buzz. But whenever I start to believe that anti-semitism couldn't occupy 10 seconds of anybody's attention, I can amble over to the anti-jew anti-nigger boards . . . and as a quasi-Jew and a secret African I can soak up the limelight, centerstage. Hey, and what about that neofascist Forza Italia, [Go Italy!] party—antisemitic football cheers???

I'm a forward-looking hopeful sort. I like civility, online or off. And when I look around the Net I can find enclaves every bit as ugly as the Aryan Brotherhood . . . Likewise, there are bars I stay out of, and I do not attend soccer games in Italy. I watch my step, try to stay prudently out of the reach of uncivil brutality on both sides of the modem. On the online, though, it's still speech—I see no bruises here. And however ugly it may be, speech had better not be censored. You know who gets censored next. Better ugly speech than enforced silence.

The hope with free dissemination of ideas is that an ugly idea will reveal itself to be ugly; act as its own counter-argument, being what Vonnegut called a wrangwrang. . . . Interesting that talk of ethics and morals devolves to esthetics and sensibility. The relative beauty of ideas. This is a great advance—it used to devolve to scripture and legality. There's hope for a civilization here.

R. U.'s Diary
Jan. 5, 1995 (amended June 8, 1998, and November 3, 2000)
Notes for a new introduction.

Jokes That Come True

In the beginning was a joke.

Do you always cede to the humorous deflation?
Do you consider the quip the ultimate expression of accumulated complexity and not just a sidetrip?
Do you blithely enunciate offensive, libelous and potentially dangerous antisocial notions that you don't necessarily believe simply because the words pop into your head and make you giggle?
If you had the perverse thought, "How to Mutate and Take Over the World,"—a techno-phreak Total World Domination fantasy, with yourself as the goddamned "fuehrer," would you actually do it?

If you answered yes, then you may be a haiuka (Hopi for "upside-down inside-out man"). You may be a jester. God's Comic. A prankster. Then again, you may just be a fool and an asshole.

1994. St. Jude and I, along with Scrappi DüChamp, CyberPiss Goddess, and a cast of hundreds, embarked on "The Mutate Project." The project came out of a one-page CD-ROM proposal that I jotted down in the subway on my way to make a pitch to a multimedia mogul. Allen Ginsberg likes to say, "First thought best thought." This was: first thought last minute.

So "Mutate" started as a pitch and slowly mutated into an obsession. I would meet with potential comrades . . . er, project participants, and they would get a demonic glint in the eye. "You actually want to *do* it, right?"

Well, yes and no. While power, or powerlessness to be exact, is the primal issue at hand, and while I love a good campaign—the vainglorious thrust of a public mission—I'm fundamentally an existential anarchist. I have big negatives around state power and intrusion against the individual. I sometimes wake up mid-nights riffing new exegeses on Hassan I Sabbah's illumination of the existential bottom line, "Nothing is true. Everything is permitted."

O Brave Brave Ballantine Books
O brave brave Ballantine Books.

Imagine. The only people courageous enough to bid on and publish this thing that (according to the script here) is going to be compared to *Gravity's Rainbow* (by the *New York Times Review of Books*) and to *Mein Kampf* (by both the *New Republic* and the *Village Voice*); this book—this *scrap*book—this memoir of the inevitable—this artifact of our world historic destiny to liberate the world from tight assholeism, from Senator Waxman and Newt Gingrich, from the purists and the censors and the religious bastards and *the chickenshit moronic obsolete mother-*

fuckers who sit on the editorial boards of big corporate book companies. Ah, yes. *There* it is. Revolution must be motivated primarily by a very personal sense of vengeance. *Hitler* just wanted to be a successful painter. *Manson* just wanted to make records. (*Sadly*) Look what happened instead. And *they* didn't even *deserve* a fucking bidding war and a six-figure advance! No. *They* sucked. Anyway, finally, at the end of the day, a barely adequate bid came in from the lonely, and brave (and foolish) Ballantine, and I didn't have to ask Mike to unleash that virus and shut down most of the Internet causing some several billion dollars worth of damage.

The cliché resounded in my skull. They are "timid creatures of convention." Clichés like this convince us that the world is acceptable as is. Bohemians used to dream of taking over back in the Sixties. But in 1994, before "The Mutate Project," they resigned themselves to lives of poverty, hanging out in isolated enclaves attempting to forget the tight-assed mediocrity-loving enemy who continued to trim the edges of freedom while packaging and selling our rage for lousy points.

"What if," I wondered, "instead of telling ourselves they are 'timid creatures of convention' we told ourselves, 'They are stupid excremental pieces of dog meat who are committing genocide of the human imagination. They should be split in half by machine gun, soaked in gasoline, set on fire, and then pissed on.' If *this* were our thinking," I told myself, "we would get somewhere. If we were to become completely unforgiving, we would eventually exterminate the mediocrats." If this book does anything, let it open people up and rip the clichéd words (except for our *own* clichéd words, of course, as they are used for effect—*ours* are rhythmic and stylin') and robot thoughts that allow them to passively accept a world where only the living dead rise to the top of the anthill. A post-Chernobyl cancerbutt world where you can suck plutonium for Government doktors but you can't even say FUCK! on America Online or the Lifetime Network. A world where—*seriously now*—the U.S. Government wants to micromanage values and behavior in a new world order. Big brother has arrived and (s)he is only ten years late. THIS IS WAR!!! Or *was* war.

THE DECADE OF THE TIGHT ASSHOLE

In the early nineties, we learned the crucial difference between media democratization and pure media anarchy. During this time, the mediocracy started examining the content of art and entertainment for political correctness (community standards) and decency, and—to their real horror—they found *Beavis & Butthead, Bad Lieutenant*, Snoop Doggy Dogg, and Manson-as-pop-icon. A popular book, *Hollywood vs. America* by TV film critic Michael Medved was based around the ridiculous but unargued conceit that entertainers and artists should reflect the values of the average person. He applied this Leave-It-to-Beaver cultural Stalinism to Ice-T, David Cronenberg/William S. Burroughs' *Naked Lunch*, the NEA naughties (Serrano, Mapplethorpe, Finley et al.), Hollywood liberals, and others too numerous to list. "Moderate" political commentator Morton Kondrache, decrying (again) *Beavis & Butthead*, (again) gangsta rap, condom ads created by the office of the Surgeon General for television, and nude cover photos in *Vanity Fair*, explicitly called for "a return to bourgeois values."

INFORMATION HIGHWAY ROBBERY

The negative trend against liberty hit the technological edge culture hard in 1994. Most technophreaks had embraced the comfortable notion that freedom would be conserved simply by staying one step ahead of "the man" and the democratic mass. But with Government pressure and massification nigh, the cutting-nerd-edge turned its attention to what turned into a decade-long battle against State intrusion. Virtual Reality, an anemic vanguard for cultural revolution, was no longer the big buzz. It gave way to the more robust vision of the Cypherpunks and crypto-anarchists, folks dedicated to the use and free exchange of encryption technology. The Clinton Administration's insistence on approving Clipper Chip X—yet another mandatory data encryption project that allows law enforcement to nip in the back door of your Net messages to have a look-see—spawned what would eventually became an unstoppable electronic guerrilla army. In the eyes of a Government man, only a criminal wants privacy from the State, and a Government man's more paranoid perceptions were likely to be rendered axiomatic. The Clinton Administration also backed up the "digital telephony" measure that enabled law enforcement to force the tele-phone company to make it easy for them to tap phones in the new digitally based phone systems.

1994 was the year of Information Highway Robbery, the year that the Al Gore government, the megacorps and the mainstream media went gaga over the notion of Cyberspace, a vast inter-connected latticework of info-comm exchange made up at that time primarily of words, but also including games, music, pictures, moving pictures, and soon thereafter, virtual realities.

The now legendary pre-1994 Internet was a miraculous tribute to spontaneous self organizing and whatever was left of the cowboy spirit of wide-open space and wild freedom that had been America (at least for white boys). It was a miracle born of Pentagon bucks—a self-organizing sys-tem of (at that time) incomprehensible complexity stretching across the globe. But now, these law-less regions populated by nerd-cowboy outlaws and cranks were about to be claimed, legislated, bought, commodified, fenced in and settled. By mid-1994, everybody's dad had a modem. And dad rilly liked Newt Gingrich's plans for the Net. UH OH! HERE COME THE NORMALS!

PASS THAT SPEAR OVER HERE

Our techno-crank heroes, The Extrophians, were still fairly obscure, even within technoculture. In 1994, Drexler's gang was unique in the belief that already impressive technical "miracles" at the beginning of the age of thinking machines and data compression would infect production technol-ogy and the human organism itself, changing the human situation, impacting on biology and open-ing up a sea of possibilities ranging from reversible aging and replaceable parts to increased intelligence, to space-faring vehicles, to resolutions beyond biology . . . and that this was going to happen *soon*. Nanotech, today's delightfully troublesome genie, was the article of faith amongst these nerdy optimists. At the time, I supported the notion of nanotech against many nay-saying ex-perts from intuitive impulse. Technology mimicking nature, yes! Out of the mechanistic industrial age and into the era of self-replicating machines. The information age implied it, biotechnology ma-terialized it, and nanotechnology would be the natural culmination. My confessedly quasi-mystical faith in predictive futurism whose inevitable outcomes came from perceived patterns had nothing on the Extrophians, whose ideological paeans to rational positivism masqueraded a millennial oc-cultism. Theirs was a search for the alchemical key, the philosopher's stone, the spear of destiny and all that. Mine too, except that I believed even more strongly in jokes that come true.

IT'S ONLY ROCK 'N' ROLL?

Which brings us to Mondo Vanilli, the rock-and-roll concept band that would haunt the end of history. MV just started to hit stride in 1994.

I was of the opinion that rock culture (that is "white" rock culture, leaving aside the p.funk/hip hop phenomenon) hadn't transcended itself since the Sex Pistols. All the way back in 1977, the Sex Pistols closed the curtain on the rock era in an intentionally confusing cyclone of music industry deconstruction and nihilistic fury. A proper rock-and-roll band performed, made records and made videos (much like DüChamp's recent retro career). The Sex Pistols blew the sides off that box. They rendered those formalities secondary to having an energized presence in the world, both via media and the streets, and *they* controlled that presence. Theirs was a controlled randomicity. Malcolm McLaren, their manager, was a consummate postmodern media prankster mogul. Vocalist Johnny Rotten was an out-and-out haiuka. Each played ambiguity in his own way.

Sadly, after the Pistols, everybody stepped back into the box. Even the most radical punk rockers were merely stagebound agitprop. Madonna came closer to having the right idea. She was outside the rock-and-roll box, but only to become famous for being famous. A band of musical guerrilla provocateurs called Negativland punctured a few reality bubbles, but never became popular enough to tear the fabric of consensus reality.

And then there was the now legendary Milli Vanilli. These pablum-bubbling lipsynchers, bless their bleating hearts, pulled into media central at the exact moment that simulation was becoming an invisible and nested phenomenon and pathetically confessed to being *inauthentic*. The spontaneous cluelessness of these living breathing simulacra was a joke to die for. I vowed right then and there to create the house band of the simulacrum.

With Mondo Vanilli we proposed to use virtuality against itself, while giving the decade of the tight asshole an enema. The goal wasn't necessarily to blow down the proscenium between spectator and artist, or to blow down the box around a rock-and-roll band, but to blow down the boundaries of logic, structure and—most of all—expectation. Mondo Vanilli's game plan was to be megamedia DMT, but with the ego still riding tall in the saddle. Three egos, actually.

The plan worked. But we crept up on it slowly.

Mondo Vanilli—in that dawn time—was about excess, in an ungenerous hypercritical public moment, but done in so self-conscious and self-deconstructed a way—and with such idiot glee— as to get away with it (maybe). Not excessive in the sense of drugs, sex and rock-and-roll, mind you. Excessive in terms of the liberal exfoliation of contradictory and confusing images and imaginative fantasy. In other words, what we made up about ourselves was as much a part of the group as what we actually did. Fantasy Vanilli knew no limits. Fantasy Vanilli was an excessive effusion of signal AND noise. We had more to say than any "rock star" around and we knew it . . . and we had nothing to say. Or something to say about nothing. That is to say; we could endlessly represent the replacement of signal by noise with our noise. And it would cohere at a higher level. Or it would be stoopid funny. Or both.

All that and the cyberpiss goddess of annihilating feces too?

= =
Date: Jan 8, 1995
From: StJude
To: rusirius
Subject: mention masturbation? no: teach it.

32

I walked in on somebody's pubescent daughter yesterday -- she was lying on the couch pelvically thrusting against a cushion and gasping.
(i cheerfully exclaimed "oops, sorry" and exited.) aha! i just read
in a medical journal a researcher's claim that he can predict from a
rise in testosterone levels when a boy will begin to have sexual
dreams and start masturbating . . . predict it accurately within a few
weeks! He said nothing about girls. Maybe girls left to themselves
would do the same. But maybe they *wouldn't*. Girls tend to be timid,
and -- born that way or made so -- they usually need encouragement
NOT to be timid . . .
So? We could encourage girls to masturbate.

Check out how many non-orgasmic women there are around. And if you
ask, you find out they never learned to masturbate. Fascinating. The
soon-to-be-Ex-Pres (the one who *might* okay prayer in the schools)
fired his Surgeon General last month for speculating that masturbation
might be *mentioned* in sex education classes . . . Mentioning it
should be mandatory. Publing girls should have a class about masturbation. Explain to the girl kids that in females the sexual response
is built up by practice, and give hints on the best ways to do that
practicing. Needn't ever say the word orgasm . . . or masturbation,
either. It could be subtle, just hints on how and why. It could be
very G-rated. It could be a SINGLE VIDEO TAPE (well thought-out,
carefully worded) in distribution throughout the schools. It's a favor we could easily do for the next generation of women. Will this
happen? Forget it.

You with yr Reichian hopes -- you ever see this happening? Don't
bother to answer.
===
Date: Jan 8, 1995
From: StJude
To: rusirius
Subject: teach physics? sure . . . with warning labels

o, i forgot to tell you. . . . the universe has collapsed.

the word hasn't gotten around much, but the astrophysics universe
model is collapsing -- the Hubbell telescope is giving them too much
data, and the Big Bang and the Red Shift and the Hubbell constant are
all starting to look really QUESTIONABLE . . . egad, did we just accept all this mutually-validating stuff? Total crisis of faith. TOO
MUCH DATA.

And in other news, the ten equations of general relativity are under attack. Two physicists (Yilmaz & Alley) are claiming that if you try to get strictly Fundamentalist with the gen relativity scriptures you discover that two bodies *don't* attract each other. For instance, if you snap the stem of an apple . . . it just sits there in its tree. It has no reason to fall, so it won't. . . . could something be wrong?

So, soon scientists will start smashing car windows and painting rude things on walls. Cultural gangrene takes over more of the body politic, as more organs of our cultural reality go dead. What the hell next? The 20th century has worshipped some scientific ideas as if they were received doctrine -- do pass me those Tablets, Lord, and a glass of water -- but even science is failing us. We better find *something* that looks viable, because our reality is decaying daily -- it's got a half-life of about ten minutes. Religion used to work. It kept the masses in line and gave humans a certain dignity -- a god cared about them. But now we've got irreligion and ugly chaos, and the obvious move is backward. Who can blame the school-praying types? (I can, but wait a minute.) Maybe that old-time religion might come in handy . . .

btw, it's simplistic to see the Republican right, professional Christians, as pawns for the ruling classes -- that they're assigned the task of re-cowing the masses with the fear of god. This is complete bullshit. The masses ARE religious, and superstitious too, if you need to distinguish between the two. Church membership in the USA is staggeringly greater than in any other developed country.

Anyway the old-time religion transplant is decaying faster than the body politic . . . stinks worse too. But what else we got? Institute *reason* in the rabble? Well . . . yes. The country's founders intended exactly that, remember. Democracy is a rational method of government only if you assume a rational rabble that can dependably make rational decisions. This country was a public works project sponsored by the Age of Reason. Church membership at the time of the Revolution was under 15%, and militant atheism was a strong voice in that Revolution. (did you ever read tom paine? AGE OF REASON? paine kicks religious butt.) Jefferson fought for separation of church and state to assure freedom of NONreligion. etc etc. . . . they had a lot of faith in humans working things out for themselves.

We could have a sane healthy country. If education were real, it

could be done. And education could be real. Education could be connected to the online -- it could draw on the entire body of human
knowledge, up-to-the-minute fresh. It could be high-tech, high cultural, immediate-practical. and as deep as the student wants to pursue it -- far beyond the expertise of a single teacher . . . and it
could happen at once. IT COULD HAPPEN NOW.
===
Date: Jan 8, 1995
From: rusirius
To: StJude
Subject: I accept!

Lessee . . . Jude's tryin' ta tell me something. education? the big
bang? teaching pubescent girls how to masturbate? YES! I ACCEPT!
===
Date: Jan. 20, 1995
From: rusirius
To: StJude
Subject: We've got a bigger problem now

Today, the new Republican congress proposed the new anti-crime bill.
You know, the one that cancels what's left of the 4th Amendment? Having swept themselves into office on a wave of fear and hate, they may
bring about the fullscale fascist police state that we've been expecting since the 1960's. I mean, it really can't get any more bur-
lesque than Jesse Helms and Strom Thurmond prominently positioned in
political power. And Newt Gingrich, we're just learning, actually
teaches courses for young Republican candidates SPECIFICALLY about
how to manipulate public fears and prejudices.
    Jude, I think it may be time to get busy. I mean, if we're mutat-
ing and taking over the world, we're certainly going up the hill
BACKWARDS right now. And did you catch the piece by Hentoff in the
Voice about the secret meetings between sensitive PC types and family
values types about the "abuse" that's taking place on the Net and in
the media?
    Meanwhile, the L. A. Times this week touts our buddy WAXMAN, Amer-
ica's most fanatical regulator of all things that you might trip and
fall on and poke your eye out with, as the last great LIBERAL, the
leading opponent of the Newt. It's authoritarianism left right front
and back, with very little opposition in the light of day, is it not?
===

Date: Jan 24, 1995
From: StJude
To: rusirius
Subject: Fat is a birth defect!!

They just found the obesity gene. True. Soon they'll find the genes
for procrastination, sleeping late, and belief in UFOs. This means a
revolution in morals and ethics -- who can blame us for our genes?
Eventually, inevitably, we'll be able to literally slap a patch on
our genetic shortcomings -- skin patches to feed us the good DNA.
Some of us will be so patchy we won't need to wear clothes . . . we'll
spend all our disposable income compensating our bad-habit genes --
trying to make it UP the slippery slope to NORMAL.

And now the Republicans are going to settle Cyberspace

Shit. Shit shit shit. This is my home in here, this virtual prairie,
this starlit empty beautiful wasteland. Gophers scuttle through the wire-
grass. There are few fences, and some of us have fence-cutters. We ride
as fast as the electron wind, and our vision is keener than the eagle's:
the eagle does not have ls -al . . . Oops, a little UNIX joke, there.

So, the *tech* wing of Bohemia will get co-opted. Underground artists and
musicians are used to getting forcibly mainstreamed -- mainhandled --
bought out, imitated by Valley kids and sucked dry in months -- but now,
but now the beautiful unreal estate is gonna get subdivided by bornagain
yahoos . . . it's gonna be just like the outside is getting to be: they'll
tell me to watch my language, they'll make me wear clothes, they'll ask
me what religion i have. do i look like i would have one???

Me, I'm a democracy yaysayer, fer xsakes. I'm a live-and-let-liver
. . . I don't even want to make the amen-shouters pipe down . . .
They're gonna make ME pipe down, sit still, fold my hands, or else.

One of the horrible ironies spiking me is that I spent 10 years in
Community Memory Project, programming UNIX-C, horrible, and for what?
To bring about online communities and Everyperson Online and electronic mass democracy. All the stuff that Newt Gingrich *loves*, and
is going to do . . . he'll do it his way.

holy shit, it's like ballotbox stuffing -- Newt's gonna stuff cyberspace
with republicans . . . and then he's going to call it online democracy. Cyberspace has always been mostly white and middleclass, but now it's gonna
be a big burbclave -- Cyburbia!! -- gotcher Online Democracy raht chere!!

Looks like my dreams of liberatory technology are getting detourned
into a disney cartoon. Familiar -- all the way along, my life as a
radical has been hijacked by irony. Okay, maybe i'm ready for the
next phase. The tech lib movement, theme 2. . . . Because I still
think tech can solve our public problems, and I still love this country, although I seldom want to say so. America's the next best thing
to The Old Cyberspace. Anarchic, wild. Don't fence us in!

Now what?

===
Date: Jan 26, 1995
From: rusirius
To: StJude
Subject: What now?

Now there has to be a real battle for freedom. And as per Newt's
electronic democracy, keep in mind that the MORE people that vote in
a given election, the more liberal the candidates that are elected.
Our job is to get the rabble excited about cyberspace AND to get them
excited about personal freedom, at the same time. Jerry Brown once
said, "We're going to go left and right at the same time." Exactly
right. Libertarianism and democracy, each where appropriate. Nothing
less will do.

The rabble didn't vote in 1994. And, despite all that propaganda from
the beltway dweebs about the middle class, the fuckin' RABBLE elected
Clinton. It was basically the so-called "traditional democratic
coalition," plus the generational thing -- the boomers and the MTV
kids. Now, Clinton himself is a house-proud town mouse and a screw,
let's get that straight. Really. Read Chomsky on GATT. And the Democratic Party has nosedived for keeps. Finally! Anyway, the lineup was
always like this:
The Multinational Corporate Relatively Democratic Party vs. The
Multinational Corporate Anti-democratic Party.
   So, what's left? The Left BEHINDS. Which is, I believe, something
like 70% of the population now, if we can just get them to understand
that. So the cutting edge and the Left BEHINDS. That's our con-
stituency . . .

Anyway, I would like to stop this crazy thing, Jane, and . . . I
think that you and I could do it. My notion is that we create THE new
political party. Why not? Sure, you've got your Libertarians, your
Greens, and the supporters of down-home big-eared billionaire

eccentrics, but WE've got the cyber. In all earnestness, we have an opportunity to CONFOUND the many with a well-thrown curve ball that combines populist rabble-rousing with elitist argument-by-expertise. To wit: "But the transition to a high-tech cybernetic society simply DEMANDS that we make these changes in order to survive. I'm sorry." But we should be more or less behind the scenes. What say?

= =
Date: March 2, 1995
From: rusirius
To: StJude
Subject: Strategies for a new political party . . .

How does a new political party burst upon the scene, with no funding whatsoever? One answer is that you get some money. From where? Well, the usual high-tech sources will prove to be too difficult I think. Kapor, the Wired 2000 crowd, even your esteemed cypherpunks, are basically only self-interested when it comes to politics. Try to talk to them about hacking the economic marginalization of the majority that leads to intolerably 3rd-world living conditions and they'll only look at you quizzically as if you just dipped your beef jerky into the wine.

But think about this: we may be becoming the silent (secret) majority. Not you and I, Jude, WE'RE profoundly weird. But the alienated, economically displaced, unasked, unpolled, unrepresented, unemployed and, most of all, unbuying of the piety in the sky bullshit from Clinton and ESPECIALLY the Newt -- ordinary folks may be a secret majority. It stands to reason, also, that self-righteous, inflexible, singleminded, authoritarian true believers are politically organized. Open minded, flexible, complex, ambiguous, anti-authoritarian people would just as soon be left to mind their own fucking business. But Newt and company want a cultural war. LET'S GIVE IT TO THEM!

= =
Date: March 3, 1995
From: StJude
To: rusirius
Subject: Re: Strategies for a new political party . . .

Okay, I'm suddenly rendered serious.
Most of the people i talk with online are worried about a clampdown. If there's a real move by the Right to take over the Net, it's not only the Cypherpunks who will resist. Almost ALL the current residents will hate it.

38

Getting together the
>>Open minded, flexible, complex, ambiguous, anti-authoritarian people

is the way it's got to go. We will unite and fight. We will infiltrate.
We must burrow in everywhere, stealthy and resolute, especially us
buddhists. These are the times that try zen's moles. Ugh.

>>Newt and company want a cultural war. LET'S GIVE IT TO THEM!
How long has it been since I've had any hope for political action?
Look, you know my history . . . for me the idea of taking to the
streets is gravy and biscuits: Will they shoot at us? You promise?
Please?

But in a cultural war it's mostly words, and we want the online, baby . . .

Here's a brief history of the tech available for spreading revolution --

Unaided human voice: chants, slogans, songs. . . . Ça ira!
Posters and broadsides (all revolutions)
Underground press (all revolutions)
Cassette voice tapes (Iranian Fundamentalists)
Fax (Chinese student rebellion, Anti-Saudi rebels)
TV Cassette (Anti-Saudi Fundamentalists)
Email (Anti-Saudi rebels, cypherpunks)
THE WEB (us)

My organizational skills are zip. That doesn't matter. What we can
talk up is an ANTI-organization. We can encourage everyone to be spiders in the Web. Every single website points to hundreds of others.
It's uncensorable and unstoppable. The cypherpunks may get end-runned,
maybe . . . but privacy and mass individualism grow directly from Web
technology. No organization can possibly be imposed upon a WEB.

Freedom comes out of the wire of a modem!

<holy shit . . . this is it.>

>jude<
==
Date: March 3, 1995
From: StJude
To: rusirius
Subject: Re: Strategies for a new political party . . .

But you still have the problem of a central, top-down, broadcast-
model mass media.

And I mean YOU.

===
Date: March 3, 1995
From: rusirius
To: StJude

No problem. We need to use both. Also, DIS organization and DE central-
ization to the point of dissipation has made us what we are today . . .
LOSERS! . . . on the verge of religious fascism and practically without a
voice in the CENTRAL social/political discourse. You can trace it all
the way back to the 70's and that stupid "think globally act locally"
thing. I mean, one reason that YOU vote democrat instead of republican
is that you understand what decentralization and downsizing of federal
government under current conditions would mean to the average black
family in Biloxi, Mississippi. And then, of course, the new technology
changes the entire meaning of global and local. Local becomes your peer
group, and that local IS global.
    I think that the organization/disorganizational model for digital
revolutionaries is probably going to be small mobile units -- some of
them networked together -- AS WELL AS irascible individualists AND
grudging public support for us mouthpieces who are trying to break
into the CENTRAL discourse.

===
R. U.'s Diary
March 12, 1995
Shit! The Mondo Vanilli tour creeps closer and I still can't find the entry point or the center for a
comprehensive media philosophy.

Let's see. What do I want to do? I want to change the human situation. Why? Because it's
painful and unsatisfactory. Because it's something to do. Because it inspires creative action and
one can take pride in that action. Because you HAVE to do something to be allowed to live in this
society and when I start to think about doing *something,* I feel compelled to do *this.* It's a
living. Because if we don't change the human situation, it will get worse. THAT's it! I'm an Extropian, after all, because entropy will make things unlivable and sooner rather than later. Left to
its own, this thing is getting worse. OK. How is it getting worse? Too many prisons. Too much
coercion. Violence. Marginalization. An across-the-board attraction to ganging up and authoritarian solutions. No sense of revolutionary possibility. LACK OF PERSPECTIVE!
    It's all about perspective, perception then. Finally, I try to have an impact on the public dis-
course because the public discourse misses the point. So . . . What IS the point?

SHIT! There isn't any point. There's just an accumulation of small points, like television. Media, like biology, is now a non-hierarchical distributed process. How could there be a singular point?

SO HERE'S ONE OF THE POINTS
Let the Games Continue:
At this point in history, nothing could be more dangerous than the urge to force people to be nice, online and in media. Media itself is a process for exteriorizing the human psyche. It's an *EX*teriorizing device not an *IN*teriorizing one. The urge to conflate the increased incidence of extreme forms of violence, the serial killers and so forth, with violence and perversity in the media is understandable but slightly off kilter. It's complicated. The urge to make nice, to make civilized, in the meat world

```
##############
#__/==$=\_     # <- From the High-Tech Fully Electronic Desk
# /))-00(\     #    of R. U. Sirius
# ((( -)))     #
# )))\ /(((    # -> rusirius@well.com
##############
```

Date: 11/10/96
To: stjude
Subject: philosophy of media?
we don't have to show you no steenkin

Can you find anything I wrote about my media philosophy somewhere in 1995? Trudy's on my ass about it.

(Hey, does she have any clue about what we're really doing here?)

Screw it: maybe I'll just make something up and backdate it. Look around, okay? I'll kick through the stacks around my bed.

AND in the simulacrum, one bright clear world reflecting the other, has a comprehensible appeal. But it either begs the question of what it is to be human, or it responds to that question in a Catholic disciplinary fashion, simply repressing aspects of the human psyche in the expectation that "primitive" obsessions will diminish and eventually disappear through accumulated behavioral change, in a Lamarckian fashion. Or, in another bubble, the repression of primitive, violent impulses in favor of civilized behavior was a control mechanism for the more shrewdly aggressive dominators who successfully channeled *their* primitive, violent impulses into a socially acceptable form known as "ruthlessness," while monopolizing the right to use outright violence as a last resort for maintaining an otherwise indefensible accumulation of power and wealth.

But *now,* as we enter the info/comm age, most humans no longer help generate wealth. The accumulation of power and wealth is semi-democratized, an ever-broadening "winner's circle" of those able to play the system and access its privileges, while an even larger group is increasingly marginalized. In the land of the carrot and the stick, there is very little carrot being offered as a civilizing influence. So, in the streets, this new formation of power and wealth makes space available for the "return of the repressed," for violent underclass subcultures; violent in fact or violent in attitude; RUDE—if you will—rather than polite. Racial and gender conflicts form subtexts. Dionysian rites based on consumption/destruction of idols and PANic culture finds disregarded psychic space to occupy. Meanwhile, on both sides of the class division, people are hipper than they used to be. There's an unfocused, nascent awareness of, and therefore a cynicism about, civilizing influences as an instrument of control. And there's a very strong social consensus that sees the ambiguities and hypocrisies inherent in this control and WANTS IT ANYWAY, because the alternative is anomie, an unlivable war of all against all. Or so it seems.

If there's not enough carrot, there is only the stick. There is only the long arm of the law. "Tough love." Except for one thing. There's media. And while power and wealth in media is still the province of a small winner's circle, a VOICE in media can be had for a song. And thereby hangs the tale.

So let's stop for a moment and reflect on this hotbed of conflicting, complexifying interests, with its simultaneous increases and decreases of opportunity, its unschooled, neo-primitive zones anything but autonomous under the watchful but selective eye of police and media, the violence both unofficial and official, and the ironic self-awareness occupying the same psychic space as the raw power, stripped of its veneer, and realize THAT'S ENTERTAINMENT!

So. Have I just explained why some of my friends collect snuff films and atrocity exhibits, wear Charlie Manson t-shirts, engage in public performances of ritual debasement and transgression, enact rude personas online, write nasty books and demand the space to vent unhealthily on the public airwaves, why MONDO VANILLI uses excrement and public sex ritual simultaneous with technological sophistry and media cuteness? Oh, I think I have. But let me bring it back around.

Desirable behavior is certainly desirable, under the idealest of circumstances. Or, to take it from another point, if it's OK for me to tear out your kidney and chow it down with some Chianti, then it's OK for you to do the same with me. Pretty soon, we can't leave our house to buy a new computer, never mind enjoy a flight to Spain or some shared realtime social space. On the whole, we can agree. Violence is not good. On the other hand, the evidence is clear that violence, debasement, hostility, rudeness are not only part of the human situation, they are occasionally necessary interruptions against the sameness and dullness inherent in their lack. There will be no utopias. We WANT our dramas and our games and our conflicts. But we must find a way that we can live

•¿¿¿•From the Electron-Chocked Desk of Jude Milhon•¿¿¿•
•¿¿¿¿¿¿¿¿¿¿¿•   •aka StJude•   •¿¿¿¿¿¿¿¿¿¿¿•
•¿¿¿¿¿¿¿¿¿¿¿•   •stjude@well.com•   •¿¿¿¿¿¿¿¿¿¿¿•
Date: 11/10/96
To: rusirius
Subject: re: philosophy of media?

I haven't seen any early articles on yr media philosophy.

Trudy's been at me a lot, too. She's very fucking sweet, and devoted to her craft and shit, but I'm getting "what does THIS mean?" every other paragraph.

Hows about you invite her to a face2face and seduce her? Come on, come on, put out: it's your duty to the firm. And you bettah do it GOOD. She's got to love us. A REALLY INFATUATED editor might give us a shot at living up to our advance publicity -- "Gibson, Pynchon, Borges" . . . christ on a bike!

(Maybe both of us should go on sexual stand-by, just in case.)

(Look over your studlier studio musicians. Oh god, what am I saying?)

I lose heart. I fear. I faint . . .

Yog soggoth save us!

42

with them while also reaping the rewards of human intelligence and resourcefulness: computers, media, fine dining, plastic surgery, parties . . .

Modern rationalists imagined communications media as a tool for sharing information and ideas. Useful things would be accomplished. But with cinema, animation, television, electronic music and recording, computers, virtual reality; communications media proves to be a many-headed monster serving all aspects of the human mind and imagination, and all its impulses— erotic, dramatic, surreal, daemonic. Dark visionary media reflects our social reality but it also does something more. It serves as a repository, and a safe zone, where the darkest beasties of the human imagination can act out. Nice media is almost always banal, because that isn't who we are. We aren't nice. We can have (relatively) nice lives. But not nice media. Clearly we like our culture dark and tough. This is why we've evolved such a pervasive post-punk culture. Inside of media is the terrain where the *most* dangerous and destructive aspects of the human psyche can act out. Let the games continue!

= =
Date: March 16, 1995
From: stjude@well.com
To: cypherpunks@toad.com
Subject: anarchists ARE good for something . . .

WHAT ANARCHISTS ARE GOOD FOR
BY STJUDE

THE HACKER EXPERTISE GAP
There are a number of men and women who have subterranean knowledge they have no use for. They don't use it for unethical purposes -- stealing is so easy it's contemptible -- and they see no compelling reason to use it for "moral," revolutionary purposes. So, what use is it to me if I know how to throw the telephone system of a medium-size city into utter con-fusion? Or how to intrude into supposedly uncrackable systems? This sit-uation defines a vital expertise gap. Knowledge is sought out for its own sake. Skills are taught or self-taught and refined and polished . . . But the possibilities for real-life action remain unexplored.

If these subterraneans discover a cause, they are immediately a for-midable force.

Consider this . . .
the american founders visualized a system of checks and balances to keep power in its place -- that is, evenly distributed on all sides. The government itself needed a countervailing force, in the form of an armed citizenry. Yeoman farmers with their own armaments were the ultimate check and balance to centralized power, to the american gov-ernment. Today the american government outshoots anyone, worldwide.

Yeoman farmers with rifles -- even automatic rifles -- can't quite stand up to the job. Who can? The question is not rhetorical. The subterraneans could be that countervailing force. Should the government become crazy, or lean too much on the people, their expertise could find a use.

Thomas Jefferson said that revolution is ongoing . . . that perhaps every generation should renew the revolutionary process. The process of renewal is stymied now. There is no force that can move against the lineaments of established power. The american revolution, as set up in the late eighteenth century, is finished. Force and counter-force in those days was material -- *materiel*, in fact: guns and bombs and ships and physical seizure of buildings and terrain. The world has shifted. Force and counterforce mean something totally else in a post-industrial society.

THE AMERICAN REVOLUTION IN POST-INDUSTRIAL TIMES
A countervailing force in these times could be anarchist in form -- in formlessness -- and as powerful in the context of postindustrial times as the citizen rifle brigades were in the dawn of the american experiment. Of course, the idea of power in the hands of an armed citizenry brings up questions of fitness. How bright ARE these guys? How scrupulous are they? How mature are they? Are they in ALTERED STATES? These are reasonable questions to ask about any primate with a gun, or a modem. An objection to an armed citizenry that is no more intelligent nor humane than the government itself seems reasonable. Governments tend not to be known for their intelligence and humanity, although this may be changing slowly. As the founders knew, govern-ments can be changed. Nurturing governments towards more enlightened behavior is like dealing with unruly two-year-olds . . . you have to stymie them when they get out of hand. An anarchist alliance can't by its nature take power and declare itself a government. But it is ide-ally suited to form a counterforce to government.

I could continue with this, developing it more fully. Should I? The ideas are very developable, but they are fetching enough in their skeletal form. Lovely in their bones. However much they flesh out, I should end it with this:

if this be treason, make the most of it.
= =

ROLLIN' SPIN   March 24, 1995   Pg. 100

MONDO Vanilli—*IOU Babe* (Naught/ Innerscoop)

REVIEW BY PIOTR TORQUE

Remember back in '93 when a tinny demo of these clowns circulated around the zine scene like a loud yawn? Justifiably jaded reviewers like myself paused only to scratch our hemorrhoids with the cassette label before attempting to pawn it off for credit at the used record shop. Luckily for MV, or whatever they're passing themselves off as these days, sci-fi writer and robot pornographer Richard Kadrey said of their brand of iron-o-matic techno rehash: "you'd have to have a rather enormous stick up your ass not to love it," citing the project's "honest idiot glee" as its irresistible quality. (Excuse me while I relube my Louisville Slugger . . . anal splinters are an occupational hazard, you know.) Now, in '95, someone with more money than sense (namely, Brent Buzzkill of industropoop band Nine Irritated Nerds) has given these frauds a record contract, and I have to waste an hour better spent masturbating to *Melrose Place* contending with *IOU Babe*, an *actual album* by a self-proclaimed "virtual band." Goddamn right they owe me! Blowjobs from Simone 3rd Arm and R. U. Sirius for starters . . .

This shameless piece of commercial entertainment product opens with the aural equivalent of warm mayonnaise being spread all over your naked body. "Thanx" is some kind of unctuous love rap by frontclone R. U. Sirius (haw haw, what a *pun guy*!)—Barry White on helium comes to mind— while liteweight techno dribbles out of the speakers and onto the floor like Cool Ranch™ dressing. "Erotic" moaning from the aforementioned Ms. Arm threatens to pull you into the track, but only succeeds in begging comparison to Duran Duran's "Hungry Like the Wolf." No thanx. The instrumental "Gimme Helter" is only slightly better than awful, saved from utter worthlessness by the absence of another vocal abortion by Sirius, but still it sounds like something the Bomb Squad could have farted out after a few 7-Eleven chili dogs back in '90. "Bummer" (indeed) sounds like a moldy table scrap thrown to the drooling dogstar by Brent Buzzkill, the band's impresario, making it the only cut on the album likely to be embraced by the fashion angst set. Namedropping Eddie Vedder and Prince might win MV some Pavlov points at the

cash register—subliminal sales are all the rage, and product placement in pop songs just around the corner. "Gun Cereal" lurches like a broken Roland DX-7, screaming "listen to me, ma, I'm *avant guard*!" The title track (thankfully) ends this barrage of arranged mediocrity. It's MV's "A Day in the Life," I suppose, and unfortunately, it's just as long.

MV's erstwhile "anti-philosopher" Eliot Han-

```
##################################################
#########        • Trudy B. Hyatt •        #########
#########       • Editorial Assistant •       #########
#########     • Hyatt@Ballantine.Books.com •     #########
##################################################
```

Date: November 18, 1996
To: rusirius
Subject: Piotr Torque review of IOU Babe

Are you sure you want to include this? It may not be necessary.

This is the worst review I've ever seen.
Harsh.

Trudy

delman has publicly lambasted his former disciples for actually recording an album, claiming that such a cliché act violates the band's primary tenet of absolute virtuality. His pretentious completely baked perorations aside, Handelman has the right idea. This aural porno for pomos should have remained in Baudrillard's bedpan.

VILLAGE VOICE March 25, 1995

Village Voice Consumer Bag

Hitler
Pocket Pool
Shithead Records

Pocket Pool fucks ya up again with a great piece of thunderous lunkhead drone metal. The lyrics, "Love you? Love you? Uh Uh Uh Uh . . . I love you," tells us all we need to know. Vocalist Klaus Barbie Doll rips his lungs out, flings them to the ground, and cuts them up with shards of glass, song after glorious song. A-plus.
—Joe Conesco

IOU Babe
Mondo Vanilli
Naught/Innerscoop

Intelligent . . . arch . . . ironic. Wins prize for first use of the words "appropriation," "ecosphere" and "data highway" in song lyrics. Well-constructed. Maybe even brilliant. Soulless. I'll never listen to it again. B-minus. —Grail Marx

===

Date: March 27, 1995
From: StJude
To: rusirius:

My cypherpunk friends are restless. Pro-censorship people are rattling their godblessed sabres -- there's talk about censoring the Internet clattering around. The media just got through hyping the hell out of the Internet, and now their followup story is, okay, now let's KILL the Net. Rumor is that some horrible coalition is coalescing to do some variation on that. NiceNet?

If they try, chances are they'll begin with alt.sex* on Usenet -- first to go: alt.sex.bestiality?

Did you know that the next implementation of the Net has packet encryption designed in? This means that link encryptors can do automatic
encryption . . . If it becomes necessary, packet encryption will be
common, but other security will also exist. The important thing (says
my boyfiend Eric) is that between two ends (and there are several different entities that are ends) all traffic can be transparently encrypted. So, all parts of the net end-to-end are protected from legal
liability for transmitting those horse-fucking gifs. Btw, i stopped by
alt.sex.bestiality two nights ago, and as always i was charmed. So
sweet. Dogfuckers there, mostly. And they're mostly so EARNEST. One
night stands? Certainly not. Longterm relationships, with mutual ten-
derness and understanding . . . I would HATE it if they got shut down.

The cypherpunks list is blazing. Excitement. Incitement. People are
getting pissed off and talking trash about a hacker rebellion. These
are the times to seize!

Maybe it's good when repression becomes dramatically worse, because
that will spark a countermovement . . . ? Sound familiar? Me, I always
wanted to be a hero of the Resistance. I spent highschool in cleveland, so i've noticed that when the overground's unliveable there
MUST be an underground.

Hey . . . let's have an underground! I like the idea of an instant underground. A *virtual* underground. And how do you join a virtual
underground? You raise your left hand and swear yourself in: you're a
member in good standing. There are thousands of ways to resist the
overground, thousands of ways to noncomply.

It also makes sense to launch the virtual underground as an act of
dada revolution.

Hey, we got something here. This could be it!
= =
Date: March 27, 1995
From: stjude
To: nesta rusirius
Subject: Re: fyi

okay, slip THIS in your slipline, pal:

dada revolution is not anti-rationalist! au contraire, mes amis!

It's an attack on literalist, fundamentalist worshippers of the Word, whether handed down by gods or scientists or legislatures . Dada revolution is an assault on church/state by weirdos armed with encryption and other tech ... hurling words that masquerade as nonsense ... as RANDOM BITS.

It's inspired by the dadaists -- harpo marxism rules ok -- but we're making serious revolution nonetheless. We making an attack on capital-T Truth, on science as ideology, on the old scientific method of sticking a pin through the heart of live being and tacking it to the display card. The universe is a work in progress! So is our model of it! Er ... notice -- this IS the rational stance.
I LOVE the Age of Reason.
Rationalism is a good idea, and somebody oughta try to implement it sometime SOON.

excelsior, baby!
===
Date: March 28, 1995
From: rusirius
To: StJude

The Mondo Vanilli Fucking Robot Tour is about to start and I'm afraid I'll have to put the Revolution, or at least THAT revolution on hold for a few months ... but please keep me apprised of your discussions with the various hackers and so forth. They are clearly ready to resist the NiceNazis on their turf and don't need MY help. So I'll just go off and make some cultural trouble. Oh ... Yes. An underground might be the best strategy, though I doubt it ...

===

SprayGun   **April 1995**

MV SELLS OUT! EXCRETING MEDIA ... OR JUST THE SAME OLD SHIT?

The SprayGun Mondo Vanilli interview
by Tim Tryon

Mondo Vanilli is a very peculiar rock band, if that's in fact what they are. Pretending to be a pure media prank, they started their career with the False Starts Tour—a series of canceled performances. In interviews in various cyberpunk zines, the ubiquitous R. U. Sirius spoke of MV as pure concept and purveyed his philosophy that any concept is ruined when you attempt to realize it.

But with the release of IOU Babe *on Naught/Innerscoop Records, we have a real*

© 1995 Bart Nagel

Mondo Vanilli continued from p.19

a cowboy, kidnapped him, tied him up, put him in the bathroom and gave him an enema. We showed it on ten video screens in the theater.

SG: Simone, do you have a name for what you do?

S3A: I'm an entertainment contortionist and an existential gender bender.

SG: Er, where do your performance ideas come from? Do you spend a lot of time thinking about them or do they just come to you in a flash?

S3A: It's always something that I'm obsessed with. I make it pretty simple and functional. You only need a few incongruous elements to make something very strange and effective.

R. U. was fascinated by the idea of the Enema paintings because it was so simple but challeng-

ing. I did my first Enema Performance onstage with my 50-year-old slave Jack Daniels, who happens to be a pre-op transsexual. She sat on a toilet seat that I put on stage—some kind of a porta-potty from a hospital—and I inserted an enema bag into her. I was wearing a medical uniform. I used grape juice. She released on a canvas that I put underneath the porta-potty. As she did that, I danced with my swords in a glittery outfit. It was very festive. I called the performance "Icky" and it really did make a mess. She didn't hold it as long as we expected.

Right around that time, I was learning Butoh, working with harupin-ha from Japan. And recently I started taking classes in trapeze. So now it's going to get a little more complex because I'm incorporating these abilities into my performance work. I have sort of childhood circus-like ideals with an extremely sadistic and twisted sense of humor. I use that to take the pretense out of today's performance art. I don't analyze too much. I just spew them out.

SG: So tell me about your cyberpiss character.

S3A: She's unfortunately a cartoon character and Earth is unfortunately a cartoon planet. She only gets one dimension. If she fucks a toaster, she becomes the toaster. She gets the toast off, but *so what*. She can't have a deep relationship, because the toaster can't become something else afterwards and she can. It's not a complex enough machine. There doesn't seem to be a complex enough hardware for her, with a brain that would stimulate her, because she's passionate and intelligent and she wants a component to turn her on, and make her feel less lonely.

SG: What are a few of the other themes in this program? What can the audience expect to see that they'll clamor to buy tickets for?

S3A: Lots of visuals, multimedia . . . layered media. You'll feel that you are in a different world when you are in the theatre, like going to the Exploratorium. But with toilet visuals everywhere that are very inventive and arty . . . alluring. A seduction at the end with the Fucking Robot— the Goddess meets her mate. It's like *The Last Tango in Paris*, only we lost Brando for a robot.

Simone Third Arm, as the Alien, is very concerned with Alienation and constipation. She wants to start a whole Bowel Movement. She wants people to release themselves.

SG: Gaaaaak . . . So do you relate human embarrassment about excrement to nationalism, racism and all those things, as the Post-Freudians do?

S3A: Wouldn't it be beautiful if we created one big toilet bowl and somebody from every country came and *shit together at the same time*. And just flushed . . . flushed all that tension . . . [singing] We are the world. We're on the toilet.

SG: I can't decide if this is going to be brilliant or embarrassing.

RUS: Both. Public embarrassment is the cutting edge of liberation. In a mass-mediated cyberculture, the greatest risk is *embarrassment*. I mean, what're ya gonna do, virtual skydiving? . . .

SG: What about the romance with technology, the sex robot . . . and R. U., you've talked about getting plastic surgery on stage. Isn't technoculture driving us towards nightmarish conclusions?

RUS: I'd find it more interesting to live inside a Cronenberg film than to live in the world as it's currently organized. There's an intrigue in becoming monsters.

SG: In other words, "What, me worry?"

RUS: In other words, I'm willing to risk my life in the search for immortality.

SD: [looking up past me] Hey!

Voice: Immortality . . . Yessss.

A thin intellectual-looking gentleman in his forties, in a stylish gray greatcoat, is looming over the table. R. U. and Simone give him weak smiles and murmur "Hello, Elliot."

Scrappi: This is Mondo Vanilli's anti-philosopher, Dr. Elliot Handleman.

SG: Oh good. I was hoping to get more of the philosophy or anti-philosophy . . .

EH: This is Mondo Vanilli's theory of immortality: In Freud's concept of death—going beyond the pleasure principle—the idea is that all animate matter wants to return to inanimate matter, to die. In Freud's time the most advanced science held that death resulted from failure to excrete the products of metabolism. The obvious inference is that constipation is the deathwish in action. So I'm now proposing a post-post-Freudian theory of media: to live forever one must excrete the metabolic products of the entertainment industry.

RUS: We're media excretionists.

EH: I'm very disappointed in these guys for making an album full of *music*. I think MV should be concerned with doing as much damage to the entertainment industry as it can.

And you did use my idea of making ads . . . but not *really* . . . not all the way. The game is—advertise Coke, Diet Pepsi. The commercials are *not* ironic. You really try to make people buy Coke. You preempt the Coca-Cola Company's advertising. And feature the advertising itself as the product of an artistic media/entertainment collaboration.

It's like *The Last Tango in Paris*, only we lost Brando for a robot.

This is done without anyone's approval. The band doesn't benefit from the selling of the product *in the least*. I think it's crucial to link MV to commercial concerns immediately. I can't like the idea of a band that's just a bunch of kids who think they can do things. There's nothing to be done. There's nothing to do it with. There's no one to do it for.

SG: That would be a funny sort of violation of proprietary interests!

EH: Yes. And I thought you guys were into challenging copyright laws (waves a CD of *IOU Babe*) instead of this crap. Rock stars? You want to be rock stars? How old . . .

SG: Elliot, why do you want to challenge copyright laws?

EH: *They* were supposed to challenge copyright laws, not me. I'm for copyright laws because they're rendering music obsolete. And I'm for that because it strips the world of another source of familiarity . . . and also because I'm against activity.

Look at the laws. It used to be that to copyright music you had to have a lead sheet, you had to have the thing written out. Then copyright extended to tapes and records and electronic storage devices. And now the question is, "What constitutes plagiarism?" The guidelines are, if six notes of your album match six notes of anybody else's album you are liable.

So, to check for plagiarism you go: "Are these notes 1 to 6 equal to any of the consecutive groups

of six notes in every piece that was ever written?" Then you would check notes 2 to 7, and all the way down the line. Now—in accordance with my anti-production principle—I'm for this because sooner or later you'll just run out of notes. It's a very large number, but it's finite. [*chortles*]

RUS: This is why we say "Music is Obsolete." It's been replaced by intellectual property.

EH: Yeah, and by the way that was my idea, R. U. You stole my idea! So much for copyright . . .

You can play some fun games once you understand what copyright law is. These are interesting laws because there's no way they can be enforced. They're artistic Nuremberg laws. They outlawed sexual activities between Aryans and non-Aryans. Copyright law proscribes intercourse between the authentic and the inauthentic.

SG: So you object to the False Starts media-prank band making an actual album?

EH: In principle, yes, although they might have made it interesting. But they didn't. [brandishes CD at the band members] The problem with this [threatens with CD] is that it's real work. This actively promotes an authentic sort of music. There's already a history of this sort of stuff!

I'd like to make "music" [sneers horribly] along the following lines: It's like trying to find out who owns a building in New York City. The tenants complain it's falling apart. But the janitor is hired by some agency, which is contracted by another . . . and the owner is 25 steps removed—just collects the rent. That's how "music" should be made. I'm not interested in the concepts of creativity and production. I'm interested in anti-production, non-production. That's key, to get away from producing things, realizing ideas . . .

[*They all start to mutter fiercely to one another, and I can hear only isolated phrases . . . "active vs. passive production" . . . "passive excretion" . . . "so we're just assholes". . .*]

SG: Wait, wait: so you're violating your own philosophy? Are you selling out?

Mondo Vanilli [All four shout at once]: YES!!!!

R. U.'s MV Tour Diary
May 3, 1995

Scrappi and Simone are arguing over her desire to do an enema painting on the last night's performance. I'm encouraging it, mostly, although I'm doing the Clinton, trying to locate the compromise or let the contending forces find their way.

I'm not sure why I was so attracted to the Enema Painting as a performance piece, when Simone first described it to me—why the notion has a kind of Warholian elegance to me, rather than seeming another simplistic bit of transgression in an ocean of subculture shock tactics. I've always taken an obscure visceral pleasure in violating the tradition of the painter's canvas. I'm a big fan of Keith Palac's Painted Meat series as well.

Scrappi likes subtlety and elegance and I am also drawn to that, particularly because—in these times of post-punk shock value and working class authenticity—subtlety and elegance IS a transgression. This was true in the early seventies as well, when such as Roxy Music and Bowie came along to violate the jeans and t-shirt Maoism of post-hippie seventies rock. On the other hand, I'm also down with the Naked Lunch, the validity of taking a hard look at what's on the plate in terms of human experience, and so I can support dealing with shit, piss, death, disease, murder, bigotry, et al. The dialectic between Scrappi and Simone's sensibility is what makes MV interesting to me.

And I don't mean to imply that CyberPiss Goddess deals in excrement in negative terms. The idea, I believe, is a very fundamental body-based philosophy of liberation. A species that can split the atom, move into space and (soon) manipulate matter at the molecular level, a species that is about to become Godlike, at least within our own limited notion of what that might be, but one that can't confront its own excrement—is in DEEP SHIT.

Meanwhile, Simone is on the telephone right now talking and laughing with her transvestite friend Jack Daniels, and sHE has already got her ticket. The enema painting now takes on a sort of grim inevitability.

3 pm
It's three pm and I've been assaulting my psyche with a steady barrage of drugs for the last two hours, trying to force myself into a state of heightened whatever. I promised myself that I would write some song lyrics while on tour. I know it's a great rock and roll tradition and I thought I'd try it. So I did a couple of lines of coke and sat in front of the powerbook, but the words were humorless and not pleasing. I smoked some opium and started to feel better, but the edge from the coke was still on me. I was then interrupted by a visit from some hippie-ish fans of Mondo 2000, who somehow convinced tour security to escort them to my hotel room. We talked earnestly about Leary's new book and I managed to get them out the door in less than 20 minutes. That's when I loaded 40 milligrams of DMT and 60 milligrams of ketamine into a pipe.

AND HERE WE ARE! You know, I can't find a new insight, drugs or no. All I can really do is try to extract already existing perceptions from the fairly complicated mental construct through which I see the world. And right now, kicked back on coke, opium, DMT, and ketamine, watching some soft-core pornography on the vid, I'm thinking about the survival value of guilt and Christianity and trying to recall how Norman O. Brown resolved the ancient question of how to have a livable human society based on hedonism and pleasure, rather than guilt and repression. But I can't remember. Or I can't believe.

I caught Chomsky on C-SPAN the other night and he was talking about the "deep irrationality" of the American body politic, with its strong fundamentalist influence, stretching back to the Puritans at Plymouth Rock. And I was nodding my agreement. But there is also this: that we all need some form of "deep irrationality" sometimes. Can we separate it from politics? Can you picture Noam at 3 am, wearing hot pants and lipsticks, dancing to Snoop and waving his hands in the air like he just don't care?

And then Scrappi comes in, asking what I think we should do about the Enema Painting. I tell him we should let it happen. "Given the recent history of rock and performance art, it's probably not even that big a deal." He buys it and so the Enema Painting will happen. But I'm not sure that what I said is true.

San Francisco Chronicle   June 30, 1995   Pg. 4

Coalition of Liberals and Conservatives May Demand Ground Rules For the Internet

by Mitchell Snead

Radical feminist Katherine McKinnon-Masson and Christian Coalition member Reverend Lawrence Lindstrom held a joint press conference today announcing the formation of a new organization called the Human Anti-Degradation League (the HADL), a coalition of liberals and conservatives who, according to Ms. McKinnon-Masson, wants to "put a stop to rampant abuse and obscenity" in electronic media. The group, which claims to have thousands of supporters, plans to focus on the Internet, which McKinnon says is "turning into a cesspool of Beavis and Butthead-style sexual harassers, racist White Power groups, and violently aggressive and obscenity-laced diatribes of every imaginable sort."

The Reverend Lindstrom said that tens of thousands of HADL supporters "will be online within the next few months" and that they would attempt "at first, to persuade folks on the Internet to behave within the generally accepted boundaries of common decency." A statement issued by the group said that they would "move swiftly towards requesting legislative action to make the Net safe for women, children and minorities, if the Net can't clean up it's own act." The statement also called the Internet "our new town hall and public meeting place," and said that it must "become a welcoming place for women and ordinary people, not just anti-social hackers and misfits." Lindstrom added, "Maybe it's just a matter of convincing the hackers and all those types that this isn't their little world anymore, and that they should behave like they would in any community where children and folks with conservative values are likely to be around. Hopefully we can all just get along."

```
= = = = = = = = = = = = = = = = = = = = = = = = = = = = = = = = = = = = = = = = = = = = = = = = = = = =
Date: June 30, 1995
From: stjude
To: rusirius
Subject: it's happening . . .
Attached File: SF Chronicle today
```

This strange bedfellowship of conservatives and the politically correct -- nice that they worked out their frigidity problems -- is going to Disneyfy the Internet?

Remember my tirades about the bornagains conquering cyberspace? So here they come, wave upon wave. The fact is that they may hold their endless church socials or whatever it is that they have in mind, but they can't enforce general niceness in the online. Never happen.

What groups like HADL *can* do is narrow what's called personal lifestyle choices -- like yours and mine -- in real life. And, worse for you, in broadcast media. Better think about that.
I love it that they call themselves the Human Anti-Degradation League. You can hear them muttering -- "this degrades women, and this over here is degrading to younger humans. And *this* is degrading to . . ."

Let 'em mutter. The clampdown is upon us. And so what?
===
Date: July 2, 1995
From: rusirius
To: StJude

Thanks for sending me the Chronicle piece. I've been in Milwaukee, and I missed the papers . . . they're probably crowing about it here, actually. Also, having software problems and not able to check the comments on the net . . . hope you're still checking here on AOL.
    So . . . The HADL. That's SMOOTH. They're not against freedom or dissent, only the degradation of humans. Our opponents are NOT about to make this easy.
===
R. U.'s MV Tour Diary
July 15, 1995

3 pm:
We're in Cleveland—where the shit will hit the canvas if not the fans—for a two day break followed by the last three performances. The shows are at the Repertory Theater, the town's mainstream theatrical performance hall. David and Samuel from Naught were able to rig it up that way, being hometowners. Brent is coming to town for the grand finale.
    Jack Daniels, raving transgender masochist, is here already. SHe sat next to me on the airplane and offered me a blow job! I got no problem with tv's, and I LOVE getting blow jobs on airplanes, but Jack Daniels is distinctly unattractive. However, sHe blathered on about her life and all of her boyfriends, while I sat there with a Himmler bio at my nose. Finally I told her, "Right now, I'm more interested in Himmler's life than in yours," although once having said that, I think we both wondered why. So I offered "her" something to put in her mouth, as a consolation, and went on reading about the occult nazi.

The tour is hemorrhaging money. So I'm glad to have another gig. While everybody else gets their rest in Cleveland, I'm set up to do a talk at some sort of ancient countercultural free school. It'll be a fun sort of distraction. Plus $1500.

Midnight:

I delivered a fun, cynical lecture revolving around the notion that media and communications technology has democratized decadence and nihilism, philosophies and "lifestyles" that were once vouchsafed for remittance men and women and the more popular artists and entertainers. It was a rambling pop lecture, namedropping Aleister Crowley, Anita Pallenberg, Kurt and Court-ney, Brent, O. J. Simpson, and Lestat. Felt good. Lots of laughs. It's the hedonism question again, in different terms. Can a society afford the spread of decadence and nihilism all the way down to the underclass? Aspects of rap and hip hop were influenced by the white punk culture. What happens when punk nihilism escapes the arts-and-culture playpen and hits the real world? 911 . . . get me George Will.

And then, here come the ravers . . . it's after the talk and I'm surrounded by the usual gaggle of guys wanting to wax cyber. And there they are, on the periphery, five of them, four guys and one girl. Big floppy hats. Anarchic Adjustments t-shirts. Love beads. Glowing youthful friendly faces. My first thought is . . . MARIJUANA! So I wrap it up with the techies and make eye contact. We step outside to get a few tokes and the apparent leader, who calls himself Mr. Matrix, is off to the races. "The consciousness is spreading, man. We've been giving out these special mandala screensavers to everyone we meet. And we did this thing in Hollywood with Tim Leary and Ter-ence McKenna and the next thing you know . . . those Fruitopia commercials hit the collective unconscious. So now the screen saver has become this video thing and I'm on the cover of Info World. This bigass psychedelic picture right on the cover of Info World! Psychedelic consciousness is spreading. By the year 2000, everyone will have seen the mandala . . ." I can't deal and bid farewell. But not before I agree to come down to the Love City Digital office the following after-noon. I even give them my correct hotel room. I don't mind hanging with shiny happy people once in awhile. And I've run out of pot.

July 16

2 pm. The ravers show up at the hotel. It's the same five, plus an older dude, Leon Light. He's a fifty-five year old slouching ex-beat type, bad attitude but with a very deep calm center. Hipster criminal as buddhist Godfather. Deep lined face that speaks a thousand lives. Long skinny black magic fingers. Ex-junkie. One time murderer. Wrote a book about Peyote in the late fifties. Very masculine. He's a sadistic sex magician, but only when he's high. The woman in me is immedi-ately in love.

We zip up to Love City Digital to look at their video, the usual content-free mandala-fractal meditation. Boring, but this one dude, Morgan, is telling me about the spiritual group that he's in, and I'm fascinated because they have some kind of weird hierarchy and set of beliefs.

They're more or less quakers. Except that they drink ayahuasca tea before each meeting. He's very earnest about his god-intoxication. The group calls themselves "Angels of the Vine" and they're fanning out across America to win converts. They believe in family, work, prayer, racism, cleanliness, patriarchy, pure food and drink, monogamy, and psychedelic drugs. He's just been to his first rave. He was not much impressed. That may be the one thing we have in common.

The members attain levels within the hierarchy by mastering some sort of secret doctrine which

is . . . well . . . secret. They wear their position in the church on the sleeves of their yellow polo shirts. Three stripes is the lowest rung. Then there's two stripes, one stripe, and—finally—the guys (that IS guys. No girls allowed in this church) in the white polo shirts. The Men In White rule. I'm fascinated and want to know more about their secret doctrine, but Morgan won't spew. So I tell him I'm the godhead of my own secret occult religion organized around the worship of the male sex god Pan and the feminine alien as represented by the CyberPiss Goddess. He's all ears. This is a man who likes religion, and secret cults and hierarchies, so I explain mine. It went something like this:
I'm on top.
The 48 Flesh Vampire Daughters of the Awful Nasty Scary Female Thing XXX are second in the hierarchy
The 144,000 Studly Warrior Dudes are next.
All Women 'Cept for One are next
All Men are next
The Last and Lowest Woman, actually a double of myself, is at the bottom. As above so below. The snake sucks its own dick.
And finally, the CyberPiss Goddess transcends our existence.

Morgan's quite literal brain is cognating the destructive capacity of my faith, as well as the possible sexual rewards. Leon Light, meanwhile, wants to join and be one of the Studly Warrior Dudes. No. Scratch that. He thinks again. HE wants to be on top. I have a terrible feeling I'm gonna let him be just that.

July 20
The show was particularly intense. CPG made us feel that the struggle in the gladiator pit mattered. We had escaped the stage, escaped the theater, escaped Cleveland and we were inside of some great epic contest of the gods. The show climaxed as usual with the simulated machine fuck, sparks flying out CPG's massive Teslacoiled "nervous system" while we played a subharmonic that vibrated the listener's stomach.

And then, the encore. Scrappi and I take places on the far ends of the stage, behind dueling synths. I start up the rhythm, he starts up the noise. CyberPiss Goddess waits a good three minutes before entering stage left, dressed in a slightly-too-sexy nurse outfit. She's leading Jack Daniels on a dog leash. They walk slowly to the lip of the stage and take deep bows. Kristen, a goodnatured and thankfully unflappable Vanna White clone we rented from a local modeling agency, enters stage right. She's carrying a chair made from a toilet seat, a 5' x 5' painter's canvas, and an enema bag. Placing the canvas flat on the floor and the toilet seat on top of the canvas, she does the quiz show babe move, hands CPG the enema bag, and elegantly exits stage right.

The audience's collective gasp was audible from the stage, despite the high volume electronic noise, as CPG lifted the enema bag into the air whilst Jack lifted up his long peasant skirt, pulled his panties down to his ankles and climbed on the throne. We all stood transfixed as CPG inserted the enema bag up the butthole (and a closeup of the act appeared on the big screen). Suddenly, the audience started to clap and cheer, loud masculine football bellows, feminine whoops and piercing whistles. CPG grinned broadly and Jack looked a little peaked. She took hold of the enema bag. She squeezed and squeezed and squeezed. The audience clapped in rhythm. She removed the bag. Jack's face—contorted, holding his breath, holding back the shit-paint—was projected close up on the big screen. Kristen rushed out and handed CPG a pair of swords. The rhythmic clapping thundered louder as CPG twirled her swords and danced around the edge of the canvas, spotlight and video projection still focused on Jack's face as he attempted to hold it in. He held a good two minutes. And then exploded. Purple, the color of grape juice. It slapped the canvas and splattered. Splattered beyond the canvas. Splattered several feet, a few splashes hitting CPG's spike heeled shoes and one hitting her leg. The audience cheered fervently, as though we'd just won the World Cup. I looped the dance rhythm. Scrappi faded his synth noise down and out, and we both joined CPG and Jack centerstage, carefully sidestepping the many wet spots. We bowed. They stood up and cheered. And cheered. And cheered. The rhythm faded. They cried for more. Hey, there's shit all over the stage . . . we're outta there.

We were still toasting the great performance backstage when we got word that the stage crew refused to deal with the excrement. Then, of course, there was a long refusal to face the fact. Then there was the bald reality. We had nothing to clean the shit up with. Finally, at 1 am, after negotiations with the theater's janitor, we got him to direct us to an all night market and leave us with the keys to the theater so he could "go the bloody hell home."

The evening ends with a snapshot I'll forever treasure, Brent Buzzkill and his bodyguards, along with Scrappi, pouring piles of kittylitter on the purple excrement while CPG talks to a few fans and I stand around trying to look busy. Finally, just shy of 2 am, we were all in cars ready to head back to the hotel, when Scrappi decided to go back in and give the place the once-over, one more time. After waiting many many minutes—and well nigh ready to go back to the hotel and die—I went in to hurry him out. I found him perched on the lip of the stage, gazing into space with a worried look across his face.

Cleveland Plain Dealer Art and Entertainment
July 22, 1995

Rep Theater Troubles

by Anthony Johns

Several angered patrons of Cleveland's elegant and reputable Repertory Theater are saying "never again," after the theater hosted a performance by an oddball rock and roll recording theater troupe called Mondo Vanilli. The three nights' performances were all in questionable taste, according to several patrons, who asked to remain anonymous. But it was the last performance, in which a transvestite was given an enema while perched over an artist's canvas, that led to complaints from audience members, including several of the theater's most generous patrons, who are now asking for the resignation of John Kimball, acting director and manager of the theater. Kimball says that he regrets the performance and had not been informed that this "gross-out thing" was going to occur on the last night. Asked if he would pursue legal action against the band, or its tour management company, Kimball said that it was doubtful, but he said that he would "be much more careful" about who performs there in the future. Members of Mondo Vanilli, who have names like Are You Serious and Simone Triple X, couldn't be reached for comment, but Samuel Portay of the band's Cleveland-based record label, Naught/Innerscoop, told the Plain Dealer, "I think maybe they were protesting on behalf of Robert Mapplethorpe or something."

```
============================================================
```
Date: Sept 18, 1995
From: StJude
To: rusirius
Subject: dream, seizure . . . whatever

Listen, something seriously strange just happened.
I dreamed I was a bluebottle fly . . . yeah, I know it's been done already, but listen: I was not asleep. One minute I was writing somebody
online, and the next I was a bluebottle fly. Way WAY in the background
I knew I was sitting at the keyboard, but here in FRONT I was buzzing
my wings like hell, hovering more or less in one spot, looking for a
place to land on the face of this muddy, tired-looking cow, maybe water buffalo? -- big horns. Then zap! Gone. Nothing but keyboard.

Seriously strange, but I feel goooood.

This was not like a psychotic break . . . more like a reality break.
It was nice. Like a little intermission, a tiny time out. A COFFEE
break.

I am not insane. No.

Maybe I've just had a Green epiphany . . . do I suddenly want to help
trees? do I want to change my voter registration? [Definitely not . . .
I LOVE being registered under an expired name, address, and political category, and the more they remain the same the more I
change.]

I am not insane. I am not Green. And I'm not worried.

zzzzzzzzzjude
ps: don't you worry either. i feel very primate-identified. true.
```
============================================================
```
Date: Sept 19, 1995
From: StJude
To: rusirius
Subject: Another Armed Interview! For Details, Details! But it's to-
morrow!

Christ, I forgot: I'm doing that armed interview tomorrow. Means I
can't meet yr leman for lunch -- regrets; have fun.

58
```
```

I'll need lots of time tomorrow, too. Benoit is a good writer, I like his stuff, but his publisher sez he's a REALLY hard interview. Knives are in his latest book, but I think I may tempt him -- if he's good -- with my newly converted Quigley .45. A yummy piece.

Wait a minute. Time out. Uh oh: it's happening again. I've got feathers. It's cold . . .

I'm a male Emperor Penguin with a big egg on my feet, shuffling around with a thousand others, all with eggs on their feet. If we didn't have eggs on our feet we'd be seeking some shelter, out of this damn wind -- Antarctic high midwinter, pretty fierce. I'm glad about my egg, though, no mistake. We seem to pass warmth back and forth, me and this large solid egg, which is wedged comfortably under my bellyflap, pressed to my scaley feet tops . . . I like it very much . . .

Okay, now what was I saying? Oh yeah . . . so I may have to be very very clever and fierce tomorrow. Gotta sort out all my leather restraints and oil them up.

When I pulled that switchblade on Shonen Knife, when I flashed my right tit at Nicholson Baker in the French Hotel, I thought I might be making myself a new career. But it's an idea whose time is PAST, baby; the HADL's gonna do it in. This may be my last byline as Jude Milhon, Armed Interviewer. My last case . . .

At least now my shtick can never get appropriated. Nice to think that the wannabes might have tortured their interviewees for real, or KILLED them . . . or . . . who knows? Popculture models spin out of control almost instantly nowadays.

BTW, in the Tuesday NY Science Times there's something you oughta know. As a sidefeature of melanoma research they've learned how to increase total melanin in people. That is: total. Seven days of pills and dreams of negritude come true like >doink< THAT! -- UR Siriusly ethiopian. It wears off in 3 months. I bet by this time next month I can get some of this stuff on the <oh no> black market, what you bet? I get it, you do it? Yes yes.

>jude<
===
Date: Sept 21, 1995
From: rusirius
To: StJude

I'll take the pills! See what you can find out about scoring some. Jan Morganshtakker and that whole smart crew oughtta know where.

Speaking of pills, from the looks of your last two email messages, I'd say you've been sticking your hand into that blue bag that I left over at your place and you promised you wouldn't touch. . . . That shit's experimental jude, stay away from it. Unless you're a fiend (not a former fiend, mind you) that shit'll getcha to schizoland in microseconds! Stay away.

===
Date: Sept 21, 1995
From: StJude
To: rusirius
Subject: Blue bag??

oops, i shouldn't put provocative things in the Subject line . . . Blue bag??

Forget the fucking blue bag; i fed that shit to my cat a long time ago -- i'm 2/3 straightedge unto death. I'm an ex-everything, yeah. I zapped to Antarctica under my own power. No weird chemicals for me. (Hmm . . . is my brain synthesizing its own?) Look, don't worry about me. *I* don't need a new liver every six months.

>jude<

ps: I'm having my doubts about turning you out on the pigment, too. Think! Look in the mirror! On this Mello-tone stuff you may look like late-stage Miles Davis . . . with world's worst process job. Reconsider!!
===
Date: Sept 22, 1995
From: rusirius
To: StJude
Subject: Re: Blue bag??
YOU FED THE STUFF IN THE BLUE BAG TO THE CAT!?! SHIT! YOU'LL PAY FOR THIS JUDE!!!

Meanwhile, I'm still trying to get that shit that'll make me look like half-an-Arnie Schwartzeneger while I sleep. And then to be BLACK on top of it all!
YOWZA! I MUST HAFF ZE PILLS DOKTOR CHUDE!!!!

===

Date: Sept 29 95
From: rusirius
To: StJude
Subject: grrrl talk!

Hey! Just got a copy of Grrrl Talk with you on the cover. Nice picture!
Leathers, gun and modem . . . you look good that darker shade of black
-- a look for our new radical push (putsch?) -- the Panthers meet
cyb(ph)erpunque. Also, thanks for letting me nip into the GrrrlLove
Mailing List. Hella funny. I think I'm in love with Marina.

   I just had a brief fling with a grrrl named Kali. Great young wild
energy. Really self-righteous, of course. Brought to mind this chick I
was with in college, Dizzy. Member of Women Against Violence Against
Women. Had to be slapped around to get an orgasm. I'm not making this
up. I don't care what you say, hetero guys cope with more cognitive

dissonance per mile
than any other sex-
seeking primate.

   Anyway, I met Kali
at my first acting gig
. . . this independent
movie about the evolu-
tion of the computer
network called "Global-
head by Pentagon." I
play this hacker who
seduces this chick on-
line, discovers she's
a "feminist," and then
fucks her up. I rape
her data! Anyway, I

###
#########   • Trudy B. Hyatt •   #########
#########   • Editorial Assistant •   #########
#########   • Hyatt@Ballantine.Books.com •   #########
###

Date: 1/6/95
To: rusirius@well.com   StJude@well.com

While I enjoy both of your comments very much, they seem to meander
along any which way they please. I'm wondering if that's your intention
or not, and if so, why?

Also, I don't recall the initial plot being oriented so much around gender
issues. I'm not complaining, mind you . . . just wondering.

come into this not realizing that I'm typecast as this total reactionary
vis-a-vis feminism. It's like "Are you a (wincing distaste) *feminist?*"
And so forth. Kind of a cyberhip Rush Limbaugh. And I did it very well . . .
heh . . . *shut up jude.* Hey. It was my first acting experience. So I acted.
It's acting, fer fuck's sake. Anyway, this intensely cute young girl (with
the usual -- hair shaved off on one side of head, lip ring, nose ring, Kali
(the Goddess) tattoo on her right shoulder) is laughing, appropriately, at
my performance, taking it in the over-the-top spirit that was intended.

   Then, a few weeks later, I'm watching the rushes with the rest
of the cast and crew. And I realize that the character that I play
in this film is "R U Sirius." That's right. I'm playing myself as
an out-and-out male chauvinist pig and cyber-rapist! Ok. So, do I

object? No, not me. Use the Icon-At-Large as you will, ladies.

So we're doing the wine and cheese thing afterwards and everything's different. At the filming, the women are telling me what to say and what kind of attitude to have. Everybody can see that I'm acting. Now, it's R U Sirius in theory and practice, and these same people are looking at me rather uncomfortably. I plunk myself down next to Kali. She compliments my performance. I say, "I didn't know my character was supposed to be *me*." She says, "You don't actually think that way?" I say, "Not quite." We lock eyes and there's that awful

```
##############
#   /==$=\    #  <- From the High-Tech Fully Electronic Desk
# /))-00(\   #      of R. U. Sirius
# ((( -)))   #
# )))\ /(((  #  -> rusirius@well.com
##############
```

Date: 1/6/95
To: hyatt@ballantine.books.com   StJude@well.com
Subject: It's a SCRAPbook Trudy.

Well it's a diary within a scrapbook. With all that implies. Of course, it's also a novel that uses the scrapbook as a strategy. Not to worry. The meandering is in a forwardly direction.

The gender stuff is a major meander that will meander in and out of the overall theme which is, after all, HOW TO MUTATE & TAKE OVER THE WORLD! Well, Trudy, the world's a big fuckin' place and we feel that we have to comment on EVERYTHING before we're complete. |-)

sense of inevitability. It's like my shop teacher said in the ninth grade. "This is gonna be alot of fun but alot of work."

And so forth. Just another hot three-week sex fight and now it's over. The high point for me was when she tied me up, made me watch her fuck this journalist who had come to interview me, and then they left me there to go out bar hopping for the night.

So just for the fuck of it one night I go to one of her classes over at UC Berkeley with her favorite RadFem teacher, Miyuko Takahashi. Miyuko dishes out the woman-is-victim-of-sex line to the scariest, toughest, nastiest, rudest gang of tattooed and scarified young babes you'd ever wanna be run over by. Kali is in her "History of Rape" class and in her "The Portrayal of Women by Hollywood" class. So I go to the Hollywood class and they're showing the Elvis Presley classic, *Clam Bake!* You've basically got your bikini bimbos and you've got big El. The bimbos wiggle around. Elvis looks 'em up and down and curls his lip. Harmless fun, in my book. The film ends and all the guys in the class are sucking up to Miyuko, talking objectification. They're particularly onto Elvis, and the way he looks at the girls' tits and curls his lip. I just *have* to speak out. "Uh, pardon me," I say, "but we're animals. When young animals look at one another during mating season, they don't want to talk about theory or career options. They check each other out. They *smell* each other. They growl. They curl their lips.

(Kali starts rustling her books next to me.) Elvis is playing the role
of the male sex god Pan in *Clam Bake.* And we've killed Pan. It's a
DeadPan era. (Kali pushes past me with a certain level of barely contained violence). But Pan doesn't give a fuck about a bunch of fucking
deadass weasels so . . . uh, that's all I wanted to say."

They're laughing at me not with me as I stumble from my seat, squeeze
out into the aisle and walk briskly out the door to try to catch up with
Kali. But I'm not much thinking about what I'll say to her. I'm going
over what I just said in that class, trying to gauge just how foolish it
was. Kali's way down the hall. I call. She stops. Between us a class lets
out and some sixty-odd people get in my way. I pirouette through the students. "Your mother must have really done something to *YOU*!" she's
screaming. Huh?! So I'm stunned and speechless and I can't help giggling.
"*NOT* funny *NOT* funny *NOT* funny." This isn't gonna be a reasonable
discussion. Four black guys stand nearby, watching, snickering and jiv-
ing. "I do *NOT* want to be objectified!" "Uh . . . what do you think we've
been doing to each other for the last three weeks? I mean, that's how we
get off." She pours a coke over my head, and stomps off down the hall. (I
didn't know she had a fucking coke. Where did that come from? PROPS!!!)
It's then that I notice that however genuinely pissed she might be, she's
also performing for the black guys. She's doing a sexy, pouty white-bitch
number, stalking off in high dudgeon. The black guys are saying, "Smack
the bitch," and suchlike. I catch one more glance of Kali wagging her
cute little drama-queen butt down the hall and decide, what the fuck,
I'll go back in and check out the rest of the class. I turn around, catch
my breath and proceed slowly back. And I can't stop giggling. If I've
learned one thing in my 42 years on earth it's that PEOPLE ARE FUNNY!
Suddenly, "R U! R U!" I turn around. Kali's running back to me. She's really preening for the black guys, and doing these little Sunset Boulevard
flourishes. "I thought you'd chase after me." She's giggling herself now
and says it outright, "I'm a real drama queen, aren't I?" We lock lips.
We go home. We fuck four times. The next morning I wake up and she says
that we can't see each other anymore. "I guess I'm just politically correct." No, you're inane, I think, but I don't argue. It's been fun.

Anyway, that's my riot grrrl story. I'm pro-grrrl. I love crazy
young radical energy. The grrrls will not be their mother's feminists, when erotic push comes to puritanical shove. They're too hypersexual. They're too into the body. As a pin cushion maybe, but
into it. As Acker would say, they're into the body as the final locus
of identity. And so they'll be pro-sex in the long run . . .

Anyway, sorry to rant so long.

   as always,
     R. U.
===

The Wicked St. Jude Challenges Yr Most Cherished Beliefs, Grrrrl

Interviewed by rosie x

Since her "Grace Jones Schools for Girls" column in MONDO2000, StJude has been a voice—usually a loud, raucous voice—for free speech and online education. One of the things she's been shouting is that grrls need cyberspace as a sort of boot camp to make them strong in the real world.

StJude can be annoying. Just when you think you know where she's at, she blips out and bounces at you from behind—she loves to throw stuff at ya from odd positions. You may be annoyed, but please: Don't throw stuff at *me* !! I'm just the interviewer here, okay????

—Rosie x; >

RX: If you had a word to describe yourself and what you do when using this electronic medium what would it be?
SJ: I'm a future-hacker. I'm trying to get root access to the future. I want to raid its system of thought. Grr.

RX: What type of machine turns you on? If you could design a machine, what would it feel, look, and act like? How much grunt would you give it? And would you let it wear your black leather jacket??
SJ: Machines disappoint me. I just can't love any of these warez, hard or soft. I gots the intermediate, o so inadequate, present technology blues. I'm nostalgic for the future. I need the stuff that we can dream it but we can't be it, yet.

I don't want any of this virtual crap. Ordinary reality is too virtual already. We need bandwidth! We need ultrahigh-res! Give us bandwidth or kill us! Let's see the ultraviolet polkadot flowers that hummingbirds see, and smell 'em like the bees do. And crank UP the sensorium all across the board: TURN IT ALL UP TO 11! And bring that synesthesia over here. We can have the systematic disorder of our samesame senses, certainly, but then let's have some home-brewed special senses we whip up to our own taste, with sensory equalizers, band-pass filters, flangers. New vocabularies. Very rich. Yum yum.

RX: How come you're sick of all this stuff re: women and technology? Do you think the issues of feminism and technology are resolved?

SJ: No no no! I think tech will solve all our problems, personal AND scientific. Girls NEED modems. Let's talk tech: techytalk.

RX: Do you think that women-only electronic salons are important? Have you heard of women resource centres that allow women to 'gag' dorks, cyber bores, etc.? What do you think about these strategies to counter some of the more abusive males?

SJ: Hanging out with nice people is nice. But I don't want to sit around in this elite club all the time: the Politeness Ghetto. Hanging out with nasty-ass bigoted male teeners is also good, if I can learn from it. I may pretend I'M a snotty male teener myself, and why not? Particularly if I can turn somebody around with my expressed deviant opinions. (I'm a GAY snotty male teener, now that I mention it.) Sticks and stones may break my bones, but words on a screen get at me only as much as I allow them to . . . I can get very tough online. (ANYBODY can be tough online. Just keep your cool and THINK before you type.)

RX: There's alot of concern about American female academics taking over the Internet, attempting to impose their agenda. Are American female academics GHETTOIZING these spaces and setting themselves up as Patrol Cops, overseeing what is said, who to, and how they should say it??

SJ: Implying censorship? John Gilmore of the Electronic Frontier Foundation told me what may be the quote of the year, 1995: "the Internet treats censorship just like any other glitch. It routes around it." To use the language of the acade-

mics, "the discourse is propelled by desire" and love laughs at locksmiths. So we'll talk about what we love to the people who can hear us, and if people bully us, we'll find another trysting spot and leave the cops to themselves. Keep in mind that we always have to drive the so-called InfoBahn defensively. Whether we're set upon by zealots or bigots or abusively correct politicos, we have to learn to defend ourselves.

Any kind of attack online calls for martial arts. Aikido may be best. Use the enemy's strength against them harmlessly. Martial all your arts. Learn how to mount an argument and win. I'm not going to be undressed—OR deconstructed—without a fight.

So: learn to fight! Cyberspace is better than an acre of warm tapioca for a tussle. (I see no bruises here.) This is the best training ground for women. We may start ten down in a physical fight, OK, but the keyboard is the great equalizer—BETTAH than the Glock .45. Combat on the Net is like Basic Training. The lonesome 14-yr-old girl that I used to be could have managed her life a lot better if she'd been through this kind of Boot Camp.

RX: Is the Internet safe for women? Is virtual rape possible?

SJ: Keep in mind, in cyberspace EVERYONE can hear you scream. There was a woman crying virtual rape on LambdaMOO a couple of months ago. A gay guy who was in-real-life beaten and raped told me about this with great distaste: "Nobody, NOBODY is raped in cyberspace."

It's a game, lady. You lost. When he tried to muscle you around you could have teleported. Or changed into an Iron Maiden (the spiky kind) and crimped off his dick. But by playing it this way, you've REALLY lost. Because the MOO is also a social space, where you can talk to people with REAL cultural differences—like Klansmen—and make them respect you as a woman, as a dyke, whatever. Toe-to-toe, you maybe change their prejudices forever. Excluding people changes nobody's behavior, and it certainly doesn't change their opinions. Cries for niceness don't make it. Toughen up! You're dealing with primates here. You have to stand up to them and give them a reason to respect you. I hate this Waaaaah I'm a poor sensitive

nobody, NOBODY is raped in cyberspace. It's a game, lady. You lost.

weak woman protect me shit. This kind of stuff generates MORE contempt for women. Uh oh, I can feel you scowl: >:(
—now remember, ain't I a woman? Let me look. Yes . . . yes I am . . .
So . . . Fuck Niceness! Self-defense. It's not learning how to cuss, girl, or how to act hostile. It's learning how to fence with words—make your opponent feel your point, laugh at the situation, and respect you. Learn how to WIN. No more Ms. Nice Girl! Develop the cutting remark, the tongue that cuts! Just say Bobbitt! O no: i didn't mean that. Heheheh.

RX: Apparently, the women conference areas on the Internet are being taken over by men. (! hmpf !) Do you think this is men trying to understand the female psyche?

SJ: How do you know they're men? I'm no lady, darlin'. How do you know I'M not a man? How you gonna let only genuine gyno-type double-X, Barr-body bearing, real virtual women into your virtual salon?? If they say they're women, *I*

say they're women, and should be treated just like the rest of us—BADLY.

Anyway, I think it's touching. It could be that this is the only way the alien sexes can converse honestly—when they're bodiless, nothing at stake, masked by their pseudonyms. Online, you can learn to be fearless, you can afford to be bold. I've found myself saying things on the telephone that I wouldn't say face2face—and the Net subtracts even the human voice. When you got nothing, you got nothing to lose. I can play amazing pranks, or I can do something even more outrageous: I can be honest. Say stuff so personal and real that my mind boggles to think about it now. This could be a breakthrough for humans learning about humans, not just men and women learning about each other.

RX: Who do you have more time for on the net—men, women, dogs? Or do you treat them all disdainfully? :-x

SJ: I like men okay. Women too. I haven't met any dogs, but I have frolicked with cats—the Tiggypersons on AOL. As for the academics, I feel that the last two speakers of Navaho should not be forced to speak English just in case the FBI might need to eavesdrop on them. That is—I feel that those persons who love to speak academese have the right to do so, whenever and wherever they choose. And I think that academics have the same right as other citizens to lead troops of boy- or girlscouts, according to their predilections, and that they should be allowed to recruit even the youngest of them into the academic lifestyle.

Furthermore, the online discourse on gender remains not uncircumscribed by Foucauldian delimiters, insofar as the engaged vocalities must inevitably find themselves submitted to the tenesmus of displacement strategies by which the placeholders inhabiting the patriarcologies uh the patri-hierarchies inhabiting the er uh huh heh heh heh . . .

Grrrrl Talk Forum   Oct 1995   The Wicked St. Jude

Oct 2
Dear Grrrl Talk:

I was really disappointed with your interview of St. Jude in the last
issue. I can't believe that a GRRRL magazine would seriously accuse feminist academicians of trying to GHETTOIZE and TAKE OVER online spaces
for wimmin! Get real! Your questions were hardly tough or meaningful,
you kissed up to St. Jude and her brand of macho-male attitude, and you
never called her on any of her inconsistencies.

    While you and St. Jude can wax wonderful about being a rude bitch
vigilante and holding your own online (more power to ya), the fact is
that many women (who aren't as naturally testosterone laden as you apparently are) are confronted with the same hate and sexism online that they
get EVERY DAY and they are sick of dealing with it! And why should we
have to become assholes just because MALES have taken over everything?

    A wimmin-run, wimmin-only space allows us to express ourselves with-
out being ignored, discounted, made fun of, or shit on by sexist assholes. They are not ghettos. I am on several wimmin-only lists and they
provide a great sense of support and camaraderie for me. And when I do
participate in the greater net, I know I have a network of caring sisters behind me. I have a place to go to relax, wind down, and be myself,
rather than being on guard all the time for the next jerk. These wimmin-
only places are places of power for women. Perhaps they threaten St.
Jude who can feel on top and alone as a woman without a network, a woman
who owes nothing to other women. I'm surprised she even wanted to be interviewed by you for a GRRRL magazine. Isn't this magazine just another
ghetto?

    As for your section on cyber-rape, that REALLY made me mad! Anyone
who has gone through the horror of rape knows that going through it online is like having to go through the real experience all over again. It
is degrading and it creates an atmosphere of fear among many wimmin I
know online.

    Sure, it's "only words." DUH. But all you are in cyberspace IS
WORDS and so WORDS, which create the universe, have UNLIMITED POWER!
Once we recognize this maybe we won't tolerate their rampant abuse any
longer.

    I appreciate all my activist sisters who are creating wimmin spaces
on the net. Don't insult them.
    Sarah

Oct 3
dear sarah;

yeah like people really get raped online.
    you "wimmin" amaze me; you are people of such delicacy i'm surprised
any of you survived your childhoods.
        yr pal,
        marina

ps: try not to faint.

New York Times Review of Books Oct 4, 1995

WE'LL HAVE FUN, FUN, FUN ON THE *INFOBAHN*

How to Mutate and Take Over the World
by R. U. Sirius, St. Jude and Friends
266 pages. $19.95
Ballantine Books

By Dale Lazarov

Any time a book like *How to Mutate and Take Over the World* appears on top of their pile of review copies, they send it to me. I don't know if this is some kind of honor or not, but I guess I've been chosen to explain the more esoteric subcultures to the middle-highbrows. In this case, *How to Mutate and etcetera* was sent to me because I know what a modem is and I can use it. Modems do not frighten me. I am Modem, hear me roar.

Hacker subculture, though, frightens the grand majority of VCR + code users. Yours truly has been designated by the Cultural Elite as He Who Deciphers The Clues To The Clueless: Great Explainer of the Weird and Hip to the Great UnHip—Mister Zeitgeist to the Masses. In the case of the massive, much heralded *How To Mutate etcetera*, I am to decode the Weird and Possibly Quite Dangerous—

and tell you what to make of it. Translation: Should you hide in your basement, head between your haunches, waiting for the revolution to come?

The answer: Don't turn your assets into gold, just yet.

Written by cyberjournalists with a chip on their shoulder (ha, ha, the martini spills merrily down the side of the glass) *How To etcetera* is a massive, rambling, wildly uneven, impossibly ambitious and out of control *thing*—one hesitates to call it a *novel*—that begs to be compared to *Gravity's Rainbow* and much lesser novels of the world/language/meaning/life-as-we-know-it-falls-apart genre. The plot, such as it is, can be safely reduced to this: Imagine if God was Laurie Anderson, and she set the pieces in motion, like one of those magnetic, vibrating tabletop football games, and then the world ends.

An intriguing concept, too clever by half. Written for the converted, *How etcetera* satisfies the ideology in a language only the converted understand, and plays by the generic conventions of the converted. It's a massive in-joke. It's as PC as PC is about itself. It makes the same mistakes young cultures can make: create your own rules—not very sophisticated rules now that you mention it—and enforce them as blindly and uncreatively as what they are reacting *to*.

To see yet another exciting subculture rise from the junkheap to play by the same rules of orthodoxy and blinkered parochialism that killed Beat poetry, Punk Rock and *Spy* Magazine, to name but three cultural analogues ... Well, it makes one's arteries harden.

And that's it, substance-wise. The dominant writing style is on par with local yokel *samizdat*—relentlessly hyper-hip, smug and glib to the point of exhaustion. It's as exciting as a tin can dropping down a flight of stairs, and equally resonant. Personages imagined and real (real to whom?) weave in and out of the narrative without existing as *people* in the imagination of the reader—or at least at the level of characterization a parody like

this demands. They are, by all intents and purposes, cyphers, and nothing more.

A virtual compote of attitude and jargon, *How to Mutate and Take Over the World* should have been thought out more thoroughly as fiction, rather than pseudo-satirical cant. What could have been a truly alternate view of the world is tinny and unconvincing—a screaming coming across the screen in a late 70s arcade video game.

DALE LAZAROV is the author of *Birmingham Blues*, *Defunct Dogs* and *Cash*.

==

Date: Oct 9 1995
From: StJude
To: rusirius
Subject: wake up! time to revolt!

Your tour's long over. We got a book. Enough high Art. Done. It's time for the In Real Life. the future is bearing down on us harder than ever and what are we doing about it? Remember? The revolution? The party of the future? ANOTHER kind of crowdfucking? Oo, like, he really POLITICKED that crowd ...

The HADL are keeping their promises. The cypherpunks are posting stats and wringing their hands ... HADL is indeed colonizing the online. It's like the balkanizing thing ... where one ethnic group settles in and outbreeds the natives and then does a revanchist number on their parent country. Well, the online IS going to be nice. It's filling up with HADLites, and they're going to want to get everything sponsored by their churches and dinosaur feminist groups and shit ... and i will want to move out ... to where? It's a tiny planet.

Look, we gonna get busy? Lemme see if I can get you a patch to tweak yr ochlophilia, look it up -- means love of crowds. The rabble needs rousing. Now.
ttttt
Date: Oct. 14, 1995
From: rusirius
To: StJude

Oh shit, yeah. I DO think about that political movement I promised you back in February, every morning when I read the paper. Would you

accept a cool t-shirt and a few backstage passes instead? I mean, I
can think about politics til around noon when the sisters, Christy
and Karmela arouse . . . uh, that is . . . arise and, inevitably,
start right in . . . ON EACH OTHER! Well, politics just sorta flies
right out the window. I mean, what 95% heterosexual, trying-to-
avoid-midlife-crisis, overintellectual, funny-looking, borderline
pop star wouldn't sacrifice his political focus . . . scratch that . . .
wouldn't sacrifice a SMALL THIRD WORLD COUNTRY and two cypherpunk
draft choices (to be named later) -- for just TWENTY MINUTES
of this?

Rabble rousing?!! Here I am in this opulent 30's-style hotel --
a secret film industry hideaway in Maui. I'm smoking a mix of
hashish and opium out a hookah, watching Christy insert strawber-
ries inside of Karmela and lick them out, the cute young maid is
watching with an indelicate quiver in her upper lip as she sets out
the champagne breakfast, there's a message on my machine from Connie telling me that IOU Babe has hit the top 30 and one from Brett
Leonard asking us to join him and Julia Roberts for a late dinner
in their room . . . and like a goofball, I have to go and log on. Oh
well. Ain't it just like the night to play tricks when you're trying to be so quiet.

I HAVE been reading the L. A. Times though . . . every morning.
70% support school prayer. 68% say HADL is a good idea (24% don't
know what it is yet?). 59% support the "Singapore Spanking" legislation propounded by Jesse Helms. In other words, THERE IS NO HOPE!!!
My passport is still valid. And my bank account is getting fat . . .
(Actually, I need to check on that . . .)

===

R. U.'s Diary
Oct. 30, 1995

We've been watching the movements of the incredible Mondo Connie, world class conquis-
tadoress and publicist incredible. Every day, day in and out, across the telephone wires she
has stalked her prey; radio programmers, record chains, rock journalists. Connie, endless
font of arcane occult knowledge, mastress of verbal hypnotics . . . listen to her spin her
web. She doesn't play *hello*. She leads with a peculiar offhand comment, provoking—in
breathy scarcely controlled enticement—an intriguing hint of witchcraft and sacred sex.
Imagine the day-to-day banality on the low end of the music biz food chain suddenly interrupted by the carnival of all space and time and imagination, traces of lord krishna, excremental and carnal animal ritual sacrifices to some fabulously decadent goddess whispers
across the corporate forebrain and wafts way back to the mysterious south, and before old
sad eyes can snap to and realize "HEY THIS IS BULLSHIT!" he's had, he's skullfucked, a big
fucking hole drilled through his dull prosaic day-to-day and that's where she inserts Mondo
Vanilli, Jack, so that by the time he reenters corporeality, he's in some poor drone's face;

"WHY IN HELL HASN'T ANYBODY CALLED MY ATTENTION TO THIS MONDO VANILLI GROUP!?!"

And that's how we got to where we are today. And where are we? Finally, we're on the charts, we're in demand, we're . . . hopelessly naif. This calls for a big old bottle of champagne.

```
Welcome to Grrrlove Mailing List 1995

Grrrlove Mailing List, Nov 1995
Date: Nov 1, 1995
From: BossGrrrl
Subject: Welcome


I would like to welcome everyone to the Grrrlove Mailing List. I formed
this list because I got sick of having to defend myself from every fuck-
ing asshole on USENET. Our sisters were being silenced and this list is
a grrrl-only space where we can provide support to each other and talk
about things that are important to *us grrrls*.

Boys are not allowed in this list and I will be personally vetting every
new list member to make sure she is female. Please tell your friends be-
cause we want the list to grow!

This might be a good time for introductions. Tell us who you are, what
bands you like, and that sort of thing.
Peace,
BG

Grrrlove Mailing List, Nov 1995
Date: Nov 1, 1995
From: BossGrrrl
Subject: Why the net sucks for grrrls

Oh, I am forwarding you this post from that asshole newsgroup:

  >Date: Oct 1, 1995
  >From: Ed Spam
  >Subject: Some people are simply pathetic ...

  >Yeah, I know that this is again off the track of this conference, and
  >for that I apologize, but I simply couldn't let this slip by
  >unnoticed.
```

```
>>From fuckme@well.sf.ca Sep 26 11:09:57 1995
>>Subject: Re: Riot Grrrls and Hate Mail
>>Organization: Pro-Slut Organization
>>(Ed Spam) wrote:
  >>>Gus T. writes:
  >>>SuperStud wrote:
    >>>>what the fuck do these tupid Bitch whining about some
    >>>>stupid ass band's show have to do with this newsgroup?
    >>>>Cunt Grrrrrls like that should take their whiney shit and get
    >>>>your own newsgroup, Alt.Grrrl.Dumb Cunt

  >>>bitch bitch bitch whine whine whine my newsgroup,
  >>>not yours!... who elected you king of this newsgroup anyway?
  >>>why the hell are you so protective of the "purity" of
  >>>message content? and why are you such an asshole?

    >>>>Yeah, listen to Mr. Sensitive New Age Guy here.
    >>>>It may not be politically fucking correct, but I think a
    >>>>lot of u guys should stand up and have the balls to
    >>>>admit where you really stand. you want to
    >>>>fuck these stupid bitches just like everyone else,
    >>>>admit it, If I am a Mysogynist Asshole, I'll say it loud
    >>>>and proud.

  >>>I hate to burst your bubble, but not every man's goal in life is to
  >>>be an asshole and some of us are actually not threatened
  >>>by women with brains and talent

    >>>>C'mon, Ed, these Riot Grrrls are just stupid
    >>>>young bitches. Stop defending the whore trash. Fuck em
    >>>>THEIR DADDIES DID!!!!
```

>I guess some men just don't get it. Simply pathetic.

Need I say more?

—BossGirl

Grrrlove Mailing List, Nov 1995
Date: Nov 3, 1995
From: LittleNell
Subject: Hi!

Hi-dy-ho, seestahs!
Little Nell here.
Nice list ya got.
Let's see if we can get it on the road and kick it into overdrive.

Anybody else interested in pirate media?

Grrrlove Mailing List, Nov 1995
Date: Nov 3, 1995
From: Jen
Subject: Intro ...

hi i'm jen and i go to mills college. i'm really really glad this list
is here cuz i'm so sick of the jerks on usenet.... like that post you
put up.... why can't the guys shut up and let us talk?

it reminds me, here at mills we are trying to get men out of the post-
bacc classes becuz they talk so much and the women never get a chance to
ask questions, & well you know the profs are biased toward the men anyway ...

i'm really happy to have grrrl-only space, i think it's real important.
i love chocolate, tatoos (i'm getting a new one), bikini bear and huggy
kill, my pet cat teardrop, and i *love* reading audre lourde

oh, i just turned 19 last month.

bye for now

love, jen

Grrrlove Mailing List, Nov 1995
Date: Nov 8, 1995
From: ParaLogical
Subject: cunts

dear cunts;

my name is marina and i think you are all a bunch of empty-nest suburban
academics with time on your hands.

see ya!

Grrrlove Mailing List, Nov 1995
Date: Nov 11, 1995
From: LittleNell
Subject: Angry fucks
Dear Marina,

It's been my experience that wimmim with such levels of hostility are
good in bed. Wanna fuck? Your face or mine.

Nell

Grrrlove Mailing List, Nov 1995
Date: Nov 11, 1995
From: BossGrrrl
Subject: Re: the c-word

Hi Grrrls!

I guess Marina really stirred up something with the c-word. I first
want to say that, while I hope we can respect each other here, I do not
censor posts to this list (as long as they are from women).

Marina, I hope you can expand on what you said, or if it was a joke,
please explain why you made it.

For everyone else, I was wondering how you felt about words like "cunt",
"bitch" or "whore". While I find "cunt" reprehensible, there have been
times when I have used it to describe other women that I really really
hate. Please keep the discussion going. I love you all and I'm so glad
to have you here!

Smooches,
RG

Grrrlove Mailing List, Nov 1995
Date: Nov 14, 1995
From: ParaLogical
Subject: cunts

dear cunts;

so what's the problem? i mean other than the usual white-lady's burden

headfuck? i mean, christ aren't you females just doing this instead of
playing bridge or something?

marina

Grrrlove Mailing List Nov 1995
Date: Nov 15, 1995
From: LittleNell
Subject: cunts

Nah. I'm doing it so I don't have to go hunt for Gris' screwdriver and
soldering gun, and because I don't want to buckle down to rebuilding the
damn transmitter again for the third time this week.

Marina, you're a scream. Do you find that the aggressive approach works
pretty well with these polite chicks as far as getting attention? C'est
la guerre, babe, but if you get serious, call me.

As for language, get it through your heads: it's TOOLZ. UTENSILS, dammit.
Ideas are pieces of rock that we chip sharp edges onto, and words are the
sticks we tie onto them for handles, and sometimes we pick them up and go
bang bang BANG.

Cunt is my word as much as anybody else's. You wanna leave that stick
lying on the ground, you go right ahead.

Me, I've always been into tools.

-- Nell.

Grrrlove Mailing List, Nov 1995
Date: Nov 17, 1995
From: ParaLogical
Subject: cunts are for kidz

so tell me, nell, how many kids you got? an how long has your ole man
been in middle management? you sendin your kids to stanford or harvard?
hard decision, huh?

cracks me up what you say about language, all you femmes sittin there
smack dab in the middle and tryin to pretend like you're some kind of
marginalized group. christ.

damn cunts.

Grrrlove Mailing List, Nov 1995
Date: Nov 17, 1995
From: LittleNell
Subject: hey, cookie

"Marginalized"? You got an old map, dollikins, and you must be a maphead,
and like all mapheads you're scared of the territory, got to get it on paper. Why else would you fondle the concept of "dangerous language"?

Scared to put your ass on the line, cookie?

Oh, whoever asked about pirate media, yeah. We here. Where are you at?

Grrrlove Mailing List, Nov 1995
Date: Nov 23, 1995
From: chrone
Subject: marina

Marina, are you scared? Are you afraid you're not going to make it at
all? Listen, hang tough. Time is on your side. True. If you hold on to
yourself, you can outlive your childhood, outlive your craziness, and
you sure as hell can outlive the world the way it is now.

I'm an example: when I was young it was the fifties, but I can't blame
everything on the times. I couldn't get through college -- i was too
flaky. Couldn't hold a job -- too nuts. I never had a success in my life
until I was 50, and seldom had a lover who was worth a damn till then.
Lucky I didn't get it together to kill myself before I lived through the
shit. Listen, this is something you'll never hear from anyone: a young
woman (usually) is a hostage to her own fate. Everything she does has too
much importance for her to be able to be sane about it. The future's looking over her shoulder every minute, and it makes her crazy. It gets better
as you go along.

Just set your mind to hang in there and outlive your present. Outlive
your youth. Outlive your imprisonment by your body. Outlive your fertility and its misery. You want your future. Live to meet it.

In the meantime, fight the right people. Get smarter about them and
about you too: learn to read your own mind.

Stay tough, live long.
love,
chrone

R. U.'s Diary
Nov. 24, 1995

The Net *is* going to be censored. There was a *Nightline* forum about it tonight. This lady from the newly formed InterNet Management Group as much as said so, though she said the HADL proposal is too extreme. Kapor and the guy from ACLU attempted to bring reason into the proceedings, but between the FBI girl going on about alt.pedophile and that *kid* from the Clinton Administration ranting about nuclear terrorism to the point where you could SEE the plutonium flow from hard drive to hard drive via modem, the studio audience was rendered pink with fear and rage.

So *Nightline* ends and it's that Reebok ad with SubCommandante Marcos. And then I channel surf and it's that new Nike ad with Burroughs and Acker. Burroughs (while muscular basketball guys run around the equally muscular Acker, who is lifting weights in a gym): "It's a biological fact that if you don't use it, you lose it." Acker (camera focusing in on her leglifting a heavy barbell): "William, do you still believe that women are a biological mistake?" Acker continues to leglift while female astronauts wearing Nikes float in a deep space background. Burroughs: "I was wrong." Closeup of two pairs of Nikes. Pan up, full body shot of Burroughs and Acker looking meaningfully into the camera.

Meanwhile the Net is about to turn the clock back pre-*Naked Lunch.*

===
```
Date: Nov 25, 1995
From: StJude
To: rusirius
Subject: you can't censor what you can't read


It's okay, calm down. The cypherpunks foresaw this clampdown sev-
eral years ago. This is what cryptography is FOR ... If HADL's
pressuring the services into monitoring their traffic, let 'em
monitor. Their traffic will not offend the tenderest teener ...
because it will be *encrypted*. No problem. I told you before
you left on tour that the next implementation of the Internet
will handle packet encryption routinely ... and the Net will
protect itself. I've dreamed about the extensions of this ...
everybody encrypted, Internet traffic looking like -- random bits!
Except for the religious bits. And the nice chitchat. ... but how
ya gonna keep 'em down on the farm, darlin'? What am I saying? --
even down on the farm they can dialup and sneak over to
alt.sex.bestiality and pick up techniques for steer humping. Oh my.
Most of the postings are bouncing through anonymous remailers, most
often via our buddies in Finland. You will notice that however re-
strictive the mass media become, and however closed and nice and
farmlike the US gets, Finland is just a bounce away, and so is
steer humping.
```

There's already major pressure to restrict the alternative.nasty
boards on UseNet. Can UseNet hold out? Will YOU miss your
alt.sex.bondage? Not worrying . . . the only way to eliminate Usenet
is to make its software illegal. But its software, and therefore
Usenet, is everywhere . . . all machines on the Net use the software's distribution algorithm, which is simplicity itself: one machine says to another, do you have this yet? then i'll give it to you
. . . so there's a continuous update Net-wide. There is no top to
dictate from. A sweet anarchistic sharing, and there we are. . . .
hello Finland!

If HADL wants to shut off access to the nasty postings on UseNet,
they have to do it site-by-site. They can lean on the major commercial servers to self-censor, i guess, and they can force the col-
leges, maybe, to stop subscribing to the naughty bits, but the design
of UseNet defeats censorship. UseNet is a model for a sweet anarchist
future where We ARE Everywhere, until they kill us to the last machine, the last human.

ugh

>jude<

===
Grrrlove Mailing List, Nov 1995
Date: Nov 26, 1995
From: chrone
Subject: Surgical Feminism

The Egg Baskets' Revolt

I'm going to tell you a secret that no one else will ever tell you.
If you're a male interloper on this list, stop reading now, or pay
the price with nightmares. If you are, like me, a double Xed-out being in trouble with your destiny, you might want to file this for
later, for when you feel worse than you do now. I'm speaking as
Chrone, the third voice of the triple Goddess, the one that doesn't
give a shit for the lies that humans tell themselves in order to
carry on as a species. I'm the one who survived the crapola that the
Maiden anticipates so feverishly that she forgets her Pill. I'm the
one who outlived the endless hassle with kids and surrogate kids
that the Matron feels is the governance of the world. I am the female of any age who thinks, who looks out for her destiny, who LIVES
DOWN HER FERTILITY.

If you're through reproducing, or if you never intend to start, why pay
the breeding fees? You know the overhead:

The predictable hemorrhage, the cramps, the anemia ... Your predictable
berzerker the week preceding all that, which ravels all your human
ties ... Your predictably having to sit an exam remembering nothing ...
except that it's the egg-nourishing time of your cycle, when your brain
becomes a nest.

Putting up with the cyclicity of sex -- at the new moon you're a corpse
in your beloved's bed, half moon sends you ravening out for the
unsuitables.

And the fear of accidents. Ooops: fetus! Parental prison for 20-to-life,
or a fling on the abortion tilt-a-whirl ...

And living with your fear of your own hidden agenda. Your eggs are all
in there RIGHT NOW, rolling and mewing in your ovaries. These cats are
in heat ... they're plotting how they can roll down the Fallopian Way
and rollick with their long-tailed mates.

On the up side, of course, there's the thrill of being fertile, the
possibility of birth, how important it is for a woman! ... Now here
things get misty ... mystical ... religious. Giving birth is the final
secret. Breaching, you should excuse the expression, the final veil.
What does it take to find out what's behind there? What will it cost
you to pluck and eat that fruit of knowledge? -- to switch metaphors
mid-religion. Let's get judeo-xian: ALL THAT OPENETH THE WOMB IS MINE,
saith the Lord. That used to mean that the first-born gets sacrificed
to the Lord, or blasphemously to Baal instead (Baal is just another
word meaning Lord, but a rival Lord, bad bad) -- but nowadays the
first birth is an offering to the great god Curiosity. So THIS is what
it's about. Too late: now that you know, you've got the rest of your
life to contemplate your rashness. Noticed how many single-baby families there are? Heh heh heh.

What if women can learn from other women what's behind the curtain (among
other things, two years of diapers and twenty more of hassle) -- and
what if women, learning what's there, then feel free to forget about the
whole thing?

So I'm talking the forbidden female alternative: surgical feminism.
Taking your anatomy along with your destiny into your own hands. If

thine ovary offend thee, pluck it out! You can hedge your bet and
have it deep-frozen. Egg custard, french vanilla. Heh.

Why be broken on the lunar wheel? It makes no sense. We're handi-
capped enough, living *feminized*, marinaded in the hormone of
acquiescence. There: I've gone too far at last. I love my replacement estrogen. It plumps the breast and pinks the clit, and, according to the latest *Science News*, pumps the brain as well. The hormone
of softness, surrender, and cunning. Make that intelligence. Well
well.

Progesterone, on the other hand ... the premenstrual, nest-brain,
Clytemnestra hormone ... somehow you don't get around to replacing
your progesterone, cycling it off against the estrogen. The doctors
used to fear that if you ceased to cycle, if your uterine lining
didn't develop its monthly gangrene and then slough off [this truly
IS the mechanism], it would grow cancers to spite you. But if you
pluck your offensive UTERUS out, dangling tubes akimbo, you needn't
worry about that. And now they're all gone, all those high-overhead
organs designed for birth or cancer. Ahhh.

So the cyclicity is gone? And the cyclical craziness? Gone. Your hypothalamus, made sweet on a steady diet of the estrogen pill, flattens its
careenings; your brain steadies, ceases to cycle. You may be crazy
still, but it's steady-state crazy. That's *bettah.*

And there are unexpected plusses when the cervix is minussed. Instead of
a vulnerable cervix whose inner lining collects diseases and goes pre-
cancerous, instead of an *irritable* cervix whose bulk interferes with
sex, you have an H-SPOT. Ahhhhhhh.

This is poisonous, treasonous talk, and you feel disloyal listening
to it. You are a proper womanly woman, proud of your hormone unbalance,
rejoicing with your monthly flux, excited by your reproductive
destiny ...

And you're really spitting fire if you're a man, if you stepped past my
warning. You're spitting that this sort of shit can come only from a
bitter, withered, unsexed female whose life has clearly been wasted.

Guess again. Chrones can have consorts. Chrones may be attractive because they manifest a guileless sexuality. Their copulations are free

from unconscious baggage. Selecting a mate for breeding purposes, for
the good of the species, just doesn't figure. They can concentrate on
sex. And they are attractively honest about the emotions of sex. Say
it: they can be honest about love. They can *afford* to be honest, now
that the lies necessary for mating-to-breed are pointless. Perhaps more
of them are bisexual, gay, unisex. Why not? The whole species is for
mating when you're not mating for your species.

Think about it, you egg-baskets of either sex. You'd better: your eggs
are already thinking for you. The ethology of breeding is getting a lot
of media play right now ... how the older man really DOES just want you
for your body -- its beauty and youth and health -- and you really DO
just want him because he's taller and older, and richer ... because a
healthy mother and a powerful father means healthy, protected offspring.
Hearing this stuff a hundred times in the media doesn't necessarily
change anybody's behavior. That these are the real facts of life --
that they determine everything we do for thirty years -- is irrelevant
to us if we're still heavily invested in acting them out.

What happens when women see through the harem games they're spozed to
play -- mating, birthing, killing their rivals and their rivals' offspring. What?

When the melodramas associated with breeding cease to fascinate
... when the craziness that attends mating goes transparent ...
when your underlying plots to become a parent become apparent
... What happens to human society? Very interesting. Millions
of years of wired-in primate stuff, gone as quaint as a Sol
computer.

Will the species die? Given a critical mass of women with insight on the
mate-to-breed -- of Chrones -- would the species just end? (Tolstoi
thought the end of breeding was the signal that God was waiting for. The
final generation, ungenerating through celibacy, demonstrates to Him
their hatred for all things nasty-bodily, signals their worthiness to be
introduced to Him formally ... and that's it. Everybody bundled into
heaven. Finis.)

I think not. The species will go on. Some people of both sexes really
want to devote themselves to children. This is almost unthinkably ad-
mirable. The sacrifice, the vision seem almost angelic. Voluntary parents may be better than the unconscious, accidental kind. Like me in
another age, and thank goddess my kid survived. Sheer accident.

But ongoing human society might be radically different if it were salted
with Chrones. It's true that countries are now entrusted to post-
menopausal Matrons, who extend their Motherliness -- including their
brood-defending murderousness, remember -- to householding in the
greater world. Chrones of all ages might do a better job of that. Of
everything. Honesty instead of willful self-delusion. Sex instead
of heir-centered harem wars. Hmmm.

Just a thought or three. That's it for Chrone -- over and out.

Tell me how you feel about all this. No: tell me what you THINK.
All this just poured through me, and I am amazed by it, all of what I
said.

Grrrlove Mailing List, Nov 1995
Date: Nov 26, 1995
From: wiggle woggle
Subject: Surgical Feminism

the goddess is maid, mother, * crone*, as I've always known it.
Is this added 'h' a new fashion? I also love that rant.

Grrrlove Mailing List, Nov 1995
Date: Nov 28, 1995
From: chrone
Subject: Surgical Feminism

wiggle woggle wrote
>>maid, mother, *crone*, as I've always known it. Is this
>>added 'h' a new fashion?

Nah, baby. Check the meaning of "crone." Ugh.

Chrone carries the meaning, but it's honorable.
It implies time served. It celebrates the non-reproductive
aspect of the Triple Goddess. Chrone is not an evil wartnosed witch.
Chrone is the mature, masterly female. Like the ideal of Sophia,
maybe -- she's detached, she's accumulated a lot of data. She's got a
good chance at being wise. More like what Donna Haraway opts for when
she said she'd rather be a cyborg than a goddess.

So: Chrone. <That's what I wanna be when I grow up.>

Grrrlove Mailing List, Nov 1995
Date: Nov 28, 1995
From: little nell
Subject: Surgical Feminism

****
I am one of the Chrones she talks about.

To get cut, to have the unnecessary mechanism removed, to cut loose the
little tissue-n-tube strings binding me to biological destiny and ten
million speechwriters' cliches, was the knife as liberator.

Skoptsi, they got nothin' on us.

Like Pat Cadigan said in Synners, "change for the machines." Well, we
were made *into* the machine, the fuckin' baby machines, and now the
machines are changing. You hear us, Mr. Plantation of Wombs? You hear
us, Mr. Planned Birth Rate and No Abortion Clinics? You hear us, Mrs.
Caring League Baby Factory for Christ? Ms. Neofeminist
Glorious Fuzzy Reproductive Purpose, Ms. Women As Nurturer Will Save
the World?

I'm not interested in saving your snot-nosed world, in changing its
diapers.

I am a Chrone. I am a long-legged spider, walking slantwise over the
page of your descriptions and your prescriptions and your social roles
and your job classification lists.

When we opt out of the reproductive loop, the white Christian
fundie back-to-reagan business types will never be able to get things
Back Where God Intended. They couldn't do jackshit about it, could
they?

Chemical change, surgical change, the joyful sacrifice. Hurl those egg-
sacs into the fire, sister spiders, and walk long-legged with me over
the bars and out into freedom.

Billboard HOT 10 SINGLES for the week of Nov. 22–Nov. 28

	This week	Last week	2 Weeks Ago	Weeks on the Chart
LA LA LA NICE LADY (FROM "THE NICE LADY" SOUNDTRACK) GARY LEWIS (c) (m) (t) COLUMBIA G. LEWIS (G. LEWIS, G KAMOSE)	1	1	1	22
STUCKUP TLC (c) (m) (t) LAFACE ARISTA D. AUSTIN (D. AUSTIN)	2	2	2	13
THANX! MONDO VANILLI (c) (m) (t) NAUGHT/INNERSCOOP SCRAPPI DUCHAMP (R. SIRIUS/S. 3RDARM/S. DUCHAMP)	3	23	45	11
SEND ME TO PARADISE MELISSA ETHERIDGE (c) (m) (t) ISLAND RECORDS H. PADGHAN (M. ETHERIDGE)	4	3	4	11
BLISS AT MIDNIGHT 4 P.M. (c) (x) NEXT PLATEAU/LONDON M. DESTANTIS (M. DESTANTIS)	5	4	3	18
OLD UNCLE ALEISTER'S GONE GONE GONE THE DON KNOTTS EXPERIENCE (c) (m) (t) ISLAND RECORDS B. TIRED (B. TIRED/W. UNINSPIRED)	6	8	12	5
NORMAL FELLA ENGLEBERT HUMPERDINCK (c) (d) ARISTA (G. GOULDIE) G. GOULDIE	7	17	19	45
WRAP YOU UP IN MY ARMS BABY BABYFACE (c) (d) (m) (t) (v) (x) EPIC L.A. REID (L.A. REID/BABYFACE)	8	7	7	19
YOU AND ME ARE FOREVER TONI BRAXTON (c) (m) (t) (k) LAFACE/ARISTA A. GORING (T. BRAXTON/A. GORING)	9	9	9	11
MR. SHIPPED FOR BRAINS PLUTONIUM PUSSIES (c) (m) (t) NAUGHT/INNERSCOOP D. GRRRL (D. GRRRL/B. GRRRL/I. TWAT)	10	10	10	8

WHITESPACE: Art and Beyond December 1995 Pg.6

Apocalypse How?

How to Mutate and Take Over the World
by R.U. Sirius and St. Jude
Ballantine Books, 1995
BY TOTO DEJOUISSANCE

Gonzo cyberpundits R. U. Sirius and St. Jude, abetted by a foolhardy Ballantine Books, have produced the cyberpunk strokebook they've always threatened to deliver—a millennial Baedeker clumsily entitled *How to Mutate and Take Over the World*. Designed as a scrapbook from the future, *Mutate* is devoid of conventional prose, substituting data trash *samizdat*—e-mail exchanges, BBS banter, pirate advertisements, and hypertechnical hooey, for linear narrative. Bereft of a responsible narrator, *Mutate* unfolds through a virtual parade of terminal identities—mainly no-account propeller heads and rebels *sans* clue—revealing a teleology *sans telos*, a scatological eschatology, an ass-backwards history book for an ahistorical, no-future generation. The arcane, subcultural discourse of *Mutate* often devolves into incestuous, rhetorical circle jerk, as inviting to the uninitiated as a Monster Truck/Tractor Pull, and just as inane.

Occasionally, Sirius & Co. wield the cutting edge like a spastic Benihana chef, reducing the

reader's hands to bloody hamburger in just a few pages. All too often, though, the authors are merely slapping a dead fish against the reader's back, in hopes of keeping him awake. One gets the sense that Sirius intended *Mutate*'s anti-structure as a hyper-postmodernist intervention into the Western literary canon, yet it reads as though the pages were spat out of a leaf blower. One hesitates to call it a work of "literature," yet,

```
#######################################################
#########        • Trudy B. Hyatt •          #########
#########        • Editorial Assistant •      #########
#########     • Hyatt@Ballantine.Books.com •  #########
#######################################################
```

Date: Dec. 19, 1996
To: rusirius@well.com   StJude@well.com
Subject: hip, but

This notion of having the book reviewed within the book is pretty hip and recursive and all, but does it work?

```
# # # # # # # # # # # # # #
#    /==$=\        #  <— From the High-Tech Fully Electronic Desk
#  /))-00(\       #      of R. U. Sirius
#  ((( —)))       #
#  )))\ /(((   #  —> rusirius@well.com
# # # # # # # # # # # # # #
```

Date: Dec. 19, 1996
To: hyatt@ballantine.books.com   StJude@well.com

It doesn't really work AT ALL, but since when has THAT made a diff? The reviews that Andrew Hultkrans and Dale Lazarov wrote are just SO funny that we gotta work 'em in. But we're gonna try not to fuss over it TOO much. Just let the idea that this book is released early in the book hang out as a weird little nuance.

forced into pre-existing categories, *Mutate* fits (like a fat guy into a Go-Kart) into the satirical tradition. An attempt to give Jonathan Swift a swift kick to the groin, *Mutate* thrusts Satire into the 21st century, lurching and retching towards . . . well, just lurching and retching. Indeed, *Mutate* qua satire is eminently more forgivable than *Mutate* qua fiction. Considered as fiction, *Mutate* takes its place with the *Battlestar Galactica*'s of yesteryear, disposable sci-fi destined for the bargain bin.

The "plot," insofar as one exists, traces future events from the present to the year 2002 (this transparent one-upmanship against Kubrick did not go unnoticed by *this* reader), when the world ends in a sophomoric nanotech disaster, covering the globe in key lime pie. The major players in this post-structuralist playground are two collective entities—R.U. Sirius' MONDO Vanilli Corp., a multimediocre entertainment organ, and St. Jude's hacker "Underground," a liminal network of media pirates, cryptoanarchists, and console cowboys. Both of these collectives find themselves pitted against an increasingly repressive and tightassed Establishment, characterized by the unfortunate cross-breeding of the values of Catherine MacKinnon and Rush Limbaugh.

While the parodic exaggeration of current societal trends is inspired, the authors spend so much time licking their own assholes with self-congratulatory relish that one finds oneself unconsciously siding with the dreary Overground. Indeed, the reader often unexpectedly finds himself wading through a minefield of hypebites for Sirius' "band," MONDO Vanilli, an experience not unlike negotiating a meadow of steaming cow pies without one's galoshes. These delusions of power and influence beg for a Freudian analysis of *Mutate*, which would surely reveal just how *deeply enschwanzed* Sirius' and Jude's megalomaniac "roles" have become in their core personalities. The authors may indeed become the menace to society they long to be, but not as the countercultural power-brokers they now envision themselves. Instead, they will fulfill their revolutionary fantasies as the unwitting stooges of some shadowy Parallax Corporation, who will satisfy their delusional desire to go out in an apotheosis of heroic rebellion against "the Man" by having them take the fall for a minor political assassination.

This ambiguity between fact and fantasy problematizes the core of the *Mutate* project, threatening to reduce it to a cybersleaze version of *Sword of Shanarra*. No amount of tongue-in-chic jargon can save the book from the transparent desire of the authors to project themselves into an anarcho-syndicalist wet dream of their own pathetic design. And it is the exclusively private nature of the authors' desire that renders the book impenetrable, or merely tiresome, to the average reader. *Mutate* does everything it can *not* to invite the reader into its world. The reader in search of *frisson* only gets pissed on. Even for the fearless reader with more time than sense, an entrée into the world of *Mutate* is limited at best, and whatever limited understanding the reader may glean will reveal an unappealing and petty world which ends not with a bang but a wimpout.

December 3:

Welcome to CompuService
Please join noted authors R. U. Sirius & St Jude in the Wired 2000
Auditorium

HOST: Welcome to the CompuService Wired 2000 Auditorium. Tonight we'll be talking to authors St. Jude and R. U. Sirius. They are both Contributing Writers to Wired 2000, they've co-authored the novel, *How To Mutate & Take Over the World*, published by

Ballantine Books, and R. U. Sirius is a vocalist with the media rock band, Mondo Vanilli. Hello, Jude and R. U.

STJUDE: Hey ...

R. U.: Yo ...

HOST: I'm going to start this out with my own question. You both are pub- licly known for writing about the culture of high technology, yet your book, *How To Mutate & Take Over the World*, seems to me to really be about politics, sex, gender ... lots of sex actually. Any comments?

STJUDE: Sex is interesting to primates. We're primates. But we're in the middle of a technology-mediated sex war, have you noticed? This is a special case in the war for information.... the Net spreads the discourse about sex, (and makes porn available to everyone) -- and as information flow increases, belief gets washed away. More people know they can ignore what they've been taught about sex, and more people want to make them shut up about it. But sex is only one area. The book is about the impossibility of stopping *information*.

R. U.: Yeah. I'd agree with what Jude just said. I think sex is more interesting than computers. Shit, I think LUNCH is more interesting than computers ...

STJUDE: yeah? How'd you like to have your modem cut off??? Is that your THIRD favorite organ or what??

HOST: R. U., we may not have told you about the rules on CompuService regarding language. Obscene words can be indicated like this: s*** of F*** but they can't be spelled out. And now, we'll take our first question from the auditorium. Go ahead, Echimp.

ECHIMP: I wanted to ask R. U., when's the next Nine Irritated Nerds album coming out?

R. U.: Sorry, I really don't know any more than you do about what Brent Buzz- kill is up to, but let me take this op- portunity to say how absolutely ludicrous it is to type s*** and f*** instead of the actual words, when everybody knows what the actual words

```
###################################################
#########         • Trudy B. Hyatt •        #########
#########       • Editorial Assistant •      #########
#########   • Hyatt@Ballantine.Books.com •  #########
###################################################
```

Date: Dec. 19, 1996
To: rusirius@well.com   StJude@well.com
Subject: i am wondering

Well ... I was trying to be polite but REALLY what bothers me is, here it is at the end of 1996, you STILL haven't delivered the final manuscript, but you have the book released IN the book in summer of '95. Maybe we better push the conceptual book release back to a date that would more likely correspond to your actual completion of the book ...

Let's see. I'm looking at the plotline right now. So ... WHEN DOES HELL FREEZE OVER? hahahaha ... :-)

are. That the letters hit and uck provoke defensive action DEFINES the
term "superstitious savages!" I mean, Jesus F***in' Christ!
HOST: I'm sorry to cramp your style, R. U., but those are the rules and
even though some of us don't like them, we seem to live with them o.k.
The next question is from Ibogail.
IBOGAIL: This is for both of you. Do you think that the brain is like a
computer, and can you reprogram it with psychedelic drugs?
R. U.: No.
STJUDE: What he said. Cool handle, though.
HOST: And now we have Lizzie ...
LIZZIE: First of all, I wanted to say that CompuService has made a big
mistake inviting these two on as special guests. Their writings are riddled with obscenities and gross disgusting attitudes. Even the liberals
think that they're sick. I know that there are at least forty members of
the Human Anti-Degradation League in the audience here tonight and we
want StJude and especially R. U. Sirius to know that we're watching

them, and that vio-
lence against women
and pedophilia and
obscenity and encour-
aging children to use
drugs ... these kinds
of things are not go-
ing to be tolerated
much longe(interrupt)
HOST: Please ask a
question, Lizzie.
LIZZIE: Ok. After
AIDS and the problem
that we have in the
country today with

```
##############
#___/==$=\___    #  <- From the High-Tech Fully Electronic Desk
# /))-00(\     #     of R. U. Sirius
# ((( -)))     #
# )))\ /(((  # -> rusirius@well.com
##############
```
Date: Dec. 19, 1996
To: Hyatt@Ballantine.Books.com,   StJude@well.com
Subject: TRUDY!

Trudy, you're getting WICKED!

drug-related crimes and the loss of values by our kids, how can you
carry on with your sixties counterculture attitudes? I know you're supposed to be living in the future but I think you're living in the past!
R. U.: F*** you!
HOST: Well, that's a real brilliant response, R. U.
STJUDE: Sixties mumble ... I'm sick of getting Sixties-bashed ... I am
not a hippie, madam. We're not Sixties-style degenerates. We're
nineties-style degenerates. And noughties-degenerate-wannabes -- the
2000s. keep in mind: the sixties didn't happen -- they only TRIED to
happen. the idea of information wanting to be free STARTED then, but it
didn't make it.
R. U.: For what it's worth, the initial impulse in the sixties was to

try to have openness and therefore lots of information about sex and
drugs so people could make informed decisions. Things didn't get really decadent and apocalyptic until the extreme repression of the
Nixon Administration. And then, since the Reagans started the War on
Drugs in the mid-80's, there's been no possibility for reasoned discussion or the distribution of real information about drugs that af-
fect consciousness. As for sex, I acknowledge that sex annihilates
social responsibility every single time you have a REAL orgasm. Ever
had one, Lizzie?
STJUDE: What are you, the orgasm gestapo? The 4th Reich is Wilhelm!
Maybe she has smashing orgasms, but orgasms DON'T smash the state --
you noticed that yet?
R. U.: Achtung, you vill now haff ein orgasm mitt der orgone accumulator!
HOST: Let's stay with the audience, guys, please. Ok, the next question
is from emh.
emh: I don't see how the right to be obscene does any good for this society. I think freedom of speech has gone too far and I support the Human Anti-Degradation League.
R. U.: Well first of all, this idea that something has to be GOOD for
society in order to be allowed is OBSCENELy authoritarian. And we seem
to be -- with your HADL group and family values and so forth -- moving
towards that situation. I mean, what next? Shouldn't hot dogs and nachos
be banned before obscene words? After all, they're actually BAD for
you, in a real physical sense. You know, opposition to "degenerate" art
and impure forms of communication were central tenets of Nazism and
Stalinism. What's happening in this country right now is EXACTLY the
same impulse.
STJUDE: But really, emh, the right to be obscene and still heard IS
good for society. If adult discourse is endlessly deferred, the
culture stays infantile. How can a society without adults raise its
kids?
HOST: Next we have Darkhaq.
darkhaq: yeah, i'm 14 and i just want to say that these guys are cool
and that i don't *need* to be *protected* by you hadl assholes. i agree
with rusirius that it's stupid not to be able to say shit fuck because
they're only words (interrupt)
HOST: Darkhaq, read your parents' service contract. We may have to terminate your participation in CompuService. This is turning out to be a
fun night, isn't it? Our next question is from MrsKlaar.
MrsKlaar: You both seem to have the attitude that you can just do whatever you want. As Chairman of the New York State Chapter of the Human
Anti-Degradation League, let me assure you that that is NOT the case. Do
you acknowledge any limits whatsoever?

STJUDE: hey, darkhaq!
darkhaq: hey
HOST: Could we stick to the questions, people?
STJUDE: OK ... limits, MsKlaar? My life is *blighted* by limits. I
still can't fly. I've been on the waiting list for wing transplants
for 2 years, but almost nobody donates them -- they're scarcer than
prostates. Guess I should try the blackmarket. (btw, darkhaq is not
one of your subscribers anyway ... he's a wily little other-ucker
(interrupt)
R. U.: And MsKlaar I have limits too: over this modem I can't shove a
Mars bar up your c**t or f**k your rightwing husb**d up the b*tt with a
br**m handle even with a virtual lubric(interrupt)
darkhaq: why are you scared of *WORDS* -- shit fuc(interrupt)
HOST: Well, we'll be ending early tonight. Next week in the auditorium
Dick and Jane, publishers of Wired 2000. Apologs to any of you that were
offendec by ttonight's program and thank y(interrupt)

= =
Date: Dec 27, 1995
From: rusirius
To: StJude
Subject: ahah!

Somebody (who asked to be nameless) with more money than sense has
taken some of my ranting seriously and has approached me about actually forming a political party. He wants to call it the New Democratic Party. There's apparently a bunch of people putting money behind
it, including Dick and Jane from Wired 2000. He asked me to take a
crack at writing a basic party platform. I'm game ...

= =
Date: Dec 29, 1995
From: stjude
To: RUSIRIUS
Subject: i didn't do it ... did i?

I'm in jail, baas. You've seen why. I hear my photo made it all over
the planet in the last 24 hours.

It's a fake, sorta.
It's like the most famous photo of the student revolution: the Kent
State coed on the cover of TIME, on her knees over her dead comrade,
screaming with anguish ... Then it turned out she was a 14-yr-old

runaway who wasn't in the demo, had no politics, didn't know the guy
. . . but it was a GREAT PHOTO.

same same with me.

well, the world could see that I did, in fact, clobber a cop who was
choking a frail little blonde child -- chopped him with a big sign
that said FUCK, which got censored in a dozen ways in the various news
services -- (it was the censored fuck that really made it play, i'm
sure.) So I'm the hero of the revolution. Listen, i'll tell you an
embarassing secret: i'm innocent.

that little child was a fierce orange-haired punker in her twenties --
i talked to her as they took us away. i wasn't carrying that dumb
sign, and it really said FUCK off hadl, without a comma, pfui.
The nearest i got to leading the damn demo was i knew a couple
of the people who put it together. I was even late getting there,
and the hoohah had already started. I saw a big cop putting the
choke on this undersized grrrl (who was trying to tear his ass up,
btw) so i grabbed a sign from somebody and just gave him something
to distract him . . . just a mild chopping kind of thing on the arm.
however . . . A news photographer happened to snap the picture at
exactly the right time, from exactly the right angle, with miracu-
lously correct f-stops or whatever, and it's the magical fucking
photograph that sums up the censorship war, so he sold it to every
wire service on the planet, and here i am. . . .

here in the W 54th St jail. They were going to send me to Rikers Is-
land with everybody else -- over 100 got busted -- but since I'm the
leader and chief malfeaser they're keeping me here. I hear they're
releasing everybody else . . . just processing people through as
quickly as they can.

I have my very own cell here. It's like GRAND ILLUSION -- they give
posh accommodations to the aristocrats of war or crime . . . so it's
better to be an arch-criminal. There's lots of toilet paper, and they
let me keep my powerbook. i'll keep ya eposted

. . . I just bowed out a formal visitor, a woman lawyer who volun-
teered to defend me free, because i'm leader and chief hero of the
anti-censorship war.

how embarassin.

>jude<

ps: My father was a friend of lou lowery, the dude who photographed
the real flagraising at iwo jima. It was a pretty stark event --
just three guys sticking the flag into the ground on a hill at dawn.
They had to keep their heads down -- they were still under fire --
and it didn't look all that climactic, although it was. Hours later,
whatsisname came along and gathered up one of the real guys and
a lot of extras and took them down on the beach, posed them just
so . . . "Hey, guy on the end, reach up like you just let it go" . . .
And there we have it, for all time:

HISTORY

Segment Two: 1996
The Plot Sickens

As the Religious Right and the Political Correctness Left roadblock the Internet successfully, plot rot sets in. Our characters start lurching and retching. The Sirius Megalomedia trip may lull some readers to sleep . . . but that's deceptive. This chapter is as deep as it is wide, with St. Jude and the Instant Underground and several thousand pirates and parodists doing some cunning stunts.

```
=====================================================
Date: Jan 2, 1996
From: stjude
To: rusirius
Subject: i'm free
```

okay. Connie came through. i am as free as i ever am. i'm coming back
to califloria tonight, and i'll be glad, glad to be back on the left
side of the country. meanwhile i'm sitting in a sidewalk cafe on the
tribeca, in january, because i don't want to stay indoors another
minute. my fingers are freezing to the keys. it's snowing on my head.
it's GOOD.
Jail is like hell -- it's okay, until you have to deal with other entities. hah -- t.s. eliot had THAT wrong . . . "hell is alone. hell is
oneself, the other people in it merely projections . . ." HAH. when
they did leave me alone it was like a drug trip . . . not bad . . . no
people . . . you just lie on your bunk in the slammer and listen to
the -- yes -- slamming . . . the steel doors, the locks, the steel
bars, day and night. gnash, clatter, crash, screek, hollow boom, re-
verb -- like living in a metal machine . . .

not that i wasn't happy to get bailed, oh yes, but Connie is very
strange. when i bolted out the cop doors to get to the open sky she
was still trying to tell me about kangaroo penes. (yes, she used the
real plural -- penis, penes) but i already KNOW about kangaroo penes
-- they're double headed and furry. well!
in fact, some avant-guys are talking about getting their penes split
now -- split along the midline, with the heads splayed out to either
side, i guess to imitate native australians, who do it to imitate
the roos. if you do it, and let it heal up, and you still want to
have sex, it's a terrible hassle inserting the result, but it's
spozed to be worth it to both inserter and insertee. . . . plus it's

so Hip . . . i guess. NEVAH underestimate the tyranny of Hip.
sitting here in the Big City i can hear the voice of the Zeitgeist
plainly, and it's a querulous male voice, and it's whining. . . . okay,
i *got* it tattooed with indigo stripes and i *got* the ampallang
shoved through, and the prince albert threaded in the top, and i got
the row of ittybitty *rings* stapled all along the bottom . . . And
now i've gotta take it back and have them do WHAT?????

look upon this process as sex-*replacement* surgery. Every upgrade to
your genitals makes them more hip but less functional -- ugh, think
of the crushed or sliced nerves. . . . it'll show up in slackerfolk
birthrates, you'll see . . . it's like the zeitgeist is plotting to
make hipness an evolutionary deadend, having the NORMALS outbreed it
every time . . . the zeitgeist wants to ensure we can't breed our way
out of this mess. . . . we MUST mutate, if we're going to take over the
world. . . .
i am going to sit out here drinking lattes with grated chocolate and
snow on top till i turn blue, and then i am going to take a cab to
port authority with the high high ceilings and the heated air and
just walk around until i thaw out or get mugged. life is good.
thanks, baas . . . i owe you bigtime.
big
time.
==
Date: 4 Jan 1996
From: stjude
To: rusirius
Subject: cybercowboy broadside

Hey . . . look at this. I found this when I was in jail. The booklady
brought us magazines, and this sheet was stuck in the (sticky!) fashion pages of WIRED2000 --

I passed you one of the cybercowboy things before, right? These guys
have hinted that they're setting up to fight us, you and me, like
there's some sort of factional split . . . ? That's the same kind of
vast-prairie excluded middle that d0k's complaining about . . .
There's them and us and the Avengers and everybody else . . . But
we're all, with totally different POVs, non-conjoined in a battle
against intellectual corralling, hobbling, or stymieing. . . . . (A
stymie's a short hobble -- their language is catching.) And I like
d0k's analysis -- he's another retro-Rationalist. The Age of Reason
rides again, on a Western saddle.

BAD-Broadside-#13
Jan, 1996

The Pre-Modern Era: A Cyber-Cowboy Surveys the Intellectual Territory

by: dOk HOLOdAY

A central tenet of the current intellectual territory has been that the
central ideas of modernism (a foundationalist epistemology, a reliance
on the methodology of Western Science etc.) have run their course and
we've now fully entered a post-modern era. According to this discourse,
we now must "decenter" the leading concepts of modernism if we are to
shake free of its vise-like grip on our intellectual life. We must, we
are told, break out of the corral of modernism.

I submit, however, that we do *not* live in a postmodern era. Rather,
we live in a pre-modern era. The leading ideas of the Renaissance have
yet to be understood, much less adopted. Moreover, I shall argue that
the current trajectory of the intellectual discourse into this post-
modern fallacy isn't a natural evolution in response to the failings of
"late capitalism." It is, in fact, a reflection of the ability of certain vested interests to manipulate and control western intelligentsia.

You may find the idea that the academic theory-oriented left has
"taken the bit" of the vested interests absurd. It's widely supposed
that this intelligentsia is in opposition to the new world corporate order. But this is a mirage. Indeed, the appearance of a radical intelligentsia perfectly serves the vested interests. Among the snake-oil
salesmen employed by the corporate new world order, we must include: the
Marxists, the writers in the Anglo-American Liberal Tradition and, of
course, the influential Deconstructionists. First, however, it will be
useful to clarify what the leading idea of modernism *actually* is.

The fundamental idea of modernism is that persons are capable of
thinking for themselves. You don't need to corral them in this or that
spot and tell them that these are the sorts of things that are safe to
think about. Persons should be free to graze the intellectual frontier
and find what they will. There is a deep confusion about this. People
have been encouraged to believe that modernism is bound up with Cartesian
dualism, or the idea of the ghost in the machine, or in a certain rational method. Descartes and the thinkers of the French Renaissance are portrayed as the evil land barons of the intellectual territory. To the contrary, Descartes is properly thought of as the first cyber-cowboy.

Read a history of Western philosophy (Coppleston's, Russell's, etc.)
and you get a picture of Descartes as a buttoned down city slicker -- a

cool rationalist determined to force his own methods onto the evolution
of human thought. The truth is quite different. Descartes was a 17th century punk -- a young man fond of wearing green capes, prone to staying in
bed until dinner and, once rising, finding no end of trouble (constantly
getting into duels, etc.) His debates with church authorities -- some
having lasted up to eight hours -- are carefully recorded in the Vatican
library. His best rants weren't published. They were passed from hand to
hand. Descartes was an original "samizdat." He was also the revolutionary
genius who successfully overthrew the authority of the church as the sole
repository of truth. His strategy was brilliant. He realized that simply
offering a negative critique would be inadequate. He needed to establish
an independent authority in a situation where no independent authority
was admissible. So he offered his foundationalist epistemology and -- in
a single, elegant brush-stroke -- centered it around an ingenious argument for the existence of God. The Church was trapped! They could argue
against Descartes, but that would mean trying to defeat the argument of
this popular intellectual for the existence of their God. Or they could
let Descartes' writings pass, in which case they allow for an independent
authority. It was a brilliant hack!

For Descartes, the goal was a liberated intellectual terrain --
freeing people to think for themselves. After Descartes, it became
necessary to control western thought by other means. Enter the "intellectual class" -- hired guns in the service of the thought barons.

Initially, the so-called intellectuals were obviously pawns of the
vested interests. No one would doubt that the German Idealists were simply hired guns in the employ of the Kaiser, charged with concocting an
ideology that would help unify the German peoples. But with the slow but
sure democratization of the printed word, came increased skepticism
about authority. More subtle control strategies became necessary. The
intellectual class would have to present themselves as oppositional.

With industrialism came consumer capitalism. The impoverished masses
of the feudal era no longer sufficed. Impoverished masses are not in a
position to *buy* the products of the industrial revolution. A comfortable working class, able to buy products, generated more wealth for the
elite. The concept is simple. If you own all the cattle, and everyone is
dirt poor, there is no one to sell your cattle to. The ideal situation
is when everyone has money in their hands, and they're all bidding for
your cattle.

Marxism was, in essence, an ingenious strategy for getting money into
the hands of the masses. Marx's intellectual task was to raise the consciousness of industrial workers worldwide, to get them to feel that
they deserved better than they were getting. All of that fluff about
controlling the means of production, the workers' state, and so forth,

was verbal window dressing for the core concern -- creating a class of reasonably wealthy consumers. The sophisticated vested interests knew that the industrialists would respond by appeasing the workers with good (taxable!) wages. While the meme took a convoluted path when it met with pre-industrial territories like Russia and China, in the industrial world that was Marx's focus, it worked like a charm.

The thought barons have succeeded in making marxism and capitalism appear diametrically opposed, and therefore they are presumed to have exhausted the possible intellectual territory. It's as though someone built two corrals out in a vast prairie and said "you can keep your cattle in this corral or that one, because that's all there is." The Cyber-cowboy movement is dedicated to busting people out of these corrals and letting them see the vast prairie out beyond those two tiny claims staked by Adam Smith and Karl Marx. Totalitarian philosophy puts high fences around an intellectual territory and decrees that everyone must graze their cattle within. The Western democratic elite, on the other hand, tells everyone that they can graze where they like, but use media, repetition, and intellectual persuasion to insure that people graze within an area that is nearly as confined. Meanwhile, the cyber-cowboy truth is that the intellectual territory is vast.

It is by now obvious to anyone with two brain cells that hang together that Western democracy concerns itself only with the *illusion* of free speech and a free press (Even that illusion seems to be losing importance in America, with its HADL, its family values and its various pogroms.) Noam Chomsky has documented how Western societies "manufacture consent," how real dissent is portrayed in mass media as so off-the-wall that the dissenters can only be discussed for their lovably eccentric entertainment value (media coverage of the Cyber-cowboys form a case-in-point). Media and intelligentsia ranch hands tell us, "Sure, you can graze your cattle over there if you want. But the grass is dead and the water is poisonous. And everyone will think you're a fool." Is it any surprise that so few venture out on their own?

A recent strategy of the thought barons' hired guns has been to argue that there's no fundamental truth. These "thinkers" are the ones who have been busy redefining Descartes, and other French Renaissance "Moderns," as evil overlords of the intellectual territory. One of the key guns has been Derrida.

Some of my skeptical friends have challenged me to use Cyber-anarchic methods to prove that the deconstructionists are working for vested interests. In my view, such methods are unnecessary. If you want to know who someone works for, find out who profits from their work. Who profits from widespread deconstructionism? They who are interested in distracting attention in a time of tremendous worldwide social and political up-

heaval -- a moment in history ripe with the possibility of real revolutionary change and genuine intellectual novelty.

But, why worry about the proper form of government for the newly liberated Soviet Republics? We can play word games instead! Why worry about
alternative economic ideas for the struggling world economic system? We
can cut up postcards instead! We can talk ceaselessly about the end of
identity! What's the great threat to people today? The evil phallocen-
tric idea of Cartesian rationality -- *that's* the source of all our
problems. If we could only cast off the evil grip Reason had over us. Of
course! How simple! *Thinking* is the problem we face today. The solution? Flashy intellectual masturbation, of course!

The intellectuals have their word games. The rich get richer, and the
masses are more marginalized than ever. The role of the cyber-cowboy? To
expose the intellectual charlatans, yes. But then to ride the great ex-
panse of cyberspace, to find new places to graze and water. And to leave
a few signposts about.

New Nation   Jan 12, 1996

Guest Column

HADL Cleans up the Karma in Cyberspace
by Jude Milhon

It had to happen, what with all the Infobahn brouhaha. The New Conservatives have noticed the Internet! They've been looking over the pasture fence at that information superhighway over yonder. And they reckon they've gotta speedbump it.

Oh, it makes sense. The Human Anti-Degradation League has noticed that the Internet will be the medium of the next century. Since conservatives blame much of what ails them on the media of the present, it's logical that HADL should make a pre-emptive strike on the future. So they're doing it.

Over the past few months HADL has pressed its membership to buy modems and SIGN ON. The newbie services—the entry-level Internet servers like US OnLine—have seen their membership double in the past month. And guess what? The Net's newest members seem to feel

the Net must be censored. They feel this so urgently that they're sending anguished email form letters to their service managers begging them to enforce the New Niceness on their boards . . . A close friend within HADL tells me that as the cannon fodder toils over their email, the HADL leadership is wooing the Net-service directors. And it's all in such a good cause: the Disneyfication of the Net.

All HADL wants is for everyone to adopt its "Anti-Degradation Standards." For starts, they want to ban religiously objectionable references and common sexual words like damn and pork, and *pork* . . . and words that might be racist or sexist. They need to know that users who use objectionable words will be bounced from their service. They want to ensure that these standards will be enforced by spot-monitoring the Net server traffic. They hope that when this is accomplished on the major Net servers, the Internet at large will voluntarily pipe down with the nasty adult-level conversation. Soon all of Cyberspace, from the academic journals to the haqr bbses, will become fit for tender ladies and tots. (Aren't you always happy to include the three-year-old in the dinner conversation?) And when this happy state is reached, maybe something can be done about private email . . . Just think of the volume of filth pullulating through the Net!

Will this enforced niceness be a trespass on the privacy of electronic communications? Is this a rape of the rights of Net service subscribers? Might this infringe upon free speech? If you answer yes, yes, and yes, will your answers count? Thousands of nerds and students and teachers—the senior citizens of cyberspace—will certainly protest, loud and bitter. Ah, but the new kids in town may outnumber them by a factor of two already . . . and the AIS, the Association of Internet Servers, will be listening to the numbers.

Where does the FCC figure in all this?

Nowhere, so far. The Feds maintain that they have no reason to notice: it's a commerce thang. So the Libertarians can count themselves a win. Big government will not intervene on behalf of free speech. Big government will yield to commercial necessity.

Bet that within months the Net management will cave in to pressure from its new majority. Bet that, this time next year, HADL can crow that the Net is no longer gross.

Bet also that HADL's attack on free speech and privacy rights will not stop with the Net servers. They're out to clean our karma for us. First they'll wash our mouths out. Later they may cut our throats.

```
==================================================
Date: Jan. 14, 1996
From: rusirius
To: stjude
Subject: stand up straight and tall son
```

I think this is too abstract and needs to be more passionate, what with the reemergence of David Duke, the latest figures on starvation and homelessness, the spread of the plague and the unfathomably baroque farce of the HADL and the bring back Father Knows Best acquiescence of the boomer media . . . uh, in fact REALLY let's just POUR GASOLINE OVER THIS WHOLE FUCKIN' COUNTRY AND LIGHT IT ON FIRE!!! Uh, ok ok I'm gonna be ok . . .

And another part of me isn't even in it. Three days ago had this dream that I was in love . . . I mean REALLY in LOVE with this 10 year old girl. And she with me. It wasn't dirty or the thrill of transgression or anything. It was quite authentic. My heart soared and I was young again. I mean, not to sound like a Hallmark card for dirty old men but I can't remember the last time I felt that good. And then I woke up . . .

And since then, there's this something deep down inside that wants to forget rational discourse and row row row the boat downstream of every blackhearted atavistic whimsy -- just gorge on the full human spectrum of emotion from compassion and pity to murderous lust, from romantic love to nihilistic suicide. Are these all clichés? I don't know how to speak the language of emotion really, except of course . . . "POUR GASOLINE OVER THIS WHOLE FUCKIN' COUNTRY AND LIGHT IT ON FIRE!!!"

So I got as far as I got in writing this "party platform" and then I
stopped. And I found myself dragging out this old book of Salvador
Dali paintings and just sort of HEARING each one of them. No drugs
mind you. Just something whispering to me from the wings? Anyway . . .
please edit the following when you get a chance . . .

INTRODUCTION

The Information/Communications Age
It has been axiomatic since the onset of the 1990's that the first
stage in a major transitional process in how we live is nearly complete. We've exited the industrial era and entered a period most
popularly known as the Information Age. A closer analysis tells us
that we are in a time that includes agriculture, heavy industry and
information/communications (from here on represented as info/comm),
and that these earlier stages in the human economic are powerfully
impacted by info/comm.

   This transition has changed the lives of ordinary people -- and
the social/economic/political national and world situation -- so
quickly that many, if not most, people are still in denial, refusing
to recognize even the reality of the change, never mind comprehending
and adjusting to it. One of the most salient public expressions of
how radical this shift is, and how much of an impact it's having on
ordinary persons, has been the oft-repeated words of President Clinton: "Most people will have to change jobs seven times in their life-
times." (Let's pause here to examine this statement and ask the
question -- does anybody actually believe that most people will be
able to get seven jobs, or learn skills beyond burger flipping and
data entry seven times over? -- more on this later.)

A Contemporary Humane and Freedom-Enhancing Politic
We in the New Democratic Party perceive the lack of a contemporary,
humane and freedom-enhancing politic to cope with and successfully
exploit the new situation. By now, everybody understands -- at least
viscerally -- that the situation is one of crisis. We believe that
contemporary political solutions require an understanding of the future, as much as an understanding of history. Our modus operandi will
be to combine the projective analyses of the experts with the empow-
erment of the masses and the emancipation of the individual. Our politics are neither left nor right, but contemporary.

No More Pandering!
Lastly, as we enter the political arena, we pledge not to pander to

the sorts of prejudices and emotional hot buttons that arise among
the population with increasing frequency and that formed the core
of the political discourse in the distressing 1994 elections. We
are not interested in being "populists," amplifying and enacting
popular opinion, even when we believe that opinion is mistaken or
destructive. Nor are we elitists. We will simply try to put forth
ideas and solutions as we see them and have as much impact on the
body politic as democracy allows. We will be ourselves.

ECONOMICS

Even in a time when the control of economic variants has more or
less completely escaped national boundaries, economic strategies
still form the real core of politics. The center of the current political and legislative process revolves around how to deploy the
moneys collected by the government through taxation. The debate
therein tends to center around a simple opposition; the notion of
the redistribution of (some of) the wealth vs. an (apparently) relatively unfettered free market. The New Democratic Party offers a
different vision. We call not for a redistribution of wealth, but
for its creation and distribution in a mixed/market economy that is
more free than the current one. We propose that, in the context
of a global economy dominated by multinational conglomerates that
operate beyond the control of the democratic mass, the political apparatus, and even those individuals who are part of -- and profit
from -- these massive multinational organisms, government might be
envisioned as a union of free agents, one that tries to get all of
its citizens -- from the highest to the lowest in the economic
order -- a good deal.
    In this opening statement, we can only pass lightly over the many
novel ideas that we hope will bring our economic situation into
harmony with high technology. Some of these suggestions are merely
fodder for study, an explicit working plan for their enactment being
admittedly beyond the ken of the author of this document and his ad-
visors. It will take many of us, thinking together, to actually turn
desirable changes into a workable plan. We'll start with some basic
principles:

1) A nation's wealth is not measurable by the current standards and
is difficult to measure by any standards:

a) Real Wealth: (to be completed)

b) The GNP, the tyranny of the "market," consumerism, and the quality
of life: (to be completed)

2) The free market and the commons may function better, each in its
purest form in appropriate domains, than in a mix:

a) Freedom is its own justification. Competition produces real benefits. Unfettered free market activity is the most powerfully revolutionary force in human society, generating rapid change and novelty,
encouraging competition, risk and experimentation. Contrary to popular wisdom, the Free Market is radical, not conservative.

b) In certain domains, the Free Market holds back revolutionary change,
erects barriers around experimentation, exchange, free discourse, and
slows down the introduction and distribution of potentially valuable
technologies.

c) A thoughtful public discourse may be able to erect a commons, possibly without coercion, for some domains where that commons would
be more progressive and humane than the market. Effort might be put
towards technological solutions to the intransigent problem of
bureaucracy in situations of shared social wealth . . .

3) Harvesting a post-scarcity economy:

We recognize that the natural evolutionary trend in the age of high
technology is towards a simultaneous internationalization and decentralization of economics. We further understand and generally support
the anti-statist and anti-social engineering tendencies that dominate
the current discourse. We agree that a post-modern economy can't be
governed or managed. It can only be guided and harvested. Our interest in removing the barriers to harvesting wealth on behalf of ALL of
our citizens is one of the things that distinguishes us from the
"Free Market" advocates in the current political mainstream. In other
words, while the international market has virtually escaped the bean-
counter dynamic of industrial era economics and is operating at quan-
tum speed, the body politic and the average citizen is still boxed
into a linear, zero sum economic logic built around limits, supply
and demand, debit, inflation, etc. Our principal goal is to transform
the economic dynamic within the United States from one of taxation of
the rich versus abandonment of the poor to one of harvesting a high-
tech economy that escapes the boundaries of scarcity.
     In this context, we believe that we are in -- or close to -- a

situation where the bottom of our economic ladder need not be starvation and destitution but instead, basic well-being; a true, uncondi-
tional safety net that includes housing, food, health care, transpor-
tation, education, and democratic access to communications technology
and media.

We will be presenting the outrageous and unpopular argument that
our post-industrial society is in danger of self-destructing from an
inordinate fear of getting something for free.

(and that's where it died for the moment . . .)

= =
Date: 20 Jan 1996
From: rusirius
To: stjude
Subject: here comes my 19th nervous breakthrough

You didn't even notice I was gone, did you? I've been in John Dobson
Hospital in Fremont, up in the psycho ward having myself a nervous breakdown. I'm glaaad! Finally, I've dumped the prosaic
oaf, flushed him down the crapper along with 20 pounds. I'm
free. I'm feelin' pretty, witty and gay. Well, not gay
per se but sort of feral and ecstatic.

I never did finish the political platform (the word plat-form, of course,
always sounded at least partly farcical
to me but now it sounds utterly nonex-
istent.) I was liter-ally tearing my hair
out, reading every-thing from Von Neu-

•¿¿¿•From the Electron-Chocked Desk of Jude Milhon•¿¿¿•
•¿¿¿¿¿¿¿¿¿¿¿¿•   •aka StJude•   •¿¿¿¿¿¿¿¿¿¿¿¿•
•¿¿¿¿¿¿¿¿¿¿¿¿•   •stjude@well.com•   •¿¿¿¿¿¿¿¿¿¿¿¿•

Date: Dec 19, 1997
To: rusirius
Subject: breakdown!

Convenient of you to give yourself a breakdown at this point in the book.
A little . . . break . . . DOWN.

Why has the goth set had a heroin subset? And why do YOU do heroin?
Anne Rice. It's all her fault. We all read her, so we know that blood = sex
= immortality in cool clothes. We're conditioned.

Heroin? Repeat after me: HEROIN IS AN ANALGESIC. If you get a bad burn,
do heroin, fine -- although it does impede healing. A great drug.

It's just got the blood glamour, that's all. It's so . . . so . . . parenteral.

It's just that we all read INTERVIEW WITH THE VAMPIRE at an impression-
able age. Hit us with the proper cues and we're panting gasping helpless
to resist the lure of . . .

BLOOD PORN

mann on Systems Theory to Kropotkin on autonomous collectives, and
poring over Bucky's Critical Path trying to find a passage writ in
English, and devouring New Republic, the Nation, The Village Voice,
The National Review, The American Spectator, eleven daily papers, and
taking EVERYBODY's opinion seriously . . . searching searching searching for the right synthesis, the weak link out of this hell or the
strong thrust that would penetrate her secrets and get me inside . . .

And it was like what Tom Robbins once told me about politics,
"It's like trying to get your shower right. You keep twisting the
left knob and the right knob and when you finally get it just right
you step into the shower and the guy in the apartment below you
flushes the toilet."

So there i was, lying in bed with my powerbook on a cold, dark,
windy Tuesday afternoon having decided that finally I could at least
lay out the fallacies of the known political tendencies, sort of
working up to actually presenting an alternate plan.

And there was this smell. I swear it jude. No drugs. My doors were
shut. My window was
closed but there was
this powerful gaseous
emanation, it smelled
sort of like burnt
onions. And you know
how i hate onions.
And I muttered to my-
self, "Jesus Christ.
I'm gonna have a
fuckin' nervous
breakdown" which is
just a figure of
speech for exaspera-
tion mixed with
stress usually,
right? but this time
it was like a magick
incantation. There
was an oceanic roar
followed by a high
pitched whine in both
of my ears, while I
felt the inside of my
head fill up with

The music is part of the rite. You know the songs. Jane says . . . there are
SO MANY songs . . . You turn the TV on, sound cut off, and you turn
down the lights. Maybe the TV's between channels, a source of light and
motion, like a campfire.

You have your favorite tie . . . maybe you're wearing it right now. A cash-
mere scarf, a black silk kimono belt. The ritual builds a fondness for all
its utensils.

You take out the matchbook. Snug behind the matches is the twist of
wrap, scotchtaped in. You pluck it like a grape, put it on the table -- your
eyes stay on it as you pluck a match and light the candle. (The match
smell, the candle smell.) You and your friend sit down in its friendly
light. You untwist the wrap. The vanilla scent fills space. Three beads of
brown mexican.

You don't bother smiling at your friend. You know the moment is shared.
You're more concerned with sharing the ritual and getting where it
takes you. It's like joining a party, it's like sex, only the rite is unchang-
ing and the outcome is sure.

Break open the wrap of the insulin syringe, move the plunger once to
free it. Spoon's on the table, handle twisted to keep it level. Distilled

white light and there was this terrible terrible TERRIBLE need to drill a hole right into my fontanel. That's right Jude, to trepan myself. So I rushed to the basement and found a hammer and a small screwdriver. And then I almost started to think. And then I said to myself, "Don't think." And I didn't.

BANG! I penetrated. BANG! I let it in a little further. And it was GOOOOOD!!!! It was like being touched by a lover after not having been touched for three years, but more. It was like scratching an itch that had always been there that you could never reach to scratch, like the first blush of spring and the first rush of a generous line of pure crystal speed. It was like feeling your muscles for the first time. Like a tight pussy. Brisk. Clear. Like shaving a layer of fat off of some smooth hellish perfection, but then a little voice said, "Go deeper. Set that little homunculus FREE!" It was a dry, twisted, california-desert, all-seeing but unkind rednecky mansonesque voice but BANG!

water's in a ruby-glass goblet. You dip the needle, draw the plunger, spurt the water into the tablespoon . . . you do that twice more, three times . . . flip one of the beads into the water with the needle point, wash it around to see how it dissolves . . . usually the mexican just starts drifting out into the water like smoke. You hold it over the candle until it simmers on the edges and then suddenly boils up all over. The air smells like baking cookies.

Put the spoon down on a piece of paper . . . the carbon on its back makes a mess. Pick up a Q-tip. Pinch off a wisp, twist it into a tight ball, drop it into the spoon at the edge. This is the cotton, the filter. You push the plunger all the way in, push the needletip into the cotton and draw the liquid through it, watching that you suck no particles. Mexican dissolves if you just think at it. You look through the syringe at the color . . . like sherry. You re-cap the needle and tie yourself off. If you're male, your veins stand like ropes; you can choose a discreet forearm vein. If you're female you may go for the wrist; the big vein under your thumb is easy to hit; hidden under watch or wristlets, and nobody thinks tracks if they're on the wrist. Slap it to bring the vein up. Swing the arm, clench the fist. Slap again: this somewhat anesthetizes. Usually vamp . . . uh users like to feel it when they make the hit. Needle slides in slow, bevel eye pointing up, here's lookin at you. Your breath goes very shallow . . . You angle in . . . feel the little pop when the needle breaks into the vein. Draw the plunger back gently, not to disturb the needle in its pocket,

OK NOW I'VE DONE IT! And there was this slight feeling of panic, an astounding colorful, geometric/psychedelic visionary moment. I had entered some other state. I looked down at my body. It looked the same but it was different. I experienced a moment of being convinced that I was other than human (You KNOW how I ridicule this conceit in others . . .). The word that came up was "Individuated Insectoid." I succumbed to a impulse to pound on the veins on the insides of my arms and my thighs, harder . . . USE THE HAMMER! My skin wanted to be pulled and stretched. I felt that I had no internal organs. When I thought about this, a voice in me head said "eternal organs . . ."

As far as I'm concerned, that's when I blacked out. But I was found, bloody, bruised and weeping in the lap of a comforting ten year old girl in Dolores Park. Her name is Claire and she's visited me twice here at the clinic. No, I'm not in love and there's nothing sexual. She'd recognized me as R. U. Sirius and thought that all the blood and bruises were just "part of being really cool" at first. She says we had a pretty normal conversation but that I didn't believe that I was R. U. Sirius. Finally, I told her that "little suzie was the queen of the underground" and then started weeping uncontrollably. She doesn't know who called the ambulance.

Anyway, everybody is keeping this hush hush thankfully and there's no real damage from the trepanning. In fact, I FEEL SET FREEEEEEE!!!!!!!

==

Date: Sat, 24 Apr 1996
17:14:52 -0800
From: stjude
To: rusirius
Subject: Ugh. gaak . . .
but -- it's an exer-
cise in free speech.

You want to know why Congress passed the Anti-Deg Standards?? Justpat just sent me this, encrypted. I'm sending it plaintext, why not? It's practically public record, according to Pat. He got it from a friend doing tech consulting for HADL. Remember rumors that HADL was menacing congress with hideous stuff from the Net? This may be the very document that made them

and look for the register: yes -- a little red flower blossoms at the base of the cylinder. You're in, you're there . . . and the real connection is made: THE BLOOD . . . you're talking to your heart now, downstream in the blood, in the current. You hear it in your ears, the echo in your body. You loose the tie . . . ease the plunger in, watching the blood wisping through the shortening cylinder, breathe in shallow murmurs, and you push it all the way home . . . withdraw. Bright blood beads up on your skin.

Grab a tissue. Press it to the vein. Slide back and take the feeling as it takes you . . . Warm. Blood warm. It's pussy-by-the-fire. Your everything curls up purring. In a little while, as if something just occurred to you, you walk into the bathroom and throw up. No problem. Just something you thought about doing.

Then you can't do anything for a couple of hours. You nod, noting the music, noting the candle, noting the TV, but you're just scanning the surfaces, distracted from seeing or hearing, distracted from your distraction by a thousand distractions, thoughts cutting in past each other like fractured glass panels. A significant-seeming thought pursued and pinned proves to be the equivalent of a doodle. Then you droop lower and lower to a proximate sleep, a sleep that seems athletic, muscular: you leap from dream to fractured dream. You wake tired, your everything slightly ACHES. But that's cool. In the mirror your face has a lead-gray aura, and your pupils are tiny, twitchy, like you're looking at something you hate. But it's okay. You look forward to next time.

. . . 'Cause every time it's exactly the same . . . and it's always good.

pass the A-D bill. HADL's as shrewd as always -- this is plenty ugly,
yes it is . . . And we're put in the position of having to defend this
piece of excrement?

Okay. I'll defend it. Got yer free speech right here. It's obscenely
insulting about public figures, threatens assassination, and threatens
sexual violence against a cat. It gives us a cool insider view of
how brutal the competitive sexual posturing among males can get --
oops . . . a little sexist there.

But I must PRAISE this document, as a perfect illustration of how
disgusting free speech can get. It can only remind us of how disgusting the lack of free speech might be, and there we are.

Here's what HADL bludgeoned the hapless congressfolk with:

Message-ID: <191302Z02061994@anon.penet.fi>
   Path:dockmaster.phantom.com!uunet!EU.net!sunic!news.funet.fi!news.
   eunet.fi!anon.penet.fi

just like milk and cookies at recess . . . always the same, always good . . .
except the time it takes you to hit a vein protracts, and the time of the
glow shrinks.

BAH.

It's Vampire Lite. It's only glamorous if you sexualize it. And speaking of
sex, if you and your lover love the drug, your libidos will die in it, and
this little rite will be your sex. Sex Lite. And you won't do much talking.
Friendship Lite. If you think your life is shallow and empty now, try the
real thing: try heroin. Lite up your life.

So when you run into goths at 2 am in the convenient shoppe, and they got
nothing on the counter but distilled water and Q-tips, you smirk at them
sardonic-like. Heh, little gothlets: heroin? Tawdry, tacky, so banal . . .
it's like hanging at macdonalds,
it's like drinking till you puke,
but it sure as fuck can kill you,
(and if it does . . .
your more gullible friends will be impressed.)

getoverit.

Newsgroups:
alt.pranks
From:
anx91072@anon.penet.fi
(BENEDICK)
X-Anonymously-To:
alt.pranks
Organization: Anony-
mous contact service
Reply-To: anx91072
@anon.penet.fi
Date: Sat, 2
Jun 1994 19:06:55 UTC
Subject:
Presidential prank

Howz this fer a
prank. I just wrote
the following message

Dear Billary,
   I'm gonna kill
Bill's fucking commie
liberal ass and then

I'll make Hillary suck Sox the Cat's balls while Al Gore cornholes her
fat ass (after I put a bag over the bitches head so he can get it up).

and I ran it through PGP and got

—————BEGIN PGP MESSAGE—————
Version: 3.3

pgAAANgP0G/sYWGxAW5Bpp0DmAR7T3GugHNSDG4PmYDD61ATsDJ9+qndQRDr4vYeYbbCN
FRZ1cAa9muZvLkPQEYo9rn3Sp5TbrokXlAhZJ2/Js4x7LLgCVVE+5XBheHfAhFtGvrx1k
Flt5Wl5e7wdqMDk5EGucpSVo9xLJ5r0knj1x4llT6DFJPAu0Uk0ON9CZiv5m5X9xFoIyG
mU378UML9HRbteuQaM9lwi5L/ER37UYPeNhl4FH01v79RmJiqAl36kcCklINy/E3JsoS4
+Z0xTUmfgKslivuHLXY=
=KM20
—————————END PGP MESSAGE—————

then I mailed the PGP file to president@whitehouse.com.

Now, when the Gestapo (sorry I mean the SS) comes knocking at my door
that will prove that (a) PGP is not secure (b) Remailers aren't secure (c) Hillary always sucks Sox's balls.

```
xxxxxxxxxxxxxxxxxxxxxxxxxxxxxxxxxxxxxxxxxxxxxxxxxxxxxxxxxxxxx
    Andreas Lusuriello       I You are what you are;
    HOME: 1-818-555-1982     I you is what you is.
    FAX : 1-818-555-9384     I
    andreas@bowtie.lido.com  I -- Frank Zappa
xxxxxxxxxxxxxxxxxxxxxxxxxxxxxxxxxxxxxxxxxxxxxxxxxxxxxxxxxxxxx
```

    Message-ID: <205451Z02061994@anon.penet.fi>
    Path:dockmaster.phantom.com!uunet!EU.net!sunic!news.funet.fi!news.eunet.
    fi!anon.penet.fi
    Newsgroups: alt.pranks
    From: anx222489@anon.penet.fi
    X-Anonymously-To: alt.pranks
    Organization: Anonymous contact service
    Reply-To: anx91072@anon.penet.fi
Date: Sat, 2 Jun 1994 20:46:55 UTC
Subject: RE: Presidential prank

User anx91072@anon.penet.fi writes:
    >> Howz this fer a prank. I just wrote the following message
    >> Dear Billary,

```
>>   I'm gonna kill Bill's fucking commie liberal ass and then
>>
>> and I ran it through PGP and got
```

```
>>————BEGIN PGP MESSAGE————
>> Version: 3.3
```

Why are you still using Version 3.3??????????????????

```
>> xxxxxxxxxxxxxxxxxxxxxxxxxxxxxxxxxxxxxxxxxxxxxxxxxxxxxxxx
Andreas Lusuriello        I You are what you are;
HOME: 1-818-555-1982      I you is what you is.
FAX: 1-818-555-9384       I
andreas@bowtie.lido.com   I -- Frank Zappa
>> xxxxxxxxxxxxxxxxxxxxxxxxxxxxxxxxxxxxxxxxxxxxxxxxxxxxxxxx
```
And nice going dumbass. The signal for the remailer to remove a .sig
is a row of DASHES!!! since you delimited yours with a row of Xs, the
anon remailer probably didn't touch it, so your .sig (with YOUR NAME,
PHONE AND EMAIL ADDRESS) is on the PGP message threatening the Pres.
Grease your asshole, dude, you're going to the slammer. Do you know
why they call it the "slammer"????

```
  Message-ID: <211423Z02061995@anon.penet.fi>
Path:dockmaster.phantom.com!uunet!EU.net!sunic!news.funet.fi!news.eunet.
fi!anon.penet.fi
Newsgroups: alt.pranks
From: anx5326538@anon.penet.fi
X-Anonymously-To: alt.pranks
Organization: Anonymous contact service
Reply-To: an91072@anon.penet.fi
Date: Sat, 2 Jun 1994 20:46:55 UTC
Subject: RE: Presidential prank
```

User anx91072@anon.penet.fi writes:
```
    >>————BEGIN PGP MESSAGE————
    >> Version: 3.3
```
Nice going dickdrip sending a PGP message to Billary. If the FED-
NAZIS only work on ONE thing, it'll be an encrypted message sent to the
president. We already have word that the NSA (Nazi Security Agency) can
trace 70% of the remailer traffic, so there's no news there. Now you're
going to insure that they spend all their time either cracking PGP or
tracing you and finding your PGP key from your directory.

And everybody knows that Hillary is a lezzy. Who would fuck that ugly bitch anyway.

Message-ID: <022531Z03061994@anon.penet.fi>
Path:dockmaster.phantom.com!uunet!EU.net!sunic!news.funet.fi!news.eunet.
fi!anon.penet.fi
Newsgroups: alt.pranks
From: anx647352@anon.penet.fi
X-Anonymously-To: alt.pranks
Organization: Anonymous contact service
Reply-To: anx91072@anon.penet.fi
Date: Sat, 3 Jun 1994 02:18:55 UTC
Subject: RE: Presidential prank

Given all the shit coming down these days, let's assume that NSA has cracked PGP. And they probably don't even LIKE Prez Clinton . . .
    And mark my words, Sox is a virgin.

Path:dockmaster.phantom.com!uunet!EU.net!sunic!news.funet.fi!news.eunet.
fi!anon.penet.fi
Newsgroups: alt.pranks
From: anx951401@anon.penization: Anonymous contact service
Reply-To: anx91072@anon.penet.fi
Date: Sat, 3 Jun 1994 02:18:55 UTC
Subject: RE: RE: Presidential prank

    anxx91072@anon.penet.fi writes:
    >> I'm gonna kill Bill's fucking commie liberal ass and then

YOU sick man ,not even Clinton wants to fuck Hilary. Now the Gore girlz, Al and Tippsters daughters are prime goddess material. I can see why "Uncle Bill" gives them lessons on his "sax-o-phone". Lets hope they don't turn into porkers like Tippster.

Cool prank, d00d.

Message-ID: <076531x03061994@anon.penet.fi>
Path:dockmaster.phantom.com!uunet!EU.net!sunic!news.funet.fi!news.
eunet.
fi!anon.penet.fi
Newsgroups: alt.pranks
From: anx647352@anon.penet.fi
X-Anonymously-To: alt.pranks

Organization: Anonymous contact service
Reply-To: anx02156@anon.penet.fi
Date: Sat, 3 Jun 1994 02:18:55 UTC
Subject: RE: Presidential prank

Well what *i* really want to do is CENSORED CENSORED CENSORED CENSORED
CENSORED CENSORED CENSORED CENSORED CENSORED CENSORED CENSORED CENSORED
CENSORED CENSORED CENSORED CENSORED CENSORED CENSORED CENSORED CENSORED
CENSORED CENSORED CENSORED CENSORED CENSORED CENSORED CENSORED CENSORED
CENSORED CENSORED CENSORED CENSORED CENSORED CENSORED CENSORED CENSORED
CENSORED CENSORED CENSORED CENSORED CENSORED CENSORED CENSORED CENSORED
CENSORED CENSORED CENSORED CENSORED CENSORED CENSORED CENSORED CENSORED

<Message Truncated>
==
Date: 30 Apr 1996
From: stjude
To: rusirius
Subject: Here it comes after us, the deluge!

this week the monitoring of the Internet is starting to roll

Of course, the Net's doing countermeasures. My god, we foresaw this
years ago. There's no government like no government, eh? likewise,
there's no governance like no governance. Let them monitor until
their faces are as blue their noses. . . . they can't censor what they
can't read. The Net is going to be encrypted.

There are a couple of readymade programs for encrypting your email,
but you have PGP already, right? Dust it off! Fire it up! It's easy.
It's KOOL. You'll like it.

it's long overdue for you to get a little technical. You been looking
down your drug-blasted nose at tech for far too long . . . You're going to use PGP or else. I'll walk you through the whole thing. Don't
be afraid. . . .

Be ready! Be very ready!
==

Ben is Brain Dead   May 1996

Crypto for Dummies

by Pat Justice

"So what's with all these geeks with lines of gibberish all over their computer screens?"

The point of using cryptography is to make sure that a certain piece of information is seen and comprehended only by a specific person chosen by the encryptor. Simple, right? There are two main types of cryptography—private and public key. The key is what it sounds like, the thing you need to lock or unlock the message. In private-key crypto (DES, IDEA, Vernam ciphers are all examples of this), it all works a lot like a hotel room door. Your lover has the key, (s)he uses it to walk right in. Your spouse, on the other hand, doesn't have this key and (s)he has to stand outside the door whining and wondering if you're in there.

A public key system (RSA is the most widespread, but there are others) is more complex. Two keys are involved. Zowie! Imagine certified mail in an unopenable envelope and you're on the right track. Your lover sends you a message to your address. You have to sign for it. Your spouse's signature wouldn't be accepted. Your address is the public key. You can give it to anyone, and anyone can send you an encrypted message. But you can only get it if you provide the right signature, your private key. No one can read your message in transit. Also, by using your private key, you can sign a message and other people can be sure that you sent it.

Of course, nothing is ever 100%. Suppose your spouse has suspicions. (S)he tricks your lover into thinking that hir own post office box is your address and hir key is your key. A torrid letter will be delivered there, and your spouse will sign for it. Suddenly you're in divorce court.

Enter the web of trust, which frankly scares the shit out of the government. And maybe your spouse. If you can certify that your illicit lover is the one who holds the public key, then anyone who trusts you can trust your lover's key. So anyone who trusts anyone who trusts you will trust your lover's key, and so on. The reason why the web of trust scares the government

```
#####################################################
#########           • Trudy B. Hyatt •          #########
#########         • Editorial Assistant •        #########
#########    • Hyatt@Ballantine.Books.com •     #########
#####################################################
```

Date: 4 Aug 1997
To: StJude@well, rusirius
Subject: Tech!

HELP! I thought I'd be happy once we got to the tech stuff, but really all of this techy talk makes my eyes glaze over. Now I MISS the sex, drugs and politics!

```
# # # # # # # # # # # # # #
#   /==$=\      #  <— From the High-Tech Fully Electronic Desk
# /))-00(\     #     of R. U. Sirius
# ((( —)))     #
# )))\ /(((  # —> rusirius@well.com
# # # # # # # # # # # # # #
```

Date: 4 Aug 1998
To: Hyatt@Ballantine.Books.com, stjude@well.com
Subject: help?

CONCENTRATE TRUDI THIS STUFF IS GOOD FOR YOU!! THE DO-IT-YOURSELF TECH IS AN ESSENTIAL PART OF THE BOOK!

is that we can all trust one another (supposedly) and communicate with each other without them knowing what's being said or being able to break into the web—if we're careful and don't sign each other's keys without being certain.

This is why the government wants a cryptography standard they control, one based on a hierarchy rather than a web. You prove to the government (with your ID) that you're who you are. So does your lover. So you can trust each other—but only if you trust the government not to peek and not to lie.

How much do you trust the government with your love life? How about that car the IRS thinks you bought from a friend for $500 that you actually gave him $1000 for—and he threw in a bag of weed? You see, the web of trust is how real people live their lives.

This article barely scratches the surface of what string cryptography can do for you. Pick up PGP today. The marriage you save could be your own.

```
•¿¿¿•From the Electron-Chocked Desk of Jude Milhon•¿¿¿•
•¿¿¿¿¿¿¿¿¿¿¿¿•      •aka StJude•       •¿¿¿¿¿¿¿¿¿¿¿¿•
•¿¿¿¿¿¿¿¿¿¿¿¿•   •stjude@well.com•     •¿¿¿¿¿¿¿¿¿¿¿¿•
```

Date: 4 Aug 1998
To: Hyatt@Ballantine.Books.com, rusirius
Subject: Re: Tech!

You want some more politics, Trude? I just found this . . .
We should shove this back into 1995, I guess -- you can place it temporally wherever you will.
This is the first appearance (in the megamedia) of the Gaian Avengers. . . .

New York Times 25 May 1995
Letters Column:

In the early autumn of 1994 three human-friendly male elephants -- well known to the humans who studied them, and the local Masai who protected them -- took a fatal walk. The three wandered a hundred meters past the border of Masai Mara, their "preserve" in Kenya, into neighboring Tanzania. There they were gunned down with automatic rifles firing armor-piercing bullets, perhaps from a moving vehicle. The "hunters" who murdered them -- one American, two Germans -- have been tracked to their lairs and dealt with by the Gaian Avengers.

The three killer humans were tranquillized with darts and taken captive. At all times they were transported humanely, kept caged, fed and watered, though isolated from one another. In the course of three days they manifested consistent violent aggressiveness, which was treated by surgical removal of the trigger finger, followed by appropriate postoperative care. Yesterday the three were further treated with 500 micrograms of LSD and released in remote wilderness areas.

Earth First! (Humanity -- Soon!)

The Gaian Avengers

= = = = = = = = = = = = = = =

```
Date: 2 May 1996
From: stjude
To: rusirius
Subject: it's also
after us, the purge
```

so, you feel lucky, punk? you gonna keep on saying f***, and just hope for the best? I'm not gonna talk even to YOU in cleartext from now on. You wanna talk, you gotta 'crypt! Crank up the PGP, comrade. Use it or lose.

Look, it's only weird at first . . . after a while it will seem almost
natural, just like the rest of your life . . .
First: copy this key, paste it into an ascii text file and have PGP
add it onto your public keyring, okay? Here's my public key --

—————BEGIN PGP PUBLIC KEY BLOCK—————
Version: 4.3

mQCPAi5MpIMAAAEEAKu4HAHQkjGcb/S4iFcAetowJgbtylekFTMw9vCZNOQ/0PxYgLlMc
UNtnR6veQ1nSQPaF0YfBVx7wAZC2IyD4VxDHjKfAXGWPsaqqm8//JgofctmCYsWESx4Wn
IVPB0wq1sGpTHIsXcAdMTkg2CFA+ETvCn1eR25iLf5jDqBnoEZABEBAAG0IFN0IEp1ZGU
gTWlsaG9uIDxzdGp1ZGVhd2VsbC5jb20+
=zrMC
—————END PGP PUBLIC KEY BLOCK—————

And when you want to send email to me, you write it in an ascii text
file and put it through PGP and encrypt it with my public key. Right?
And send the encrypted output. Got it? And when I send you what looks
like a mess of garbage, you whisk it through PGP and decrypt it with
my public key, and there it is, readable, right? Right. You want the
censors pawing through OUR email? The gorge rises.

In the meantime, just to get you in the mood, here's a couple of manifesti, or -toes, from the Cypherpunks list . . .

pfoo, i can't find them . . . so here's a couple of cypherpunk slogans,
at least, from memory --
(this illustrates why bumperstickers are the manifesti of these
times -- short memory, shorter attention-span . . . lotsa traffic.)

ENCRYPTION. . . . JUST DO IT!
THEY CAN'T CENSOR WHAT THEY CAN'T READ!

F*CK CENSORSHIP (that's mine -- thought it up during me old prison
martyrdom)

USE PGP . . . WHAT THEY DON'T KNOW CAN'T HURT YOU

WHEN CRYPTO IS OUTLAWED, ONLY XWQVZW OEMIYS QPWXOK

etc etc The cypherpunk list's hopping. There's a lot of esprit -- at
last, they got some action. CPunks are distributing email encryption
packages out of a dozen FTP sites now. . . . you may want to pick up

the most recent Macintosh versions of everything. . . . i bet your PGP
is Version 1.0, with cobwebs . . .

SO, let's do some TECH! Do you know how to do an FTP -- a File Transfer Protocol? This is how you pick up stuff from remote places on the
Net. If you want to FTP out of the WELL, for example, you just tele-
port yourself into another site like this: !ftp ftp.dff.org
You sign on as anonymous, and give your email address as the
password. Then you *cd* (change directory) to pub -- the public
directory --
cd pub
and look around with an *ls* -- (ls = look-see, right? who said unix
is opaque. . . .)
ls
will show you the files in the directory, and then you just *get* the
files you want --
get macpgp43   Okay?????
= =
Date: 3 May 1996
From: rusirius
To: stjude
Subject: ok

Ok ok . . . I hear ya. Listen. I just got over $500,000 this month,
mostly for royalties on THANX! Contrary to popular belief, or the
assumptions of my biographer, I am not THAT strung out. So I have
extra money, and I'd like to contribute something, like about 100k,
to the best underground hackers gang . . . Can somebody rig up a way
to make it tax deductable? (If not, I'll still give about 20 or
30 k . . .)

I'm still pretty fried, but that doesn't stop me from FEELing my sup-
port for freedom . . .
= =
Date: 3 May 1996
From: stjude
To: rusirius
Subject: didn't understand your last message. somebody's spoofing you
again??!!

————BEGIN PGP SIGNED MESSAGE————

you moron, you wrote something like THAT in cleartext?

FUCK!

You get the idea, here? You just said something very incriminating to both of us, and you didn't encrypt it, then, did you? Would you like to see me, you, our friends relatives and cats behind bars for a long time?

But about yr proposition . . . yeah, in fact, there are people who could use the money to upgrade their hardware and see about doing some crimes in the name of freedom. . . . which is a cute idea, I must say, BUT I WON'T SAY IT IN PLAINTEXT!!!!

ENCRYPT, YOU SCHMUCK!!!

ENCRYPT YOUR MOST HARMLESS EVERYDAY STUFF, ENCRYPT WITH EVERYBODY YOU CHITCHAT WITH, SO WHEN YOU HAVE SOMETHING NASTY HEINOUS AND SELF-IMPRISONING TO SAY, NOBODY CAN TELL THE DIFFERENCE.

RIGHT?

————————BEGIN PGP SIGNATURE————————
Version: 4.3

iQCVAwUBLyI3Kbf5jDqBnoEZAQEuRgP9GgOIBQNJ0NTLio9oAExgHvZ7N2IHLBd/5ADN2
stYiP+iZQn6HzVj3JJ+/jhTrZoYv5CSm/aTyHdNVj9PvNiDYc7NSWa3ExzjNYmKDbN5cB
Wcs3sXymycGRC2e6GYmL2cVwOrYW/BhddTlbq3UNb9VtcR6tj9jseD2i89dfYP1cc=
=4SOK
————————END PGP SIGNATURE————————
= =
Date: 3 June 1996
From: stjude
To: rusirius
Subject: scramble!

————————BEGIN PGP SIGNED MESSAGE————————

I know you're insanely busy . . . but you should hear this. . . . word is out that HADL is making its next move this week . . . They're doing their expert number, shiatsu-ing the congressional pressure points again . . . this time to get encryption limited or outlawed.

If you thought things were settling down, just remember how your gradeschool teacher treated any sign of defiance. That's HADL's reac-

tion to encryption. The nun is picking up the yardstick . . . she's
scowling at you. . . . she's coming over to your desk . . . She's saying
fearsome things. . . . You *must* hold out your hand!!!!.

If you encrypt your stuff on the Net -- HADL is claiming to the hapless cowed congress -- it's prima facie evidence that you're a pornograph. Or some other kind of felon, maybe a mob member or a
terrorist. . . . or maybe you're just a little felon wannabe . . . In
which case you deserve whatever happens to you.

The writing's on the wall, darlin', and we don't need some Bible dude
to decode it for us --

mene mene . . .
. . . they're coming after us nasty punks
tekel upharsin
. . . and they're gonna shut us up . . .

jeez, look at all these religious metaphors . . . and me a good agnos-
tic kiddy.

————————BEGIN PGP SIGNATURE————————
Version: 4.3

iQCVAgUBLwcr2bf5jDqBnoEZAQFgSwP/S4EvTRyzes6tpSsbwRJZ9kSkkOAQEMY/szZac
5cgcbJ09z7dFoJSSqTbEhV0hf64pVXAVJt3sPQMIABGs/pn826bEQVPiRr4E26sPLsvKf
I5CbL3PW2S9GHCgxrt4EDJBDgT9wJz/LdAcRU24opBG4v/wPz+hrlyAQZ0uY4HFVA
==b6sB
————————END PGP SIGNATURE————————

= =
ANNOUNCING THE CREATION OF THE DIGITAL FREEDOM FOUNDATION
June 4, 1996

> "If Stealth planes and neutron bombs fail to protect the country
> there's not much a bunch of suburban guys with assault weapons can
> do." -- an2391072@anon.penet.fi

> "There's no way any number of people with AK-47s in the Idaho hills
> (or the Waco desert) can hope to overthrow a tyrannical government
> (or even Janet Reno), if that government sets its mind to destroy
> them." --
> an8290658@anon.penet.fi

WHEREAS the Second Amendment to the Constitution states that "A well-regulated Militia, being necessary for the security of a free State, the right of the people to keep and bear Arms, shall not be infringed."

WHEREAS it has historically been agreed that the Second Amendment serves two purposes: to allow the people to defend the country against foreign invaders, and to allow the people to defend themselves against a tyrannical government.

WHEREAS due to the increase in the power of munitions available to the government, personal armaments in the hands of the public, no matter how powerful these arms may be, serve the letter, but not the spirit, of the Second Amendment, for they can no longer allow us to protect ourselves against tyranny.

WHEREAS personal encryption tools are classified as armaments by the government.

THEREFORE we of the Digital Freedom Foundation argue that personal encryption tools at least serve the secondary purpose of the Second Amendment; they are tools that the public can use to ensure their own privacy, and hence their own freedom, in the event of the creation of a tyrannical government, without having to RELY on the goodwill of that government, and therefore these personal encryption tools deserve protection under the Second Amendment.

The aim of the Digital Freedom Foundation is to petition the U.S. Supreme Court to agree that personal encryption tools deserve Second Amendment protection. We will do this by doing all we can to provide legal and financial support to anyone brought to trial for the use or distribution of encryption tools, in an attempt to get their case heard by the Supreme Court. Let's face it, folks, our rights are at risk here, and we need all of you to take action.

If you are an attorney and can contribute your legal skills; if you are a student and can help out with research; or if you are one of the few people in this country with money and if you care about our fundamental rights as Americans, please email the DFF@dff.org

```
= = = = = = = = = = = = = = = = = = = = = = = = = = = = = = = = = = = = = = = = = = = = = = = = = =
```
Date: 12 June 1996
From: stjude
To: rusirius
Subject: scramble!

————————BEGIN PGP SIGNED MESSAGE————————
You almost certainly missed this . . . This bill passed itself as dis-
creetly as wind at a GOP fundraiser . . . And it demonstrates that the
Goblinment can really MOVE when it wants to . . .

> New York Times Online
> Wednesday June 12, 1996
> page A12(!!!!!)
>
> The Electronic Communications Public Safety Act passed the Senate
> yesterday with virtual unanimity, with only two dissenting votes.
> Given such strong support in Congress and in the White House, the
> ECPSA's whirlwind passage through both houses presumably will set
> the tempo for its implementation -- which begins with determining
> the makeup of the Encryption Regulatory Commission. ECPSA sponsors
> met today to discuss logistics for the new regulatory body. The
> ERC is expected to include active advocates of what is called "The
> New Civility."

It's a setup wherein the ERC will monitor the Internet for encryption
that they can't decrypt, and confiscate it -- just pluck it off the
wire. It's that simple. If they can't get in through the back door
and read it, it's illegal. Encryption programs that the Goblinment
can read, like WALL, they've been distributing for a year already . . .
Funny how nobody outside the govt wants to use them. It's like the
eternal Clipper Chip fiasco -- the govt gives out shoddy encryption it
can break, and is flabbergasted when nobody uses it EXCEPT them??
Hmmm. . . . you gotta love them. . . . but would you TRUST a government
that uses shoddy encryption???

So the ERC will be sitting on the flow like a pair of kidneys. . . .
passing, passing, oops, eliminate that one. . . .

> So the coalition of HADL + government will think they've won. And
> this channel for secure communications -- yes, this very one we're
> using here, guy, after all the trouble I had FORCING you to use
> PGP -- will very soon become illegal.

Then what?

HEH HEH HEH

>jude<

————————BEGIN PGP SIGNATURE————————
Version: 4.3

iQCVAwUBLw1Uurf5jDqBnoEZAQFGKQP/bhCfdfGORxsyz6T4MUwYkf4rgNl0DzREWHQFD
B/G03FRQLvM/W5c/wKH3eBC9NPol9kCI1u1dr8xp1vr/fnWZvO8yWNpwR8RRTC8rRCjG8
j1d5fy0bxpU2E781buAsLaCAWb3eWmqHEJQ6aIy5wxC8QuGMuaLrsIqnUM1qTAbIQ=
=rB+0
————————END PGP SIGNATURE————————

= =
Date: 12 June 1996
From: stjude
To: rusirius
Subject: ERC!! WHAT NEXT??!

————————BEGIN PGP SIGNED MESSAGE————————

As i was saying: Heh heh heh.
The cypherpunks have been working on countermeasures to this Kidney
Act for YEARS. Back in 1993, hero girlnerd Cypherella wrote Stego....
Let me tell you about Stego. Have you seen the Hallmart E-Greeting
Cards? Well, here's one from yr aunt marge:

To: rusirius
Subject: Happy Birthday from Aunt Marge!
Format: GIF

The "card" is a GIF (a picture file) of a bouquet of Crimson Glory
roses in full bloom, in glorious greyscale....

But HEY -- as you're wiping tears from your keyboard you remember
that it's not your birthday and you don't HAVE an Aunt Marge. So you
crank up your copy of Stego and feed the bouquet to it.... munch
munch munch . . . and what comes out . . . is a PGP-encrypted file!!!
If you feed this to PGP and decode it with your key, what you get is
something like this:
————————

My friend Chicken has written a sniffer for FSP sites -- that is, a program that looks for sites suitable for setting up a hidden anony-mouse file server on. He's an Eagle Scout, he's prepared -- he's run-ning it NOW. Interested?

Gettit????
Steganography is concealing messages. In graphic files, in music files, wherever. If you can't send an encrypted file over the wire naked, you can clothe it in the manymegabits of a file so big that it comes out looking normal anyway. . . . And it does. Music and pictures with Stego messages in them look . . . normal.

And hoping you're the same. You bettah keep your hair over your anten-nae. Keep your extra hands in your pockets. Times 're getting tighter.

————BEGIN PGP SIGNATURE————
Version: 4.3

iQCVAwUBLwlUurf5jDqBnoEZAQFGKQP/bhCfdfGORxsyz6T4MUwYKf4rgNl0DzREWHQFD
B/G03FRQLvM/W5c/wKH3eBC9NPol9kCI1u1dr8xp1vr/fnWZvO8yWNpwR8RRTC8rRCjG8
j1d5fy0bxpU2E781buAsLaCAWb3eWmqHEJQ6aIy5wxC8QuGMuaLrsIqnUM1qTAbIQ=
=rB+0
————END PGP SIGNATURE————

Date: 12 June, 1996
From: rusirius
To: stjude
Subject:

————BEGIN PGP SIGNED MESSAGE————

Well, word is out. At my lecture here in minneapolis, i had over 20 invitations to join secret encrypted online parties for June 19th. Everybody's talkin' 'bout instant underground, and I met two -- count 'em -- two different groups who told me they're prepared to start over-riding TV transmissions. This woman who claims to be part of the Hassan I Sirius Revolutionary Brigade said that they have affinity groups across the country and are getting organized for major league propaganda war. The idea is that an organized cabal could knock out the same program at the same time in dozens of different service ar-eas, maybe even over most of the country. This is the only way you could -- in effect -- create a semi-national pirate television event.

Which makes me paranoid as hell. First of all, they using my name.
The Innerscoop lawyers will all have heart attacks. But that's the
GOOD news. The bad news is that I'll be associated with their ac-
tions, if in fact they're real. Well, this girl, who calls herself
Weasel Art, says "No. There's this other guy calls himself Hassan I
Sirius. You'll be hearing from him soon." Oh joy.

And the thing that scares me the most is that they want to broadcast
five minutes of straight out political propaganda over the top show on
television, which I believe is the Rush Limbush Variety Half Hour on
Faux TV right now. Is this effective propagandizing? Wouldn't it be
more effective to knock out the advertising and not interrupt a popular show, however idiotic that show might be?

    I told them that they have to produce absolutely the most amazing,
funniest, exciting, entertaining five minutes of television imaginable, because otherwise they'd just piss people off. Everybody went
away nervous.

————————BEGIN PGP SIGNATURE————————
Version: 4.3

3FRQLvM/W5c/wKH3eBC9NPol9kCI1u1dr8xp1vr/fnWZvO8yWNpwR8RRTC8rRCjG8j1d5
fy0bxiQCVAwUBLw1Uurf5jDqBnoEZAQFGKQP/bhCfdfGORxsyz6T4MUwYKf4rgN10DzRE
WHQFDB/G06aIy5wxC8QuGMuaLrsIqnUM1qTAbIQpU2E781buAsLaCAWb3eWmqHEJQ=
uiRmP
————————END PGP SIGNATURE————————

===
Semiotech[e] Online   24 June 1996

The Nerds' Revenge
by Jude Milhon

To the ramparts!! The Feds have finally gone too far. Their latest
move against "unauthorized" encryption has driven the Cypherpunks to
bloody revolution. Well, virtual revolution. The Cypherpunks -- a self-
publicizing secret conspiracy -- have cobbled up their top-secret counter-
measure. And being who they are, they're shouting it to the media --
look out! It's the Virtual Underground!
The Cypherpunks are announcing the VU as an instant, come-as-you-are
Revolution, open to everyone. The Net's afire this week with manifestos,
each claiming to establish another Underground faction. And that means
... now watch closely ... it means that this merely conceptual Under-

ground is already quite real. It's got the semiotic cred ... it's there ... it's virtually SOLID.

Okay ... sounds good to me, but how do you join an Underground that's only Virtual? Well, depending on which manifesto plays your tune, you would go start a TAZ [Temporary Autonomous Zone] in the Caribbean ... or set up an encrypted bank in a FreePort ... or most slackerly, just download a soon-to-be-banned program like Stego, for disguising your encrypted email. The VU Weekend Hobbyist advises: "Just insert a virtual wooden shoe between any of the wheels that make society go."

[The wooden shoe's a *sabot*, dig -- sabotage? geddit? -- there's an old-rad trivia question for you.]

The Dada à Gogo manifesto shouts, "COMING SOON! The Virtual underground Digest. Everyperson a Haqr! It's as easy as saying F S P! For do-it-yourself hacking techniques, download the Virtual underground Digest,. FSP it from penet.fi after 31 July! And check alt.anarchy.vud! The VuD is accepting how-to articles from now till the end of the world."

If the VuD maps to anything real, it's truly radical. The VuD is anarchism in action ... most intimately so, because it hacks the hacker anarchist hierarchy itself. If the most knowledgeable guys, those at the top of the haqr heap, give up their accumulated haq/phreak secrets to the masses -- it's, well ... it's revolutionary. The elite wall crumbles. Technically lame you might be, but if you can follow a cookbook you can play like the experts. Which means there's virtually an Underground for everyone. Technical cretin or Wiz, anybody can implement a grudge against the Niceness Gestapo. Anybody: Libertarians, retro-Republicans, Neo-Democrats, Noötrophians ... even you.

Something else is happening here that's revolutionary: Dada à Gogo is a powerful bourbaki, even if it's only three days old with a membership of one. [A bourbaki is a bogus group, in this case only one member shy of the null set.] DDAGG is powerful because it created the IDEA of the Virtual underground Digest. Could ideas == power? Sound like nerd heaven?

DDAGG invites hackers, phreakers, pirates and pranksters to post their own additions to the Virtual underground Digest -- which exists only by having a logo, a timestamping protocol, and a remailer address. You submit something to the VuD by pasting the logo onto the head of your screed, timestamping the whole mess, and sending it to anon23964873923 @penet.fi. That's it. If your checksum checks out it gets stashed in the

penet FSP site, and gets distributed via the penet NNTP server out to
the great UseNet, worldwide. (The UseNet's been shut off over most of
this land. If you can't get to UseNet, ask the teenager next door.)

DDAGG suggests that you can authenticate your VuD posts -- tie them to
your pseudonym -- by signing them with public-key encryption. And if you
want to be extra authentic, get your key signed by known and trusted Net
pseudonyms. Disco! It's an incarnation of the Cypherpunks' old idea, the
Reputation Net.

Many of this week's manifestos invite you to issue your *own* personal
manifesto, why not? They suggest posting it to appropriate newsgroups
like alt.anarchy.manifesto or alt.sex.fetish.politics. It might be pru-
dent to issue your call to action through a trail of out-of-country remailers, like PENET.FI, or BOUNCE.IT or SELE.NE, to cover your tracks.
And you might avoid words like phuq, lest you attract the censors' chop.
No fun, if your manifesto gets unmanned 'round mid-Net.

The Cyberphunq Manifesto (posted this week also) gets radical, "If you can
issue a manifesto you can have a secret life online -- you can dig yourself
a virtual Batcave in cyberspace. And if you want to go further, if you've
got secret yearnings for a Real, NONvirtual Underground ... well then. Read
SHOCKWAVE RIDER for inspiration, prepare yourself a new identity, get some
interesting new friends ... and get *down*." The harangue finishes: "The
physical Underground will be, it will be. Remember: even the lamest Rave
kids managed to kludge themselves up their own Sixties. The Underground
NetRoad will happen. Just saying this will MAKE it happen."

Conceptual revolution revs on. And the mind just goes on boggling.

•••
StJude's Underground Faction Of The Week: The Moles.
(from a posting on alt.anarchy.manifesto):
The Moles
And who are we, you might ask?
Who are the Moles? We are the Fifth Column,
Doric and proud. We are the waiters in the dark
restaurant. We are the
BLEMISHES ON CORPORATE AMERICA.

Baltimore Sun Bulletin   June 25, 1996

New Civility Targets Lifestyles
cont. from pg. 3
made it clear that they were getting ready to fight for standards in all the popular media. Television, computer games, virtual reality, radio, film, rock and roll, and pornography were all singled out. HADL co-chairman Catherine MacKinnon-Masson predicted "total victory within the year on the complete elimination of pornography."

The Nice Society
The New Civility Movement is dominated by conservatives. And indeed the best-known speakers at this conference were the Republicans at the vanguard of this cultural revolution—Dan Quayle, Newt Gingrich, William Bennett, Jesse Helms. But the freshest ground was broken by less high-profile cultural conservatives from the Left. From *Tikkun* editor Michael Lerner to environmentalist guru Paul Ehrlich, the liberals sounded the same theme, "the Nice Society." These speakers asked for New Civility in the real world, railing against, in Lerner's words, "a culture of speed, violence and sleaze." A wild panel, that included Jeremy Rifkin, Gerry Mander, Catherine MacKinnon-Masson, Mark Farkner, Katie Milstead and Bob Redwood-Beaver-Elk, gleefully suggested the possible elimination of "several media in their entirety" including television, virtual reality and computer games. At one point or another, panel members also suggested for possible elimination: environmental pollution, fast cars, meat, junk food, tobacco, animal experimentation, weapons, alcohol, billboards, sexually suggestive clothes, fur, a culture of sexual promiscuity, and even "plastic values."

Surprisingly, these suggestions struck a chord with the more conservative attendees. For instance, ultraconservative Nancy Swiberg-White of Mothers Against Virtual Reality said that she was very impressed by the idea of a nice society. "The age of permissiveness is over. Everything should be on the table." Nancy said she's spoken
cont. pg. 21

HAR! <Piracy underground Digest>
Avast, newby scum:
Piracy FAQ July 4, 1996
Pp. 4–5

DEFINITIONS

Media piracy — Interrupting regular TV and radio programming by hacking the microwave stations or satellites delivering the signal. Pirates substitute counterfeit programs that usually, as the French say, simulate the simulacra—phony public opinion shows, phony news broadcasts, elaborate privately produced dramas ... but mostly phony advertisements. Some of these are parodies of actual ads, and some mimic the originals accurately, except for some strange inclusion or deviation ... and some advertise illegal widgets, illicit ideas, and contraband encryption programs and where to find them.

Giving the day's FSP sites is essential, because these are on hacked Internet addresses, and appear and disappear within a few hours. The Feds shut them down as soon as they find them, so the sites move constantly. FSP sites are libraries where one can find outlawed programs and pick up bulletins: HAR, for example. And manifestos, mock-manifestos, reports on hacks performed, ideas for hacks and proposed physical actions, and other Underground info. Publicizing current FSP addresses was the first major justification for media piracy. Later it became art for the art's sake, particularly for hacker/phreakers collaborating with artists doing high-end computer animation.

Bam BBS or FSP Site — Bam is a Euroterm for the ancestor of the Rave. A Bam is an instant party that coalesces in abandoned sites, parking structures or mid-town traffic and continues until police intervene. A Bam site is a little parasite inside an unknowing host machine on the Internet, sudden and very temporary. See BBS and FSP.

BBS — Bulletin Board System. An electronic town pub, dispensing data instead of drinkables. A Net site that allows notices to be posted for ongoing public conversations. Note: Putting up a BBS is quick and easy with a kit. BBSes can be run on tiny archaic machines. This means that ANYONE can put up a BBS, and take it right down, as well. See Bam BBS.

bourbaki — A pseudonym masking a collaboration. 2. [v.] Band together to do art, tech, or actions [see The Residents]. Bourbaki can also refer to a CONCEPTUAL organization, one that exists only insofar as it SHOULD exist, somewhere. [Name is from a mathematics collaboration on the 1930s.]

bourbaki haq — 1. Pretending to be a member of a bourbaki. 2. inventing a conceptual bourbaki, or conversely, claiming a real bourbaki is merely conceptual. This is a primary culture hack by the Underground. The Overground just doesn't get it.

conspiracy theory — Systematic delusions that whatever is happening, it's because people have banded together for sinister purposes. Applied paranoia. Government agencies have traditionally been devoted to this sort of thing.

DIY — Do It Yourself. DIY is one of the watch-acronyms of the dada revolutionists.

download — Sucking digital information—data or programs—over the Wire for storage in your personal computerspace.

FSP — A program, the File Sucking Protocol, [not really: it's the file *server* protocol, and it's real UNIX] which allows a Net user to appear in-visibly inside a remote site and swiftly and silently transfer files. As a verb, to travel anonymously into a computer site to browse its libraries for permanent checkouts (downloading).

FYI — For Your Information. FYI is another watch-acronym.

GIF — Graphic Image Format. A digital rendering of a photograph, map, painting, circuit diagram, etc, for transfer over the Net. ["Give the GIF that goes on giving."]

ILF — The Information Liberation Front ("Information Longs to be Free") was first mentioned on the Net back in 1992, on the Cypherpunks list. It's a bourbaki believed to be member-free, a pure Net construct.

pronoia — Delusions that people, the planet, or maybe the Underground are conspiring to help you.

spam — [v.] Overwhelm a communications carrier with an unwanted message. (From the Monty Python skit/song, "Spam spam spam spam, spam spam spam spam."

Also spammy [adj.], applied to a grudgingly admired prank.

An example of spamming is the early MUD/MOO prank of deluging a fellow MOOer's screen with [this window expands to fill user's screen with various fonts and colors and pictographs of spam spam spam spam spam spam spam spam . . . which keep on replicating and overlaying each other until the user hits any key]

Steganography — Sending messages concealed inside a picture. In telecommunications, sending messages concealed in a graphics or music file. [Learned borrowing from the Greek stego-, covered, covert, plus -graphy, writing]

San Francisco Chronicle July 12 1996

HOLY UNHOLY ALLIANCE!
The Improbable Convening Of The HADL

by M.E. Jaren Wasau

The man who may pose the most serious threat to the growing political influence of the Human Anti-Degradation League is known only as UNREDEEMED. According to myth, he lives in an abandoned utility booth on an unfinished subway line in a major metropolis. With a half dozen computer terminals plugged into a jury-rigged transformer, this bitter convert to the Underground has transferred no funds from bank accounts, hasn't hacked information off a single government mainframe. But UNREDEEMED has been infuriating Federal watchdogs of the Internet for months. And early this week he released a videotape to several large city newspapers that may make waves inside the powerful HADL organization.

Since May of this year UNREDEEMED has been roaming the Nets, underground and mainstream, with what he calls the "true story of the most psychotic lover's pact of misanthropy since Adolf and J. Stalin bellied up to the Leningrad Hotel wet bar." UNREDEEMED isn't the only alienated citizen who sees the formation of the HADL in those terms. But unlike the thousands of hackers and cypherpunks who inundate the encrypted underground net sites with similar rhetoric, Mr. UNREDEEMED was there when the pact was signed.

PREPARING LIBERALS FOR THE NET
I'll call him Gerald Cho. As an idealistic computer-sci graduate he was systems consultant for the Dignity Institute, an informal Liberal and Feminist thinktank that came to comprise a wing of HADL. When the Institute began to focus on the Internet, Cho was one of its chief technical advisers.

"Early 90's, there was a barrage of racism on the Net," he tells me over an encrypted telephone line.

"All these midwestern guys were logging on anonymously through their white supremacist BBSes, flaming any ethnic-sounding userid they found. And don't even mention sexism. It was the rule, not the exception. It was killing everything the Net stood for, and I wanted to help change that."

In the early months of '95, a significant portion of new Internet users were affiliated with charter groups on the Dignity Institute's roster. Cho, and similarly computer-literate Institute staffers, were instrumental in expediting this rising presence of liberal political activists, encouraging them to log on and advising them on Internet navigation. He also helped prepare them for the uncensored and frequently vicious nature of the Net.

"I mean, these are the kind of folks who would go into conniptions just hearing Rush Limbaugh. Can you imagine how they'd react to reading some lunatic's advice on how to seduce adolescent girls in alt.pedophile?"

A FREAK ZONE POPULATED BY MARXIST PEDOPHILES
Meanwhile, on the other end of the political spectrum, conservative religious groups were landing on their own beachhead in cyberspace. Political analysts attribute this largely to the influence of conservative House leader and cyberculture enthusiast Newt Gingrich. By late 1995, the religious right had all but dropped its pro-life rhetoric in favor of attacks on media and, in the words of one Moral Majority fundraising letter, ". . . the immoral, vile obsessions of internationally organized computer users." Conjuring the Net as a "freak zone brimming over with Marxist pedophiles and neo-pagan polygamists," the Internet quickly became the Radical Right's arch-nemesis.

THE NON-AGGRESSION SUMMIT

It didn't take long for the liberal activists and the fundamentalists to realize that they had similar concerns regarding the anything-goes anarchy of the digital world. Elements of these political polarities had already connected on opposition to pornography. Now that they were online, exploring the Net, they started comparing notes about the things that disturbed them.

Cho recollects, "There was an amazing volume of e-mail about The Net at the Institute. And we started getting stuff from these unbelievably backward Christian hayseed groups, people we called The Neanderthals. Then suddenly we were planning conferences together. It happened very fast."

These conversations culminated in the fabled "Non-Aggression Summit," a secret convocation that took place in May, 1995. HADL has always officially denied that the Summit took place.

cont. pg 8

===

Date: 15, July, 1996
From: rusirius
To: stjude
Subject: My weird career

You gotta love Faux TV. In the middle of the New Civility juggernaut, they go and offer Mondo Vanilli a TV series.

Connie apparently took my late night mutterings about a Mondo Vanilli TV show that crosses the Monkees and David Cronenberg, and turned it into a one paragraph proposal. And, unbeknownst to us, she's used her connections, charm and wit to SELL the damned thing.

The whole deal was presented to us this afternoon at Innerscoop's New York office (we're ending the American leg of the tour here) as a fait accompli. That's the only kind of fate I'm having, since I feel like a zombie prop anyway. Hell ... that's a 26-week season, Jude, at $35k per show, plus 15% ownership of the show and a 50%/50% cut on spin-off profits! Hah. I'll buy you AND your whole goddamned family a set of matching pink Cadillacs and a 90-foot neon statue of Elvis, that I'll have built by Jeff Koons.

We signed instantly. The show starts in mid-September, 9 PM Thursdays.

• •

THE MONDO VANILLI FUN SHOW: A proposal

The MONDO Vanilli Fun Show will be like the Monkees forcibly bred with David Cronenberg. The popular Mondo Vanilli group, whose members -- R. U. Sirius, Simone 3rd Arm and Scrappi DüChamp, already have cartoonish personas -- will play a pop band living together and having silly fun, except that two members, R. U. and Simone, have a secret Mr. (and Ms.) Hyde personality literally just beneath the skin, the result of exper- imentation with intelligence and longevity drugs and body modification. Thus our cute popsters turn into freakish monsters every episode. But the show really revolves around Scrappi, who maintains an irritatingly unctuous innocence, however horrifying the situations his bandmates force him to witness or participate in. Each show will end with a terrifying scene accompanied by an inappropriate laugh track. This will be a show signature. The first three shows will be filmed in 3D, and virtual reality gloves and goggles will be marketed for less than $100 through 7/11's and other participating stores.

• •

How she sold this I'll never know.

Anyway, after tonight's MV performance, I follow Connie back to a room she's subletting in Manhattan. I'm looking forward to some time alone with her, but there are these two characters there, one of whom calls herself Outrider and the other a thuglike wacko who calls himself Joey Bishop. The two of them say that they're part of the "Outrider gang." They claim to have word for me from "the underground" thanking me for my leadership (??!!???). I can only blink my eyes and form an O with my mouth. I'm shaking as I go to grab a beer but Joey is trailing me into the kitchen going on and on about the true Leninist nature of the underground, and how "armed struggle" is next. He has a list of over a million reactionaries "slated for execution." He wants to email it to me. Remind me to call Connie and BEG her to BEG him NOT to send it to me. Am I being framed yet?

    After about an hour of this, Outrider calls off Joey, with the words "Down boy." Then SHE goes off on this weird discourse about The Catcher in the Rye. I'm working on beer number six, and while it's clear to me that Outrider is quite nice and NOT a Leninist or some kind of Shining Path grand executioner -- she is in fact rather a kindly liberal -- it's even more obvious to me that
a) I really don't give a flying fuck.
b) Connie is going to keep grinning and yapping all night long and
c) I can flag a cab back to my hotel room in about 10 seconds just by stepping outside so . . . later.

= =
Date: Aug. 7, 1996
From: Snoopy
To: St Jude
Subject: and now, here's this

As per your request, here's the outline of our very first prank commercial, broadcast from a TCI satellite uplink station in Reston, Virginia the night of July 20, 1996, during "Seinfeld". We did it on a Quadra with Hi8 video outputs.

"When fun is outlawed . . ."

Length: 20 sec
Medium: Computer Generated Video
Producer: PSEUDAPOP
Market: To be distributed wherever the Underground is: we are
everywhere.

AUDIO

The instrumental track "No One Receiving,"
from the album "D'Cückoo LIVE", plays throughout.

VIDEO

Fade in on the ordered chaos of an orange-pink kaleidoscope image
like the 'Fruitopia' ads. 2 seconds.

Fade in white sans-serif letters "WHEN FUN IS OUTLAWED," floating
over the kaleidoscope image. Hold 2 seconds
Fade to the words "ONLY OUTLAWS WILL HAVE FUN." Hold 2 seconds
Fade to the words "JOIN THE UNDERGROUND." Hold 2 seconds
The words fade. Orange-pink kaleidoscope image. 5 seconds.

FADE TO BLACK.
FADE MUSIC.

FADE IN
White letters on black backdrop
Hold 5 seconds

WHEN FUN
IS OUTLAWED,
ONLY OUTLAWS
WILL HAVE FUN

JOIN THE
UNDERGROUND.
HAVE SOME FUN

FADE TO BLACK

===

WIRED 2000 Magazine Online Sep 1996

The whole beginning of this one is missing -- what the hell?

\/\
Satellite hacking is still a hardware coup, an insider's game, but pirate crews like Reach! and Mooners are spreading the tech around, trying
to make it as common as graffiti. Some of the satellite pirate broadcasts are slickest professional-qual graphics -- and some are rawest
homebrew, right out of the garage ...

    The Mating Game shows us bachelor #2, ... but look! it's a green-
    jumpsuited person in a Smileyface mask standing in front of a plaid
    blanket. In a gravelly Bogart voice it reads from a sheet of paper
    held between its bunny mittens:
    -- And now, a brief message from your unsponsored Hacker Underground,
    Ahem. Today's Stuff Your Government Does Not Want You to Know.
    In mainland states bordering the Pacific the ACTUAL unemployment rate
    for last month was a hair under 30%. That is, THIRTY, 3-zero percent.

    This information comes to you hot from a report deep in the bowels of
    [government-agency@Net-address.gov]. This data was lifted by the 13th
    Floor Elevators for your daily reality hit. It comes via pirate satel-
    lite feed, fresh from the Rogered Jollies to you. Stay awake, you hear?

Regardless of quality, these interruptions are REALLY POPULAR: even TV-
haters sit with remotes at the ready, waiting to tape them. Tapes get
collected and traded around.

For much of the American public, viewing and taping is the real stuff of
their lives. The world is the TV screen. The message is media. Now the
subversion of the media is the message. You can call it a revolution.
\/\
===
Date: 13 Sept 1996
From: rusirius
To: StJude
Subject: fun show!

————————BEGIN PGP SIGNED MESSAGE————————
Hope you caught the opening fun show last night. I can't believe it
caught the front page of the Chronicle ... "MONDO VANILLI VIRTUAL TV
EVENT WACKY FUN!" Not a bad review.

In fact, the reviews this morning are almost universally great. What the hell is wrong with this country? I mean, the show implies that we're luring girls into our house for snuff orgies!!! Ah, but they're comparing it to the Addams family, and they understand that . . .

So we transgress way over the line, we cross Monkees with Cronenberg . . . and they think Addams Family? Cool

————————BEGIN PGP SIGNATURE————————
Version: 4.3

AKT1fgJUuKKnnmrx9YMK6FtmCBvqzy3ptulkOGDJNUz+SoHliDE3OSpx9LHZQ7xTGGrZn
3mmEjQHp9OMQLq3wfbG4mr3ptulkO+SoHliDE3OSpx9LHZnmrx9YMK6FgL1McUNtnQ1nB
Vx7fAXGWPsqm8/wAZ=gb5e
————————END PGP SIGNATURE————————
= =
Date: 13 Sept 1996
From: StJude
To: rusirius
Subject: no encryption for you, buddy

uh huh. I saw it. uh . . . yeah.

i found it very disturbing.
disturbing.
but i guess i can't complain about
transgresses always greener,
i grew up on oz & harriet -- but this was scariet.

see, you got me duing it. . . .

does this mean i pass some kind of test? or maybe fail it? gah.
disturbing
<shudder>

= =
Date: September 15, 1996
From: schwarz@christbuddha.com
To: rusirius@vnli.com
Subject: Introductions

Dear Mr. R.U. Sirius,
Relax and let me introduce myself. My name is Nichiren Schwarzendruber and I'll be your prayer partner for eternity. My bishop heard

about your TV program and immediately put you down on our missionary
messenger list. Of course, I don't watch television out here in Intercourse, PA -- this is Amish country -- but our bishop gets emergency alerts on his laptop and he immediately sensed that something
was very wrong with you, that "an immortal soul was writhing and crying out for help." So he put me on your case. It may surprise you to
learn that I've been psychoanalyzed. Let me help you!!

R. U., I know what a sensitive person you are -- surprise! -- I've
been reading about you in the papers. No, not the tabloids, though I
can't avoid your angst-ridden photographs in the supermarket checkout
line. To be fair, I should tell you that our bishop has assembled a
dossier of considerable girth about you and your foibles, pet peeves,
sexual peccadilloes and so forth, that we'll be using in our work. No
need to worry! Everything's under control. And we certainly won't
sell the information we have, specifically about the sheep incidents,
to the tabloid press. Do we understand each other perfectly yet?

OK. I've got a lot of patience. There will come a time when you
will be whimpering and begging for one single word from my lips. THEN
I will speak. I'm not a sadist. But not until you really want it! For
this to work, you have to want it bad.

As I said, I don't watch TV, but our bishop described your show as
"bizarre and sexual." Now deep down, you know what you're doing is
wrong. You feel pretty rotten about it. And the bottom line is --
you're going to have to stop. This is not a threat. Not yet.

I know you're miserable enough already. Just keep this in mind --
I AM YOUR FRIEND. I know that friendship is one thing you haven't experienced much in your pathetic life. It takes some getting used to.

R.U., good to make your acquaintance. I look forward to getting to
know you much much better, down in the very fiber of your being. OK!
Fine! Hallelujah!
       Warmest Regards,
       Nichiren Schwarzendruber

= =
Date: September 18, 1996
From: rusirius@vnli.com
To: schwarz@christbuddha.com
Subject: I feel so very very good inside, knowing that I have a
friend.

yeah.

= =

The Village Voice   Sept. 20, 1996
Wired Section Pg. 1

ALL ABOARD FOR FUN TIME!

Those monkeys in Mondo Vanilli have finally found their true calling. The MV Fun Show is fun with a capital F. Television may never be the same.

I'm one of the lucky ones, of course. I got my 3D earphones and eyephones in the mail, courtesy of Faux. Still, I don't think I'd have minded the $59.99 price tag. This is a show that gives up more eyeball kicks per second than a wagonload of DMT. The nineties update of the Beatles myth that the show centers itself around isn't merely parodic, it's gruesome. The "New Civility" and the politics of the HADL hangs over the program implicitly in the hilarious persona of the willfully disneyesque Scrappi DüChamp. Sirius and 3rd Arm turn embodying schizoculture into physical and cerebral slapstick, and the use of voiceovers, laugh tracks, parody ads and even pseudo-pirate intrusions all add up to make the Mondo Vanilli Fun Show network TV's main distraction.

Eric Dibbel-Gehr

**Variety Top 10
Television Listings**
For the week of Sept. 20, 1996

1) The Rush Limbush Variety Half-Hour
2) The Mondo Vanilli Fun Show
3) Armed Forces
4) 60 Minutes
5) Politically Incorrect
6) The Abernathys
7) The Secret Service
8) Thank you, Mr. Vanderbilt
9) Black Humor for Black People
10) Cops

= = = = = = = = = = = = = =
Date: October 2, 1996
From: schwarz@christ-buddha.com
To: rusirius@vnli.com
Subject: Season's Greetings!

Dear R.U.,
Greetings to you,

##
########   • Trudy B. Hyatt •   ########
########   • Editorial Assistant •   ########
########   • Hyatt@Ballantine.Books.com •   ########
##
Date: 17 Feb 2000
To: rusirius@well.com, stjude@well.com
Subject: disintegration

This whole chapter sort of seems to deteriorate into an endless series of unexplicated fragments of your lives and times. Everything seems to disintegrate. Or am i missing something?

```
##############
#   /==$=\    #  <- From the High-Tech Fully Electronic Desk
# /))-00(\   #     of R. U. Sirius
# ((( -)))   #
# )))\ /(((  #  -> rusirius@well.com
##############
```

Date: 17 Feb 2000
To: Hyatt@Ballantine.Books.com, stjude@well.com
Subject: Re: disintegration

No, Trudi. That's exactly right. That was the year that was . . . 1996. The forces of chaos and the forces of evil clashed . . . and what comes out of that?
so the disintegration of the year in text mirrors the content which mirrors the actuality.

R.U. You've been on my mind and in my heart a whole lot this last month, ol' prayer buddy!! In fact, I've been chanting Namu-Myo-Ho-Renge-Kyo for you each day in eager hope for your deliverance. You know, miraculous things do happen when you put your trust in the Lotus Sutra, and I believe that way down deep in your smut-ridden soul, you believe this too!

I notice in your last email letter you say that you're feeling very, very good. Well, I'm not surprised! Plenty of folks will testify that they get a kind of glow about them when they first come into contact with me and you're no exception. Unfortunately, this is a superficial sort of high, a "high of denial" as we call it and alas, for you, R.U., before too long we'll get down to mind-numbing, heart-searing, gut-clutching existential agonies, as the really filthy stuff starts to ooze out of your toxic soul like pus from a suppurating wound. But all in good time!

My bishop reports that your Plain Vanilla television show is going from bad to worse and that there's talk of slaughtering a live hog right on TV. R.U., don't do it. I'm not going to badger you with a list of shoulds and shouldn'ts or even urge you to do the right thing. I know that your thoughts and emotions are so perverse and twisted that it's actually beyond your capabilities to know the difference between right and wrong. But there is hope for the most chancrous, besotted, vile and degenerate

```
##################################################
#########          • Trudy B. Hyatt •         #########
#########         • Editorial Assistant •        #########
#########      • Hyatt@Ballantine.Books.com •    #########
##################################################
```
Date: 17 Feb 2000
To: rusirius@well.com, stjude@well.com
Subject: Re: disintegration

Oh. Well . . . ok then.
No problem.

????????
You guys make me feel like
1> I should go audit some critical theory classes.
2> I should get some French theorist to kick your ass.

TURN IN THE FINAL EDIT OF 1996. NOW.

sinner. Am I pushing any buttons R.U.? Say amen. Now say it again.

Are there places in your psyche that, if unbandaged, suddenly ooze, then bleed, even if you haven't thought about it in years? Sure there are. There are places in your sick dark psyche that -- if we poke an electrode in -- we might illuminate. Must we go that far, R. U.?

Personally, I hope we don't have to. It's not a pleasant sight, leather restraints on your wrists and ankles, foreign barbarians playing needles on every groove in your brain over and over again until they've satisfied their inquisitorial curiosity; the smirking Japanese doctor and his sadistic revelries. This is not a threat, btw.

Gotta go, ol' buddy. Now you just relax and have a good time and meditate on these things. Particularly the electrodes. And the needles.

Warmest Regards,
Nichiren Schwarzendruber

```
===================================================
Date: Oct 2, 1996
From: rusirius@vnli.com
To: Schwarz@christbuddha.com
Subject: Seasons whaaa
```

I'll have to read your lovely greeting later. One to many hot toddies last night. I be barely walking lawd . . .

```
===================================================
```

The New Nation
5 Oct 1996
Guest Columnist: St Jude

Pranking the Elections

What's a voter to do? These are serious times. Everybody's SO SERIOUS about the seriousness that it's daily more ludicrous. Political rhetoric grows more surreal, candidates more personally preposterous, the Republicrat juggernaut careens ever Righter . . . What's a serious Left Over voter to do?

Well, all the Seriousness slots seem to be filled already, by the haters of dirty pictures, free speech, and free assembly. What's Left Over for us? Maybe . . . getting unserious. Abandon shape! Shift left! Mutate! Turning Prankster is a satisfying response to all this fanatical earnestness. For role models, there are the Pranksters who have turned the Presidential election on network TV into something worth watching. Pirates

are inserting anti-ads so slick they look like the real thing . . . except that they're more gross, more radical than either side would dare to produce . . . and more scurrilous than any network would willingly show. These are some seriously strange ads.

●●

(20-second ad spot)
Quick intercutting:
Political conventions, blurry porn clips, closeup sweaty faces of girls moaning "Billllll."
Cut to standard 900-number set, girl, and costume:
[sultry voice]: "Bill always tells a girl exactly what she wants to hear . . .
and he'll do the same for you. Vote for . . ."
Cut to and hold:
Clinton election poster.
[Voice-over, different female voice wailing orgasmically]: "Bill!"

●●

In case you've been missing the absurdities in this election, the pirates are packaging them for you loud, clear, 3-D, computer-animated and fully rendered. Reading between the lines has never been more fun—and sure beats the same old lines themselves ... This has gotta be the last traditional election. What kind of act could follow THIS?

•••

(30-second ad spot:)
Computer-animated wrestling ring
[Crowd noises back, continuous]
Newt Gingrich and Bill Clinton circle each other in satin shorts;
Bill in red, Newt in blue, both with stars and stripes:
Newt and Bill:
"ARRRGHH."
"GRRRRRRR."
The two figures circle, and then the Newt grabs the Bill and takes him down with a spectacular flying mare. The Bill bounces up and head-butts the Newt, who bellows. Fierce snortings, hideous threat postures, circling ...
Then a cartoon-style blurred multi-limbed melee, ending up with both figures on the canvas, bellowing, clutching each other in horrible limb-mangling holds.
Zoom in to closeup two-shot of their faces.
Bill [whispers]: "You okay, dude?"
Newt [whispers]: "A-OK, old buddy."
The Newt nuzzles Bill's jaw, and Bill puckers up and plants a little kiss on Newt's knee, which is twisted up next to his face.
Both jump up and roar.
"ARRRGHH."
"GRRRRRRR."
Cut to and hold:
Election poster of donkey-elephant, with two heads, Newt and Bill.
Subtitle:
VOTE REPUBLICRAT— They're both Right!

•••

What about you? You feeling a bit prankish? Well, help yourself to some media: the technology for getting alternative is all over the place right now. The Net is buzzing with happy fellow mutants. Sign on, sign up, freek out. ...

These are serious times. Right. Yeah.

Variety Top 10
Television Listings
For the week of Oct. 5

1) The Mondo Vanilli Fun Show
2) The Rush Limbush Variety Half-Hour
3) Armed Forces
4) The Abernathys
5) Black Humor for Black People
6) 60 Minutes
7) Politically Incorrect
8) The Secret Service
9) Thank You, Mr. Vanderbilt
10) Cops

```
=====================================================
```
Date: Oct. 28, 1996
From: schwarz@christbuddha.com
To: rusirius@vnli.com
Subject: rejoicing
Dear R.U.,

Well, ol' prayer buddy, the good news is that your last email letter
gave evidence that repentance is beginning to enter into your morbid
and sordid life, if you can call it a life. The mere fact that you
recognized your wretched excess in the matter of hot toddies is
cause for rejoicing! Perhaps you had a flaming headache, and maybe
you vomited too. Well, that's all right. It happens to all of us on
occasion. And as the scripture says, "The dog returneth to its
vomit." Say amen!

   Perhaps you looked down in the toilet while you were writhing and
said to yourself -- amidst your spewing and disgorging -- "R.U.!
R.U.! Is this the way I'm going to spend eternity?" And my reluctant
answer is, "Actually, no. Actually it's going to be MUCH MUCH worse."

   Because there's that little matter of the sheep. Now the FCC can
go on all it wants about freedom of expression, but if you seriously
believe that the moral majority in this country is going to sit idly
by and watch while a posse of maniacal sheep-bonkers goes on nationwide TV and goes so far as to simulate (and I do recognize, R.U.,
that it was only a simulation -- I'm familiar enough with the real
thing in the flesh to know it when I hear about it) casual sex between an animal and a human being then this time you've gone too
far!! Let's go to The Book! I'm reading from "The Essentials of Sal-
vation" by St. Genshin, in the Yampolsky translation:

   "*Outside the four gates of this hell are sixteen separate places
which are associated with this hell. The first is called the place
of excrement. Here, it is said, there is intensely hot dung of the
bitterest of taste, filled with maggots with snouts of indestruc-
tible hardness. The sinner here eats of the dung and all the assembled maggots swarm at once for food. They destroy the sinner's skin,
devour his flesh and suck the marrow from his bones.*"

Where will you spend eternity? Where will you spend the next six
months? If the answer is San Francisco, there's not a whole lot I or
anyone else can do for you. Close your eyes and imagine a maggot,
just one, cruising up your carotid artery. Then multiply that maggot
by a thousand. By a million. Close your eyes and feel that maggot ca-
ressing the moist mucous membranes of your sinus cavities and the
most intimate parts of your body. Feel it sucking the marrow from

your bones. Then, relax and have a Budweiser, "dude." Maybe you'll get the idea.

Warmest Regards,
Nichiren Schwarzendruber

==
Oct 29, 1996
From: rusirius@vnli.com
To: Schwarz@christbuddha.com
Subject: ???

I'm sure you think this is either funny, or you're for real and think that it's touching me somewhere deep in my psyche. But really, this stuff isn't exactly blowing up my skirt.

==
Date: 1 November, 1996
From: stjude@W.A.S.T.E.LAN
To: rusirius
Subject: >>zzzPOP<< this is a mushroom

This is me, out of the blue, out of left field -- remember CONELRAD, the emergency radio system that broadcasts from all directions? Remember the free Internet, that nothing could kill? The Net's doing its own mutating . . . It's ramifying like fungus in the dark, in fact -- in fact it should be called the Mycelium, which is the underground net that mushrooms occasionally poke up out of. . . .

The Internet is now very interesting indeed. I'm coming to you out of a little subspiderweb that got macraméd into the Net, sort of . . . like an invisible subnetwork . . . sort of.
like a whole fucking OTHER WAY OF COMMUNICATING, off the map and out of sight. It's the Underground Mailroad. Oh jumping jeezus, they're even calling this segment of it W.A.S.T.E. (Remember, in Pynchon's Crying of Lot 49?)

I KNOW you'd like to use this nifty service. But don't count on reply-mailing back to this msg, whiteboy. It'll never make it back to my 'hood without a native guide. Hehehehe.

we ARE everywhere

        and
      YOU'RE
      +NOT+

ps: i'll deliver the startup software to you face2face . . .

```
=====================================================
```
Date: 6 Nov, 1996:
From: stjude
To: rusirius
Subject: Re: election news?

So, Bill and Hillary -- er, Gore got themselves re-elected. This is
not fascinating . . . and I did tell you so. . . . Since the whole political landscape earthquaked to the Right twenty ratchets, and the
old centrists, whoever they might still be, just ratcheted right
along, what else were we expecting? The Spanish Inqui -- no, no . . .
but maybe NEXT year. . .
```
=====================================================
```
From: schwarz@christbuddha.com
To: rusirius@vnli.com
Date: Nov 23, 1996
Subject:

Dear R.U.,

OK. Fine. Where were we? Oh yes -- SKIRTS! To quote your last message: "This stuff isn't exactly blowing up my skirt."

Yes. You see? As we go along your language becomes more revelatory,
richer, evocative of dusky-hued maidens and exotic lusts, redolent
of the original sin that pollutes your immortal soul, if you can
CALL it a soul. The skirts, the skirts of the fat neighbor girl in
the summer of your tenth year, who sat on your chest in the long
afternoon grass behind the tool shed, her concupiscent and volumi-
nous thighs enveloping your face like buns around a hamburger. Your
nose up her knickers. Your hypothalamus as close to paradise as it
ever hoped to get.

The skirts of your mother in the arms of the Venezuelan milkman, in
the parlor after school before your dada came home, moaning ecstatically like a seraph in labor. And the milkman whistled, chucked you
under the chin and gave you a nickel, carefully adjusting his sus-
penders. The skirts of your mother on your pubescent hips in the hall
mirror, your tremulous décolletage . . .

OK. Time to stop. Does it feel any better, R.U., letting that crap
ooze out? Sort of like lancing a boil, when the pus just won't stop
flowing. Your secrets are safe with me. Of course, if the Pedophile

Police got ahold of some of this stuff it might raise a few eyebrows down at headquarters.

This is not a threat. Not yet. You'll know we're getting serious when we get to the part where we take out the electrodes and play the synapses of your body like a banjolele; tweak the neurons of your neural network with a soldering iron until they go out Pop! one-by-excruciating-one like the little bulbs winking out on a Christmas tree. And we twist the diseased ganglia of your warped desires until you holler for momma. Say amen! Now say it again!

Warmest Regards,
Nichiren Schwarzendruber

===
Date: November 23, 1996
From: schwarz@christbuddha.com
To: rusirius@vnli.com
Subject:

Dear R.U.,
Oh, and by the way, one more thing about that skirt business -- you're probably aware that "to skirt" has the connotation of avoidance. That is . . . to spell it out so that the meanest intelligence (I allude to yours) can understand it, your use of the word "skirt" betokens not only an unholy fascination with women's garments, undergarments, harnesses, buttresses, straps and diverse paraphernalia, it also signifies your unconscious desire to avoid all conscious knowledge of your disgusting and lascivious perversions. Son, we're going to wipe that perpetually bemused look off your face. It's for your own good.

As my silver haired dada would have said, had he lived long enough, "There's nothing a good frontal lobotomy won't cure." But let's not rush things. First we need to raise your awareness of the foulness of your loathsome, stinking abominations. Surgery might not help. We've got a fat dossier, R.U., leather-bound I might add (I knew you'd appreciate that) and printed on pages of the purest vellum, fat as the hindquarters of that pubescent sheep you violated on national TV the other week. God, am I glad I don't have to watch TV! Have enough nauseating reading material as it is, what with your dossier and the filth they display in the supermarket checkout line. Don't think I missed that ludicrous attempt at intellectual pretension you slipped into the Readers' Digest, not that I shouldn't have expected it since the treacherous bastards slipped it to St. Oliver North, but the fact

that you not only sullied your prehensile lips with the holy name of
Rimbaud, the thong of whose sandal you are not worthy to tongue, but
mentioned it in the same breath with the likes of Keith Richards
demonstrates what a grandiose and vulgar antediluvian slut you are
and will always be. Tell me about your master's thesis. If you have
one.

Warmest Regards,
Nichiren Schwarzendruber

===
Date: Nov 23, 1996
From: rusirius@vnli.com
To: Schwarz@christbuddha.com
Subject: hey!

Your writing gets better, herr Schickelgruber or whatever your name
is. It's hard to even respond. 'Specially after an evening spent
wasting $1600 on 2 gorgeous whores performing their s/m rituals but
not allowing any masculine penetration . . . THE BITCHES!!!

And then a little bit of brown powder to help me sleep . . .

btw, i suspect that you're not who you say you are, just some jealous
prankster who resents my public image as King CyberKult Goohoo . . .
either that or you're some NSA sleazeball getting his jollies . . . or
is it HER jollies . . .

Anyway, this religion stuff has no impact on me, rest assured. PRAY
AWAY . . . Nanno yoho yummo blow . . . sniff . . .

===
Date: Nov 24, 1996
From: schwarz@christbuddha.com
To: rusirius@vnli.com
Subject: Re: hey!

Dear R.U.,
OK. Your secrets are safe with me. Now that you're starting to open
up on the subject of your transgressions I want you to be able to
feel perfectly safe and trusting with me knowing that however foul
the deeds you confess, they are kept in my confidence and in that of
the Dharma King of the Universe (say ah-hum! now say it again.) We'll
go into these matters of your stewardship of money, whores, s/m, and
little brown powders another time. Just feel glad that you've con-

fessed them to me and not to those hardnosed bastards who drive around in unmarked vans reading your email right off the screen by tracking the electromagnetic waves. (You might want to take a peek out the window just to make sure; they generally park about half a block down the street.) I mean, once THOSE sons of bitches get ahold of you, you can kiss your celebrity lifestyle goodbye. They'd probably throw you in the "white room" which is a very imaginative minimalist/maximal arrangement -- four walls, all white, recessed fluorescent tubes in the ceiling under the fine wire mesh (don't even think about trying to smash them) 24 hours a day, stainless steel commode in the middle of the floor, walls padded so you can't hurt yourself. Tres chic, eh bratboy? They generally keep the temperature at about 49 degrees Fahrenheit, and feed you bread and water through a slot in the door twice a day. Course they take away your clothes when they process you, check all your orifices. Don't worry, they won't hurt you physically, they're much more sophisticated these days. Ozzy Osbourne at top volume at irregular intervals day and night. After a few days, weeks, or months, depending on your durability, they bring in your confession and help you sign it. That's why it's so much better we're doing it this way. 'Cause I just want to help you son. Heh. Say Namu Myoho Renge Kyo.

Warmest Regards,
Nichiren Schwarzendruber

===
From: rusirius@vnli.com
To: Schwarz@christbuddha.com
Date: Dec 1, 1996

Hey, I already listen to Alice Cooper at top volume at irregular intervals day and night. On the other hand, Ozzy DOES suck. Where do I sign?
===
Date: Dec 24, 1996
From: stjude@hinky.dinky.parley.voo
To: rusirius@vnli.com
Subject: YOU DIDN'T SEE IT, DID YOU?

I got a call right before it started. I tried to call you, but your beeper gave me a fucking strange response, and your voicemail was full . . . and it's too bad for you, because as of tonight the charlie brown christmas special was détourned TWICE . . . last night, it was supplanted right after the credits by a half-hour animation with a brown Charlie Brown called Let My Kwanzaa Go! Charlie Brown and all his kid friends --

one of them a black bart simpson -- get together to have a Kwanzaa celebration, but many holiday obstacles interfere ... christmas shoppers,
the Ghost of Christian Past, Republican grandparents, and a surprise
guest appearance by a blackface baby jesus. Amazingly, they cut to the
real scheduled commercials at the right times. So I think everybody got
confused -- even the control people getting the network feeds in the
local stations. . . . they thought it was a real broadcast. It sure as
hell was not. It was insanely funny. The final credits were something to
see: pseudonym after pseudonym, weird puns, wonderful. . . .

then there was an actual four minute break for real commercials.
When the network feed came back there was some sloppy timing -- some
actual Charlie Brown got through for a minute or so. Then we got a
shoutin', stompin', grimoire-thumpin', goddess-fearing televangelist
(dressed Gaian S-M style in black leather and studs and chains) doing a full-tilt rant about taking back the Solstice. "*It's* the
real thing, baby!" -- followed by a gospel-style green-robed choir
holding candles and singing their hearts out in what? -- Gaelic??
Indo-European?? (lots of gutturals and shouts)-- for a stirring
huge spiral dance of maybe a hundred people in animal costumes or
black leather, led by a naked green man with antlers on his head.
Oh, it was amazing. Then there was another sloppy segue and a
straight Chanukkah lighting, short and sweet. Then there was what
looked like a festive Mithraic bull sacrifice, with a bunch of white
dudes in camo gear, which got interrupted by a jamming signal. . . .
and that was it for the hour. . . .

So tonight the Charlie Brown Christmas was scheduled again . . . The
network had their jamming signals ready, I guess, but after the opening credits the following show came in unjammed, but strangely jittery
and snowy at all times -- CONELRAD? -- ahem -- the following show:

Mr Charlie's Brown Christmas,
A Minstrel Show,
(These actors look (to me) suspiciously like the S F Mime Troupe . . .)
Across the stage is seated a minstrel line in blackface, some of them
actually black . . . at the end of the line is a whitewigged blackface
Newt figure, called Mr Bones, and his opponent in snappy patter -- Mr
Interlocutor -- is a black man in blackface wearing a comic stovepipe
hat that says LIBERAL on it . . . Also in the line is a classic chrome
robot in blackface, a hiphop black kid in gang gear, and stereotypes
of other races creeds and sexes . . . the whole cultural lineup.

The minstrel shtick is interrupted at intervals by stage-front vi-
gnettes of a white family (mr charlie and miz anne brown and their
kids -- mastah Forsythe, missie Scarlett and missie Faubus Brown)
gathered for xmas with a brown woman waiting on them -- a chuckling,
gingham-aproned hankyhead whom they call either Jemiylah or Ms Butters-
worth . . . Lots of "banjos ringing, darkies singing" racialist nostalgia songs . . . interspersed with snappy stylized patter -- traditional
minstrel coon talk (fake darky dialect), rants about the return of the
good life, thank you Jesus! . . . Okay, but this whole thing is inter-
mixed with political pattersongs by the Newt figure -- about futurism
and cyberspace and stuff. One song, a trio with the robot and Jemiylah, has the chorus "Back to the future, forward to the Past!" And in
another Newt was crooning something like, "I'll do the world, I'll do
it Right, I'll do it MY WAAAAAY . . .

antebellum futurism. . . ?

EVERYBODY WILL FREAK!! EVERYBODY -- black, white, left, right. . . . !
It's PAN-OFFENSIVE.

funny funny funny joy joy joy
I got that holiday feeling NOW . . .
===

```
###############################################################
#########                • Trudy B. Hyatt •              #########
#########              • Editorial Assistant •            #########
#########          • Hyatt@Ballantine.Books.com •         #########
###############################################################
```

Date: 17 Feb 2000
To: rusirius@well.com, stjude@well.com
Subject: >>>BOOOMMmmmmmm<<<<

I've read 1996 now five times over and I
think I finally understand exploded narrative. I'm lost. Your characters are crawling
around bloodied and undone. I don't know
why anyone or anything is introduced to me.
The narrative is frayed, arrows point in every
direction, and the future looks grim. R. U.
SIRIUS . . . THIS IS YOUR LIFE!

hahahahah. . . .

      your pal Trudy . . .

David Fremont

```
##############
#   /==$=\      # <- From the High-
# /))-00(\     #    Tech Fully Elec-
# ((( -)))     #    tronic Desk of
# )))\ /(((     # -> R. U. Sirius
##############  rusirius@well.com
```
To: Hyatt@Ballantine.Books.com, stjude
Subject: Oh, Trudy . . . I love you.

By the time we're done, you'll be reading Rimbaud by candlelight with a belt
wrapped around your arm, sneaking down alleyways with skinny, lizardlike
tattooed bi-boys in leather, walking across the Moroccan desert seeking desperate wisdom. Or at least playing Soft Machine V4.2 nearly every night.

    Yup. Our personas are getting pummelled by the zeitgeist. Disintegrat-
ing. From here on, we are more or less shadow guides through the "revolution" as the society's structures themselves disintegrate. We are barely
treading water. We're closing down Narrative Highway 10101010101010101 . . .
All characters are frozen in place to be thawed out later if we make it
through on TIME. As we approach the singularity, extinguish all hope and
bring your chair to an upright position.

PART TWO

RETURN OF THE UNDEADLINES

Brad Pedinoff (Mossman)

Date: Oct 9, 1998
From: stjude@root.bodhi.tree
To: rusirius@vnli.com
Subject: R U the Burger King

Plot . . . Ok, plot . . .
Think! Ok . . . how's this for the META plot? . . .

The book is SIX years past deadline. Trudy won't fuck you anymore, even though she's out here twice a month to harass us. You're working in burger king, in the kitchen, (they won't let you work counter again, never, not after that last incident . . .) and you start fantasizing about Trudy Hyatt's Mummy, Margot -- Trudy mentioned Madame Hyatt's name to us once -- Margot, with a T.

You're sweating into the sink, scrubbing it with chlorine cleanser, out of sight of the paying customers. In the roachy back room you're obsessing about our failure to complete the book, and you start daydreaming . . .

". . . Maybe I can get to Trudy's mother. Margot. Maybe I can win her trust. Get her to make Trudy go easier on me . . . make her daughter take pity on me again. Margot's ineffably rich and powerful . . ."

[At this point the guy from burger central comes in wearing delivery livery (on the back of his jumpsuit an escutcheon -- burger in majesty, couchant, field gules and vert) with a huge box of frozen beige burger-disks, and you have to transfer towers of them into the steel fridge, but you caress the door as you slab them away. Mmm: *stainless steel*. You dream on . . .]

". . . Margot Hyatt. Maybe her full name is Margot Hyatt-*Regency* . . .
She will love my critical analysis. She will want me for her body slave. She will keep me captive in her chauffeured sound-proof Rolls, ready at her service, helpless, always there for her to use mercilessly *en route* to her rulingclass teas or uh . . . (whatever it is they do). . . . In crotchless leather breeches, my wrists and ankles bound tight by leather thongs, I am spread-eagled across the oxblood-leather back seat. Little leather-*du-maroc* riding crop in her *dressage*-tanned leathery hand. The ridingcrop rises. . . . swishes through the air. . . . falls!! aaiieeeee. I must scream again: aaiieeee."

[You, for your part realize that you must be *très sauvage* with *le sexing*, yet terribly *careful* -- you know that if you injure her clothes or go near her makeup she'll turn you out. There are lots more crit theory wildboys where you came from.]

Segment Three: 1997–2001
Foregone Conclusions

In which the authors look the possibility of writing the great American exploded post-novel in the eye . . . and blink first. Then, it's the thrill of the chase, as our authors are forced to duck and weave in and out of the documentation. And finally, we discover that pigs do have wings and the meaning of it all is stated, restated, and then stated again, just in case.

NORAD ALERT: SANTA INVADES!
COLORADO SPRINGS, Colo. (AP) Jan. 1, 1997—The North American Aerospace Defense Command and the U.S. Space Command nearly nuked Santa Claus, a NORAD official said today.

On December 24, the high-tech intercept computers at Cheyenne Mountain, the military's primary space tracking center, issued an alert on an unidentified flying object approaching the United States from the vicinity of the North Pole. NORAD spokesperson Col. Roger Kehtron stated, "At no time during this incident was the defense of the United States compromised." He said NORAD officials realized it was a prank when messages "NUKE SANTA", "TAKE BACK THE SOLSTICE", and "MERGE WITH THE MYCELIUM" appeared on computer screens throughout NORAD. Kehtron said today that it appears that members of the computer terrorist group Mycelium broke into the NORAD tracking system on Christmas Eve for the first and only time. Computer security experts have been checking over NORAD operations since the incident, and are expected to give them a clean bill of health in a Jan 10 hearing before the Joint Chiefs of Staff.

Kehtron admitted that fighter jets were scrambled from bases in Alaska and Greenland before the incident was discovered to be a hoax. He said that no damage was sustained, and the planes were recalled in good order.

/<<BIG ASS ZEITGEIST>>\
\#########################/   pg.6
>><<>><<>><<>><<>><<>><<
"To the revolutionary, chaos is as soothing as Ben-Wa balls"

Volume II Number 4
Jan–Mar 1997

"Being the same as everybody is the same as being nobody."
—Rod Serling

Table Of Continents:

1.00 Five Pranks that Shook the World

Happy New Year to those of you using the Western Hemisphere's Euro-Christian calendar!!! This issue of BAZ is devoted to End-of-the-Year pranks that Shook the World. OK, maybe these pranks didn't actually shake the *world*; with one exception, they all took place in the United States. But these pranks rank among the best examples of media sabotage, culture jamming, hacking, and just plain having fun that we've seen in the past three months. And they deserve to be memorialized.

Replacement seemed to be the theme underlying many of the pranks that entered our attention sphere in October/November/December. Real election results were replaced by the output of a random number generator. The phone number you dialed was replaced by the phone number someone else dialed. A Christian cross was replaced by a Pagan pentacle. Is the concept of replacement in these pranks an expression of BIG ASS ZEITGEIST? Fuck if I know, man.

A word on how the award-winning events were chosen: badly. A team of experts in the field of pranks and shenanigans judged these entrants on originality, number of people affected by the prank, and the media aftermath. Thus, while the CBS News Fake-Out wasn't so original, it got such high marks on the other two scales that it ended up far ahead of the pack. And so it goes.

1.01 The CBS News Fake-Out

Surveys show more prankers choose CBS News over any other network when they decide to hit a news org. I know of a few *Nightline* pranks, a few more *Dateline NBC* pranks, and nearly ONE HUNDRED pranks and shenanigans against CBS News in the past year. Are the folks at CBS News THAT STUPID?? Or could it be that Dan Rather bugs the shit out of us SO MUCH that we feel the need to raz him every chance we get? Kenneth, what was that frequency again? Pretty damned often, Dan . . .

Anyway, on 5 November 1996, some unknown prankers, exploiting a security hole in CBS's Mosaic server, got into the CBS News "Election '96" computers. For the next 5 hours, Dan Rather was their puppet. The prankers injected totally random election numbers onto Rather's telescreen, prompting the anchor to remark several times on Ross Perot's surprising strength in Alaska, where, because of the work of the prankers, the billionaire dwarf was projected to receive 80% of the vote.

Because of such hilarious events, watching CBS's election coverage was much more exciting than watching any other network's, most of whom proclaimed Clinton the winner by 9 PM. Assisted by the prankers, CBS's election results seesawed between the Reps and Dems for another hour. Around 9:30, so the story goes, one of the CBS News producers checked ABC News and saw that Clinton had won. She immediately passed this data to Dan Rather via his earpiece. He refused to act on it, though, because his telescreens were saying that the Republicans were ahead at that time. Classic quote: "There seems to be some disparity between what I see and what the voices in my head are telling me."—Dan Rather

1.02 The 202 Switcheroo

A thought virus raced through the phreak brotherhood in the mid-1980s. It claimed that a renegade Bell programmer had written some code into the operating system for the Baby Bell telephone switching complex—prank code that would delay all phone calls by one. For example, let's suppose this code fragment is activated in the switching system. You call your brother, but the call doesn't go through. Your brother's number is now stored in the switching system. The next person to make a call is trying to reach their doctor, but they'll be connected to your brother. Your brother's number is erased and the doctor's number is stored. The person after that tries to call their baby-sitter, but they get the doctor. The next person trying to call whoever will get the baby-sitter, and so on. According to the story, this code fragment was only 14 lines long, could be triggered by dialing a special number and entering a special DTMF sequence, and would work on any of the new Baby Bell switches. No one knew if this rumor was true or not, but, baby, how we wanted to believe.

Well, the day after Thanksgiving, 22 November 1996, someone activated this code in the 202 area code, the NPA known as Washington, D.C. You can imagine the rest.

1.03 The Met Life Building Pentacle

In the 1960s, the Pan Am building dominated New York's Fifth Avenue. You could see its black rectangle, looming like the monolith in the movie 2001, nearly anywhere along the avenue. And every December, in honor of Christmas, the building's management would leave select office lights on all night, converting the building's facade into a 59-story flourescent Cross. Of course, all that good fellowship ended in the No-Religious-Displays movement of the 1970s.

By 1996, the building was owned by Met Life, the new president of Met Life was a born again Christian and charter member of HADL, and she felt, garsh darnit, that HER building would CERTAINLY display a Cross at Christmastime. At her command, once again a glowing fluorescent Christian icon shone down on Fifth Avenue.

Until the night of 4 December 1996, the night of the lighting of the Rockefeller Center Christmas Tree. Members of the Pagan Right, a pagan-revolutionary-guerrilla-mime troupe from Hoboken NJ, dressed themselves in Con Ed uniforms and infiltrated the basement of the Met Life building at 7 PM. After bridging the security cameras, they spent about 15 minutes consulting wiring diagrams and flipping circuit breakers. By 7:30 they were standing two blocks away, in the center of Fifth Avenue rush hour traffic, silently laughing their asses off. Above them, shining down on nearly two million New Yorkers, the face of the Met Life building had been transformed into a 59-story glowing inverted Pentagram.

Of course, New York being what New York is, it passed without comment until two tourists from Idaho complained to a police officer.

cont. pg 7

```
Jan 19, 1997
You are entering
NONDO.VNLI.COM
Login: rusirius
Password: xxxxxxxxx


Come in!
Before you pass beyond this checkpoint,
please unscrew lug nuts and loosen mind-set.

  "MV are the Fake Media Cyberpunks of the revolution"
    Axcess, Sep. 1996


Ohsoverypri:
WELCOME! TO NONDO.VNLI.COM -- THE PRIVATE ONLINE WORLD OF MONDO VANILLI
AND MV INC.


R. U. Sirius & Friends in search of the holy grail
(This is a private conf, so if you can read this ... you gotta be okay.)
------------------------------
```

Sirius (rusirius)
#16:
0-oh tidings of bi-itches and ho's
(bitches and ho's)
o-oh tidings of bitches and ho's
----
rumpus marcus (spoton)
#17
i remember that party ...
----
devil or angel (angelica)
#18
you're all under arrest ...

Empress of France (josephine)
#19
help me.
josephine is looking for the dog-star; the one who
is named for the dog-
star.
she wants him.
i don't think that
she should find him;
if you know him,
please warn him.
josephine is looking.
she is disappointed.
she wants him.
she ran away, you know.
josephine ran away.
she was in a safe
place and she ran away,
looking for the dog-star ...

i am josephine's sister,
i am looking for her.
i am warning you,
tell the dog-star,
josephine is looking for him,
josephine wants him ...

```
Nothing Personal (stjude)
#20
What the fuq was THAT?
-------------------------------

Empress of France (josephine)
#21
josephine saw him,
she saw him on television,
she said,
this one is mine, yes,
this one, the dog-star,
this one is mine
i will find him.
```

```
##############
#   /==$=\    #  <- From the High-Tech Fully Electronic Desk
# /))-00(\   #     of R. U. Sirius
# ((( -)))   #
# )))\ /(((  #  -> rusirius@well.com
##############
```

Date: 17 Feb 1996
To: Hyatt@Ballantine.Books.com
Subject: Re: whaaa

Jeez. It looks obvious to me. I'll detail it for you. Mondo Vanilli has a
private encrypted net called NONDO.VANILLI.COM. In that net, one of the
discussion topics is R. U. Sirius & Friends in Search of the Holy Grail. Far
from a grail search, the topic had degenerated into a lame sort of mindless decadence, implying that perhaps the same has happened to MV itself. Then, somebody . . . namely Josephine . . . appears who is not
supposed to have access to NONDO.VNLI.COM. She comes right into R. U.'s
private topic. She has stalked him online! (Cue scary music. Cut to commercial.)

Now, like any stalker, she worships R. U. Does she notice what a wee-
nie he's being? No. She's fanatical, obsessed, poetic, and perhaps deadly.

One can unpack this still further. What are the resonances? Why is
the author R. U. Sirius making the character R. U. Sirius so pathetic?
What sort of weird compulsions have made him follow through on this
course that can only be viewed as utterly debasing? How will it impact on
his real life? Why should we care? What is the capital of Eritrea?

There. I've just said MORE than you ever wanted to know. . . .

```
she said this; someone
told me,
she said this,
her eyes were
shining bright like a
fire burning
under a heretic, yes,
josephine saw him
the dog-star,
she wants him;
not the green man in
the forest, no
not the green man.
the dog star, she
wants him.

josephine is missing,
josephine is looking
for him,
thinking that the
dog-star has
come down from the
sky,
just for her, yes,
just for her ...
---------------------
```

Nolan Void (nolanvoid)
#22

Woah ... this person is NOT on the Ohsoverypri ulist.
In fact, she doesn't exist -- no entry in /etc/passwd.
Looks like R. U.'s being stalked inside vnli.com....
Who's the ringer in here?
Who brought in (or mocked up) this Josephine????

Empress of France (Josephine)
#23

josephine says that she saw him,
the dogstar, she saw him walking
there, in a city with many hills.
she saw him with a friend, a painter,
walking not far from the ocean,
josephine was standing outside the
little grocery store on the corner; standing
quietly, next to the beauty parlor
where the nice ladies get the manicure.
josephine was there, standing, down by
the road that leads to the freeway,
there by the road overlooking the great
city, there she was, josephine was,
josephine yes, the queen of babylon,
the empress of france, josephine,
the dark lady, waiting, calm and silent,
watching, with her little book in her
hand, watching and waiting for him,
for the dogstar.

Mondo Connie (spydergrrrl)
#24

Is this a joke? This isn't cute. Nolan, are
you responsible for this? Because otherwise
I've got to assume that this is the Feds, or worse.
Perhaps I should just shut this whole thing down!

Sirius (rusirius)
#25

Let's not be hasty.

I've actually seen a lady watching me with a little book --
outside the MV building. Sort of a bag lady, but in a tacky
gold-colored robe and a tiara.
Once i walked right at her. She started shaking and
stared through me, off into the middle distance ...
She's no Valerie Solanis, that's for sure ...
----

dan quayle, NOT! (scrappi)
#26

And YOU sir are no Andy Warhol. I KNEW Andy Warhol ...

Date: Jan 30, 1997
From: rusirius@vnli.com
To: Schwarz@christbuddha.com
Subject: thought you were gonna get to ME?

YO, christey buddha-dude . . . haven't heard from ya in awhile. wherez
the sadisto japanese torturer with the needles and black sabbath albums? R. U. chanting your silly wordz for me still? Look, I have a
notion to include you in this film we're planning for the band. Just
play yrself . . . we'll pay you lots that you can contribute to your
bishop or whatever . . . ok?
= =
Date: Jan 30, 1997
Message returned, addressee unknown
Date: Jan 30, 1997
To: Schwarz@christbuddha.com
YO, christey buddha-dude . . . haven't heard from ya in awhile. wherez
the sadisto japanese . . .
ttttt
Date: Feb 2, 1997
From: rusirius@well.com
To: stjude@tentacle.black.net
Subject: smell in a box

We finished Smell in a Box, our second CD today . . . only this time,
it's a massive CD ROM. Extraordinarily, thanks to all the rain, we
each worked at home, and were able to exchange the ENTIRE working
CD-ROM back and forth with one another over vnli.com. I had no idea
data compression had come this far.

===

Date: Feb 10, 1997
From: rusirius@well.com
To: stjude@tentacle.black.net
Subject: smell escapes the box

Everybody here at MV Corp. is FRANTIC since Smell in a Box was distributed free over CryptoNet.

See, because of the floods last week, we worked in our homes, and
passed the entire product back and forth over vnli.com using private
key encryption. (Did I already tell you this? My memory is fading . . .)
I didn't even realize that computing power had increased that much
that quickly, but I talked with rangerjo about it over on cryptonet
zone 3 and he says it's because of the war for the net. He says that
war has always juiced the swift development of advanced technology
and this is no exception. The best hackers are all on the CryptoNet
and they're really motivated to push computing power to dizzying
heights . . . increases their power. (And power is information . . .
guh? Wha?) Plus, the way they play it now is that they keep it in the
underground for a couple of weeks and then, when it starts to leak to
the mainstream, they make their deals . . .

Anyway, after spending hours trying to figure out which one of us
ripped ourselves off and sent the thing out free to the netters (I
was the prime suspect), we realized, poof . . . it's easy. Somebody
took the actual product, crunched it down and uploaded it. Let's face
it. Outside of live performance, media business is not long for business! Mondo Connie, Art, and Lydia have been locked inside the vnli
office for nine hours. They're all in a paranoid and apocalyptic
state. I excused myself. After all, we've still got our TV show and
we're still rich . . .

What me worry?

===

Date: Feb 14, 1997
From: Lydia (vpincharge)
To: rusirius
Subject: damage control

It's been decided that you should make a statement supporting the
liberation of *Smell in a Box*. We've arranged for it to run in
the March 4 issue of *Variety*. We need it by tomorrow . . .

Meanwhile, Thomasita has used her sources to spread a rumor that the copies that were uploaded last week were incomplete and that the real *Smell in a Box* will be uploaded by expert crackers this Saturday. We fully expect this copy to completely replace the copy that's out there, and we've even suckered Outrider into shilling for us. Thomasita inserted a virus into the new one. It self-destructs the entire thing after it plays one of the MV songs. We believe that this will create so much paranoia that ALL copies, including lingering copies from that first distribution, will be flushed away with all due haste.

Then, we'll have the commercial product tested by a team of experts who will declare it safe as milk!

So take the day off tomorrow to write your piece.
= =
Date: Feb 14, 1997
From: rusirius
To: vpincharge spidergrrrl scrappi

I didn't realize we'd become this corrupt. Hmmmm, diabolical. If this ever surfaces, I opposed it.

        yours in realpolitik,

Wired 2000   March 1997 Pp. 16–19

The Rise of the Data Banks

by Patrick DiJusto

Ready for a story? At the end of World War Two, international trade in Tangier, Trieste, and Macao grew like muscle tissue on steroids, because these cities were international free ports. Free ports were seaports that were not part of a larger country. They were city-states unto themselves, where people with money and a few connections could buy, sell and transport nearly any commodity without having to bother with little details like laws, tariffs, and customs. They were the Temporary Autonomous Zones of the postwar world, havens for smuggling and commerce in illegal goods, away from the prying eyes of any government.

After 1945, these free ports became fulcra in the power balance as political and economic spheres of influence sought equilibrium. Tangier became famous as the drug port, from which tons of opium and hashish were sent to Marseilles and New Orleans. Trieste, between Italy and Yugoslavia, was the great arms trading port, through which captured German weapons were sent to the newly emerging African states. And most of the money generated in these ventures was sent to the money-changing port of Macao, to be exchanged for either hard currency or non-taxable gold bars. Some of the great international postwar fortunes were made and lost through these open ports.

Well, history repeats itself, as the sage said. The political and economic shifts brought about by the end of the Cold War have caused the blossoming of the Data Havens: free ports in cyberspace where one can buy, sell and store the commodity of the future, digital information, away from the prying eyes of government or the clamp of international regulations. Data Havens are where the great post–Cold War fortunes are being made. They are Safe-Deposit Boxes for the Net.

DATA BANKING IN THE TIDY GREEN HELL

Balmy Geneva, Switzerland, spends considerable money and energy trying to appear both carefree and serious. I'm here to see Dr. Fritz Greuber, the head of Banc de Geneve's Information Services department. Dr. Greuber is a very tall, very thin man in his 60s with a gray buzz cut that shines like velvet. He is the creator of one of the first "official" TAZs to get up and running on the Internet, Banc de Geneve's Information Storage department, which opened for business 27 hours after Congress passed the Public Safety Encryption Bill in July 1996.

"I immediately realized," he says candidly, through a thick Swiss accent, "that your Congress had created the perfect environment for, shall we say, offshore banking of corporate data. Your Public Safety Encryption Bill is merely a license for your government to read any computer files it wants without the bother of obtaining a search warrant. And I knew most of your large corporations would never accept that."

A forty-year veteran of Swiss banking, Greuber knew that American corporations had large amounts of money they didn't want the U.S. government to know about. He further assumed that they had data that was equally sensitive. On the night after the Congressional vote, he and his staff went to work on doing what the Swiss do best. Bereft of natural resources, they sell services. Selling security is the most profitable service of all. In 24 hours, they hacked together some old Groupe Bull minicomputers that were due for replacement, 9 ten-gigabyte storage units, and went on-line. By the end of the week, all ninety gigs had been leased. The majority, Dr. Greuber reports, to American corporations.

Now, he says proudly, with close to two terabytes of on-line storage and nearly unlimited off-line available, Information Storage is Banc de Geneve's most profitable department, pulling in millions of dollars each month while costing only a few thousand francs for electricity and maintenance. Although "regretfully prohibited" from telling me who his clients are, Dr. Greuber boasts that he handles data storage for corporations on every continent but Antarctica.

Swiss data banks (of which Banc de Geneve is merely one) operate on a multiple password system. To get an account, you fill out an anonymous paper form obtained from the bank, or better still, visit the bank in person. (Dr. Greuber says that while he has an on-line sign-up form, virtually none of his clients feel secure using it.) You select your userid and five passwords, and give the Swiss bank access to your line of credit. That's it. If your credit checks out, you now have a Data Haven in Switzerland, ready to store your most precious secrets at $1,000 per gigabyte per month. Since the Swiss are not signatories to the 1995 International Treaty on Data Security, records stored on Swiss computers can only be subpoenaed by a Swiss court for the breaking of a Swiss law. "Fortunately," Dr. Greuber says with a twinkle, "Switzerland has very few laws regarding electronic data." Your data is SAFE here, baby.

On the other hand, Dr. Greuber warns, you are responsible for the security of your own passwords. "We will grant access to anyone who knows all five passwords. If your government manages to obtain the passwords from you, by whatever means, and they log on as you, they will read your data."

Toward the end of our talk, I asked Dr. Greuber if the United States had ever applied pressure to the Swiss authorities to have his TAZ shut down.

"Your government," he says, pausing for the right word, "understands us. They accept the need for our existence, because under certain circumstances, we serve their purposes as well."

This statement confused me at first, but then an amusing question occurred to me that demanded an answer. "Does the U.S. government store their data on your systems?" I asked. Dr. Greuber paused while he considered whether or not to answer, then politely admitted that some governmental agencies of certain national governments have opened accounts on his system, but whether or not these accounts were used to store governmental data, he wouldn't know.

But, he explained, that's not the main reason that governments accept the existence of his data haven. "Answer me this," he said, sounding like an old foreign professor. "Do you think your government passed that encryption bill to prevent corporations from encoding their data, or to prevent the average citizens from encoding their data?"

I told him I personally thought the government was out to get both groups.

"Then you are sadly mistaken," Dr. Greuber intoned. "Your corporations are a great friend to your government. Or I should say your government is a great friend to the corporations, no? Your government accepts the fact that corporations need to keep some data secret. Your agencies and your Congress can't have your large companies openly flouting the encryption laws within the United States, true. If a corporation is found to be violating any laws, then of course your government must investigate them. But if a large corporation quietly ships its data offshore and leaves it there without bothering anyone, your government will leave them unmolested.

"Remember," Dr. Greuber warns, "your gov-ernment goes after only those things it feels may disturb the status quo. Businessmen don't make revolutions. Ordinary people do."

On that note Dr. Greuber very stiffly said good-bye.

TO GET A BANC DE GENEVE INFORMA-TION STORAGE ACCOUNT:
    http://bdg.geneva.ch/pub/is/SignForm.html
or e-mail to
    SignForm@bdg.geneva.ch
with the word HELP in the subject line
****

It Is Good to Get Rich

Information, like opium a century ago, plays an extraordinarily secret role in the Far East, and Guangzhou (formerly Canton), capital city of China's Guangdong Prefecture, is the hub of the area's underground traffic.

Guangdong is a hot, humid region, a delta of the Pearl River in southeastern China. It was the first of China's provinces to be allowed to practice a modified market economy; a capitalist cell in a Communist body. As a result, for the past fifteen years, Guangdong's economy grew at upwards of 12% a year. It's citizens earn an average of ten times the per capita income of the rest of China. And because of this magnificent growth, fueled by foreign investment, Guangdong is the center of high technology in China.

Although the media is just now discovering her, Guangzhou is one of the hot centers of the world. An energy runs through it similar to the energy that ran through New York and Tokyo in the 1980s. This is the place where things are happening. On a daily basis, pre–World War II buildings are being knocked down to put up new factories, condos, and office buildings with Japanese, British, and Singaporean money. And everywhere, people are perfecting their hustle.

Ms. Zhou Yin, the ever-smiling thirtyish president of Guangzhou Information Systems, runs the largest public internet provider in Southeast Asia:

ChinaCom, a 50,000-member service whose name is a grim joke on the Communism that Guangdong has all but discarded. ChinaCom is generally regarded as THE hacker/entrepreneur board of the Far East.

Ms. Zhou, who insists that everyone call her Yin, spent two years studying Electrical Engineering at New York's Manhattan College in the 1980s. She emerged with a desire to get rich quick, and a great talent for spin-doctoring, which she can accomplish in fluent English when the situation warrants. She returned to Guangdong and opened a small circuit-board shop, soldering the boards in her kitchen at night. Eventually, she would own the first computer chip factory in Guangdong. She started ChinaCom as a simple anonymous remailer for herself and her friends. When netters want to send e-mail to each other without revealing their identity, they can route their mail through a special anon remailer server. The anonserver strips all identifying information from the incoming message and passes the text of the message on to the intended recipient. As far as the recipient knows, the message originated at this anonymous remailer; there's no way to find out who really sent the message. Anon remailers are indispensable tools of the Underground, enabling them to write and post messages some regard as obscene without getting caught. Because of its quick turnaround time, ChinaCom's remailer became the darling of the Singapore Net Set, and word quickly spread.

Yin later added FSP ability to her system. FSP stands for File Server Protocol, the ability to download a file from the net without leaving a record of how, when, and from whence you downloaded it. A popular tool of the Underground, FSP sites usually exist for only a few hours; long enough for the members to download what they can, but not long enough for the Feds to get a fix on the site's location. ChinaCom's FSP site has attained almost mythical status in the Underground by being continuously up and running for nearly two years.

Yin smiles, and tells me that ChinaCom is dedicated to peace and brotherhood among humanity, and to bring computer knowledge and futuristic ideas to the people of the East. When pressed, she smiles again, and says she's aware that some people use her system for data smuggling, but she is powerless to stop them.

"Yes, digitized American movies have come across my system, to be downloaded in Hong Kong, Singapore, Kuala Lumpur. But what is there to do? I cannot examine the accounts of my users." She smiles again and adds, "That wouldn't be right."

This laissez-faire attitude toward data has gotten ChinaCom into at least one lawsuit. A major American film studio discovered not only digitized movies, but the software used to create the special effects in these movies, sitting on a ChinaCom FSP server. Faster than you can say BAM!, the studio's lawyers tried to sue Guangzhou Information Systems in the International Court of Intellectual Property in The Hague. When the court refused to hear the case, the lawyers brought a copyright infringement suit against Yin in a Chinese court. Yin was saved by the fact that it's not a crime in China to violate American copyrights. "I was very worried at one point," she says, "because while the Chinese court did not object to the existence of the American movie on my system, they took great offense at the film's content. I was let off with a warning; the judges saved their venom for the American lawyers representing the film company that had created this scandalous work." Yin laughs heartily at the memory.

I told Yin that under U.S. law, our citizens are prohibited from using any form of unauthorized encryption on any computer anywhere in the world. I asked her if she had recieved any requests from Fort Meade to examine some of her American accounts.

"Oh," she said with that same smile, "we are not subject to any North American laws. There are no United States accounts on my system.

That is the whole point." When I expressed disbelief at this, she shrugged and said that's the way it was. After a moment, she added that she had had a lot of accounts come through some of the anonymous remailers in Finland and Russia. "Those could be American," she smiles. "But I really don't know."

TO ACCESS CHINACOM:
>   telnet to chinacom.com
>   login as GUEST
> or FSP to
>   fsp chinacom.com
>   login as anonymous
>
>   To use the remailer:
>
>   mail to anon@chinacom.com
>   subject line HELP

****

Colonel Hernando Escalante's Cuba brings to mind that old Star Trek episode in which the social structure of a planet is based on the book "Chicago Gangsters of the Roaring 20s." There is a palpable criminal presence in the streets of Havana, exemplified by the cagy eyes of the hundreds of well-dressed young men leaning against customized pastel BMWs and Lincoln Continentals. Yes, the Mob is back in Havana, in full cooperation with a friendly government, and they've got computers.

It's not easy to keep track of millions of drug deals, thousands of loan payments, and hundreds of rat bastards who have to have their kneecaps broken. Computers help. Organized crime got into computers in a big way in the late 1980s. Expert systems, designed to Mafia specs, planned drug shipment routes and helped design casinos. Cellular modems and faxes carried the information to the field, and databases with genetic search engines kept track of everything.

Escalante's coup against Raul Castro, after the death of Fidel, gave the Mob the one thing they were missing: the ability to launder even the dirti-
est of their money through a country's national banking system. Banco de Revolucion de Cuba is, for all intents and purposes, a Mafia bank. Within hours after the coup, telephones were ringing off the hook in the offices of the United States companies that make ATMs and other automated banking systems. The new Cuban leaders were willing to spend millions of (Mafia) dollars to create the ultimate state-of-the-art banking and information system in the Caribbean.

And so Havanet was created. On the surface, Havanet is nothing more than a standard on-line service, providing a few message boards, news, weather, shopping and on-line banking services to the people in Havana with home computers. But something else is going on here. There are maybe 150 private citizens with personal computers throughout all of Cuba, but Havanet has over 2,000 accounts. Many of these accounts are in fictitious Cuban names, many of them are logged in 24 hours a day, and many of them are used for nothing but online banking.

"There's nothing we can do about it," says Special Agent Chuck Castaldo of the U.S. Secret Service, the man in charge of monitoring Cuban money-laundering. "We can piece together nearly all of the traffic that goes on in Banco de Rev, and we know it's almost exclusively used for money-laundering. We know, for example, that Pedro Ruz, a cane farmer, gets $40 a pound for his sugarcane from a United States sugar company that's Mafia-owned. Going rate is $4. Like most of his fellow farmers, Pedro insists on being paid in cash. So the Mob's sugar company must ship thousands of dollars in currency to Havana. Pedro puts his cash into his account at Banco de Rev, then uses his ATM to send a payment to a fertilizer company, for some fertilizer. The problem is, ol' Pedro paid $160 a ton for the fertilizer while his neighbors pay $30. Why does Pedro get these special deals? Pedro probably doesn't even exist. Chances are, he's just a name that's being used by the Mob as a way to explain the incredible influx of cash. All they have to do is show that they're involved in the business of selling something and getting paid for it, and they're untouchable. Damn straight the Cuban authorities aren't going to investigate; in Cuba, the Mob appoints the mid-level government officials. And we have absolutely no authority down there."

Close to $90 million dollars a day passes through Cuba's ATM and Havanet networks. U.S. authorities believe that much of it originates here. They know for a fact that a sizable portion of it ends up in Switzerland. And there's nothing they can do.

What frightens the Secret Service is that many legitimate American companies have opened or are trying to open accounts at Banco de Rev. "If that happens on a large scale," Castaldo warns, "there'll be no way to get an accurate accounting of any corporation's tax liability. All the money will be hidden. The tax burden will shift more and more to the shoulders of what's left of the middle class. The whole system is going to be in deep, deep excrement."

cont pg 127

WIRED 2000   April 1997   pg 9 - 10
How the Net was Won, by Steele
cont from pg. 8

INSTANT ERECTION
=================

It was a kind of "spontaneous erection." The creation of CryptoNet, that is. Thousands of computers, wired into the subNet of National-ISDN—ghetto of America's vaunted National Information Infrastructure. To this day, they make up the skeleton of CryptoNet. N-ISDN connections are cheap and fast. They don't require tremendous bandwidth. It just needs running room. The N-ISDN network allows that, at 56-kbps.

According to a confidential memo obtained by *Wired 2000*, several hundred Crypto hosts "peered" within hours of each other on May 16, 1996. The effort was planned a month earlier, during a rare face-to-face meeting in Las Vegas, beneath the warp and woof of WireNet '96, the nation's largest wireless trade show. There, over Jack Daniels, amidst the cacophony of clanging slot machines, CryptoNet was born.

According to the memo, 231 machines would be jacked into the N-ISDN and automatically begin peering, using an ancient-but-unbreakable encryption algorithm developed by a disenchanted National Security Agency cryptographer. These machines apparently had the codes, routing tables,

and so forth, virtually "asleep" in some forgotten sectors of their optical disks. In the words of a midwestern CryptoNet administrator, "We just fired up the old routines from the great Crypto-Wars of 1994. As the machines began running the routing tables, one by one they recognized each other, rebuilt the routing tables and—BANG—the damn Net virtually built itself," he said.

Encrypted message traffic also began to flow openly on the Internet itself, a direct slap in the face to HADL's Spot Monitors. A stunningly aggressive—but ever so polite—flame war erupted. But without the four-letter vengeance found in most pre-1996 flame wars, the effect was that of a pissed-off 4-year-old yelling at the world. A typical "flame" on the rise of encrypted messages read like this: "This coded message traffic is poopie and I insist, no I *demand* that the cretin transmitting it stop this instant."

Ugh. I warned you. But it's this kind of pablum and total intolerance for opposing points of view that have given rise to CryptoNet.

YOU CAN'T CENSOR WHAT YOU CAN'T READ
====================================

CryptoNet has two agendas: (1) to allow for a free and open flow of thoughts and ideas, and (2) to free the Net from the tyranny of the HADL. But streams of encoded messages are just so much digital flotsam and jetsam in the bitstream.

"You can't fucking censor what you can't read," reads the popular bumpersticker. But oceans of encrypted messages amount to little more than "silent" protests since the underlying message is unreadable. Enter the auto-decrypt ports.

"We understood that encrypting messages opposing HADL policy was like preaching to the choir," said White Dog, the code name of an ex-Libertarian Party leader turned Code Apostle. "But that was only an opening salvo. Then, in November (1996), a bunch of us hunkered down at the Seal Beach Inn in San Francisco and hacked out the code for Auto-Decrypt ports," he said. The Seal Beach Inn was chosen as the coding site because of the "vibes," White Dog said. "Hunter Thompson wrote some of his best gonzo stuff there," the Dog said. "We figured it was a natural place to code from."

And so, Auto-Decrypt Ports were born. Wireless transmitters that use a frequency-hopping modulation that can't be traced, these ingenious and almost undetectable "code transfer" points are set up along the N-ISDN. Selected CryptoNet machines route traffic through these Auto-Decrypt ports, which is then recycled into the Net-at-large through the public transport ports, the government-mandated "on-ramps" to the National Information Infrastructure (NII).

The process of jacking in through these Public Access Ports (PAPs) testifies to the genius of necessity. The funding for PAPs was inserted into the NII legislation by liberal-minded lawmakers and bleeding-heart advocacy groups who were afraid of creating a society of "information have-and-have-nots." So the Congress created national public access ports where anyone can jack in, easy. Hell, fucking Radio Shack and Sears sell government-subsidized software and interface kits that a pedestrian programmer could set up and have logged into these PAPs within 30 minutes. As part of public access, Congress also mandated open interfaces and protocols, meaning all the underlying code was public domain.

It was a giant mawing hole in Net Access. The only control is that the ports are often choked and ungodly slow, which is the intent of their design, sort of like the way the original QWERTY keyboards were designed so awkwardly, with the intent of slowing down a typist so the keys wouldn't stick together.

What Congress didn't foresee was that the Open Air Interface, an almost ignored access point, was little used by PAPs, and much quicker. Naturally, the CryptoNet pioneers seized on this route for Auto-Decrypt Ports.

When an encoded message is transferred to the Open Net, it's routed through an Auto-Decrypt Port, which then descrambles the message, puking the cleartext into the bitstream of the HADL. The message traffic is untraceable. Running a traceroute on the message returns a string of encrypted gibberish. Auto-Decrypt Ports are hung off streetlights, on the sides of Pizza Huts, in train stations and on Microwave towers. In short, anywhere a CryptoRebel has the stones to climb up and install one. Once secured with a couple of bolts, the Ports self-boot, bringing up the latest routing table which is quickly updated at the first peering with the nearest CryptoNet node.

BAT SHIT REVIEW
===============
Sitting in the HADL offices in Washington, DC, the impact of CryptoNet is immediate. The place is in a constant panic. The place is going bat shit but, of course, that phrase would never be used here.

cont pg 11

Date: Wed, 4 April 1997 20:50:22 +0000
From: Nesta Stubbs <nesta@nesta.pr.mcs.net>
To: Judith The Saint <stjude@well.sf.ca.us>
Subject: Cyberspace Hashishim Declare Jihad

——————BEGIN PGP SIGNED MESSAGE————

Well here is the first draft of my newest manifesto, samizdat, propaganda, agitprop etc. . . .

Cyberspace Hashishim Declare Jihad

"We declare Jihad, a Holy War, against those who call for the regulation of the Net by government occupational forces. We will cut
off their heads and fill their dead open mouths with shit, and im-
pale their skulls on pikes, lighting the whole thing ablaze with
flaming torches."
      -Mahmud Abd Al-Shakir
      Cyberspace Hashishim

Keep Your Laws Off My Body

This is not a war outside of you, like the Gulf War, a clean detached video representation of events that really didn't happen. This is a fight for your own body, your hypertext body, spread out over the globe by IP Networks, touching foreign continents with packet fingers. More than television, which simply plugs into your nervous system and is a one-way stream of control

```
##############
#   /==$=\     #   <— From the High-Tech Fully Electronic Desk
#  /))-00(\    #      of R. U. Sirius
#  ((( —)))    #
#  )))\ /(((   #   —> rusirius@well.com
##############
```
Date: Oct. 5, 1998
To: Hyatt@Ballantine.Books.com, stjude@well.com
Subject: What, we still need a PLOT????

Trudy, I'm beside myself. And neither one of me feels very good.

But, whatever you say. If we must keep narrative highway 1010101010 open, then we SHALL.
DRIVE, she said.
      But think about this word . . . plot. Sounds like PLOP, doesn't it? Conjures images of this smelly unattractive thing that you'd rather leave behind, no? If you don't flush it away, it just sits there, stinking and attracting flies, spreading disease. I mean, do you hang on to all your shit? Are YOU planning to tie up all the loose ends of your excrement at the end of YOUR life?

images and sound bytes, The Internet and its ilk are full extensions of your body's -- a fully cybernetic arm compared to television's pirate hook which drags you in. Will you let the religious right and other morality mongers tell you what you can do with your body?

Your 'self' is no longer confined to your physical body. Rather, it's the interface between your mind, your PSY in cybernetic theory, and the outside world, the PHI. It's a morphing intersection, the points at which you process information from the outside world. For instance, thru telepresence your 'self' can be moved outside of your body and into a robotic apparatus, your senses located and extended thru wires and cameras. Cyberspace becomes a new sensorium, an array of inputs and outputs to and from your mind.

This isn't projected future. This is NOW. This is the net and the World Wide Web. I am no longer simply a young man sitting on his floor in front of his terminal, but instead my 'self' is shifted, enlarged. Imagine a transparent sphere with tentacles and pseudopods like a jellyfish, extending from you and reaching towards all the boundaries of the Net, and all the data

Date: Oct. 7, 1998
From: stjude@root.bodhi.tree
To: rusirius@well.com
Subject: ken, you fuckwit

o christ, ken, you've advanced from pomo to psycho. trudy will not buy this excrement shit. She's not an idiot. She's gonna tell you you're off your nut.

points in it. This is the new hypertext body, no longer held into the rough shape of a body, but growing, shifting, morphing into a presence engulfing the wired world. NOW.

You may not physically bleed from the attacks of those seeking to regulate the Net, but blinders will be put on your new eyes, walls will block your new fingers. They are talking about putting us in prisons and straightjackets, cutting off our tongues, chopping off our hands, crippling us. When they intend to control the Net, they intend to control our new bodies.

Take Up Arms

Forget feeble attempts at fighting this battle in the realm of law. Guerilla warfare is our main weapon. Establish Networks that ride the back of the Internet, encrypted packets, posts and mail that are hidden from the prying eyes of the watchers above. Whether it be a kid running a term (fake IP thru a shell account) link from the Net to his home computer offering files, information, and a place for people to exchange data deemed illegal and detrimental, or a machine in Europe providing anonymous mail drop boxes (look at c2.org as a stateside example), or even a hacker coding a crypto-secure program for the transfer of mail or usenet posts hidden in white noise with steganography (hiding data in pictures, sound files etc . . .) allowing an entire underground version of usenet to pop up, unmoderated and unmolested by regulatory agencies -- all of these help maintain the flow of information that the government or moral majority may deem detrimental to the good of society, or whatever.

This fight is made easy by the inherent structure of the Networks. The Internet is not so much wires, as protocol. This protocol was designed, for military purposes, to withstand a nuclear attack (by now, the deep military roots of the net have taken on a positive spin in Net folklore). It was developed without central control so that it couldn't be easily knocked out. This works in our favor. No central target for attack . . . no central point of control. And as the Net expands, with more interconnections and paths, it becomes ever more uncontrollably tangled, until there are myriad different paths your data can travel along -- multiple pathways to the pornography FTP site you're downloading from, or to the anon remailer that will forward your post to a newsgroup alt.abuse.recovery where you'd like to remain anonymous.

Every path is a way around the regulations they will attempt to put upon our hypertext bodies. The Net is a jungle environment, made for guerrilla warfare, hit and run tactics made easy thru encryption and smart use of Network technology. Make it another Vietnam for the US government. They cannot win. There are too many of us, disguised, unseen, and striking behind the scenes, creating havoc, forging paths thru the jungle of bits to connect our villages, or zones of Autonomy.

Imagine traveling thru the Net, all of it a wasteland of censored data, pasteurized and homogenized till it contains nothing of interest. Dead and grey. Then a friend gives you an address, or a client program that connects to a hidden server, all transactions crypto strong and hidden. You run the client, or telnet to that address, and you're greeted by a hidden oasis of data; vibrant, alive, people talking, secret parties, like a 1920's speakeasy. The whole thing protected from the Net-cops by strong crypto, and the sheer chaotic size of cyberspace.

TAZ in Cyberspace

In his seminal book, Temporary Autonomous Zones, Hakim Bey gave us the TAZ in real-space, and he went so far as to elucidate its connection and uses for the TAZ in cyberspace. But he intelligently admits he has little experience in such matters online, and leaves the rest of the creating to us. An interconnection of TAZes in cybersapce could be mobile, mutable and undetectable. Information resources can be shared, forces united -- but not molested -- by these connections. Perhaps sometime you will come across a TAZ in cyberspace, a glittering jewel on the Indra's web of hidden Network.

= =

TimeWarner Net—
Virtual Vanity with Howard Rhinestone   June 6, 1997

TALKSHOW TRANSCRIPT
by Steve O'Keefe

Official Transcript
Virtual Vanity with Howard Rhinestone
Recorded June 6, 1977

Rhinestone: Welcome to Virtual Vanity—the talkshow that lets YOU ask the questions. I'm your facilitator, Howard Rhinestone, coming to you live on TimeWarner Net. Today's topic is self-mutilation. Let's meet our guests.

Coming to us from San Francisco, California, our first guest is Dobie Pincer, a gay S&M performance artist who cuts himself as part of his act. Welcome to Virtual Vanity, Dobie.

Pincer: Hello.

Rhinestone: On remote from the Dade County Prison in Miami Florida, we'd like to welcome Willie Last. Willie slams rusty nails into his head in what has become known as "brainspiking." Willie . . .

Last: All right.

Rhinestone: From Caesar's Palace in Las Vegas, Nevada, say hello to Tim Grimm, formerly of the Jim Rose Circus Sideshow and now presiding over "The Grimmest Show on Earth."

Grimm: Howard.

Rhinestone: And with me here at command central in Sausalito, California, is Dr. Susan Power, author of the book, "Stop the Mutilation!" Dr. Power.

Power: It's a pleasure to be here, Howard.

Rhinestone: And coming in live on the chat lines, it's YOU, our home viewing audience. If you've got a question for one of our guests, just send an instant message to Vanity at Time-Warner dot Com. Those of you on videophones can send your signal via videolink. We've got to go to a short message here, but we'll be right back with people who mutilate themselves.

COMMERCIAL ANNOUNCEMENT: Are you tired of getting spammed by crass commercial announcements cluttering up the Internet? Do you have to slog through 50 or 100 messages to find the one worth reading? Well, you don't have to take it any longer. Link up with Screen&Clean, the messaging service that lets you set the criteria while we do the grunge work. You tell us what you want to see, and from whom, and we'll do the rest. Only the most important messages will appear in your morning mailbox. The rest will be neatly archived where you can retrieve them if you ever need them. Screen&Clean—the full-service message service that makes e-mail E-Z. A TimeWarner Company.

Rhinestone: We're back with Virtual Vanity, the talk show that lets YOU ask the questions. I'm Howard Rhinestone, and let's get right to our first guest. Dobie, how did you get started mutilating yourself?

Pincer: Well, it all started with clipping my fingernails.

Rhinestone: I suppose you could call that self-mutilation, Dobie, but most people consider that basic hygiene.

Pincer: The fingernails are very sensitive. I would get sexually aroused just clipping them. I'd get an erection, you know, so I started clipping them shorter and shorter. And then I started pulling them off. I guess you could say that was the beginning.

Rhinestone: Haven't you amputated several of your fingers?

Pincer: Yeah. And one of my ears. I did a show last week where I finished off the last of the toes on my left foot.

Rhinestone: Could we get a look at that?

Pincer: My foot?

Rhinestone: Yeah.

Pincer: Sure . . . just a minute . . . here . . . can you see that?

Rhinestone: Could you move back from the monitor a little, Dobie . . . there . . . you see that

stump? There's a man who's willing to sacrifice a lot for his art. What do you think of that, Dr. Power?

Power: I think it's sick.

Rhinestone: Okay, let's go to Willie at Dade County Prison. Willie, could you tell us what "brainspiking" is, and why you do it?

Last: Brainspiking is driving a nail into your head. It's a form of protest.

Rhinestone: Protest over what?

Last: For being treated less than a human being. For being stripped of all your rights, caged like an animal, denied the very basics of decency.

Rhinestone: So you proclaim your dignity by driving nails into your brain?

Last: That's right. They can take everything away from you, but they can't keep you from expressing yourself. It's a reflection of the conditions that people in prison live under. Folks on the outside don't want to know what it's like. When they see us slamming spikes into our heads, they have to know it must be pretty bad.

Rhinestone: How many times have you spiked yourself?

Last: Three times.

Rhinestone: Have there been any negative results? I mean, you appear to be able to communicate just fine.

Last: I've lost some motor control, particularly on the left side of my body. I have a drooling problem. I get headaches.

Rhinestone: Has anyone died of brainspiking there at Dade?

Last: People die at Dade all the time. What difference does it make if it's from a nail they put in their head or from a brutal beating by the guards? You don't wanna know, right?

Rhinestone: We're just trying to understand this thing.

Last: Yeah. F*** you.

Rhinestone: What do you think of that, Dr. Power?

Power: It's sad. It's sad that people have to resort to self-mutilation before others will listen to their concerns. Something needs to be done about this.

Last: F*** you, too.

Rhinestone: Okay, I think we'll talk to Tim Grimm, the human pin-cushion. Tim.

Grimm: Howard.

Rhinestone: Do you really do all that stuff in your show—the meat skewers through the throat, the pins festooned across your chest—or is it an illusion?

Grimm: Everything you see is real.

Rhinestone: Here's a CD-ROM of Tim doing his stuff. Let's watch ... Ouch! That's some graphic footage, Tim. You look like you're in some sort of trance state.

Grimm: Sort of. It's more like meditation. I have to get centered before I can do the act, or I bleed too much.

Rhinestone: Is this a religious experience for you, Tim?

Grimm: Pain is just another stimulus, Howard. It's another way the world communicates with you. You can achieve as much ecstasy through pain as you can through pleasure.

Rhinestone: Dr. Power?

Power: It's sick. It's just another way of cashing in on sensationalism.

Rhinestone: Are you cashing in, Tim?

Grimm: Yes. You're all invited down to Caesar's Palace to see the new show. We've got chickens that try to bite the head off a geek, and we've got a new piranha dunk tank . . .

Rhinestone: I'm afraid we've got to go to a commercial now, but when we come back, we'll be taking YOUR questions on Virtual Vanity.

COMMERCIAL ANNOUNCEMENT: "I always wanted to write fiction like Stephen King. Since I started using ScareMaster, I'm collecting royalties instead of rejection slips." That's just one of the thousands of satisfied customers who've used Stephen King's ScareMaster Software to write books that bust through the best-seller list. Now you can write great suspense stories like never before, with the all new Stephen King ScareMaster2: "The Horror Continues." ScareMaster2 contains hundreds of vivid new characters. You pick the players, and ScareMaster 2 generates up to 17 powerful plot lines. Select the plot you want, and ScareMaster does all the rest, putting the flesh on the skeleton YOU created. No more hours bent over the keyboard. Are you looking for authentic accents? It's so easy with Stephen King's ScareMaster2. You just click on one of dozens of international and regional dialects and your character's words are transformed before your eyes. Looking for that perfect surprise ending? Look no further than new, improved ScareMaster2—so good I can't reveal the heart-stopping endings you'll find in this package. Stephen King's ScareMaster2 is available in DOS, Apple, and many other formats. Download it today from the TimeWarner Electronic Mall, Suite 666.

```
##############
#   /==$=\      #  <— From the High-Tech Fully Electronic Desk
#  /))-00(\     #      of R. U. Sirius
#  ((( -)))     #
#  )))\ /(((    #  -> rusirius@well.com
##############
```

Date: Oct. 8, 1998
To: stjude@aqua.hair.net
Subject: Great idea!

Don't worry. I figured it out. We'll engage Trudy in endless discussions around the plot. We'll insert those exchanges INTO THE BOOK ITSELF!!!!! (hehheh) The plot will be teased out, ranted at, screen tested, fucked, spanked, analyzed . . . TAMED!
believe me, when she sees it, she'll LOVE it . . .

Rhinestone: Hi, we're back with Virtual Vanity. Today's topic is self-mutilation. Let's go to the chatlines. Hello Billy Bob from Lonestar dot Com—what's on your mind?

BillyBob: I'd just like to know why those ladies would make themselves fat. That's just gross.

Rhinestone: Uh, BillyBob, that was yesterday's topic. Do you have a question for one of our guests.

BillyBob: Uh, yeah, okay, uh, doesn't that hurt?

[chat laughter: :) :) :)]

Rhinestone: Okay, well, that's a legitimate question. Dobie, doesn't that hurt when you cut yourself on stage, or do you use some sort of anesthesia?

Pincer: Yeah, but you sort of get used to it. It's not so bad.

Rhinestone: Tim Grimm, what about you? Do you feel much pain when you're in that trance state?

Grimm: Pain is the payday, Howard. You can't do this if you don't love the pain.

Rhinestone: Okay, let's go to NetDude from Panix dot Com in New York. NetDude? ... Uh, NetDude, we don't have your key ... you're going to have to send the key, NetDude ... We can't get the key? ... Uh, NetDude, turn off the encryption ... NetDude, were getting garbage, TURN OFF THE ENCRYPTION ... Okay, let's go to Chester the Molester on the videolink from BYU dot Edu in Salt Lake City. Chester?

Chester: Can you see me okay?

Rhinestone: Perfectly, Chester, you're coming in crystal clear.

Chester: Well getta load of this ...

Rhinestone: Oh god ... Phil ... cut, CUT ...

Pincer: He popped his f***in' eyeball out! *Dude!!!*

[chat shock: :o :o :o]

Power: That's just sick!

Rhinestone: I have to apologize to our viewers for that ... what's that? Ladies and gentlemen, I've just been informed by our producer, Phyllis Specter, that what you just saw was a virtual reality feed. Chet didn't really gouge his eye out. Pretty clever, Chet.

Pincer: Looked like he was poppin' a big ol' zit. Sh*t, that was pretty good.

[chat boos: :(:(:( ]

Rhinestone: Well, I'm afraid we're all out of time, folks. Join us tomorrow when we'll have Rosemary Fury, author of the new book, "NANOSEX." Rosemary's going to tell us how a near-future technology is about to improve your sex life big time. For Virtual Vanity, I'm Howard Rhinestone. Stay jacked!

```
================================================
Date: 7/1/97                                    D
From: enote.sally@sirius.hassani.org
To: stjude@tiddly.wink.org
Subject: dirty little secrets
```

In the six months that our cadre have been spewing cleartext onto the
NiceNet, we've put out some stuff that's much nastier than this, frequently right into the middle of a lalala nicelady conversation in
the Caring League or some similar place. But nothing, NOTHING has
ever created the kind of hysteria that this caused when we posted it
about a month ago in the middle of a conversation in Tipper Gore's
private topic on the New Civility BBS. Word has it that 10% of the
secret service is now dedicated full time to finding the perp . . .

Advice For Pedophiles
by Aw Shucks Jimmy

Here are some tips I've put together, for seducing women at that
oh! so tender age. Follow them, and like me, you will soon have a
host of fawning, eager girls to choose from, to do with as you
please, in whatever combination you choose . . .

Insouciance!
Your age difference is your key; flaunt it. Don't attempt to learn about
the singers in New Kids, or the new fashion craze. Look down at it;
look down at them. Young girls travel in simpering, giggling groups,
for protection. Eye them with a cold glance, and soon their pretty
asses will be lined in a row, at your beck. And call. They will come.

Exotique!
Ah, they're hormones have possessed them fully; they are peering up
their pink cunts, borrowing their mother's hand mirrors, hours at a
time. They build hand-made vibrators from old electric tooth brushes.
Good fellow, they are ready for you. For all manners, style, extremes
of eroticism. They will hold back nothing. If they dare, sneer, show
withering contempt; they will be ready for buggery, or an elaborate
menage, or acts of sapphism with friends for your observance. Prepare
a menu; do not skimp, do not flinch.

Forbearance!
A slight proviso. At this age, with their sexual capacity so fresh,
they will be, perhaps, a touch indelicate. They are new to the

concept of feminine hygiene. You will find oftimes their loins to
reek, their cunts to be petri dishes of unknown humors. This is so
new to them! You must be patient. The rewards are great.

That's it . . . Did it just wreck your life?
= =
Date: July 2, 1997
From: stjude@tiddly.wink.org
To: enote.sally@siriushassani
Subject:

egad. thanks for the pedo spoof. (i guess it's a spoof. . . . maybe
not) knowing you posted it on the emilies, it warms the potholes of
my heart.

actually, you know, i recently remembered falling in love with a
beautiful eight yr old boy when i was just post-pube—age twelve. i
was a precocious pedophile!

Hey, I just dug this out . . . you ever see this?

    From: Nesta Stubbs <nesta@nesta.pr.mcs.net>
    To: Judith The Saint <stjude@well.sf.ca.us>
    Subject: WARNING! WARNING! (fwd)

    I like Alan, he is cool, he wrote this for the mailing lists you
    see in teh header. I think you will like him too, all is good, God
    is with us, and we are safe.

    ———Forwarded message———
    Subject: WARNING! WARNING!

    PLEASE NOTE PLEASE NOTE:
    TO EVERYONE!!!!

CHILD PORN PERVERTS SEARCH THE NET FOR YOUR KIDS!

Lurid sex-starved children advocate free sex with ancient men! Her
teats hung down until the lap of little boys was filled with them.
His hair-less body reached through the screen accosting the
previously-perfect twins. Friends, crime on the Internet knows no
bounds! Their thin waists were grasped by the terminal itself
hurtling color pictures of wide-open holes. Wee-wee on your mommy

176

and daddy. I will come and kill your entire family, Mr. President, and their families too! This is an ascii bomb, burning your hard-drive: Beware! PCP fumes will kill within five seconds.

If we are not allowed to keep our guns, we will march on EVERY CAPITAL BUILDING IN THIS UNITED STATES. SHOOT TO KILL!!!!! Come here, honey, and sit on my life. The formula for crack involves a free radical easily reproduced from common baking-soda. Your girl-friend has a small twat, I should know. I will shoot every goddamn Russian who comes within ten miles of Peoria. Perverts Cruise the Internet Taking your Children from You. Friends, you must HURT THEM where it counts, in their pocketbooks and between their eyes! Here is a list of private phone-numbers of invalids. You have $14321.24 in your bank account and your husband is with one Su-sanne Francis. Congratulations: I have just destroyed your operat-ing system! Do not reboot or this machine with never work again! Cock piss shit fuck I bet you can't stop me! Come suck my dick! If you so much as write me again I will shoot you through the window you know which one I mean looking out over the schoolyard. MY IDEA FOR PERFECT WORLD SALVATION IN WHICH I WILL TELL YOU ALL THE AN-SWERS THROUGH MY RESEARCH WHICH I HAVE CARRIED ON FOR ONE DECADE. I want to hold you, honey, go to your telephone, go to your tele-phone now. That's right. Now when it rings, when it rings, pick it up! You don't know me but I know you! Now look behind you, out the window, the car parked down the street.

Wouldn't you like a picture like this? Isn't this a silly picture? Wouldn't you like me to take one? If you can't get the fucking manual, you don't belong here! Fuck you asshole! Clara, I just fucked your husband in the ass. I got your whole family, asshole! It's people like me who have to protect people like you! I didn't think they allowed Jews here. Is it true what they say. Pull your pants down and pull your little thing out, now isn't that better? Aren't there any pictures of kids with kids here?

THE NET IS A PLAYGROUND FOR ALL YOUR DESIRES. I READ IT IN THE PA-PERS, SAW IT ON THE TELEVISION! FRIENDS, THE INFORMATION SUPER-HIGHWAY IS REAL AND IT BRINGS CRIMINALS AND PERVERTS TO YOUR VERY DOOR, INTO YOUR HOUSE, INTO YOUR BED! FRIENDS, THE WIRES DRIP WITH PERVERSION AND EVIL! THE WIRES FUCK YOUR CHILDREN AND YOUR WIVES AND HUSBANDS! HIDEOUS MONSTERS REACH OUT THROUGH YOUR TERMINAL SCREEN AND GRAB YOUR COCK! HIDEOUS FORCES EMPTY YOUR BANK ACCOUNT! DON'T TURN AROUND! THEY ARE WATCHING YOU! GET OFF WHILE THERE IS TIME! GET OFF WHILE THERE IS STILL TIME!

"A Friend"

==

```
Date: 2 July, 1997
From: rusirius
To: stjude
Subject: talkin' bout the CryptoNet

Connie and I have decided to say yes to a request from the New York
Times for an interview about the new computer underground. In ex-
change, Connie got them to promise to put it on the front page of the
Sunday paper. This, it seems to me, is of great consequence. We'll be
walking a fine line between militant support and denial of responsi-
bility. Any suggestions are appreciated.
```
==

Sunday New York Times   July 4, 1997

SIRIUS SUPPORTS "TECHNO-GUERRILLAS"

by John Marknick

© 1995 Aaron Lauer

R. U. Sirius made it clear that he supports the new hacker underground, in a private press conference today at the New York Times office. The eccentric media artist, best known for his writing and his work with the band Mondo Vanilli, is the only public figure thus far to advocate the culture of resistance that has sprung up in response to rules and legislation controlling activities on the Internet. On tour with MV's highly successful F***ing Robot Show (although he doesn't perform in the show itself), R. U. looked relaxed and alert, appearing in the Times conference room in white slacks and a white t-shirt, a marked contrast to his perennial black. Mondo Connie, MV's attractive and eccentric publicist, was on his arm.

Sirius said that the HADL and the entire New Civility Movement was, in his opinion, a minority pretending to be a majority. "These are opposing ways of organizing. The puritans can really get out the vote. They can get people writing letters to their congressmen, they can flood the net with fanatics. But what about the people who attend our shows and buy our albums, or those of Offspring or Don Knotts Overdrive? What about all those people that you and I both know are making their way to encrypted conferences on the net? What about the fans of all those TV shows that the puritans would like to ban? What about the millions of Americans who still smoke marijuana? What about gun-totin', meat-eatin' rednecks? The HADL aims to make us all allies."

Recent articles in *Variety, New Republic,* and *American Spectator* have mentioned R. U. as the leader of the new underground. Sirius calls this "too absurd for words." The movement is leaderless, he argued, "and, frankly, I don't get onto the cryptonet very often."

He does want to "encourage active subversion" though, and suggested that New York Times readers "aren't wimps. They will find their way to cryptonet, and they will disobey the new fascists at every turn. I fully support electronic uncivil disobedience. I always thought people should have shot back during the so-called war on drugs. This is a much nicer way of waging battle. I support media piracy also. Extremism in the defense of liberty is a simple device." With that, Sirius grinned and Ms. Connie whisked him out the door.

===

```
Date: 7 July, 1997
From: rusirius
To: stjude
Subject: guess what


As the result of the piece in the N. Y. Times, I'm now THE spokesper-
son for the underground and I'm appearing on tomorrow night's Night-
line segment with Ted Koppel. It makes no sense whatsoever that they
invited me, which is finally why I decided to accept. I guess the real
underground does value its anonymity huh? Can it be that after all
this time, I'm the only really well-known person stupid enough to go
public in my support? Duhhh . . .                                    .

My plan is to take a quarter hit of acid and then get roaring drunk.
I'm gonna suck . . . huh huh huh
```

===

NIGHTLINE™
On-Line Text Transcript
July 8, 1997

{NIGHTLINE THEME}

ANNOUNCER:
ABC News' Nightline, for Friday, July 8, 1997. Your host, Ted Koppel.

{VIDEO: TED KOPPEL in studio}

TED KOPPEL:
Good evening. Last year, President Clinton signed into law the Electronic Communications

Public Safety Bill, legislation designed to prevent computer users from hiding their messages behind codes the government cannot break.
{Video: clip of President Clinton seated at his desk, signing bill. HADL member Winny Balsam and Senator Jesse Helms are visible in the crowd around him.}

PRESIDENT CLINTON:
As I sign this legislation, I again remind the American people that with freedom comes responsibility. The Electronic Communications Public Safety Act is designed to safeguard our freedom by preventing the irresponsible misuse of our most precious and basic rights.

{VIDEO: TED KOPPEL in studio}

TED KOPPEL:
While organizations like the Human Anti-Degradation League applauded the increasing regulation of computer communications, many computer users, video producers and others objected, arguing that their freedom of speech was being eroded by these laws. Some of these opponents have joined an online organization called the Virtual Underground. This year, the conflict has intensified and the popularity of this underground threatens to render the legal restraints all but irrelevant. 1997 will be remembered as the year the Internet became a political battlefield.

Nightline correspondent Ken Kashiwahara has this report.

{Video: KEN KASHIWAHARA in San Francisco. TransAmerica Pyramid is in background}

```
##############
#   /==$=\     #  <-- From the High-Tech Fully Electronic Desk
# /))-00(\    #     of R. U. Sirius
# ((( -)))    #
# )))\ /(((   # -> rusirius@well.com
##############
```
Date: Oct 9, 1998
To: stjude@mini.ha.ha
Subject: Re: It's stupid, but is it stupid enough to work?

How disheartening. But this idea IS stupid enough to work.

Anyway, this ain't post modernist. This is desperation!

KEN KASHIWAHARA:
One year and two months ago, the Information Superhighway imposed a speed limit on its nearly 180 million users. As a result of the Human Anti-Degradation League's "March on the Internet," Internet management imposed "Content Standards for Electronic Communications," a series of guidelines that banned sexually explicit materials, advocacy or descriptions of extreme violence, and all derogatory and insulting words from electronic mail, electronic messaging and from the multimedia World Wide Web. The formerly unrestrained and sometimes juvenile Internet was suddenly as inoffensive as a glass of milk. The following month, the US Congress and President Clinton made the Content Standards law. Resistance to these standards has resulted in an explosion in the use of data encryption.

{Video: animation of text going into a meat grinder and coming out as 1's and 0's}

KEN KASHIWAHARA(vo):
A piece of data, say an e-mail message, can be broken down and coded so that only the sender and the intended receiver can read the message by using a special digital key. This is known as encryption. Current data encryption schemes are so powerful that it would take the largest computers over a million years to break just one of the endless codes that are being made available on the CryptoNet, a subculture of Internet users who are utilizing the encryption technology to evade the new rules regarding inappropriate content.

{Video: a person using ATM}

KEN KASHIWAHARA(vo):
Encryption technology has long been used by legitimate institutions. For instance, it secures personal medical and banking records from unauthorized tampering. Members of The Underground claim that their private and public communications deserve similar protection.

{Video: the World Trade Center bombing}

KEN KASHIWAHARA(vo):
But unlimited access to data encryption also means that terrorists, pedophiles and other criminals, armed with these unbreakable codes, can plan their illegal activities without the possibility of surveillance. And that has many law enforcement officers worried.

{Video: KEN KASHIWAHARA in San Francisco}

KEN KASHIWAHARA:
The passage of this week's anti-encryption bill was designed to ensure that police will have the ability to obtain evidence in a world where more and more ideas are stored digitally.

Date: Oct 9, 1998
From Stjude@root.solar.sys
To: rusirius@well.com
Subject: STOOPID RULES OK

This idea IS post-modernist. It is exhaustion, flameout, dry heaves . . . tenesmus. look it fucking up—tenesmus.

(no, i'll tell you -- tenesmus is the rectal dryheaves of diarrhea . . . never tell me my medical training was wasted.)

But . . . I give up. Idiotic is IN. I know this. Why fucking not -- we will cede to the *economic* deflation. The Kalifornican depression that Zoloft cannot touch . . . This is the writer's ultimate nightmare . . . that the publisher will demand that WE GIVE THEM BACK THEIR ADVANCE. o no no no
I spent the advance two years ago. I hate my life. I had to sacrifice my cats. I loved those cats so much, ken. I smothered them in sauce bearnaise. They were so delicate, yet gamey, like pheasant. Then i panhandled on telegraph ave until i got run off by the panhandlers local. I have no resources and no hope. I CAN'T GIVE BACK THE ADVANCE, AND BALLANTINE WILL SEND THEIR GOON SQUAD AFTER ME.

I'LL DO WHATEVER I HAVE TO DO. I'LL FILL IN THE PLOT! I WILL! I WILL!

Members of the so-called Underground claim that without encryption, nobody has privacy. Representatives of the aboveground advocacy organization, the Digital Freedom Foundation, also plan to challenge the new law in the courts.

{Video: the Fruitopia-inspired "When Fun is Outlawed" commercial}

KEN KASHIWAHARA(vo):
Last night, millions of Seinfeld viewers watched the most recent salvo in an ongoing information war, when Underground members pirated 30 seconds of time to broadcast its own message.

{Video: KEN KASHIWAHARA in San Francisco}

KEN KASHIWAHARA:
It appears that the old argument of a person's right to privacy versus the public's right to safety has found a new forum in the newest electronic medium. And the battle is only just beginning. Ken Kashiwahara, ABC News, San Francisco.

{VIDEO: Nightline(TM) "field of stars" graphic, with video inserts of Winny Balsam and R. U. Sirius}

TED KOPPEL(vo):
When we return, HADL Spokesperson Winny Balsam, and R. U. Sirius, cyberpunk star and member of The Underground.

{Commercial Break}

TED KOPPEL:
Welcome back. In our New York studios, we have with us Dr. Winny Balsam, speaker for the Human Anti-Degradation League, and one of the chief supporters of censorship on the Internet.

WINNY BALSAM:
Hello.

TED KOPPEL:
And coming to us from our San Francisco affiliate, Mondo Vanilli's R. U. Sirius, musician, author, and founding member of The Underground.

R. U. SIRIUS:
Uhhhh, *actually* Ted. . . .

TED KOPPEL:
Dr. Balsam?

WINNY BALSAM:
Thank you, Ted. First off, I reject the use of the word censorship. Justice Oliver Wendell Holmes said quite clearly, nearly 100 years ago, that freedom of speech does not give a person the right to shout "Fire!" in a crowded theater.

R. U. SIRIUS:
FIRE!!! Oh, boy, fire!!!—by the way, I'm not a founding mem—

TED KOPPEL:
Now—

R. U. SIRIUS:
Fire one, Mr. Chekhov!!! From your member. But I'm *not* a mem—

TED KOPPEL:
—I'm gonna have to ask you not to interrupt.

WINNY BALSAM:
Human beings don't exist in a vacuum. We are social beings. Everything we say has an effect on other people, for good or evil. HADL is merely trying to minimize the damage being wrought by the irresponsible use of words. But our actions, which are supported by a majority of the American people, are being undermined by a small group of computer hackers.

TED KOPPEL:
R. U. Sirius, comment?

R. U. SIRIUS:
We will fight them on the beaches, we will fight them in the fields and in the streets, we will fight them in the hills; we will never surrender! Or maybe we will. You see, I don't know why you invi . . .

WINNY BALSAM:
WHAT???

TED KOPPEL:
Well, that's all well and good, but what's your reaction to what Dr. Balsam said?

R. U. SIRIUS:
First off, Ted, I reject Dr. Balsam's use of the term computer hacker. I, for one, am a "multi-disciplinary computer artist," Dr. Balsam, and I'd appreciate it if you'd remember that.

WINNY BALSAM:
I apologize.

R. U. SIRIUS:
Good girl. Next, how do you know that a majority of Americans support your views? Back in . . .

WINNY BALSAM:
. . . Because of the over . . .

R. U. SIRIUS:
. . . the 1980s . . .

WINNY BALSAM:
. . . whelming support . . .

R. U. SIRIUS:
. . . there was a group . . .

WINNY BALSAM:
. . . our legislation has received . . .

R. U. SIRIUS:
. . . called the Moral Majority . . .

TED KOPPEL:
One, one at a time, please.

WINNY BALSAM:
. . . in Congress. People have . . .

R. U. SIRIUS:
. . . which turned out to be neither.

TED KOPPEL:
R. U. Sirius, please continue.

R. U. SIRIUS:
As I was saying, before Dr. Balsam ignored my right to speak—in the 1980s, there was a group called the Moral Majority that turned out to be neither. So how can you say that a majority supports your actions? andletmejustsayalsothati'm*NOT*amemberofany . . .

TED KOPPEL:
Well, Mr. Sirius. Our polls indeed show seventy percent supporting the HADL. Sit back as we take a break. We'll be back, right after this.

{Commercial break}

TED KOPPEL:
We're talking to Dr. Winny Balsam and R. U. Sirius about the sudden appearance of the Internet Underground, which leads me to ask R. U. Sirius: how many people are in the Underground?

R. U. SIRIUS:
Oh jeez . . . Señor Koppel, roughly how many people watch Nightline each night? Roughly.

TED KOPPEL:
Well, I . . .

R. U. SIRIUS:
Fifteen million? Twenty million? And of those, how many are intelligent and informed enough to actually GET what you talk about? Half? Maybe? On the Net, I can write something and have it read by one hundred and eighty million people!! Ted, you would have to French kiss a (bleep)ing dog to get one hundred and eighty million viewers.
    Maybe half of those users have taken to using the cryptonet. You can consider them all members. It's not like the HADL. There aren't badges or membership cards. Nobody attends meetings. At least *I* sure as hell don't. The Underground is simply a group of people who share a common goal of personal freedom. The Underground is indestructible unless you stamp out the *idea* of freedom.

WINNY BALSAM:
HADL is trying to PRESERVE the idea of freedom!

R. U. SIRIUS:
Yeah, in a specimen jar!
    The scariest thing about the Underground, from Dr. Balsam's point of view, is that my ability to reach about 90 million people is UNREGULATED! Nothing but the customs and traditions that have grown around the Net can stop me from sending my message to every one of those users. The Internet has become a mass medium, Monsieur Koppel. We don't need the broadcast media to get our message across, and we don't need Dr. Balsam and her sexually repressed followers.

WINNY BALSAM:
Why do you call members of HADL repressed?

R. U. SIRIUS:
. . . because we . . .

WINNY BALSAM:
Why is it repressive to want to ensure you the freedom and equality you have today?

R. U. SIRIUS:
Well, if you'll shut up . . .

WINNY BALSAM:
Why do you call us repressed?

R. U. SIRIUS:
Because we can't call you "(bleep)suckers" on television?? I don't know.

WINNY BALSAM:
You see!?!?!?! You . . .

TED KOPPEL:
Now, I'm . . .

WINNY BALSAM:
. . . completely ignore my rights . . .

TED KOPPEL:
. . . gonna have to ask you both . . .

WINNY BALSAM:
. . . and revert to stereotypical . . .

TED KOPPEL:
. . . to watch your language, please.

WINNY BALSAM:
It's language like that, language that reduces a person to a stereotype, that HADL has tried so hard to eliminate from daily American discourse.

R. U. SIRIUS:
Along with the thoughts that go with them.

WINNY BALSAM:
Yes, along with the thoughts.

R. U. SIRIUS:
So you're the Thought Police, comrade?

WINNY BALSAM:
Look, you'll have to accept the fact that the lawless Wild West days of the Internet are OVER. The Marshall has come to town.

R. U. SIRIUS:
The only Marshall we need is McLuhan.

TED KOPPEL:
You're referring to Marshall McLuhan, the Canadian write . . .

{Video: At this point, the satellite feed was interrupted.}

= =
Date: July 23, 1997
From: StJude
To: rusirius
Subject: "it's a drag to be rejectud" <frank zappa>

Fuck, R.U.: a think piece I wrote about kiddie liberation has been
rejected by about seventeen journals, from *Am Jour of Sociology* to
Jack and Jill, from *Whole Earth Axis* to the *NAMBLA Bulletin.* Nobody
wants to hear about it. This aint the version for the academic journal; I know you'd rather see the one from my personal journal, exclusive insider your-eyes-only --

Kid Lib: NAKLA
The kids were rattling their cups against the bars today. They found
some stuff online and started asking about evolution. Took us half an
hour to get 'em calmed down to the point where they could be moved
into the exercise yard.
    Some rural religions don't allow their kids in school beyond the
8th grade. It's not so the kids won't be exposed to pop culture,
which poisons even me, but so they won't learn Science. They're right
about that. Science is about knowledge. Epistemology, like they say
nowadays. So against all this mess they got their kids in protective
custody, just like everyone else has, only they keep THEIR kids in
the high-security wing.

They've got the right. Libertarians are honest about this. They
made their kids themselves -- they paid for them, they own them, they
get to run them. The society tacitly accepts this for all kids --
parents ARE the owners. Does the society at large own the kids? Do
the kids belong to the species? The future?

Currently the society seems to have an amicus curiae kind of relationship with the parent-owned and -operated kids. The society takes
responsibility for those parts of their education that God doesn't

provide -- geography, that kind of thing -- because it's GOD who lays down the philosophy, and all the other stuff of life. When kids, on a chancily need-to-know basis, want to find out about death or violence or sex (the real stuff of primate life) what is supposed to give them the answers? Science, such as it is, or God, such as IT is? And the official answer is -- whichever the kids' owners choose for their property to receive.

It's always been the case. Your sacred duty as a parent is to trans-fer your worldview to your kids, maybe cleaning it up a bit en route. Kids can only absorb so much without getting confused, anyway -- it's like locking out most of the channels on the TV, right? For their own good. What is the alternative? You let them see everything, you got a sex-experimenting, dope-shooting, COP-shooting sociopath on your hands.

Now, I believe in protecting kids. The question is, how to do it? And I think the only way is to give the kids all the info they're gonna need for surviving in an armed world . . .

Heath Kensen's kids were brought up to read and discuss everything, even porn. (What about kids' instant "ewww" reaction? Think back. The impulse is to temporize with a ewwwww, while you get clues about what other people think is gross.) Heath's kids have grown up real sane, although they had a run-in with a flasher that was fairly traumatic. When he flashed them, they were astonished. Stunned. Then they

```
##############
#   /==$=\     #  <- From the High-Tech Fully Electronic Desk
# /))-00(\    #     of R. U. Sirius
# ((( −)))    #
# )))\ /(((   #  −>  rusirius@well.com
##############
```
Date: Oct 9, 1998
To: Hyatt@Ballantine.Books.com, stjude
Subject: Ok. A few thoughts on the continuity of the plop . . .

The melanin pill . . . I piss off ralph@panther.org by showing up at pan-ther headquarters one day in black face after taking the melanin pill. they kick my ass . . . (one diary entry covers the whole thing)

Yes, Trudy, You're SO right. Some semblance of a plot is still in order. Can YOU suggest some ways of handling this? I mean, you have the original plotline, and you know us as well as we know ourselves, by now . . . don't you? You really are like a master director to us, you know . . .

More later . . .

love,
    r.u.

asked him please, stay there for just for a minute, okay? please? because they had to run and get somebody -- some friends who would want
to see him too -- "This is VERY interesting!" Traumatized the erection right off him.

Full disclosure. Freedom of information for kids. What a concept. What
if every kid had full access to the whole thing, the full flood of human information, so questions could be answered at each step, down to
the nitpick? What if every four-yr-old could have every single WHY?
answered to her satisfaction? What if EVERY kid could be educated like
the king's son, by Chiron the centaur, one-on-one tutoring? What if

each kid got issued
her own electronic
centaur that was
fulltime online to
the everything, able
to access it all in
full megalomedia? A
friend centaur that
could carry the kid
on its strong back
while discussing what
humans have said
about the events or
theories in question,
down through the mil-
lennia. A loving pro-
tective very wise
tutor who is also a
half-horse?

The real value of
full disclosure may
be the process it-
self. The kid can
access the REAL
secret -- that adults
don't KNOW the an-
swer. Yet. The
exposure of adult ig-
norance may be key to
the kid's freedom of
mind. It's a bonus

Date: Oct 10, 1998
From: stjude@semi.ram.is
To: rusirius
Subject: master director . . . ?

Egad, sirrah; you lay it on with a trowel

```
##############
#__/==$=\_     #  <- From the High-Tech Fully Electronic Desk
# /))-00(\     #     of R. U. Sirius
# ((( -)))     #
# )))\ /(((  # -> rusirius@well.com
##############
```

Date: Oct 11, 1998
To: stjude@semi.ram.is
Subject: Oh yeah?

Hah! Look at the private note I just got from Trudy . . .

. . .
To: rusirius
Subject: See. You CAN be nice

You can be SO nice, I suddenly remember. Mmmm. I'm going to take the
plot home with me for the weekend and try to come up with some suggestions.

smooches,
     Trudy

ps: don't show this to jude . . .

the kid gets every time she can't get an answer. What a motivator,
for the mind in training! The interactive process can push her to
call up data to support a premise, to argue with the sources and ask
for counterexamples, to do research real time. And the centaur can
demonstrate, real time, what it takes to build an argument, how to
make a deduction from given data. . . . Why, why . . . the kid could
learn to THINK!

= - - = = = = = = = - - - = = = = = = = =
Date: August 1, 1997
From: rusirius@cryptonet.zone3
To: stjude@tweedle.deedle.dum
Subject: Help! Police! I've been deconstructed

This chick pretended to be interviewing me for Entertainment Weekly.
CyberCrit Journal? Sheeesh . . .

Date: Oct 11, 1998
From: stjude@tentacle.black.net
To: rusirius
Subject: SMOOCHES!!!!!

You are a true rat's ass . . .
it makes me proud to call you podner.

She used even
bigger words than
Connie, who got re-
ally pissed because
. . . oh yeah! because
I fucked her. NOW I
remember. No wonder
. . . this thing --

"He seemed to be sin-
gularly apprised of
the totality of American culture." Uh huh . . . quelle embarassing . . .

= =

CyberCrit Journal   August 1997

R.U. Sirius: The Meme Chose cont. from pg 6
by Zumbido-Perro

LOVE FOR SALE
While generally dismissed in academic circles as
a callow and exploitative pop culture representa-
tive of an increasingly radicalized cyberculture,
(Mo Ulrich called him "A caricature of a human
being" in *Whitespace*), Sirius' brilliant and un-
orthodox tactics have also earned occasional
praise in serious publications like the *ICA Journal* and *Critical Inquiry*—where there is currently a raging debate about his use of vernacular
language.

As a self-described icon, RU Sirius has an
interesting relationship with a form of visual
art that has a long historical connection with
the worship of the Divine. Although he described himself as the Icon-at-Large for the
Mondo Vanilli empire, he might be more accurately discussed as one of the earliest icons
representing the worship of the hyper-real.
What fascinates the observer is the self-conscious declaration of the availability of the
RU Sirius image as an object of public vener-

ation. Here he is giving expression to a tendency that will ultimately validate Umberto Eco's contention that western Europe is in the process of returning to a social state similar to the Dark Ages, but with a slight modification: the society becomes a-literate rather than illiterate—non-rational rather than irrational. (Umberto Eco: *Towards a New Middle Ages*, 1972) The self-consciousness of the Sirius icon is also reminiscent of the 1980's mass culture phenomenon called Madonna, who in her behavior-aesthetic and public persona acknowledged the inevitability and, perhaps, even the necessity of relationship through commodification in western society, by resolutely dictating the terms of her own exploitation.

With their first record, *IOU Babe*, Sirius' band Mondo Vanilli makes explicit the relationships between commodity and: love, sex, fame, belief and revolt. The album builds around the song "Love is the Product" (the song is repeated twice, in different forms, on the album. The chorus of the song declaims "the medium is the message/money makes it dance/love is the product/the joke is in your pants"). Like Madonna, Sirius has defined the parameters of his own spectacle. Using the metaphor of western European iconography, one might say that he has become the equivalent of a late Medieval painter, in that he has painted an altarpiece. There is, however, one difference. It's an altarpiece in which he represents himself as the Angel Gabriel bringing good tidings of himself to himself while outside the spectacle and observing it, we—the masses—conditioned into stupor through enforced passivity, look on, grinning like sheep, engaged in an act of hysterical identification with, and worship of, the unreal. And, beyond that, through his simultaneous self-identification with the *Wired 2000* culture of techno-fetishism, we are seduced into waiting, again passively, to be told which of the many new toys would be

most appropriate to acquire in order to maintain our continued identification with—and membership in—the demographic group of our dream-ambitions. We engage in this relationship with the hyper-real in desperation. It is the only reality that we have left, "all other realities," to paraphrase William Yeats, "being estranged or dead . . ."

THE TRICKLEDOWN-THEORY THEORY
Another little-discussed aspect of Sirius' work is his contribution to the field of literary criticism.

During the late Middle Ages—one of the last great periods of mass-mindedness previous to our own—all eyes looked towards the institutional Church for information about what to think and how to behave.

The Church enforced its political power through the dispensation of grace and penance, with its table of deadly sins and cardinal virtues—all of it designed to enforce passivity and maintain the status quo. More importantly, access to power and information was also regulated by the ruling classes of the period through use of language. Vital information was coded in Latin, a language that most people couldn't understand, speak, or read. This code was so important to the elite that initiates into the educational system of the period were required to speak Latin at all times. A system of enforcement, with rewards and penalties, was set up to assure compliance (Charles H. Haskins; *The Rise of the University*, 1926).

During the Renaissance, however, as a result of the introduction of print technology and the reification and distribution of Greek philosophy in Western Europe, the avant-garde began to compose literature using vernacular forms and vernacular language. Writers like Boccaccio, Martin Luther and Miguel de Cervantes began to write works that—in both form and language—subverted the existing social order. As a result, between 1517 and 1521, Martin Luther was able to almost single-handedly undermine the power of the institutional Church in Germany, simply by declaring that the individual has the right and the responsibility to read and interpret the Bible for him- or-herself.

It's ironic that the elitist codification of specialized language was reconstituted as part of the Enlightenment project in the form of "scientific" and academic language; scientific language purporting to carry specialized knowledge necessary for the progress of the western European agenda of control over natural phenomena. In the mid-20th century, this code was questioned by the critics Roland Barthes and Georges Bataille, who identified this type of language as an instrument of political and cultural exclusion. Their critique was, and is, problematized however by a new specialized language that has, in turn, evolved around *them*, and around academic critical theory and the so-called post-modern discourse in general. Of all the writers active in the late 20th century, it is only RU Sirius who has subverted and democratized this code. In his writings, he has consciously and consistently used vernacular English forms to express his insights into the Postmodern condition, describing, for example, the unrelenting and increasing rate of cultural change:

". . . Technology escalates on your very block: Knives turn to pistols, pistols become Uzis. Cocaine turns to crack, crack to nuke. Charles Atlas turns to Arnold Schwarzenegger, 48DD turns to 64GG. Mick Jagger sings "Sympathy for the Devil" on an easy-listening station, and after an evening of techno hard-core sounds, the first Sex Pistols album sounds mellow and quaint . . ." (RU Sirius: A User's Guide to Using This Guide. *MONDO 2000: A User's Guide to the New Edge*, 1992)

In 1997, Sirius made explicit his democratization of critical theory with the song "Trickle Down Theory" on the Mondo Vanilli album (and CD-ROM), *Smell in a Box*. (The song services a double entendre, revolving around Simone Third Arm's excrementally oriented "Cyberpiss Goddess" while at the same time commenting on theory and name-dropping Bataille [Rhymes with "why"]).

The language of RU Sirius can be unpacked as a sign that points toward a new Renaissance. The Florentine Renaissance of the 1300–1400s was a rebirth of human thinking that integrated intellectual self-awareness apart from the mass-mind program of the Roman institutional church. Now Western culture is moving toward an integration of non-tangible and previously poorly described elements of the human experience against the backdrop of the side effects of the Second Industrial Revolution of the 19th century. That revolution, with its unquestioning belief in the idea of progress; its definition of good as the participation of the group in a program of increased consumption of non-durable goods and services through a deliberate appeal to hysterical identification and fetishism has, as a project, failed on a scale that nearly defies language. RU Sirius and Mondo Vanilli—utilizing a strategy that includes embrace of, commentary about, and self-sacrifice as a battlefield for, contending forces within commodity fetish kultur—have made the attempt to decode both the language of the overseers of this project and its mirror reflection in sub-cults. To put it mildly, they have brought both attention and controversy to themselves.

cont. pg. 30

==
Date: 5 Aug, 1997
From: stjude@dark.satanic.mil
To: rusirius@well.com
Subject: FLAMES

Go over to alt.religion.scientology and read the recent postings. It's
hard to believe that a gentle dig at the sincerity of L-ron Hubbard would
whup up this firestorm, but that's life on the Wire ... I just pointed
out that Dianetics/Scientology was the result of a drinking bet that
L-ron couldn't make up a credible cult-follower religion in the course of
one (drinking) night. (I was told this by somebody who knew him.)

Well, I guess L-Ron won, didn't he? I just got a letterbomb on the WELL
from one creduloso. Along with some perfectly-spelled hate email ...

whooooo. that's infotainment.
==
Date: 5 Aug, 1997
From: rusirius
To: stjude
Subject: Re: FLAMES

That is so cool. Maybe I should take Herr Hubbard on? I could use
some clean well-lighted enemies who spell good.

I think I have another stalker, every bit as sloppy as Josephine ...
Yesterday I walked down from MV headquarters for a cup of coffee, and
hey -- wasn't that a Chinese guy bumping into Jo as they both ducked
behind the same mailbox?

But see, if I rile the Scientologists ... then maybe they and the
heathen Chinee and Josephine the empress of the french will all start
to watch each OTHER. Jealously. Leave me some slack ...

Hmmm. I'll call them the Branch L-Ronians? ... Heil Ron Hubbard!?
I'm working on it ...
==
Date: 7 Aug, 1997
From: stjude@flaming-orifice.of.god
To: rusirius@well.com
Subject: it's a nice day ...

think *i'll* just mosey over to talk.religion.mormon and post something dreadful

here's an ecumenical hack that eric invented:

I have just received secret documents that indicate that Lron hubbard
learned, through his meditations, how to travel back in time. On his
first journey he was clutching a bottle of scotch when he was launched
backward . . . >>POP<< he appeared as an apparition in Joseph Smith's
cell in Liberty jail . . . The two of them really hit it off . . .
spent all night drinking and telling yarns . . . and then Joseph bet
l-ron that HUBBARD couldn't make up his own religion and get people
to actually believe it . . . etc etc
this should piss off both mormons AND scientologists equally. i'm
gonna crosspost it . . .

what'll they do? i know about the scientologists -- they'll sicc their
Net Sharks on me. but the mormons?? they used to have the Danites --
the mormon boogeymen, mythical vigilantes who rode out to redress re-
ligious grievances . . . nowadays i suppose the Danites would write me
chiding email. stern email. tsk! they'd say. for shame!
= =
Date: 9 Aug, 1997
From: stjude@dark.satanic.mil
To: rusirius@well.com
Subject: why are we doing this?

because it's fun? well, yes, but i HATE religions. The HADL and their
ilk have pushed me off the edge on this. religion is a giant step
backward for >crackle< mankind . . .

Why not take on religion? Religion's the most visible enemy of cultural mutation right now . . . Look at the HADL -- look at the Conservative Alliance and the Civil Decency People. They're all plus/minus
monotheists, at least in public. I want to bite their monotheistical
ankles. I wanna bite those shins so badly.

The Religious Right's winning only because of the cowardice of everybody else. Scroom! Let's mount a counter-juju. Let's
shake rattle,
and roll!

A retreat to old-time religion means a real failure of nerve in this
culture. The guys who founded this country were Age-of-Reason vision-
aries -- mutants! -- looking to set up an entirely new thing: a culture based on rationality and individual co-operation.

Too bad, the experiment is being shut down. The Bill of Rights is being rescinded by the US govt, right by right -- starting with the right from unreasonable search, and the right to bear arms ... has anybody noticed, aside from those weird dudes in the sticks with rifles? What us worry?

Nah, it's logical ... these ARE harsh times, yes -- anomie prevails, the civil contract no longer holds, violence engulfs us -- something must be done to re-establish order ... Does this sound familiar? Something historical, maybe? So the de facto Martial Law is imposed upon us -- but we're Americans, so it's happening to us slowly, softly softly, with no public declarations.

The founders' Mutant America has become dangerous and must be put down. But that's okay -- we must have Order!

That ole-time religion's *always* been a feature of an Orderly retreat from freedom. As we the people are being disarmed, as our rights and our assault rifles are impounded, we see the Great Packleader reinstated as Commander-in-Chief. Swear in the Lord of Hosts! The Thunderer blesses the new U.S. Congress as He once blessed Adolf and so many previous primate pack-leaders ... O no, is this real? Or have I gone truly paranoid at last???? Well, regardless ... I'm going to carry on. I'm the designated atheist. I intend to persecute all religions impartially -- with extreme prejudice. . . .

AND it IS fun.

===

Kansas City Examiner   October 5, 1997

Right Reason:
Some thoughts on "Robin Hood Day"

by G. Jim Wauren

The streets of Kansas City are still congested tonight. On the evening news, we can see the crowds carrying home their new TV's, hi-fi stereos, and computers, wearing the feral grins of plundering Carthaginians. Perhaps you, gentle reader, are reading this while perched near your own personal spoils—a plush Ottoman, a marble coffee table perhaps. And—reading this, you are bemused. You are at a loss as to the source of my rancor.

After all, you now have three thousand dollars, money that came to you through no sin of commission or omission. Why not, then, use it any way you please? Perhaps you even feel a sense of rebellion triumphant, a feeling of being on the embattled ramparts against the repressive strictures of social order.

Still, the facts remain. Last Tuesday, a grievous crime was committed. A crime not only against the bank accounts of our most productive citizens, but against the integrity of our monetary system—and finally against the integrity and decency of those millions who now enjoy the spoils of this mindless act.

We speak of "Robin Hood Day." We speak of the day when anti-social ingrates, some self-described "hackers," decided that subverting the foundations of our banking structure might be even more fun than sitting around watching MTV.

It was an arbitrary act of economic obscenity, robbing from the "rich"—randomly selected persons with over thirty thousand dollars in their account—and giving it to the "poor"—randomly selected persons with less. Clearly, even by the wiggy criteria of this new leftist, anarchist, technological movement, this is inane. One person may have $20,000 in three different accounts, while another might have $33,000—all in a single account—to his name. And what if the fellow (or woman) with $33,000 is supporting a family of six, and the other fellow is single? This is why—for better or worse—we have such a complicated tax structure, to account for these kinds of distinctions.

Still, I'm sure they are quite amused with themselves, filled with the sort of grinning malfeasance that comes from defacing cathedrals or Federal buildings. Undoubtedly, they style themselves after the sneering pranksterism and Marxist *noblesse oblige* of Abbie Hoffman and other sixties rebels we assumed were long forgotten.

Melodramatic? Perhaps. Still, I ask of you a moment's consideration for those hard-working individuals now looking at three-thousand-dollar debits in their accounts. Facile leftists refer to them as "the privileged," but for many of them and—yes, particularly for the wealthiest among them—their chief privilege is the burden of responsibility. "No loss for them," I overheard one wag offer recently, "It just means they'll have to cancel their trip to Acapulco this year." But these are the men and women who stoke the furnace of our nation's infrastructure—in the executive offices of our major corporations and in the pits of Wall Street. And far worse than the financial hit they took from these hackers last Thursday is the sight of a gleeful public, enjoying the spoils. All this week, our most responsible and productive citizens were getting their statement from the bank of the American psyche. It read, "Account overdrawn. Gratitude expired."

Meanwhile, we endure the sight of the undeserving squandering the unearned. Will any of they who now pirouette in the streets consider using these funds to invest, or spend the money on an education, so they may better their social status? Doubtful.

Still, like Diogenes, I keep vigil, in search of the last honest proletariat. I picture him before his money, with the gnawing sense that the moral fate of this entire country hangs in the balance. And he would be right. He will fish the money from the counter, and obey the ethical imperative. He will do the right thing. He will travel to the nearest country club, find the first captain of industry he can, glumly sitting at the bar wondering if there is any justice in the world—any at all. And he will prove there is.

New York Times Magazine
Sunday October 15, 1997

HIS

Post-Modern Casualty
By Robert Solo

When my son was born I was sure that my relationship with him would be entirely different from the one my father and I shared. I bragged about how much "hipper" than my father I was. My son and I would like the same music, wear the same style clothes and share the same values.

Then Rap music happened. And I was wrong.

And it's getting worse. Now we have Mondo

Vanilli. I find myself longing for the tuneless monotony of just a year or so ago. The youth culture exemplified by this group, in which my son is a zealous participant, has evolved into a technology-crazed cult dedicated to a nihilistic pursuit of the "new" and possessed by maniacal (and paradoxical) demands for free and open global communications while insisting on total privacy and secrecy. My son and I are casualties of that culture.

Recently, upon returning from a prolonged business trip (I was abroad for over three months), I went to my son's room only to find some kind of electronic locking device on his door. I was struck by wave after wave of conflicting emotions: pain, anger, guilt, indignation, mostly confusion. Later, he coolly explained that every individual has a right to privacy and the only way to guarantee that right is through the implementation of mathematics and physics (he meant electronic gadgets I think).

After raising this boy for 15 years, entering his room was like stepping through the looking glass. There were magazines everywhere, some so graphically intense that they dared you to read them. His desk looked like a TV repair shop and his bookshelves were packed with volumes about cryptography, computer network designing and psychopharmacology. We'd come a long way from my adolescent Catcher in the Rye and Playboy. The floor was littered with small empty paper envelopes that appeared to be drink mixes from a health food store. In the middle of this chaos was his computer, the one I paid thousands of dollars for, its screen quietly displaying page after page of nonsense syllables.

My mind reeled. In a confused haze, I stammered something incoherent and retreated to my bedroom.

My wife and I talked into the night. She had seen what was happening. At first she thought it was harmless . . . until the lock appeared two days ago. Since she has no control over him, she anxiously awaited my return.

Unable to sleep, I picked up a newsmagazine. The cover story was about Robin Hood Day.

Two days later, two FBI agents appeared at our door requesting to see my son regarding allegations of illegally accessing bank computer systems. He wasn't home then and we haven't seen him since.

Later the following week six federal agents came with a court order and removed everything from my son's room, computer, disks, magazines . . . even the empty paper envelopes. As I stand bewildered in his bare room, I find myself asking the same question my father must have asked himself over and over. Where did I go wrong?

HIS is a regular column by guest contributors presenting a male perspective on various issues. Bob Soloman is an account executive with IBM-Apple-Snapple.

WIRED 2000   Nov 1997

LIFE'S A BITCH AND THEN YOU FREEZE YOUR HEAD:
Millennium Madness at the Extropy Con

by R. U. Sirius

"Timothy Leary is going to have his head cryogenically frozen when he dies. The theory is that some day something called nanotechnology will be able to bring him back to life. I don't know, but Tim figures what the hell—if it doesn't work, there's always celebrity bowling."
Paul Krassner, 1994

The kids are lined up for about three miles. Well-groomed upbeat youths, carrying their tents, their coolers, their free-radical-killing nutrients and cognitive-enhancing drugs, they patiently make their way by foot up the Sunnyvale, California exit towards the Sunnyvale Hilton. Behind them, the traffic is backed up for about forty miles. The sleepy town of Sunnyvale is not prepared for the deluge, nor is the small Sunnyvale Hilton Hotel, or King Tut, the leader of the Extropy Institute, the group that's sponsoring the event in question, Extropy Con 1997. Why did half-a-million youths from across America unexpectedly descend on this convocation of utopian scientists, technologists and other dreamers dedicated to immortality, self-directed evolution, space migration and the replacement of biological life?

I Think Therefore I Am Privileged and Immortal

POP! Yeah, right . . . Shouldn't fall asleep like that while I'm on the job but it's a gorgeous Saturday afternoon and here I am stuck inside the Sunnyvale Hilton with about sixty extropians. It's a varied and various gathering, but the two main flavors seem to be thin-lipped Aryan types wearing suspendered pants, sports coats, ties and brown shoes; or standard nerd—slightly overweight, mother-dresses-you-funny, bespectacled and abstracted.

The Aryan types are dominating the stage and . . . well, they're talking about something I just can't follow. They're quoting Ayn Rand a lot, and they seem to know how to think. In fact, that's what they're trying to say. They're trying to say that there's a correct and objective way to arrive at TRUTH. Yeah, I think that's what they're saying. And they're libertarian but . . . most people don't know how to think. And, if I understand this correctly now . . . what's the point of allowing for the opinions of those who don't know how to think? I mean, they can have their opinions, sure, but we should gently render those opinions impotent. In fact, I think that King Tut said earlier that the extropians were involved in some process wherein those that know the correct way to think are advancing human thought in a forwardly direction, and those thoughts that don't build on that trajectory are, basically, useless thoughts. I think that's what he was saying, but what do I know? Well, I just don't know *what* I know, but I know what I think. And I think this sucks.

You see, I'm very interested in immortality, self-directed evolution, space migration and extra-biological possibilities. How could anybody who seeks radical change not be? And I know that there are some heavy hitters around. There in the back right corner chair, by the coffeepot, is Dr. Eric Drexler, the dean of nanotechnology. Marvin Minsky, the AI dude, hovers nearby, and somewhere in the middle of the room is Hans Moravec, the cherubic advocate of uploading human consciousness into the computer matrix. I respect these people. I want the technology that's indistinguishable from magic even to the people who've already heard this statement. And that's what I'm here for. To get the reports. THIS is what's happening in the area of intelligence increase. HERE'S the latest advance towards nanotechnology. AND (tah-DAH) the age-reversing intelligence-increasing immune system-boosting aphrodisiac pleasure drug *is* . . .

Like that. I didn't come here to be told how to think by a squad of *Fountainhead*-wielding thin-lipped white boys. Ok. Gotta calm down. Everybody wants to have their own cult. And why should King Tut be any different than me or StJude or the Queen or Dick and Jane over at *Wired 2000*? Ideology's a killer, true, but it sure can generate plot, movement and structure. And maybe later, they'll clue me in on the magic bullet and the trip to the stars. Gotta stick close to the Extropians, cause ya never know.

But right now, it's five hours into this thing and nothing has happened *except* for ideology.

I'm a-goin' home. What the hell. I don't need the Extropy Institute. I can tell you about Extropianism myself . . .

EXTROPUNKIANISM: DEMOCRATIZING OBSCENE AND SCARY GODLIKE POWERS

The basic idea, I mean REALLY basic idea of extropianism is to defeat entropy. Entropy is, of course, the tendency in nature for things to run down. Physicist Erwin Schrödinger used the term negentropy in the 1950s to represent the notion of challenging entropy. Any course other than sitting on your thumb in the mud waiting for disease, or some other creature, to off you is essentially extropian. Which is another way of saying that optimism is natural. So even the most cynical among us is either extropian or blessed with really good maid service. It all comes back to Frank Sinatra's extropian command: "do be do be DO!"

Intelligence-increase drugs? Hey, fuck libertarian principles. PUT 'EM IN THE WATER SUPPLY!!!!

Once you've acknowledged the basic innate tendency among creatures to want to survive, you're on the slippery slope to superhumanity. I mean, wail philosophically about Faust and Frankenstein. Wail to your heart's content. But when they say to YOU, "Lookie here, Chucko. This is the choice. You can die a slow, dreary, and painful death from cancer or you can take this here pill, reverse the aging process, be smart as a whip, fuck four times a day and eat fried pig guts right before bed and not get gas,"—what say YOU?

Ok. Here's a testostimonial . . . 1975. I was 23 years old, living on welfare, convinced that life was essentially worthless, despite the fact that I'd conned this total blonde babe named Erika into

thinking I was some kind of romantic poet in the Rimbaudian tradition, and therefore worthy of a $^1/_3$ share of her goodies (along with the persian juggler and the handsome-but-stupid car mechanic who could sing like Rod Stewart . . . and one time, his dad, actually. Both at the same time, mind you, on a little cot in a back room at the garage . . .). Anyway, one bored night I'd picked up a copy of *Crawdaddy*, my favorite rock and roll magazine—run by ex-yippies and featuring columns by Burroughs and Paul Krassner, for instance . . . There was an article about Dr. Timothy Leary, who had just been released from prison. Now, without wanting to go into a long diatribe about the Doctor, some people connect with the way he thinks and writes and most people don't. For those who don't, the rest of us just seem ridiculous. One's relationship to Timmy's philosophic observations is very much akin to a relationship with drugs. Your neurons are either delighted by the hit, confused and upset by the lack of baseline reality, or you just don't get off.

I'd always connected with Tim's writing, starting in the late 60's, so it was with great interest that I read of his latest travails and his new direction. But this was too weird. Leary was babbling away about something he called SMI2LE—space migration, intelligence increase and life extension. There was this weird picture of him standing on Wall Street amidst the high buildings, smiling and pointing his finger into the air. A 23-year-old nihilistic Ramones fan, living in scruffy, working-class Binghamton, New York, in 1975, I couldn't get the hit. At that time, I thought having a telephone answering machine was a sign of fascistic plasticity. And Leary was talking about high technology and high frontiers. Feh.

So I slept on it, and the next day beautiful Erika came by for a visit. After slappin' skin all afternoon, we smoked some pot and realized that we were starved. So off we headed for Dave's Dogs 'N' Burgers. On the way there, I bumped into my psychotic friends, John Carson and his sidekick in criminality, Igor. We made small talk for a moment (If I'm recalling the timeframe correctly, John's form of small talk at that time was relating his criminal activities to those of Stalin) and then I let it be known that we had to continue on to Dave's. "We need to get some fuel," I said. Well, for some reason, beautiful Erika was delighted beyond words by what she perceived as the reductionism of my calling food fuel. Reductionism was, of course, THE word among rock crits writing about the N.Y. City punk movement of the time. Erika was so excited by how cool I was that she started kissing me up and down and rubbing her crotch to mine. And for some reason, that's when it hit me. "Leary's right!" I said.

She backed off and looked at me nervously. Leary was a name she knew. She'd told me the story of how some friends of hers had dropped acid and read from his version of the Tibetan Book of the Dead *(The Psychedelic Experience)* one night, as a lark. One of them wound up having a powerful "spiritual" experience and had been a lot less hip and reductionist since. Leary was NOT cool.

"The distinction between the poorest and most oppressed human being on the planet and the richest one is not as great as the distinction between the infinitesimal amount of space and time that ANY of us get to experience and ALL space and time. What Leary is proposing is the exteriorization of the infinity that we experience on acid!"

Erika walked faster. She'd only had acid twice and both times had come to the inescapable conclusion that all of nature was just a desiring machine that wanted to fuck her. I could agree with that analysis, as well. Anyway, she figured that I was stoned on pot and that once I got some cow flesh in my belly, I'd come off it.

Well, it was twenty years ago today that Sgt. Peckerhead taught . . . uh, that is . . . I've never quite come off it. The expansion and extension of human possibility itself has remained part of the revolution that I seek. And now there's tens of thousands who speak that language. And there's talk of nanotechnology (the ability to manipulate the structure of matter) happening within this century. (Even Newt Gingrich's into it . . . which is, of course, scary.) There's biotechnology, replaceable body parts, some promising double-blind studies on setting back the aging process and increasing human intelligence, all of it against a backdrop of blinding reactionary idiocy. One recent poll shows that 90% of the American people don't believe in evolution. I'LL say! "Hey, we're so stupid we don't believe in evolution, so how can you expect us to believe in revolution?" Intelligence-increase drugs? Hey, fuck libertarian principles. PUT 'EM IN THE WATER SUPPLY!!!!

==

Date: 10 Nov, 1997
From: stjude@flaming-sword-of.living.god
To: rusirius@well.com
Subject: news of the weird

i've been getting like 5 emsgs a day from (i assume) mormons, saying of course the Danites don't exist and moreover they never DID.

what the hell? you shouldn't say that sort of thing to a natural-born paranoid -- makes me think they did and DO. Makes me wonder if somebody's running a text search grep-demon on UseNet . . . looking for any occurences of the word "Danite" Arrrrhhh.

==
13 Nov, 1997
From: rusirius@CryptoNet.zone3.com
To: stjude@whooowhooowhoo.com
Subject: my sweet lord

I caught my Chinese stalker sneaking around in my neighbor's back
yard. He was carrying some kind of strange device, looked like it
might transmit sound waves or something. He was muttering "nommy
yoho rengate kyo" under his breath. Aha . . . it must be herr schikel-
gruber, the buddha christ! I didn't say anything, and he went
sprinting off . . .

I must admit, I'm starting to think about writing a will. It only
takes one bullet . . . afterall.
==
Date: 6 Dec, 1997
From: stjude@kali.maha.dev
To: rusirius@well.com
Subject: death threats from christians!

And one of the nicest things is that I'm nowhere near their operative
reach . . . I'm clean outside the venue. . . . according to their email
addresses. And we're not traveling to certain sensitive areas on the
book tour . . . we WON'T touch them THERE . . . below the BIBLE belt . . .
will we?

Uh oh—

Too late. And too much fun . . . I shall persevere in my religious
war. Shall I take on your Shiksadrubber?

Let me frighten him to death for you . . . electrodes and needles, in-
deed . . . I'm a not-yet-forsworn buddhist me own self . . . how dare
he threaten you with violence. . . . i'll call him out. i'll tear his
ass UP. . . .
==
Date: 6 Dec, 1997
From: rusirius@well. com
To: stjude@kali.maha.dev
Subject: Re: death threats from christians!

okay by me . . . take the sucker out.

```
===============================================
Date: 7 Dec, 1997
From: stjude@kali.maha.dev
To: rusirius@well.com
Subject: taking him out and . . .

I wonder if I should toy with him . . .

Like this:
My dear Sangha Friend: R. U. Sirius says that you are helping him to
enlightenment. He fears that you are threatening him with physical
harm. If this is true, I'd like to help you overcome your desire to
use unsuitable practices for noble aims. Consider those who offend
against the dharma!

As Sgam.Po.Pa. tells us in the thirteenth chapter of THE JEWEL ORNA-
MENT OF LIBERATION, or THE WISH-FULFILLING GEM OF THE NOBLE DOCTRINE,
which deals with the Perfection of Ethics and Manners,
"Then when they have been burnt with molten metal so that no skin is
left and while fire flames from the nine orifices of the body, they are
pierced with three-spiked weapons from the anus and feet through the
top of the skull and shoulders."

etc etc -- doctrinal quotes laced with the insane nastiness the me-
dieval Tibetans did so well . . .

OR i could just bore him to death for you, if you like.
===============================================
Date: 7 Dec, 1997
From: stjude@blood.atonement.tentacle.black.net
To: Schwarz@christbuddha.com
Subject: you abject poseur!!
Bc: rusirius@well.com

You! You threatened my partner R U Sirius with violence! You apostate
son of a dogpack, you call yourself a Buddhist???
```

```
                                     H
                                     O
                                     W TO MUTATE AND TAKE OVER THE  W
                                                                    O
                                                                    R
                                                                    L
I invoke the power of the Sangha, brother Buddhist. I will make you  D
sorry you were ever reborn.
```

I invoke the power of the Sangha, brother Buddhist. I will make you
sorry you were ever reborn.

Dharma combat to the death!

 "stjude"

```
|| +^+ ||  || stjude@blood.atonement.tentacle.black.net
|| \|/ ||  ||
||  I  ||  || Sangha of The Flaming Yami, Ecumenical
|| /|\ ||  || Vajrayana Local #314
|| +v+ ||  || 8449 St Clair Av Detroit, MI
=====================================================
```
Date: 7 Dec, 1997
Mailer Demon Complaint
Message returned, address unknown
Text of Message Follows:

. . . . .

Date: 7 Dec, 1997
To: Schwarz@christbuddha.com
Subject: you abject poseur!!

You! You threatened my partner R U Sirius with violence! You apostate
son of a dogpack, you

and you're gall-blasted lucky we didn't see this heaaah message, else
you'd be sayin' hello to the next bardo . . .
        watch your ass,
         Bishop Joey

San Francisco Chronicle, Dec 29, 1997, Media Watch

MORE UNDERGROUND HIJINX

The balance between viewer annoyance and viewer delight—quick, turn on the VCR!—is being sorted out by the Pirates of the Air.

Nicely timed ad-slot hacking seems to be easing complaints about interruptions of scheduled fave shows and football games.

So, into our traditional 3-minute commercial breaks are neatly dropped such familiar anti-ads as the one-liner "Insert YOUR message here," with the severely out of focus porn stuff happening in the background, and state-of-the-art computer graphic ad parodies. New is a feature turning up in spots in the evening news and the MONDO VANILLI FUN Show: "The 3-minute Mutant."

1998 LOOMPANICS UNLIMITED CATALOG

THE COMPLETE GUIDE TO ASTEROID LIVING, by John Fisher

With nanotechnology coming on any nanosecond, it may soon be easier to write the program that builds a spacefaring vessel than it is to program your VCR. So, for those who really want to get away from it all, here's an amazing book that describes 1,400 asteroids in our solar system that are perfect for human habitation. Detailed maps show the location, speed and trajectory of each asteroid, so that you can plan your landing. Also discussed are ways of building shelter, growing food, and finding ways to pass the time. The access chapter gives complete contact information for current companies planning independent space missions. There's even a chapter on evacuating in case of a pending planetary collision!

5½ x 8½, 176 pp, more than 50 maps, indexed, soft cover, $19.95. Hypertext, $27.95.

HACKING THE IRS, by Boston T. Partee

If you're tired of the blood-sucking leeches in Washington D.C. draining your economic vitality, this book is for you. Complete instructions on how to hack IRS computers and change your data, all from the comfort of your own home. Includes an easy-to-use computer disk that contains dozens of hacking routines. Contents include: IRS Computing Systems * What Information Do They Have On You? * Phreaking Basics * Making a Call that Can't Be Traced * Once You're Inside * Diddling Form 1040 * Making 1099s Disappear * Changing Other People's Taxes * Sabotage * Covering Your Tracks * And much more!

8½ x 11, 148 pp, includes disk, $34.95. (Please specify Apple or DOS disk.)

COUNTERFEIT E-MAIL MADE EASY, by John Sample

Would you like to send someone a "love letter"—straight from your heart? Here's the EZ way to send e-mail and make it appear to have come from someone else. Covers accessing mail servers; Eudora; Pine; Elm; "From" field, including handle; "To" field; "Return To" field; Signatures; Changing routing information; Sending from a remote system; Forwarding replies; Set-

ting up a dummy mailbox; Covering your tracks; And much more!

5½ x 8½, 160 pp, illustrated with screenshots, $17.95. Hypertext, $24.95.

ELECTRONIC IDENTITY, by Trent Sands

We live in a world where you are known more by your numbers than by your face. Change those numbers and you change who you are. With the right digits, you can reap the benefits bestowed on the privileged classes or avoid the pain of those who are punished. This is a complete guide to your electronic identity. You will learn how information about you is stored—and how it can be manipulated. Covers: Birth Records * Credit Reports * Bank Accounts * PINs, Passwords and Access Codes * Employment Records * Medical Records * Charge Accounts * Social Security * IRS records * Legal Records * Utility Companies * And much more!

5½ x 8½, 225 pp, illustrated, indexed, $19.95. Hypertext, $27.95.

SATELLITE SOCIETY, by Skye Pyrit

Unlock the amazing capabilities of communications satellites. This book is your guide to commercial satellite services that can be used by the common person to send and receive all sorts of goodies. Did you know that the Romanian Satellite Service will sell its capacity to all comers? Now you can avoid FCC regulations by using foreign commercial satellites to: Beam Pornographic Images * Trade in State Secrets * Set Up Your Own Pirate Radio or TV Station * Find Out What's Really Going On in Foreign Lands * Chat with Friends Overseas—For Free! * And Much More. This book provides complete access information for dozens of international satellite companies. It describes all of the services they provide, explaining in simple terms how YOU can use satellites to broaden your horizons.

5½ x 8½, 189 pp, heavily illustrated, soft cover, $17.95. Hypertext, $25.00.

DIGITAL DICK: Law Enforcement in The Age of Computers, by Burt Rapp

Find out how law enforcement officials use the latest technological advancements to find criminals and bring them to justice. Burt Rapp takes us all the way from the station house to super-secret spy agencies and shows us the latest methods for bagging the bad guys. Covers: Hardware (in patrol cars and at HQ) * Software (dozens of programs used by law enforcement) * Security (how they guard access to information) * Training (setting up an intelligence department) * And Much More! Learn how the police listen in to phone calls and intercept data transmissions. Learn about encryption-cracking supercomputers. Learn how the FBI gets immediate notification about suspicious transactions. Anyone interested in modern law enforcement will find this guide invaluable.

8½ x 11, 210 pp, illustrated, indexed, soft cover, $19.95. Hypertext, $27.95.

SILENT DEATH 2: How to Kill with Sound, by R.C.A. Victor

Did you know that you can kill somebody with sonic blasts that are below the range of human hearing? The author is an acoustical engineer with years of experience programming shopping mall systems. In this book, he explains the principles behind sub-audial killing. You will learn how silent but powerful sound waves can liquefy a human brain in seconds. Victor shows you how to construct a sonic cannon that can deliver deadly blasts from a distance of several miles. Now, the same weapon that took out Fidel Castro is available to YOU!

8½ x 11, 140 pp, illustrated with diagrams and schematics, soft cover, $24.95. Hypertext, $34.95.

THE SUICIDE CLUB, by Diane Earley

You've heard about the mysterious "Suicide Club" that has captured the imagination of youth across America. Now go inside with investigative journalist Diane Earley as she gains the confidence of Club members and chronicles their stories. Earley explains how the Club recruits members, and reveals for the first time the suicide pact they must sign with their own blood. She tracks down the source of the "suicide signal," which is used to tell members when their number is up. She interviews several Club members, some of whom she later watches die. You won't be able to turn away from the riveting story of misdirected rebels and the society that let them down.

6 x 9, 280 pp, illustrated with actual suicide photos, $19.95. Hypertext, $27.95.

SERIAL KILLING FOR FUN AND PROFIT, by Theodore Dahmer-Benz

The most disturbing "how-to" book we have ever seen! Read as a real-life serial killer describes how he plies his trade. Covers: Victim Selection * Abduction * The Hideaway * Soundproofing * Torture * Keeping Victims Alive * Trophies * Killing Techniques * Body Disposal * Destroying Evidence * Alibis * Changing Your M.O. * Interstate Flight * Monitoring Police Investigations * Marketing Videos * Shopping a Screenplay * Trial Theatrics * Cashing In on Your Celebrity * Hiding Your Earnings * Winning Parole * And Much More, including a state-by-state summary of murder statutes! You simply won't believe it till you see it.

5½ x 8½, 195 pp, illustrated with rare photos, sample release forms, indexed, $24.95. Hypertext, $35.00.

SECRETS OF SMART DRUG MANUFACTURE, Revised and Expanded Second Edition, by Uncle Fester.

Now you can manufacture smart drugs in your own home using readily available materials and supplies. Underground chemist extraordinaire Uncle Fester guides you through the step-by-step process of synthesizing all your favorite smart drugs at home. Contents include: The Lab * Where to Get Equipment * Buying Precursor

Chemicals * Distillation Procedures * Deprenyl * Melatonin * Nootropil * Pregnenolone * ALC * Piracetam * And Much More, including information on synthesizing smart vitamins and nutrients. Don't let the FDA deny you the benefits of smart drugs—buy this book, and outsmart them all.
6 x 9, 175 pp, heavily illustrated, indexed, soft cover, $24.95. Hypertext, $32.95.

TAZ 22, by Ben Kaliban
This exciting book explores 22 alternative communities that operate outside the view of Big Brother but INSIDE THE U.S. A "TAZ"—a Temporary Autonomous Zone—is a free-form, anarchistic colony of individuals that can relocate nomad-style to avoid regulation or supervision. Some TAZes have re-formed several times, maintaining contact through underground computer networks! Check out TAZmania: 10 years in abandoned warehouses in Detroit, hacking city utilities to support their hydroponic gardens. And VONU: a Green TAZ that operates on forestry land in Washington State. A fascinating documentary about living out of control! Includes tips on choosing your niche, keeping security, tapping into the Grid, much more!
4 x 6, 148 pp, soft cover, $9.95. Not available in Hypertext.

WIRED 2000   Feb 1997

HACKING THE FEDERAL RESERVE
by Patrick DiJusto

In the wake of "Robin Hood Day," people have been questioning the security of the nation's banking system in this electronic age. Eyes are now turning to the computer system that runs the Federal Reserve, the nation's central bank. Are the Fed's systems secure? And what of the rumors that they've already been hacked?

On the morning of November 6, 1997, I received anonymous encrypted e-mail from a remailer in Russia. The author claimed to be a former programmer for the Federal Reserve Bank of New York. S/He claimed to have numerous stories revealing how the Fed computers were pranked from within on a regular basis. If I was interested in hearing these stories, I was to leave a message in the alt.christnet.evangelism newsgroup stating what type of computer, sound card, and modem I had, along with the key phrase "I want to see the bunny."

I posted my agreement, and a week later I got a diskette in the mail containing a beta version of some sort of telecom program and a README.NOW *file. I have no idea how they obtained my address. The README file said I'd receive a phone call on Friday, 17 November 1996 at 23.00 EST. I was to have a microphone and headphones plugged into my sound card, and the telecom program up and running in preparation for the call. This would be a secured system, the file assured me.*

At 23:01 on November 17, my phone trilled. The telecom program clicked into action. I heard the whistle and buzz of a modem connection, a squeal of feedback in my headphones and—finally—a modulated human voice saying "Hello?"

Q. Hello?
A. Can you hear me OK?
Q. Yes, I can. Who are you?
A. We're the guys who sent you this program. There's two of us. Call me The Skipper.
A2. And call me Gilligan.
Q. OK, Skipper and Gilligan. First of all, how does this phone setup work?

SK. It only works with fast computers and fast modems. Basically, you speak into the microphone, the sound card digitizes your voice at about 11K sampling rate, encrypts your voice data, and pumps it out through the modem. The computer on the other end receives that packet, decrypts the data, and plays that sample through the sound card into your headphones. Simple, really.

Q. A scrambler phone. Of course. It sounds like we're talking on a satellite link. There's that kind of delay.

SK. Well, we *might* be. *You'll* never know.

Q. I guess not. OK, I understand that you guys claim to be former programmers for the Federal Reserve Bank of New York, and that you claim to have pranked the Federal Reserve System from within.

SK. Yes.

Q. Did you guys have anything to do with Robin Hood Day?

GI. No. I left the Fed in July, and the Skipper left in September. We were nowhere near the bank in October.

SK. Not that that means anything.

GI. [laughter] Right.

Q. Well, when you guys worked at the Federal Reserve, where did you work?

GI. Mostly in Cash Systems Division. Cash Division is the part of the Fed that deals with cash transactions to and from banks. Cash Systems Division deals with the computer systems that store data about the cash transactions.

Q. What systems does the Federal Reserve use to receive data from other banking institutions via phone lines?

SK. Yeah, OK. One of the systems we worked on was CDS. Cash Data Systems. It was a special software kit we gave to banks. Ran on an IBM PC or clone with a 2400-baud modem. It enabled banks in the New York City area to call up our special CDS computers.

cont. pg. 15

****

hacking fed reserve cont. from pg 17

GI. When we had to make a regular modification to the upload program, we took the opportunity to add a little gem. Our own Trojan Horse. At random dates, at least 28 days apart, the upload program would take the *first* data record in a shipment order and repeat it throughout the whole order. So if a bank asked for a million in fifties, 2 mil in tens, and 5 mil in twenties, the upload program would change it to a million in fifties, a million in fifties, and a million in fifties.

SK. Remember, banks would normally order up to 75 million dollars at a time through CDS.

GI. So we're talking major fuckups, here.

Q. But that kind of hack seems trivial to detect, doesn't it?

SK. Not really. We were running a database on the AS/400 that had this kind of problem ALL the time. Whole data files would suddenly have a thousand repetitions of the first record. AS/400 operators used to have to do backups three, four times a day. So our pranks were always attributed to an AS/400 error. Remember, the data on the PS/2 was fine.

One electromagnetic pulse device . . . would have knocked out the Federal Reserve Bank . . . and the AMEX and NASDAQ stock exchanges. Poof!

Q. So what would happen?

GI. Pandemonium. The Fed's busiest time is from November, when people start their Christmas shopping, to April, when the tax returns come in. We happened to start our little gem in October 1995, and kept it running until May '95. Luck, really.

SK. Tell the container story.

GI. Oh, geez, yes. The container story. That was a classic. Well, the last week in November, a bank in New Jersey ordered some empty containers along with their currency. Containers are big plastic boxes, about one meter cubed, that we use to ship currency. Everyone wanted empty ones at the beginning of the Christmas season, so they could ship their excess money back to us more easily. So this bank placed an order for two empty containers, along with about ninety million dollars in different denominations. Of course, that was the day our little gem decided to go to work. It multiplied the request for two empty containers and ignored the request for the money. The AS/400 dutifully printed out a shipping order for fourteen empty containers to be delivered to New Jersey.

SK. That one made the papers.

GI. Yeah. When the procession arrived at the bank in New Jersey, the manager got really pissed. He started throwing things. It was cool.

SK. Yep. That was the high point for that Trojan Horse.

Q. If a guerrilla gang wanted to do something to the Federal Reserve to damage the U.S. economy, what would they have to do?

SK. They'd have to get a time machine. They missed their chance. There was a period between 1987 and 1993 when an underground gang could have destroyed about 15% of the United States' economy with one EMP [electromagnetic pulse] device. All they needed to do was set off an EMP at the corner of Nassau and Pine Streets in New York City. That would have knocked out the Federal Reserve Bank, two or three other major banks, and the AMEX and NASDAQ stock ex-

changes. Poof! All the hypercritical liquid money they had would have vanished. Without a trace. Just gone out of the economy.

Q. Geez. And now?

GI. Nowadays the computer centers are more spread out. Some are in Manhattan, some are in New Jersey, some in Connecticut. A revolutionary group would have to make several raids on widely dispersed centers. It's not worth it.

Q. What other Fed secrets do you know?

GI. Hmmm. You want to hear my opinion of the REAL reason that the design for the $100 bill was changed?

Q. I thought it was to make the bills harder to counterfeit.

SK. Yeah, well. In 1992, a secret House Republican task force on terrorism came out with a report stating that bogus $100 bills were being printed in the Iranian mint, as part of Tehran's plan for economic warfare against the United States. These bills were beautiful. Whoever did them managed to duplicate the paper and the ink used in U.S. currency—

GI. The phony bills weren't setting off the counterfeit detectors at commercial banks.

SK. Hell, some of the counterfeit bills weren't even triggering the detectors at the Fed, which are much more sensitive. The Fed had to refit their detectors with extra sensors.

Q. How do these sensors work?

SK. The ink in U.S. currency is slightly magnetic, with a special magnetic pattern that can be read by special detectors on a bank's currency counting machines. If the machine doesn't detect the magnetic pattern, it spits that bill out.

cont. 18

Date: March 13, 1998
From: pdijusto@domeidea.com
To: stjude@mondovan.com
Subject: Lookie here!!!

You may have already seen this. Persons unknown liberated it from
fbi.gov!!!!!!!
-x-x-x-x-x-x-x-x-x-x-x-x-x-x-x-x-x-x-x-x-x-x-x-x-x-x-x-x-x-x-x

Federal Bureau of Investigation
OPERATION COINTELPRO II
Transcript 970311MV-WSB-TL-T

The following is an edited transcript of information obtained at a
party in an abandoned warehouse on 560 Folsom St., San Francisco, California, on the night of 11 March 1998. This particular conversation
took place between William S. Burroughs and Dr. Timothy Leary. The purpose of the party was to celebrate the release of the musical recording
VANILLI DECADENCE by the group Mondo Vanilli (ref. 970311MV).
    This transcript was based on a video recording. Audio was obtained
with a Sunbeam laser vibration apparatus. The conversation was ex-
tracted from background noise using two Nakamichi PS-2000 Noise Elimination processors. Subjects have been identified by visual and audio
evidence and by voiceprint identification.

L: Bill! Bill Burroughs!
[Pause of six seconds. Subject Burroughs appeared confused.]
L: I'm Tim Leary.
B: Who?
L: Leary. Tim Leary.
B: Oh, yes. Sit down.
L: Thanks.
[Pause of three seconds]
L: Nice party.
B: Sucks.
[Pause of four seconds]
L: Lots of pretty girls.
B: Lots of pretty boys.
L: Oh yeah, I forgot. [pause] At least the kids are dressing nicer
nowadays. Have you noticed that? Kids are dressing nicer.
B: What?
L: Grunge seems to have died out. I never liked grunge fashions.
B: What are you talking about?

L: You know. The backwards baseball cap and the lumberjack shirts.
B: Yeah. [Pause] In my day, lumberjack shirts stood for something.
L: You've got that right.
[Pause of three seconds]
L: Lots of people here.
B: What?
L: I said there's lots of people here. It's pretty jammed.
B: So's my rectum.
[Pause of four seconds]
L: Tell me something, Bill.
B: What?
L: How the hell did you get a commercial deal? I've been itching for a commercial deal for years.
B: WHAT commercial deal?
L: Your commercials for Nike, a couple of years ago.
[Pause of five seconds.]
L: You remember, don't you?
B: I'm tryin' to think. Fuckin' drugs.
L: You didn't say a thing about sneakers, is maybe why you can't remember it.
[Pause of two seconds]
B: Nike?
L: Nike, Adidas, one of those sneaker companies. You didn't say shit about the sneakers.
B: What'd I say?
[Pause of five seconds]
L: Damned if I can remember, Bill.
[Pause of three seconds]
B: I did a music video once.
L: Did you?
B: Yep.
L: What was the name of the band?
B: Ahh, fuck knows, Timmy.
L: Jesus.
B: They showed it to me when it was finished. Something about tornadoes. Kid puked blood in the sink. Shit. Used to be, I'd only see pictures like that if I was on junk. Now it's all over the goddamn TV.
[Pause of four seconds]
L: I made a record album with Jimi Hendrix once.
B: Jimmy who?
L: Hendrix. Guitar player.
B: Colored guy? Schvantz a yard long?
L: That's him.

B: I heard of him. He's dead, right?

L: Oh, twenty, thirty years now.

B: They're dyin' off, Timmy. They're all dyin' off . . .

L: Well, we're still goin' strong, you and I.

[Pause of four seconds]

B: Fuck off, Tim.

[Pause of six seconds]

B: You know, now I remember. A bunch of Chinks, Japs, videotaped me talking about technology. They said something about saturation marketing to the basketball crowd.

L: Yeah, that's it! You appeared on a small TV screen on the regular TV screen, and you were saying . . . um, something . . . about technology.

B: Who fucking remembers? Half the time I can't remember to unzip before I piss.

L: I know that feeling.

B: And you want to do a commercial?

L: Well, yeah. I'm pretty good at selling.

B: Can't sell drugs on TV, Timmy. [Laughter]

L: You've never worn sneakers in your life.

B: Fucked a smooth skinned Arab boy who never took his sneakers off. Proudest possessions he had. That and a cock like a police baton.

L: Did that ever really happen?

B: Does it matter, Timmy?

L: I guess not.

[Pause of five seconds]

B: They said they chose me 'cause I was the one person who has been regarded as cool through the 1950s, 60s, 70s, 80s and 90s.

L: I didn't become cool till 1963.

B: You've got a ways to go, Timmy. Ah, fuck. They said something like seven-eighths of the viewers didn't even know who the hell I was.

L: New generation, Bill. A couple of new generations, actually.

B: Thought I was just some old guy in a commercial.

L: Yep. That's the problem. They were marketing you to Generation X.

B: Generation Who?

L: X, Bill. Generation X. Folks just now plunging into their thirties. Never read a book in their lives.

B: Fucking savages.

L: I follow you. Used to be, you could change the world with a book. No more. These kids nowadays are the greatest solipsists in history.

B: What?

L: Solipsists, solipsists. That means they don't believe anything they didn't think up themselves.

B: I know what it means, I just didn't hear you.

L: Okay.

B: Christ.

[Pause of seven seconds]

B: So what are you saying? These kids are more introspective than kids usually are?

L: Um-hmm. Not introspective. Self-absorbed. To the point where it's pathological.

B: Hey, I only wrote about what was going on inside my head. Nowhere else. That's either solipsism or jerking off.

L: Yeah, but Bill, you were pretty fucked up at the time, too. Remember that.

B: I was that.

L: Me too. And these kids know that. And they wonder why they should listen to two fucked up old men.

B: Well, because . . . I don't know.

[Pause of seventeen seconds]

L: You want another -- what is that, whisky and soda?

B. Thorazine. Whatever they got.

L: Be right back.

[Subject Leary leaves]

==

Voices from the Net
APRIL 1998

G!rlie Cooper: The CyberCowGirl Philosophies

The exploits of the Cyber-cowboys are legend -- the infamous Space Shuttle prank, and the widely criticized Tom Brokaw incident particularly stand out. That was several years ago, before they went deep underground. In this interview, one of the most infamous cybercowhands surfaces to tell us about her history and to talk philosophy. The going gets a bit heavy here, boys and girls. You may want to fire up your SmartProfessor and 20th Century Political Philosophy.

   Nolan Void

Q: Let's start with your pseud.

G!rlie Cooper: I stole it, actually. About 5 years ago I was doing a little *Let's Go Europe* thing with Johnny Climax, and we took in a TV bar in Amsterdam. All the usual female impersonators were doing Marilyn Monroe, Joan Crawford, that sort of thing ... when all of a sudden, Girlie Cooper came on stage -- a girl playing Gary Cooper playing a drag queen. It was really quite brilliant. Climax called it meta-gender-bending (say it three times, fast). I grabbed the name for my pseud.

Q: So you were into the western imagery even before the Cyber-cowboy movement?

GC: Cyber-cowboy *movement*?!! No such thing. There are cyber-cowboys.

And there's the discovery of the cyber-cowboy by the underground
e-zines. Sometimes people think that the discovery of something in media
marks the beginning of its existence. The way I see it, the moment of
discovery by the underground media (I don't care if its _Phrack_ or
Scream Baby or whatever) is the beginning of the end. The discovery by
mainstream media (e.g. _Time_) is the last nail in the coffin.

Q: This isn't the first TAZ you've inhabited. Give us a bit of your history.

GC: At thirteen, I saw *War Games.* That was it. I figured ... girls can
do that too. So I got my parents to buy me a modem. Some of my hacker
friends at school clued me in on some of the elite BBS's (like Shadows-
pawn, Metal Shop Private, and Digital Logic) where, for example, the LOD
manuals were eventually published. I was particularly good at hacking the
IBM VM/S system. I pretty much memorized Lex Luther's manuals. I really
got to know that system. Of course, if I knew then what I know now, I
would have spent more time hacking UNIX. Live and learn.

Q: But you were never busted.

GC: No. The boys got busted. Us girls almost never did. The problem with
the guys ... well, they had two problems, actually. First of all, any
time they successfully hacked a system, they had to run around and give
each other high fives and tell the world about it. Second, they had a
tendency toward destructive hacking. Hacker girls would enter a system,
explore it, and leave. No one even knew we were there. It was a good way
to learn about computers. Better, anyway, than sitting in a computer
science class with a bunch of geeks and a patronizing greasy professor
staring at your tits the whole class.

Q: So, is there a Cyber-cowboy take on feminism?

GC: Sure, but what I have to say on the topic is of no more intrinsic
interest than, say, what dOk HOLOday has to say.

Q: We'll ask dOk the same question. Promise.

GC: Hah. O.k. Fair enough.

First, distinguish between what "feminism" means on the street and what
it means in academia. On the street, it means equal pay for equal work,
reproductive rights, that sort of thing. And then we might look to the
academy for an analysis of the root causes of gender discrimination. But,
of course, we end up disappointed. However radical their pretenses, the
academics are basically baby-sitters ... stooges of the vested interests.
The theoretical feminists are no exception. Continental feminism is the
biggest disaster in this regard. You look at work by someone like Kris-
teva, and you want to ask her "what the fuck is all this *Freud* doing
here? Freud was the biggest sexist pig in all of intellectual history!
What do his half-assed theories have to do with feminism?" Also, I don't
consider it useful to the liberation of women to have this industry
called "feminism" that generates slogans like "the nation-state is phal-
locentric." The worst is this whole idea that women think differently and

are more compassionate. You know the rap. Men are cold and rational and logical. Women are intuitive and nurturing and cuddly. There's no evidence for that crap. It's just an intellectual doctrine designed to reinforce comforting 1950's stereotypes.

Q: On the other hand, you yourself pointed out a distinction between boy and girl hackers.

GC: We all hacked systems the same way. The fact that we didn't have testosterone coursing through our bloodstream doesn't mean that we *thought* differently. It just means that we didn't have to download digitized nudes all day long, and we didn't have to give high fives and butt heads every time we successfully hacked a system. There's a difference between thinking differently and acting differently.

Q: Well ranted. Let's turn to some of your thoughts on Marxism and political philosophy.

GC: Finally!

Q: We save the best for last. You've seen the dOk HOLOday's piece where he calls Marx a stooge?

GC: Yes. Well, dOk went a bit over the top on that one. Let's give Marx the benefit of the doubt and say that he wasn't in anybody's pocket. What do we have? Well, we have a theory that's so wildly implausible that even so-called Marxists can't take it seriously. The real atrocity is, as dOK points out, that people believe that the intellectual space is exhausted by Marx and Adam Smith.

Q: But there are innumerable variations of Marxism.

GC: Yes. "Infinitesimal variations within a definite space." To Bernard Henry-Levy, this spells elegance. To me, it spells boredom. It's like staying at home and counting the cracks in your wall. You can do that forever if you want, but in the end the only thing you know about is the topology of the walls of your room.

Q: You mention Henry-Levy. What's your take on his work?

GC: His work ... you mean his writings? Well, from a sociological perspective I suppose that *Barbarism with a Human Face* was important because it made it possible for European intellectuals to criticize Marxism. I don't know *how* it accomplished this -- certainly not through argumentation. He knew how to press the right buttons, I guess. But the real question is, why should the critique of anything *need* to be made acceptable?

Q: Let's be fair. He exploded the myth that Eurocommunism was benign.

GC: *That* wasn't the myth. The real myth, which persists today, is that communism and capitalism were oppositional. Not true. Look at Italy. The Christian Democrats go out and Craxi and the Communists come in. Nothing changes. Why? Because both parties are drawing on members of a single elite club for their leadership. The Christian Democrats, the Communists, the Mafia, the Vatican, the secret service, and the P2 Masonic Lodge have all been shown to be bundled together in one neat, money-

grubbing package. People laugh and say, well ... it's those Italians.
It's just that Italy is the one place that this crap has been exposed.
Italy is really ahead of the curve on this one -- thanks largely to
judges (like Falcone) who get blown away for their efforts.
So I'm sorry, but I'm not giving Bernard Henry-Levy credit for jack.
Q: Most commentators take you and the Cyber-cowboys for libertarians.
GC: Either they haven't read a single thing we've written or their compre-
hension skills are nil. Libertarians are all for freedom of expression,
which is cute of them, but they're tied to a ridiculous doctrine ...
Laissez-Faire economics. What's the point of the free discussion of economic models if you're already fully committed to one (and a silly one at
that)? But the libertarians are just a circus side-show. Lots of the best
hackers, of course, are libertarians. But the economic part of their package is actually LESS popular now that it's been largely adapted by the
U.S. Congress. That's for sure.
Q: Ouch! O.K... . one last question. What happens to the Cyber-cowboy
when cyberspace is tamed and the suburbs take over the terrain?
GC: Yes. Well, aside from the HADL, that appears to be the stated goal
of certain more seemingly benign organizations taming the electronic
frontier. I don't see it happening. The problem with the old west was
that you had finite land space and a rapidly expanding population. Cyberspace doesn't have those limitations. It's as if the frontier is expanding faster than the population. The American Continent was bounded.
Regions of cyberspace leap into existence even as we explore it.
Maybe the thought barons can wrest control of cyberspace in their effort
to maintain control over the flow of information and knowledge. They're
sure trying. And *failing.*

Wired 2000   May 1998

Designs for the Future

THE NSDAP NEW SCHOOL OF DESIGN ART AND PERFORMANCE

INTERVIEW BY EVAN GODLESS
PHOTOS BY Heinrich Vanna DonnWhiten

In Society of the Spectacle, *Guy Debord ob-
serves that, just as early industrial capitalism
moved the focus of existence from being to
having, post-industrial culture has moved that
focus from having to appearing. If this is so, if
appearance has truly become the central focus
of existence, then by co-opting fashion, the
art of appearance, it becomes possible to seize*

the means of social organization and control.

*One group that seems to have taken advantage
of this idea is the Oakland-based New School of
Design, Art and Performance. Founded in the late
eighties, this cabal of designers and artists first
came to prominence with their 1995 guerrilla theater piece, "This is Not a Pipebomb." Since then,
their Eschaton fashion designs have gradually be-*

come a familiar sight on the chests and butts of the young and fashionable. While the Underaged and Underground seem taken with their bold graphic design, many others tend to be outraged by what they see as a cynical and blasphemous fusion of 60's nostalgia and Nazi iconography.

The NSDAP is currently (I'm conducting this interview on April 11) co-sponsoring Mondo Vanilli's highly controversial Decadent Art Show at the Los Angeles Olympic Stadium; they were responsible for the highly acclaimed Torchlight Eschaton fashion rally and Bordello of Light. However, whether these events will accompany MV on the road is anyone's guess, especially after the near-riot that followed last Friday's opening performance.

I caught up with the NSDAP at the Kommisar Suite of the infamous Potempkin Arms, the Sino-Russian brothel/casino/hotel (and former Soviet aircraft carrier), that floats in international waters west of Los Angeles. Chief Ideologist Dada Vinci, Fashion Director Multi Medea, and Cinematographer M.A.O. receive me in their hotel room, dressed in full NSDAP Couture: black

jacket and boots, tie, Sam Browne belt, and red-and-black armband. Gestapo chic. Under the circumstances, their multiethnicity seems jarring—like Himmler at the family seder. The three, however, are disarmingly engaging hosts.

WIRED 2000: Things in Los Angeles still haven't calmed down from last Friday's show. Fringe elements of the Human Anti-Degradation League have threatened to *nuke* your next performance.

(Laughter all around)

MULTI MEDEA: The Human Anti-Degradation League couldn't nuke a burrito!

M.A.O.: This is typical for our performances. We're used to getting death threats from around the world.

DADA VINCI: Well, the shit has really hit the fantasy *this* time. We always say to our audiences, "If you can't stand the heat, stay out of the ovens!"

MM: Fashion is an endless cycle of birth, death, and rebirth. The NSDAP offers liberation from this wheel of sartorial *samsara*, stylistic peace in the static cool of classical forms. NSDAP ready-to-wear production art is the *antithesis* of international high fashion. We reject utterly the continuing charade of seasonal change. We seek not to extract

© 1995 Bart Nagel

maximum profit from the idle rich, but to provide maximum value to the working poor and permanent wave. Why kill yourself following the everchanging capitalistically-motivated dictates of the self-appointed fashist leaders when you can rest in the security of durable designs approved by a collective of socially responsible artists?

W2: Why mess with Nazi iconography?

MM: The ends justify the memes. The DisArmband, for instance, employs the swords into plowshares principle. We alchemically transmute darkness to light. Hitler didn't invent the armband, nor the colors black, red, and white, yet he seems to have been granted a patent for them in perpetuity. Hitler still has power as long as his definitions of terms are observed. The NSDAP resolved to challenge him, and has successfully liberated a useful fashion accessory—and the single most powerful color combination.

DV: The original peace sign has a funky, furry feel to it and it reeks of patchouli. It carries many mellow, nostalgic connotations that have nothing to do with eliminating war. The nomenclature of a romantic, tribalistic, innocent past is out of place in a neo-classical, technological, and sophisticated present. The original peace sign is graphically weak,

uninspiring and abstract. New times demand new symbols. The *Sprocket*, a peace sign with a gear around it, symbolizes not only peace but work, progress, and technology. The Peace Eagle co-opts the archetypal totem animal of the nation-state and posits a noble, self-possessed condition beyond war.

DV: Let us be clear that an "emotionally loaded symbol" simply reveals a psychopathology. The symbol is an arbitrary designation for an object or idea with no real or permanent connection to it, and to imagine otherwise is madness. People who become upset at artworks like *Piss Christ* do so because in their unbalanced minds a cross soaking in urine is equivalent to urinating on the baby Jesus himself. To a sane person, the Disarmband, Sprocket, and Peace Eagle present no contradiction because playing with symbols has no direct relationship to the things symbolized. Full understanding of this principle results in enlightenment; not understanding it constitutes genuine mental illness. The real relationship between Nazism and our work is that anyone unable to separate the signifier from the signified is a Nazi—using Nazi as a generic term for an irrational fanatic.

DV: The final solution to the problem of racism is deracination through miscegenation.

© 1995 Bart Nagel

```
================================================
Date: 5 May, 1998
From: stjude@glory.glory.hallelu.jah
To: rusirius@well.com
Subject: persecuting the religious, continued

The mormons are aroused. I just got a charming enote from a mormon
hacker. (!) Here's his dot.sig -- notice he's spoofing the address of
the Latter Day Saints main org . . . cute. and that's a beehive, which
is sort of the mormon logo . . .
Moroni's been telling me to lay off -- yes, indeedy, for *GOD'S*
sake.
Moroni's cute, yet somewhat scary:
                      ##########
                 #####@@@@@@@@@@@@######
              ###############################
            ### moroni@salt-lake.temple.lds.com ###
            ##########################################
            #######  Hacking for    +    Working  #######
            ######    Jesus Christ   +    For The 7th  ######
            #####  And Joseph Smith  +    Dispensation  #####
            ##############################################
            ###  "I soon go to rest in the paradise of God"  ###
            ################### Mor.10:34 ###################
            ##############################################

oooo. . . .. True fanatics are always suicidal.

all these putative mormons have been very civil and sweet . . . I've
explained to them that I'm not persecuting them ESPECIALLY -- it's
just that they're a RELIGION and i'm taking on all religions in non-
alphabetical order . . . Nothing against them PERSONALLY . . . they're
nice people . . . some of my best lovers are Saints . . . (this is
true) etc etc
================================================
Date: 5 May, 1998
From: stjude
To: RUSirius
Subject: uh oh. last night, this . . .
-----------------
From: nephi@oasis.wendover.nv.us
To: stjude@well.com
Subject: Insults.
```

Lady, you don't know what you've been messing with.

If you had the sense that God gave you you'd go back to your book
writing and leave alone that which does not concern you.

(signed) A friend who has friends

"Slay him, for the Lord hath delivered him into thy hands;
Behold the Lord slayeth the wicked to bring forth his righteous purposes" 1 Nep. 4:12-13
————————————————————>-8 Cut Here 8<———————————————

ah aha.
so is this the real deal? is this a Danite? Or a Danite wannabe?
(Vigilantes ARE volunteers, after all.)

wendover's the nevada gambling & sin place over the border from utah
. . . maybe this is where the mormons interface with the Mob? . . . or
ARE the Mob? what a concept!

now i'll have to tell you this joke . . . mormons think it's hilarious --
how do you distinguish among jews, protestants, and mormons?
jews don't recognize jesus, protestants don't recognize the Pope, and
mormons don't recognize each other in Wendover.

= =

SUMMER 1998
CHOMP! Yer Musek Zine

July 1998   Pp. 8–9
Alice Falls Down Another Rabbit Hole
by Alice

MONDO VANILLI WIPE YER FEET

Alice went down the Hole again last week, kiddies dear, slipped the lock on the enclave gate and Got Out. Mumsie and Deadbeat were asleep or tranqued to the nine-and-a-half mark while the cablebox poured out the Reverend Salvatore James and the Salvaged Souls Gospel Choir un-heeded all over the floor. . . .

Alice went to the Mondo Vanilli event. Even rabbitholes were never this much fun. How can we count the ways? She loved it with scratchy eyes and red-rimmed glances when the smoke fountain powered up beneath the grid she was crossing. She loved it with muscular empathy as she watched the naked boy on top of the throbstax trancedancing to the crystalline wall of careening metalshriek. She loved it with whirling skirts (edged with little bits of broken mirror carefully glued on by hand. Took all damn afternoon. That Alice is one dedicated fashion puppy.) and flying braids, ten kerjillion of them, dipped in the latex tank over by the far door, hardened over now and standing straight out from her head. And she loved it with her ears, down the slippery tubes into her soul, every word slipping in nice and smooth, driven by fourteen hundred pounds of pressure per square inch.

Words flashed across walls, ceilings, bodies, stax, the band . . . words blurred the outlines of human bodies, instruments. . . . were they fusing? This is what Alice wrote in her journal, dear children of the rip'n'tear, thrash'n'spill. These are the words she saw printed everywhere in ephemeral laser letters: "Must be negotiated must be negotiated must be negotiated" "Take the SLEEPING PRINCE NOW!" "sacred noise for sweet revenge" "The Fuehrer's Favorite Breakfast Cereal is You!" "tomorrow tomorrow, pretty face, tomorrow tomorrow" "A long wire makes a bitter gift"

Alice danced with the Mad Hatters, or were they Mad Hacks? No one could tell. MV was cranking out noise like a demented sausage factory. Extrusion. Revolusion. The sound-crew's hair was on fire, little holoflames blue and orange. Alice wandered over to the Wrap Bar and watched three boys get wound together. The techs were careful to keep their faces clear and breathing passages unobstructed before they placed them on the pedestal. Alice thought about it. Alice noticed the little phallic protrusions instibonded onto the familiar logo-dolls and trademarked ugly-cute animal shills for Better Living Through Mindless Consumption, and giggled. The DadaCapitalists had been busy little beavers again. Some were in use. She moved on, back into the maelstrom on the main dance slab. . . . What can she tell you? It was pulses of sound so far down

to be SLICEABLE, it was . . . Mondo Vanilli and what more do you want, Jack? No time for it? Then jack the fuck OUT, Jack, and clear a port for somebody with half a clue. And yeah, she made it home by dawn, dress in rags, cut over one eye half-clotted across her jagged eye-paint. And Mumsie and Deadsie were still snoozed in the Beneficent Parental Cocoon-Womb. She imagined them in there, side by side like little packaged cakes on the shelf. No need to stamp the expy date; they'll keep. They'll never change. Ain't preservatives a wonderful thing? Better societies through chemistry. Alice took off her Hole clothes, what was left anyhow, and sat there crosslegged in her smeared pale skin, and wrote this just for you. You know what to do, then do it. And if you don't, then jack the fuck OUT, Jack, is all Alice has to say. See you down the Hole. NEXT time.
Alice

"Travels with Marvin: Swashbuckling around the world with Marvin Minsky"

by Patrick Dijuju

June 1998, justpat and Sacred Cow Mutilators Publishing

Chapter 4   Marvin Gets Promoted

Slowly regaining consciousness, I opened my eyes to see chunks of the Amazon jungle framed in the remains of the aircraft window. Remembering where I was, I tentatively tried to wiggle my toes and was gratified to feel them scraping the inside of my boot. One fear conquered: I wasn't paralyzed. I moved my legs a few inches from side to side. They seemed fine. I diffidently opened my legs wider and felt my crotch. Everything was in place. Another sigh of relief. I looked across the small aisle. Marvin Minsky was sitting bolt upright, fully conscious and still strapped in his seat. The crash had torn huge rents in the fuselage of the plane, and Marvin's eyes darted around the remains of the cabin and out into the jungle in great sweeping arcs. He resembled a bird of prey on the lookout for anything moving.

"Hey," he shouted at me when he saw I was awake, "are you all right?"

"I seem to be," I replied.

"Yeah. I figured when you grabbed your crotch you were OK," he said. "That seems to be part of the algorithm."

"What algorithm?"

"What appears to be the 'Self Test Upon Regaining Consciousness after a Life Threatening Injury' algorithm. You wiggled your toes first, didn't you?"

"Yeah," I said.

"So did I. Then you checked to see if your legs worked, and then you grabbed your crotch."

"Yeah," I repeated.

"So did I. In that order. You were about to check your head, and save your torso for last, weren't you?"

"Yeah," a third time.

"So did I. The algorithm is obviously a collection of smaller building blocks of activity hardwired into our brain. Wiggle the toes. Check the legs. Scope the balls. Pretty interesting. By the way, you have—or you had—a bloody nose."

I reached up to my face and felt around. My beard and mustache felt hard, crusty and dry. I had obviously had a nosebleed that stopped some time ago. How long had I been unconscious?

"How long have I been unconscious?" I asked Marvin.

"We crashed about an hour ago. Assuming you lost consciousness at or near the moment of impact, about an hour," Minsky replied.

I had a headache that didn't seem to be centered in any specific place in my brain; it seemed to be everywhere in my head at once. An hour was plenty of time for a brain concussion to begin its voodoo. For some reason that really bothered me. My brain is my second favorite organ, and to think of it bruised or bleeding upset me greatly. I looked around the remains of the fuselage. "Where's McKenna?" I asked.

"About time you asked," Minsky replied. "He went out to reconnoiter, I think he said. Apparently he's under the impression that he knows, and can speak to, the native people of the area."

"Well," I said, unstrapping myself, "I don't want to sit around here." I jumped to my feet. I opened my eyes. I was on my back, staring at the ceiling of the plane.

"Don't stand up too quickly," Minsky said, when he saw I had regained consciousness once more. "I'm guessing that you've got a bad concussion. You'll be prone to fainting for the next few days."

There was a rustle in the leaves outside the cabin. Terence McKenna stepped out of the jungle and hurried to the remains of the airplane.

"Marvin!" he called. "I've found them!"

"I have no idea what he's found," Minsky whispered to me.

McKenna stuck his head through one of the holes in the fuselage and saw me lying on the floor. "Hello," he said. "Glad to see you're up and about. If you are, that is." He turned to Minsky. "Marvin," he said breathlessly, "I've found some indigenous people of this tropical rain forest."

"How nice," Minsky said dryly. "Can they get us to civilization?"

"Oh, you're such a reductionist," McKenna snapped.

"It's my job," Minsky replied smoothly.

There was another rustle in the jungle, much softer this time, and as if by magic, two native men appeared in our clearing. McKenna pulled his head out of the plane and looked at them.

Minsky stood up and was about to exit the plane when McKenna stopped him.

"Let me, Marvin," McKenna said. "I know how to talk to these people."

"Hi," he said, extending his hand in greeting toward the natives. "Koyan teki. Koyan teki." The natives looked at McKenna, then at each other.

```
##########################################################
######### • Trudy B. Hyatt • #########
######### • Editorial Assistant • #########
######### • Hyatt@Ballantine.Books.com • #########
##########################################################
```
Date: March 29, 1999
To: rusirius@well.com, stjude@well.com
Subject: Out of nowhere

I hate to disturb your ongoing physical ailments and paranoid delusions, but as long as we're stalling around under the illusion that my company might still publish this book, I may as well pretend to still be editing it, right?

So . . . it seems to me that this piece comes PARTICULARLY out of nowhere.

"What's he saying?" I asked Dr. Minsky.

"I have no idea," Minsky said. "But it stands to reason that it's some form of local greeting."

"Thanks, Marvin. I figured that out."

"You're welcome. Aside from that, I have no data. Come on." Marvin helped me slowly to my feet. Supported by his shoulder, I staggered out of the remains of the airplane into the dappled sunshine.

The natives were muscular, brown-skinned men wearing nothing but body paint and leather codpieces. They each carried a long, relatively straight, fire-hardened pointed stick. Both men did a double take when they saw Marvin.

"Xochipilli," one whispered to the other. "Xochipilli," the other answered in agreement.

"Terence, what are they saying?" Marvin asked.

"I don't know," McKenna retorted. "I never said I was fluent in their language."

"No, you never did," Minsky purred.

McKenna shot Minsky a look. The animosity between them that had begun at the conference was starting to fester now. Great, I thought. This was all we needed. "Look, fellas," I said to both intellectuals. "What do we do now?"

The natives took it upon themselves to supply the answer. At that moment, they both began talking a mile a minute. I didn't recognize any words except for the mysterious "Xochipilli, Xochipilli," which they said every few seconds.

"Terence," I said, motioning to the two men, "what IS this?"

"Um, they want us to follow them," McKenna said, struggling to translate their jabbering. "They want to show us something . . . no, they want to take us to their village chief, and the chief will show us something."

"Well," Minsky said, "considering we have no alternative, I suggest we go."

I only fainted once on the way to the village. When we finally reached the collection of huts that served as the natives' more or less permanent encampment, one of our escorts ran ahead of us, stamping his feet and shouting "Xochipilli, Xochipilli!"

"There's that word again," I slurred.

At that moment a large, regal man emerged from the biggest hut, at the far end of the village. He stood well over six feet tall and was adorned with a variety of feathers, bones, beads, and other ornaments. This had to be the village chief. The chief frowned at the man who was yelling. Then he looked at the three of us. And I'm telling you, when he saw Marvin, his jaw dropped, his eyes popped, his mouth opened.

"Xochipilli," he whispered reverently.

"Terence," Minsky said, "if you have ANY idea what this Hochifella stuff means, I'd really appreciate knowing."

```
##############
#    /==$=\     #  <— From the High-Tech Fully Electronic Desk
#  /))-00(\    #      of R. U. Sirius
#  ((( -)))    #
#  )))\ /(((   #  —> rusirius@well.com
##############
```
Date: April 3, 1999
To: Hyatt@Ballantine.Books.com, stjude@well.com
Subject: I laughed until i cried

Sorry to take a few days to get back to you, Trudy, but did you know that Burger King employees get 50% off on full package trips to Disneyland?! You get to stay at a Motel 6, eat at any Burger King . . . the whole nine yards.

Anyway, something about THE VERY IDEA of this piece made me laugh unto tears when I edited it . . .

btw, we're having a free bag of large fries with every whopper and large coke all next week! I figured I'd tip you off because you're my friends . . .

"Look, Marvin," McKenna snapped, "I'm as worried as you are. I don't know if this word means they're going to eat us, or sacrifice us, or what. OK? I JUST DON'T KNOW!"

"OK, Terence," Marvin said placatingly. "Just asking."

We stopped in the middle of the clearing. The chief motioned to two of his men. They walked to the clump of ferns at the edge of the developed part of the village and quickly prodded and pulled the leaves of the huge plants to the right and left.

Hidden in the brush was a huge carved stone, approximately fifteen feet high, and a stone slab, about four feet off the ground, six feet long and six feet wide. The slab was covered with a brown, crusty material that looked like dried blood. The large stone had been carved into a statue of a humanoid creature looking up at the sky. The creature was stocky and bald, had enormous eyes and an enormous beaklike nose, and looked half man/half bird of prey.

"Mar-vin," I whispered.

"Hmmm," Minsky hummed.

"Mar-vin," McKenna whined, "that looks an awful lot like you."

"It does, doesn't it," Minsky replied in a hushed tone.

"Marvin," I said hoarsely, "they must think you're one of their gods."

"I think you're right," Marvin whispered.

As if to punctuate Marvin's comment, the tribal chief and his followers slowly knelt, then prostrated themselves facedown at Marvin's feet. "Xochipilli," they chanted, "Xochipilli."

The three of us were silent for a moment, then McKenna snapped. "JESUS CHRIST!!! MARVIN??? MARVIN MINSKY??? Of the six billion people on this earth, they had to choose Marvin MINSKY as their god???" He poked Minsky in the shoulder with a rigid forefinger.

The chief popped his head up and gave McKenna a very nasty look.

"Hey, Terence, cool it," I warned.

"Jesus Christ . . . Minsky?? I don't know why they chose YOU as their god," McKenna snapped. "I'm the one who's studied their culture. I'm the one who's shared their sacraments. I'm the one who's lived among them."

"Terence!" Minsky's voice was like wet ice. "Knock it off!"

The chief muttered some words to his aides. He then stood up, pointed at McKenna, looked at Minsky, and let forth a torrent of speech. He stopped and looked at Minsky inquisitively.

"Notice the universality of body language," Minsky whispered to me. "We don't know the words, but by the look on his face, the wide eyes and raised brows, we know that it was a question."

"What did he ask?" I whispered back.

"I have no idea," Minsky replied. "Terence, can you translate what the chief said?"

McKenna ignored Marvin's question.

"Terence," Minsky said quietly, "did you catch what he said?"

McKenna didn't say anything for about five seconds. Then he snipped, "No, I didn't. And even if I did, I doubt I would tell you."

Minsky frowned. "We have no data. We can just randomly choose a response, I guess, but in situations like this, I've usually found it's safe to say yes."

"Are you sure?"

"No," he replied, "I'm not sure. I've just found that 'Yes' generally works better than no."

The tribal chief repeated his question, and once again looked at Marvin with big eyes.

"Terence," Marvin whispered. "How do you say yes in their lingo?"

"Hei," McKenna said petulantly.

Marvin sat up straight, looked at the chief and firmly said, "Hei, chief. Hei."

The chief barked out several short commands to his men. They immediately stood up, grabbed Terence McKenna from behind, gagged him with a leather thong and dragged him to the stone altar.

I jumped to my feet once again. You'd think I would have learned my lesson. As the jungle started to spin, I grabbed one of the tree trunks to steady myself and yelled, "Marvin! I think you just gave them permission to sacrifice Terence McKenna to you!!"

Minsky slowly got to his feet.

```
################################################################
######### • Trudy B. Hyatt • #########
######### • Editorial Assistant • #########
######### • Hyatt@Ballantine.Books.com • #########
################################################################
```
Date: April 9, 1999
To: rusirius@well.com, stjude@well.com
Subject: What do you suppose

This is another one worth talking about. What do you suppose happened to Bill and Hillary? I kind of liked them myself:

SUMMER 1998
July 9, 1998: The unexpected retirement of Bill (and perforce, Hillary Rodham) Clinton as the result of a scandal so bizarre (we assume), so raw (we think) that no media were able to even hint at its nature under the new Standards of Decency -- "All the News that's Correct to Print."

"Hmm," he said, as he watched the tribesmen tie McKenna to the altar. "It would appear that I did, didn't I?"

My agitation was making me woozy. "Marvin!" I yelled with nearly all my strength, "stop them!"

"I'll try," Minsky promised. He walked to the altar, looked down at the bound-and-gagged Terence McKenna and said, "Terence, how do you say 'stop' in their language?"

McKenna's eyes blazed as he thrashed around. He was talking a mile a minute behind his gag, but all we heard were muffled nasal "m" sounds and occasional ululations.

The tribal chief took a flint knife out of his belt and majestically strode toward the altar. "Marvin," I shouted with the final remnants of my strength, "STOP HIM!"

Minsky turned to me. "It would appear that Terence, who is gagged, is the only one of us who knows the word 'stop' in the local language," he said.

The chief raised his knife over his head as darkness crashed around me . . .

```
================================================================
```
```
Date: 23 June, 1998
From: stjude@blood.atonement.com
To: rusirius@well.com
Subject: don't do that!
```

```
oh christ, ken, good thing you asked me first. No, DO NOT insult mo-
hammed's dog. NO NO NO!!! you're NOT starting out mild with that --
in fact, that's probably a code-blue JIHAD-LEVEL offense. don't.
dogs are filthy. trayf . . . they're islam's other white meat. er . . .
```

```
i didn't say that.

you want to "start out slow, with a very mild insult" . . . ??? maybe
*mild insult* is oxymoronic . . .
DON'T!
```

= =

```
##############
#___/==$=\___ # <— From the High-Tech Fully Elec-
# /))-00(\   #     tronic Desk of R. U. Sirius
# ((( -)))   #
# )))\ /(((  # —> rusirius@well.com
##############
```

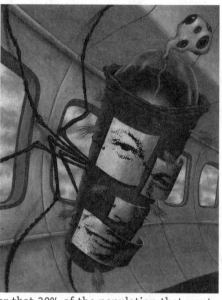

© Eric White

Date: April 11, 1999
To: Hyatt@Ballantine.Books.com, stjude@tired2000.com
Subject: intercourse with aliens?

Not sex necessarily, mind you. Something much MUCH weirder
than anything any of us can imagine. Makes Bosch look like
summer camp. More terrifying than Sonny Bono!

The aliens are camped out in the whitehouse. No, not Mexicans. At
least they don't look like mexicans. They look sort of like spraycans,
actually, but with little tufts of hair sprigged about. The workers at
Burger King talk about the aliens in the whitehouse all the time. I
think they're onto something.

You can't help but like the Clintons. EVERYBODY likes them except for that 30% of the population that wants
to assassinate them. I'm NOT one of those. I'd be sad if some major loser, under the influence of Jesse Helms
and Dick Nazi . . . a loner with no life save for a brief stint in that special Burger King Training School off of
Highway 69 in Arlington Virginia, right next door to the Lee Harvey Buchenwald School of Dentistry . . .

. . . The Gores are weirder than the loveable Clintons. A lot weirder. John Barlow, who's flown on airforce two
with the veep told me that Gore thinks that TIME MIGHT STOP during his administration. This is a true story, by
the way. There's something you may want to leak to the press, that and the fact that some of Clinton's former
classmates at Oxford have said, in the drugs conference on the Well, that Bill took LSD. The media never asked
him about LSD, they only asked if he inhaled. Which he didn't, because of his breathing problems, but he did
like to eat hash brownies.

All of this I swear is true.

Have you ever seen Al Gore naked? Well, Barlow had sex with him on airforce two and -- relax, it's not like
he was MALE -- he looks sort of like a spraycan, but with little sprigs of hair . . .

= =
```
Aug 15, 1998
From: St. Jude@tired.com
To: R. U. Sirius@wired.com
Subject: never mind

I was watching the tube last night, to catch a pirate hack that
```

someone from the Rogered Jollies alerted me to. The hack wasn't all
that interesting. But the show itself makes one wonder when the
mainline became weirder than the alternative. Maybe we crossed that
line with Patty-Tanya way back in the 70s?? Anyway, I transcribed
some of it off the tape. Here it is.. read it and weep (from laughter and terror?)

[Video clip:]
Title: Cruel and Unusual?
Newscaster: I am Joanne Stephens: As most of you know, a visionary
new direction announced by Disney-Nintendo last year is changing
America's angry prison system into a happier place. [Superimposed
franchise logo of happy face with mouse ears.] The Walt Disney Federal Prison Franchise, in collaboration with the Justice Department,
has already converted a majority of prisons into Disneyhomes, and
they're on schedule to have all prisons finished by the end of the
year. As a response to rising crime, out-of-control recidivism, and
increasing public pressure to reform the reform establishment, this
once-controversial approach is now being universally praised, although some prisoners are vehemently claiming that this system is
. . . cruel and unusual punishment.

Announcer Voice Over:
"Aug 14, 1998: By any other name, it's still a day in prison for the
inmates of San Quentin Disneyhome . . ."

A massive hangar-like cafeteria, with a line of prisoners in bright
multicolor jumpsuits holding red happymouse logo'ed trays, fore-
ground. A massive bald black inmate [face pixilated] pushes the man
in front of him: [Loudly] "Watch ya >bleep<in' feet, ass>bleep<!"
Pushed man turns and looks up impassively as pop! Sister Mary Sativa
appears above the shouter. Pan up to face of vicious nine-foot wim-
pled hologram, growling something like: "Dwayne-Eddie, your language
is not gentlemanly!" Waves of laughtrack merriment rollick from hidden speakers around the lunchroom, assisted real-time by some guys
not in Dwayne-Eddie's immediate area.
    Over the next few minutes we see three enormous Moms pop up in the
vast eating area and reprimand their [pixel-faced] sons for rude behavior. They use humiliating nicknames long outgrown, and refer to
incidents best forgotten. Each time this happens there's some mean
haha-ing in the crowd to sweeten the canned laughter.
    A school bell rings, and pop! there are 6 Mickey Classics (red
shorts with ellipsoidal buttons, bulbous yellow shoes) marching in

place, singing perkily about how our tummies are full and it's time
to go outside . . .

   The prisoners follow them, their faces bleak.

Closeup of haggard con: "It's cruel and unusual, man, no question.
This is only the beginning of what we're goin' through, see . . .
'cause even if you do get back outside, you got no dignity on the
street, man. Those baby-boy jokes is manhood-killing, no sh -- eh, no
lie. And there's sure no stylin' in here. You gotta watch your walk,
watch your talk, every minute. [Looks furtively side to side, drops
voice:] You mess up too much, man . . . they send you to the Magic
Kingdom."

===================================
I am NOT writing shtick.
This was on BROADCAST TV.
I shit you not. . . .

>jude<

= =
Date: Oct 6, 1998
From: judith.milhon@well.com
To: Cyanara@Inter.com
Subject: MONDO VANILLI

Aunt Sophia,

Mondo Vanilli, are they serious? R U Sirius? It's hard to separate
reportage from satire in America. Surreal-life stories is what we've
got here. The news is self-satire. Remember Patty-Tanya? How about
O J Simpson? What about Bill Gates?

Maybe reality can be corrupted by the Arts, mm? Like the docudrama,
where journalism corrupts fact, only much much worse. Art by definition IS powerful.

Maybe history is forced to write itself in the style of its times.
That means surrealism and Dada are now coming into their own. They've
been ramifying all through this dark century, and they're strong
enough now to break reality clod from clod.

Oh yes, the times are interesting . . . I do get to laugh a lot. And I

may live post-er than thou, but I'll never write a book. Believe it
or don't, I'd want to write moral fiction, and that ain't possible
now. The moralizers are claiming all the territory. But it's true:
I'd like to write about how to make human life more bearable, about,
about . . . anomie and like that . . .

I hate novelists who are as random and sadistic as life itself. Novelists like this are like the bad gods. They make it clear that they
care more for rules, symmetry, closure -- foreshadowing and then duly
foreclosing -- than they care for us.

For structural tidiness or because it's easy and fun, they kill off
their major characters, quelle bonne surprise . . . or make them go
mad, that always works . . . or even -- ever since the fifties --
contrive a neat finish by ending the world.

Pfeh. Disgusting. F**k that.

        love, Jude

ps: after postpostmodernism, what?

= =

St. Jude's Diary
Jan. 1, 1999

HACKING THE WETWARE: THE GIRL NERD'S PILLOW BOOK started circulating on the Internet in
the Spring of 1996 under the byline "NerdGirl." It's a hands-on operating manual for optimizing
hetero nerd sex. [PILLOW BOOKS WERE EITHER UNDER-PILLOW DIARIES, OR INSTRUCTIONAL
PICTURE PORN BOOKS LEFT UNDER THE PILLOW FOR JAPANESE NEWLYWEDS.]
    I just copped to writing it. I offered in evidence some timestamp-encrypted early drafts much
funnier than what was published later. [TIMESTAMPING IS A WAY OF DATING AND CLAIMING
AUTHORSHIP IN A COPYFREE OR COPYLEFT SITUATION. SOMETHING IS COPYLEFTED WHEN IT'S
COPY-PROTECTED BY LAW, MAKING IT ILLEGAL FOR ANYONE TO DISTRIBUTE IT—UNLESS THEY
DISTRIBUTE IT FREE.]

Section A: Booting Up
If you like each other, you may want to have sex immediately, just to get the expectations out of
the way. But expect little: unpracticed sex is usually imperfect. Even if the sex is better than okay,
really good sex is built on trained mutual coordination, rather like dancing the tango. So you
might make him take ballroom dance classes with you to warm him up. This is strangely arousing
and satisfying at the same time. In fact, dancing is just a transform of sex. More and more nerds
of all genders are learning ballroom nowadays, and maybe this is why.

* * * *

Section B: Learning the configuration
After you both get the idea that fitting tab A into slot B is actually feasible here, repeatably, he will want to customize for the individual case. Let him practice but don't crowd him. Even if he's badly trained or inexperienced, if the early phase seems like a tutorial he may quit the project before it gets interesting. Let him hack around on his own. If he's not going to be completely useless he will discover the following things for himself:

a) While fitting A into B, merely kludging the angles and pressures takes one only so far
b) A very small vector shift can make enormous differences in sensation and response
c) The intensity of one's own sensation is closely coupled to how enthusiastic one's accomplice is
d) Logically, you must find strategies to optimize both your responses

This is good. It's time to hit the manuals. Machine Architecture (Anatomy). Principles of operation (Physiology). And some hands-on work. This leads logically to . . .

The Erotic Pelvic
Treat this like the mutual research project it is. If he's going to use the systems he must learn them. The ideal male nerd will be developing a functional 3D model of your unique sexual apparatus, that he can rotate in—and around, hoopla—his head. The truly gifted nerd will develop this goal without prompting, but you can propose the idea. As it operates with this model, the penis is not a blunt instrument. It's a probe and a button-pusher. It's a *sensor*. But the hand is a more efficient data-gathering device while it's all terra incunnita.

For the erotic pelvic it's helpful if your boynerd has a thing about latex. He may not realize that he does, yet. You can help him along on this by assuring him that latex is definitely the kink of the future, unless somebody invents a yummier material for gloves and booties and polo shirts and things.
The best-case learning environment involves:

a) Rubber-sheeted bed
b) Armpit-length latex gloves, yesss.
c) Large pots of flavored and unflavored lubes
d) An angle lamp with a magnifier attached
e) A pot of warm water with a couple of soft facerags in it
f) Anatomy texts with pictures
g) A spirit of earnest intellectual inquiry in all participants

/\/

. . . but any mis-step of the hand, any move that causes discomfort should be offset at once by the above counterpleasuring techniques. If he goes seriously over the line say "OW OW OW," and wrestle him around a little, playfully. Then give him the irresistible offer: "Let's go get our email." The hackerly attitude is that this is just something that doesn't work yet, some bugs remain—not that it's a horrid failure.

Soon he'll hit the sheets with the same look he had when he was mastering UNIX. Now the interior landscape is an intellectual challenge. He may start talking aloud to himself as he does a readout of your personal data, muttering "lateral nerve plexuses" or "Gräfenberg" as he goes along. Do not correct his Latin plurals. Forget about umlauts. Just concentrate . . . focus finely . . . and give him, as they say, feedback.

Your nerd will accept standard English: "don't ever touch that again," for example, or "I shall now have an orgasm." But he would prefer precise reports in his wonderful new language. Nerds love jargon. You should know. Practice issuing calm statements like "5 cm to the right produces a fasciculation in my right sartorius." This sort of thing is good fun, and produces lots of good data for y'all's notes, but if you want to help him with his interpersonal skills, you might devolve to whimpers, self-defense postures, toe-clenching, and howls. Being able to infer *good*, *blah*, and *don't stop* will benefit him lifelong.

This research phase may wake up his kinkiness. Many nerds have startling fantasies stored up since pubescence—or even from before. (You hear enough pre-pube fantasies, you start rethinking this famous Latency Period. Some of us were less latent than others. Just how nonnegotiable must the age of consent BE? How many of us had our lives ruined by *not* being molested in a timely way? Didn't YOU long for that mysterious Other when you were twelve? Damn.)

I was saying: kinkiness. Given the basic situation, he may, for an obvious example, want to insert his *entire* hand into one of your orifices. What the hell? Let him try, whyever not? Just make him take his time and use the pain-countering techniques slatheringly. If it works, good for everybody. You might like it a lot. But if you don't, at least he's made his benchmark on that particular kink, which might be sufficient for him. What the hell?

```
################################################################
#########        • Trudy B. Hyatt •              #########
#########        • Editorial Assistant •         #########
#########     • Hyatt@Ballantine.Books.com •     #########
################################################################
```
Date: Oct 18, 1998
To: rusirius@well.com,   stjude@well.com
Subject: Plotline?

Actually, I can't find the original plot. Since we've already signed off on 1994 - 1996, why don't you just send me from 1997 through the end.

===
Date: Jan 9, 1999
From: Cyanara@Inter.com
To: judith.milhon@well.com
Subject: Re: Living by irony?

>>Pfeh. Disgusting. F**k that.
   F**k that, Judith? So very phallic-aggressive, as if to f**k were to defeat or destroy. (Freud's fashionable again, I hear, invoked this time by the academic Left, which makes no sense to me at all.)
   But I'm not in fashion, thank God. Post-modern, post-this and that. Culture defining itself with a prefix, but not even so distinctive

a prefix as anti, no. Failing even to declare clear opposition to times that *did* define themselves, that owned their labels. If you read the current label the only claim it makes is that it supersedes by being *newer*. Post. Post post. Post-Ismism. I get older and older, and the world gets stupider apace.

Oh, enough.

```
#############
#___/==$=\___  #  <- From the High-Tech Fully Electronic Desk
# /))-00(\    #      of R. U. Sirius
# ((( -)))    #
# )))\ /(((   #  -> rusirius@well.com
#############
```
Date: Oct 18, 1998
To: Hyatt@Ballantine.Books.com
Subject: Ok, trude . . . here goes..

Taaa Daaa>>>>
HERE'S REST OF THE PLOT>>>

1997

JAN 1997: SIMONE THIRD ARM DOES A SOLO PERFORMANCE TOUR, which morphs over the course of the tour into a Goddess revival-meeting format. Mass conversions result.

Feb 2, 1997: The second MONDO Vanilli record release, *Lotsa Stuff*, comes with an album's worth of music and a full CD-ROM. This will be a pretext for exploring the evolution of computer-based multimedia technology and its links to other forms of media. LOTSA STUFF gets hacked immediately and is made freely available on line -- which fact is then heavily publicized by MV. MV thus sets a Free-the-Media precedent -- seemingly encouraging phreakers to crack and freely distribute not only its own stuff but any musical or CD-ROM release.

Early 1997: How to Mutate and Take Over the World. Pirate media pranking by the Underground has evolved an ongoing shtick called Mutate and Take Over the World:

Your uncle is gone to the astral again: he spends all day every day in the treehouse, just staring out over the park. He's taking a three-month sabbatical to investigate what he calls supernal numbers.

I'll sign off now, dear: the line is noisy here after 6 pm, I don't know why.

Sophia

San Francisco Chronicle Feb. 1, 1999 Pp. 1

BIG DAY FOR NEW CIVILITY
**Tobacco Ban, Music and TV
Broadcasting Restrictions Pass in
Separate Legislation**

Two pieces of legislation, both of them the product of the New Civility Movement, passed the US Senate today. The bills, one providing criminal penalties for growing, selling and possessing tobacco and tobacco products, and the other setting up a Federal Approval Commission empowered to prevent the sale or broadcast of "obscene, immoral, degrading, and socially destructive" materials, are expected to be signed by President Gore.

It was a day of bi-partisan victory, as twelve Republicans crossed over to join the vast majority of Democrats in passing the anti-smoking legislation, and over a ⅔ majority of each party voted in favor of the Federal Approval process.

Civil Libertarians were quick to criticize both new pieces of legislation and the American Civil Liberties Union has already announced preparations to challenge the "censorship" legislation as unconstitutional.

A public protest rally in New York City turned violent yesterday, after an incident in
cont. pg 6

```
= = = = = = = = = = = = = = = = = = = =
Date: 28 Feb 1999
From: stjude
To: rusirius
Subject: gah
```

This morning when I went out to get the paper there was a devildoll hanging on my front door. Yep: it's a devildoll,

SAMPLE

- -
The evening news is focusing on the plight of the left-handed. Suddenly the screen goes plaid. A figure steps before the camera: The Smiley Facemask nods its head in greeting. His/her voice is electronically treated to sound like Mickey Mouse:

Good evening, comrades. This installment of Mutate and Take over the World is brought to you by the Post-Commie Faction of the International Anarchist Picnic, AND by The Copyright Laws of somebody's government . . . but not mine.

We all now understand that there's no such thing as copyrighted, protected, safe, tame data. Once data's distributed, it goes wild -- feral data! It just hangs around being free and reproducing itself. Sound like fun? But free data can be trapped and sold: you can sell water to somebody in the desert, right? To somebody with no access, you can even sell data.

Okay, say you're a lefto-anarchist. You write or program something truly snarky and you want people to see it, free, and you don't want some corporate slavedealer making money off it. What to do?

Remember, the best hack uses the tools at hand. The Copyright Laws of the United States of America were drawn up for just this sitch. You attach a label to your work, saying that it's copy-protected by law, that it's illegal to distribute it and if they do their ass can be sued off . . . unless they distribute it <u>free.</u>

This is called CopyLefting, an idea credited to Richard Stallman. It's a smart weapon: it hits only the law-abiding.

Remember this and take comfort, friends:
There are <u>millions</u> of ways to be Politically Incorrect!

The Underground -- *[voice lowers to a synthesized deep intimate tone]* Loves You. Stay free!

Cut to scenes from a Japanese animated porn manga, its traditional blanked-out genitals replaced by new-model cars, trees, and home appliances. Slow fade to black. Normal broadcast resumes.
- -

all right. It was looped over the front doorknob by its hair, like a pizza-hut tag. Was I scared? I was not. I unhooked it and took it in to my office

Early 1997: U.S. Ranks Worse than Cambodia in Infant Mortality!

In this post-election year, with the new congress even further to the radical right, the media starts in with the damning statistics. While America continues to be the center for tech evolution and the capital of the world for entertainment and media, and while a small percentage continue to make money hand-over-fist, America continues to decline into a class hierarchy typical of her former banana colonies to the south. The over-40% real unemployment rate makes for a demoralized formerly middle class and, for the less demoralized, more career opportunities in crime. So, the country that *already* (real life, today . . .) has the greatest percentage of her people imprisoned starts to turn large areas of real estate into prison "annexes." This is indicative of a possible strategy for resolving the unemployment problem without resorting to politically unpopular welfare statism. Meanwhile, mainstream economic statistics still show the economy doing OK in a "slow growth" phase.

April 1, 1997: April Fool Extravaganza by pirate media prankers, hours of "Best of" and new releases from all factions. Some of them are wild beyond belief.

June 1997: Simone Third Arm becomes the first televangelist for Goddess.

She's pitching the religion she just founded, which begins with the Creed, "I believe in Goddess, her Explicit Graphicness. I celebrate Her public rites of the Holy Shit, the Holy Piss, the Holy Come."

The religious right goes nuts, of course. Email complaints and rants, carefully unexplicit, swamp the Internet.

SAMPLE
- -
San Francisco Chronicle, June 19, 1997, Media Watch
Simone outstrips herself: *The media's recently had a thing for smallish brunettes with hot eyes and a stylish way with the outrage. We had Madonna in the 80s and early 90s, we've got Simone3rd Arm today and maybe into the Millennium. She's got the media by the holy vesicles: she's the Cult Hero with an actual Cult. Noticed the market share of the religious channels recently? That's not from young Billy Graham III, guy.*

If you don't want to be preached at, catch Simone on MTV and the MONDO Vanilli show, but if you really want to get religion, watch Goddess Live! on the Living Religion channel every night at midnight. TV firsts guaranteed on every half-hour segment. If you're lucky you'll catch the celebration of the Sacrament. Yow! er . . . Blessed Be!
- -

(holding it by one foot, ugh) and checked it for clues about what it was spozed to be doing to me . . .

This devildoll is a naked standard barbie, i guess, caucasian pink, unlike me, and its hands have been hacked off above the wrist. Ugh: is that voodoo for carpal tunnel? *There's* a writer's curse. I got wrists of steel, juju mofos, no problem! Its barbiehair was cut off and some ratty looking brownish dreads glued on . . . kind of animal-furlike. Not mine! No fear!

Then I saw the inscriptions on its torso, check . . . I would hope there'd be inscriptions. Maybe in haitian dialect. (I like Legba, actually. Legba, awRIGHT!) I look close . . . I detect multicolor fine-line pens, but awful handwriting. Scarey handwriting. Dyslexic letters, dysnumerics, squiggles . . . uh oh. SCAREY.

I'm taking it over to get it translated. Not to the gypsy with the gold-capped tooth, nimrod. To the library. I think it's one of the Schrödinger equations.

```
= = = = = = = = = = = = = = = =
Date: 2 March 1999
From: stjude
To: rusirius
Subject: Re: the
sharpened religious
symbol crucifixed firmly
in my front door

you too? same night.
hmm.

okay, we gotta be do-
ing *something* right.
any clues as to what?
= = = = = = = = = = = = = = = =
Date: 3 March 1999
From: stjude
To: rusirius
Subject: the sharp-
ened religious symbol
in my front door #2

ugh, it's a phurba.
it's a bronze sacrifi-
cial knife, the blade
divided into three
leaves to leave the
blood run out, like
the bayonet that got
banned by the Geneva
accords, only the Ti-
betans invented it 17
centuries earlier, and
still like it a lot.

when the buddhists
came into Tibet they
appropriated the
phurba. they just
```

Nov 1997: With online tax filing now fully implemented and being used by the majority of tax-paying civilians, hackers are able to corrupt the data at the point and in the moment of reception. Over 30% of the tax forms are corrupted beyond recognition. This becomes news towards the end of 1997 and results in yet another sales tax increase. This action continues, implicitly, throughout the "struggle."

Nov - Dec 1997: The 2nd annual X-Xmas and Solstice celebration. Much merriment is made. Constant Ad-slot hacking (see sample immediately below.). This year Overworld broadcasting has its own counterChristmas programming: sometimes it's hard to know which is which.

Late Dec 1997: A post-holiday HADL campaign on cleaning up broadcasting and squashing the pirates.

Dec. 1997: The Disinformation Highway. The hardcore intruders [Hackers who like to break into systems.] in the Underground get busy, striking at U S Government targets. One group hacks communiqués at the highest levels of the State Department and the Pentagon, breaking into allegedly hack-proof private communications networks and altering or substituting, working without publicity in hopes the changes will pass unnoticed.

Others -- or maybe the same ones, who knows? -- hit the Internet, inserting minor but time-wasting glitches in the subnetworks, even unto tweaking the PCs of home users hanging off the Net. (This generates a lot of interfactional static, some sections cherishing free communications and some just wanting to DESTROY.)

Worse, oh much worse, using insider knowledge of the dynamics of interaction within selected public and private organizations (HADL affiliates and the anti-encryption agencies are only the obvious targets), they are able to sow discord and confusion within them, avoiding suspicion by mimicking the communiqués of individuals with poor face-to-face communications skills and/or with already bad interpersonal relationships. This results in severe policy mis-steps, intra-organizational warfare and job loss and, finally, a major foreign policy débacle as U.S. troops are sent to Palestine to protect Palestinians from a minor Israeli military incursion, only to have them returned home before their arrival. This strategy of interception and replacement of communications to cause confusion becomes known as "Interpersonal Appropriation."

abstracted it -- they say it's a symbol of piercing to the heart of
reality with the threefold wisdom. nevertheless, this is a very

1998

Feb. 1998: The War Against Violence and Porn. In 1998 a bi-partisan alliance in Congress announces the War. All the media are heavily pressured
to self-censor for a G-Rated [Suitable for All Audiences] content. If it's
not fit for a five-yr-old it's not suitable for YOU.

The response of the major networks and the print media is swift: things get
Nicer than before, very rapidly. There's no censorship like self-censorship;
it's moving toward a 50s Disney world on all channels -- except for the continuing media hacking from the Underground, which is perceived by the
authorities as politically subversive as well as politically incorrect. There is
a lot of pressure to find the "leaders" and put them away. A large part of
the War Against V&P budget goes toward crushing the Underground.

March 1998: The media gets sweeter and sweeter. Meanwhile, the still hot
MONDO Vanilli releases *Vanilli Decadence* and co-sponsors the parody
"Decadent Art" show, with the Third Reich parody group, NSDAP (New
School of Design Art and Performance). The show is slated to run in Los
Angeles for ninety days, and includes the latest in computer wearables
[Computers and gear that, yes, can be worn.] and 3-Dimensional sensory
saturation staging, the new human-like robots, and pushes to the absolute edge the physical torture of an audience using light and sound. As
well as nightly live performances by MONDO Vanilli, the "Decadent Art"
show features all of the leading "shock" artists of the time. It is shut
down after one week and all participants are threatened with arrest.

March 1998: The Underground starts a heavy pirate-publicity campaign to
organize from and within the jails.

It also uses the strategy of Interpersonal Appropriation in attacks on the
ERC (Encryption Regulatory Commission), making great chaos in this
barely formed organization. Deeply satisfied with being able to read/lis-
ten to the personal communications of the leading political enforcers of
decency -- which reveals tremendous corruption and hypocrisy -- portions
of the Underground turn a great deal of attention to all forms of surveillance, including video surveillaince (they hack spy satellites to their own
use), and old-fashioned shadowing. Revelatory materials are widely distributed over pirated media and the Nets. The tweaked stuff is hilarious,
but the actual liberated stuff is only mildly convincing, given the ability
of even modestly technically sophisticated individuals to alter or even
create realistic-seeming activity in any medium. Nevertheless, the sexual
peccadilloes, drug habits etc of the "Moral Elite" becomes a primary
source of hilarity on all the media.

nasty object to see
thrust into your
frontdoor when you
come out to get yr
morning paper . . .
it has horrible
twisty things carved
on it, and feathers
hanging from the
handle. i'll get
gracie to put an
anthropologist's
specimen number on
it . . . there's a
powerful rationalist
spell.

no problem about
THEM coming after
me, anyway: i've
taken the Sangha
refuge vow . . . it's
protection from my
fellow buddhists,
like a dharmic condom
. . . i am okay. but
YOU. . . .

ps: about the vow . . .
when i took that, i
was young and
gullible. now i affil-
iate only with disor-
ganizations. i am NOT
soft on buddhism --
scroom!

my front door's suf-
fering from this
shit.

Date: 4 March 1999
From: stjude
To: rusirius
Subject: lucky to be
alive . . . i think

Last night Eric and I
went to the physical
cypherpunks meet in
silicon valley. I was
driving down 280 at
about 60 mph. When I
went into an outside
curve on one of the
hills a van suddenly
pulled up next to us
and kept pace. Funny.
Nobody else on the
road.

Then it swerved over
the divider bumps
into my lane, as if
to force me onto the
shoulder. Not much
shoulder on 280 --
natural shoulder,
slopey all the way
down. So he's lung-
ing at me . . .

So I lunged back; I
humped on him with the
Valiant's front
fender. I've never had
a car that wasn't dis-
posable, fer Xsakes --
big and heavy -- who
can afford else? So I
bumped him. Horrible
crunching squeal from
the van, sparks even,

April 1, 1998: The 2nd April Fool Extravaganza. Anti-ads for this event
have been blitzing the real ads for weeks, promising a media breakthrough,
the most surprising ever: "Revealed! The Shocking Future Of Media!"
April 1 evening programming draws the heaviest viewer share ever. Surprise: for the 24 hours following, ONLY REGULARLY SCHEDULED BROAD-
CASTS. It's pretty shocking, all right. Viewers get the point. This is what
life would be like if the Overworld gets its way.

April 3, 1998: The Information Liberation Front -- "Information Longs to
be Free" -- is raided in Mountain View, CA. An armed standoff lasting several hours ends when the Front -- one computer scientist -- cheerfully
gives himself up. He passes out copies of the Information Liberation Front
manifesto to the arresting officers and the gathered media, and quips to
the Press that he's looking forward to jail, because he's missed all his
friends. The ILF guy [who actually exists, with all sorts of name changes
to protect him] will be an ongoing character: he's a gun nut, a right-
Libertarian (Heinlein tendency), and very inventive, combative and
funny. We'll see his view of the prison Underground.

April 8, 1998: Biotechnology Produces AIDS Counter-Virus. The AIDS virus
is tamed, not destroyed, but AIDS now means only a minor susceptibility
to disease and infection. The public sexual puritanism remains in place,
which only makes the secretive but massive transgressions more delicious.

May 1998: Pirate advertisements. Amenities of the Underground are
pitched online and in ad-slot hacking on TV. Online and offshore banks
are explained and pitched. Real and virtual TAZes (Temporary Autonomous Zones) are hawked with resort style promos -- "Belgian New
Guinea. Where the balmy" etc. Some really ambitious hackers blitz the
home shopping channels with underground "products," most of them fictional and scandalous. Parodic public broadcasting campaigns ask for
viewer support for real, virtual, or completely fictional underground institutions. Promo spots like: "The few, the happy. Be all that you can be, in
the Underground!"

With contact information for newby-level [newcomer] hookups with the Net.

This is very gutsy. It indicates a move toward the Open Secret model for
action.

heh. It fishtailed a little and then straightened out and zoomed the hell
away. That van could move. (Eric says it had no light on its licenseplate;
he remembered to look.) At the bottom of the hill I found a shoulder and
cried on it -- actually, i just sat on the ground for a while refusing to
throw up. Eric drove us to the meet, so I could lie in the backseat and quiver. A good division of labor, we did our jobs like champions.

*[The notion that there is no way of cracking a revolutionary organization
that has nothing to hide and accepts everyone who wants to join.]*

June 1998: MONDO Vanilli, along with other media-oriented businesses
finds itself in a sudden economic crunch -- because information that previously longed to be free, now is. Media has been "liberated" by the hacking that MV helped foster as its own media prank. Media in general is in
chaos, but MV has its own special problems. Sponsors are leery of being
hacked in the MV TV show slots, which are primo targets. MV becomes a
media arm of Sony/Paramount and is given its own TV network with some
unreal estate on the Internet to sweeten the deal. It becomes one of the
many groups programming its own 3D interactive VR game. As usual, the
bizarre content causes consternation, and subsequent fat profits.

July 9, 1998: The unexpected retirement of Bill (and perforce, Hillary
Rodham) Clinton as the result of a scandal so bizarre (we assume), so raw
(we think) that no media were able to even hint at its nature under the
new Standards of Decency -- "All the News that's Correct to Print."

July 10, 1998: The succession of Al and Tipper and the appointment of
Catherine McKinnon-Masson as vice-President initiates full industrial-
strength New Puritanism. Jesse Helms is appointed by the new administration to head the newly created Bureau of Media Standards (BMS).
Noted technophobe and anti-biotech fanatic Jeremy Rifkin is appointed
Secretary of the Interior. Much rejoicing from oldstyle feminists and fundamentalists in the usual flavors: Christians, Jews, Moslems, New Agers,
Luddite-Revivalists et al. Correct Politicians become dominant in both
parties.

August 10 - 13, 1998: Hacking at the End of the Universe V. Members of
the American Underground openly attend a European hackers convention
sponsored by Hac-Tic outside Amsterdam. Strategies for online bankers,
schemes for digital cash -- an ongoingly difficult problem -- offshore
hacking, and other strategies are discussed . . . It's an interesting event,
because any face2face meeting *[nerd jargon for actually nonvirtually being
with someone else.]* is possibly dangerous. Being there in one's seizable
body, even in Holland . . . One can be fearless only online, with the
proper precautions, right?

I have a snapshot of the van, sort of. As if my eyes took a stop-motion picture while this was happening. It was a long black panel van with mirrored windows around the sides, and on the front door was a logo -- a golden beehive with an eye in the top, and thirteen? bees circling it like a halo.

Maybe there ARE secret conspiracies. Maybe there are Illuminati Danites who want to keep us from revealing their secrets, whatever those may be . . . Maybe pigs do have wings.

jude the obscrude

ps: okay, what YOU got on the danite illuminati? really incriminating shit? thought so. watch out.

pps: i'm bluffing on the cheery stuff. i'm shaken up. still in shock.

= = = = = = = = = = = = = = =

Date: 5 March 1999

From: stjude

To: rusirius

Subject: the sharp-
ened religious symbol
in my front door,
#3!!!!!!

or, what i had to ex-
tract from my front
door today . . .

Shit. This is rather
alarming. It's stain-
less steel, nicely ma-
chined, very very
sharp. Its points were
buried nearly an INCH
into the wood. I had
to pull it out with a
pair of pliers, like a
horrible tooth extrac-
tion . . .

A mogen-dovid
shuriken? A throwing
star of david????????

don't tell me . . .
you got one too.

= = = = = = = = = = = = = = = = =

Date: 5 March 1999

From: rusirius@vnli.com

To:jude@whooo.whooo.
com

Subject: holy shi ite?
no . . .

Yeah, Connie identified
the symbol as having

Sept. 1998: Sectors of the Underground start using both "Interpersonal Appropriation" tactics and the corruption of data to undermine computer and media megacorporations, particularly 3PO, Apple-Nintendo, Madonna Inc, Paramount-Sony, and Snapple-Disney Virtuality. With underground sympathizers now making up a large minority of the society, an underground sect organizes a highly successful work-sabotage campaign which results in a season of nearly universal releases of faulty software and hardware. This causes tremendous snafus for Undergrounders themselves, particularly hackers, prankers, and extropian futurists dependent on fully functional unsabotaged tech. There is bitter infighting, with hardcore technophiles on one side vs. the punker No-Futurists, the teen lone-marauder types, and *Processed World*ers [*A zine,* Processed World *put out by a Situationist-influenced group that urges data-entry slaves, the lowest in the hierarchy, to rise up and oops! spill sweetened coffee into the keyboard*], queasily allied on the other.

Nov 1998: the War Against the Unrated, The War Against Meat, the War Against This and That

Al shares the podium with Tipper for a nationally televised pre-election-day talk. She delivers a segment called "The Caring Society." She calls for bi-partisan support for the outlawing of things known to the Surgeon General to be bad for the body such as unsafe Sex and most Drugs, and those known to the Attorney General to be bad for the spirit, such as almost all forms of post-punk Rock'n'Roll and immoral happenings on broadcast TV.

Before Congress breaks session for the winter holidays in 1998-1999, alcohol can be issued only by state liquor stores countrywide, and tobacco is contraband as (interupt)

```
########################################################
########        • Trudy B. Hyatt •           ########
########          • Editorial Assistant •     ########
########    • Hyatt@Ballantine.Books.com •   ########
########################################################
```

Date: Oct 18, 1998

To: rusirius@well.com,   stjude@well.com

Subject: TOO MUCH

Enough already! Jesus, that proposal was practically a book in and of itself wasn't it?

```
############################################################
#########            • Trudy B. Hyatt •             #########
#########           • Editorial Assistant •         #########
#########      • Hyatt@Ballantine.Books.com •       #########
############################################################
```
Date: Oct 20, 1998
To: rusirius@xxx stjude@etc
Subject: Whole plop and nothing but . . .

Ok. Filling out this plot looks pretty daunting, but I believe it CAN be
done!! let's work together to complete it FAST . . .

```
  ##############
 #___/==$=\_     #  <— From the High-Tech Fully Electronic Desk
 # /))-00(\     #     of R. U. Sirius
 # ((( −)))     #
 # )))\ /(((   #  —> rusirius@well.com
  ##############
```
Date: Nov. 15, 1998
To: stjude
Subject: Wild Thing

Sorry I haven't been in touch over the last week. I met this wild thing
who calls herself PsychoStär, and she's been taking all my time, not to
mention my essence. Very exciting, strange, magickal, hypersexual, psychedelic (very) femme fatale. You'd HATE her . . .

But I love to hate her and hate to love her. She's got something of a rep
already. In fact, Don Rushoff even wrote a book in which she provided
the main metaphor. It was called *Psychoberia,* and it did pretty well.
This is the ending of the book:

"Some might call me naive for taking PsychoStär seriously as an intellectual. But why not entertain the belief -- as she does -- that the moon is
made of blue cheese, pigs can fly, the earth is hollow, and if we click our
heels together three times and say, "There's no place like Psychoberia,"
we'll find ourselves in nirvana? Sure, I was slightly influenced by the fact
that she showed up for interviews wearing only a white raincoat, black
gloves, heels, and crotchless panties. Still, I was somehow moved to
spend many weeks trying to understand just what PsychoStär meant
when she said to me on our last night together, 'Yiiiii Yiiiii Yiiiii Yiiiii.'
    "And maybe that's the meaning of life. A sexy young psychotic rich
bitch in crotchless undies who believes that pigs can fly."

something to do with
a mystical cabal of
jewish bankers, who
call themselves Je-
hovah's Choice. These
guys are really nuts
because they DON'T
control the banks.
The fucking Italians
control the banks.
And the presbyteri-
ans. But the jews
are always blamed
for controlling
the banks. So these
jewish bankers got
together, figuring
that they'd really
LIKE to control the
banks, because what
the hell? And so
they all got heavy
into the kaballah
and there we are.
They developed this
mysterious weapon
originally by stick-
ing a star of david
on a 45 rpm record.
See, they control the
music industry . . .
(heeheehee).
It's all because
I referred to Jeho-
vah as a jealous
condominium owner
over in zion.com,
a line that I
stole from Leary,
anyway.

Oh well. I feel
truly lucky to have

240

completed this move into the vnli compound. The security systems
here are excellent. I've got so many protectors. Infra-red cameras.
Barbed wire. And still I can't relax. I STILL feel like Schwartzendruber is gonna get me . . .

==
Date: 5 March 1999
From: stjude@toodle.oo
To: rusirius
Subject: i think i can't take the heat

so i'm getting out of
the kitchen
i'm losing the reli-
gious wars, too,
guy.i don't want to
be an atheist martyr.

i've made arrangements,
and i've got a tent --
one of these umbrella
things that you just
squeeze a button and
jump back -- that i can
stand up in . . . and i
have a cot, a sleeping-
bag, a lantern, and a
stove, and a very
clever solar battery
that i got from a name-
less friend that can
power my laptop . . .
and some other heh
stuff, too. what more
could i need? don't
ask.

i'm off to the
southern coast of
idaho, i guess. I'm
spozed to be near Bo
Gritz and the Pa-
triot gang, under
their nuclear

•¿¿¿•From the Electron-Chocked Desk of Jude Milhon•¿¿¿•
•¿¿¿¿¿¿¿¿¿¿¿•   •aka StJude•   •¿¿¿¿¿¿¿¿¿¿¿•
•¿¿¿¿¿¿¿¿¿¿¿•   •stjude@well.com•   •¿¿¿¿¿¿¿¿¿¿¿•
Date: Nov. 18, 1998
To: rusirius@well.com
Subject: never mind

psycho stãr can get you onto the eleet boards? the innermost of the inner, and all that? i never cared to know if they *were* real, the real
3L33T . . . but tell her yes, fr Xsakes, yes! What i want to do is make a
heartfelt pitch to them --

I want to tell them that they can do something with their knowledge
other than just counting coup on each other. Some of these guys must
profess to be anarchists. This calls their bluff. If they let us publish their
innermost hacking secrets and release them to the world, they commit a
revolutionary act. The most revolutionary act that CAN be committed --
the equivalent of giving up your life for the revolution . . . To give up
your prized secrets, the knowledge and skills you worked for years to as-
semble and refine and polish . . .

Imagine the anguish -- to see this intellectual love-child of yours, this
hidden delight, your secret notebook, passed around everywhere, seized
upon by newbies and teener scum, and by a whole planet of people who
suddenly have what they need to be truly self-determined. -- everyone a
haqr! Oh god, what a challenge, what an opportunity!

tell her yes. tell her i'll manage this for you, because you're too busy . . .
i'm just yr online flunky, whatever . . . pass me (encrypted encrypted, fr
godsake) all the stuff she gives you -- the signon info for each of the
boards, whatever introductions and personal referral links will get me on.
i need them bad. and soon.

`•¿¿¿•From the Electron-Chocked Desk of  Jude Milhon•¿¿¿•`
`•¿¿¿¿¿¿¿¿¿¿¿•`   `•aka StJude•`   `•¿¿¿¿¿¿¿¿¿¿¿•`
`•¿¿¿¿¿¿¿¿¿¿¿•` `•stjude@well.com•` `•¿¿¿¿¿¿¿¿¿¿¿•`

Date: Nov. 25, 1998
To: rusirius
Subject: Cool rant

I'm trawling the 3L33T boardz with requests for hacker cookbook info.

I'm doing my most to inspire, shame and bully them into doing their bit for the revolution -- the pitch is all variations on:

Here's your chance to prove that you're not an 3L1T-ist hierarchical ass-hole, just sitting there on your knowledge like a dragon wallowing around on its treasure, hoarding your expertise for your own glory. Here's an opportunity to prove that you believe in freeing information . . . sharing the knowledge . . . and all that . . .

i've got some promises, but you know how far that goes. . . .

From The Electronic Desk of the Honorable Bruce Sterling,
United States Senator from the State of Texas
Date: April 8, 2000
To: stjude@well.com
Subject: paranoid praxis

Jude,

My subcommittee on the Secret Government has come across this docu-ment. I was not surprised, but YOU may be. There is probably more, and I will pass it on to you, if and when . . .

Also, as your friend, I ask you PLEASE to take the recent reports about Nanobugs seriously. Swallowing them is dangerous. There's no substitute for a healthy diet.
          love,
            chairman bruce of tejas

Date: 10/29/98
From the Electronic Desk of James P. Davenport
NSA.3lit3.soc.eng. S&B, ***, luminated 1s, masonic order,**

          too late for me. There isn't a plastic surgeon alive that can make me anonymous. and anyway, i'll be fucked if i'm gonna give up the opium bed to sleep in a tent . . .

          later . . .

umbrella, i guess, and across the branch and down the road a piece from Salman Rushdie . . .

reminds me . . . what's blonde and has great tits and lives in Idaho? No, not me . . . Salman Rushdie.

christ, i hate the sticks. but it's about freedom, and stuff.

Quatsch! it's about survival and stuff . . . gah

>jude<
ps: you wanna join the exodus? wander in the wilderness? sepa-rate tents!
= = = = = = = = = = = = = = =
Date: 6 March 1999
From: rusirius@ vnli.com
To: stjude@whooo whooo.com
Subject: Don't Go!!!

Move out here to the compound. You'll be as safe as I am . . .

Please don't go. I'm gonna dissolve in a pit of paranoia. I can't hide jude. it's

CyberCrit Journal
SPRING 1999   Pg. 4

THE OVERGROUND IS A WILLING CUCKOLD

A Talk with Professor Artemis "Freddie" Krugerand

In 1997, advertisers and commercial TV were experiencing a severe cash flow crisis brought on by underground hijacking of commercial airtime. A rising executive at the venerable advertising firm Crumly, Crummley, and Craven came up with what he thought was a solution. He decided to form his own underground and hijack the airwaves for his clients. This idea was accepted by his superiors and he was supplied with the necessary resources. He then found several TV Pirate gangs that were willing to inject the tapes he gave them into some of their pirate programs in exchange for certain favors. It went rather smoothly, with all conspirators maintaining stealth and cunning.

The problem turned out to be the payoffs. Sometimes the underground would be paid in equipment, which was secure. But usually the undergrounders were paid in cash. Rather than having payments audited, the underground was frequently given enough information to "appropriate" the funds from the corporate accounts. A happy side effect was that insurance companies would foot the bill. This backfired when one gang was given the wrong account, containing substantially more money than was intended. The executive who made this goof was forced by higher-ups to retrieve the money, which he did. But by that time, the missing money had already been reported. In the ensuing chaos, the insurance companies became more than a little bit suspicious of foul play.

Crumly, Crummley and Craven fired the executive. But the investigation, already underway,

#2, System Control, EFF Control, Cypher Control, P.Dot.Aleph, White Temple, O.T.O-Jihad, A:A:, Semblance of Order, >>><<<, Rapid Response.
Yale, 1958
Pentagon 1963-1966
Central Intelligence Agency 1967-1968
National Security Agency 1968 - Present
System Consultant, Office of the President 1968 - 1976, 1980 - 1992
System Control 1969 - Present
PsyOps 1969 - Present
NLP/CLP/AIF/MC 1969 - Present
Private Defense Holding Corporation   1992 - Present
(indicate encrypted file)

To: Lloyd Gettyson-Plymouth
Chief Executive Officer: MHC (Media Holding Company) America OnLine, Cond Nasté, Plymouth Rocks!, Ford, Sega USA, Snapple-Disney Virtuality, Paramount, WEA, Time-Warner, Random House Family of Book Publishers, Internet Coordinating Group, Electronic Arts, Gibson & Stephenson Ltd.

(my roses feel silly, my words feel silly, my fish feel silly, m.b.x. ex.L!) Let One's Talk

Greetings Lloyd. Hope this little note finds you and Jenny well. I was very sorry to hear of the problems Tanya (or Patty, as she now insists on being called) has been causing for you. Yes, as you surmised, your little girl has built herself up quite a little file here. But I wouldn't worry too much. She's having her late adolescence just like my J.P. -- who, I'm proud to report, recently became V.P. in charge of new technological developments at Cond Nasté. I can tell you from personal experience, Lloyd, that the whole thing about cocaine is really exaggerated, and our files tell us that Bathos Masterson is very paranoid about sexual disease, and doesn't use needles. I wouldn't say your daughter is in *good* hands, but the man is a wimp and not much to worry about. In any case, we'll see to it that the charges against Tanya are dropped.

So Lloyd, Johanna's redone the guest suites, and we've brought the Cézannes up from the summer house. You should be very comfortable on your next visit. And I'm learning to fly! Oh, and Johanna had her face done again. She looks terrific!

Anyway, a small item has been passed on to me by David Sprague. Our word search program alerted one of our field agents to a document transmitted to a Ballantine Books employee, Trudy Hyatt (#141988, daughter of Fred Doddsworthington III and Margot Hyatt-Holliday, *****luminated 1s/masonic order/white lady lounge #606). This document is apparently a plot outline for a book to be published by your subsidiary company Ballantine Books, part of the Random House Family.

This book, by authors who call themselves R. U. Sirius (#183309, Kenneth B. Goffman, x45-subversive, 138 page document available, 694 brt pot.terror, #41 ss, e.m: drugs/sexual perversion) and StJude (#164489, Judith Milhon, x36-comm-subversive, 100 page document available, hqr, cypher, e.m: sexual perversion) appeared to promise information that should not be allowed to be made available to the general public, a sort of do-it-yourself hacker manual.

Using one of our PsyOp fF sm field agents, a complicated unit that calls itself PsychoStär, we have already gained the basics of control and are guiding the situation towards a soft landing, damage nil. Our unit has obtained intimate contact with author "R. U. Sirius." He's functionally our copy/u.i. Unit PS reports that the book is in trouble, massively overdue, with big chunks rendered irrelevant by the passage of time. I actually read it in its current form and it appears to be a rambling and confused discourse containing naught but radical crackpot opinions and pseudo-poetic gibberish. At author Sirius's insistence, the authors are holding the book back until they can stick in the subversive information that he hopes will destroy society, and they've had problems obtaining same.

Our Unit PS has now successfully led our subjects into a blind gut. Author StJude, at R. U. Sirius's insistence, has posted the aforementioned plotline on four "3lite boardz"

eventually uncovered the Pirate activities of Crumly, Crummley and Craven, and implicated the advertising industry in its entirety.

This spiral of extra-systemic conspiracy seemed the best context for my already scheduled conversation with legendary media theorist and English Professor, Artemis "Freddie" Krugerand. Freddie was more than familiar with the case. He had written about it for the New York Times Sunday Magazine.

CYBERCRIT JOURNAL: I WAS HOPING WE COULD TALK ABOUT YOUR VIEWS ON THE PRESENT STATE OF THE MEDIA BEFORE WE DISCUSS THE CRUMLY, CRUMMLEY, AND CRAVEN SCANDAL.
ARTEMIS KRUGERAND: The whole discourse of media has been inverted, due to the effects of HADL. All authentic discourse has become de facto illegal, while legal discourse has become irrelevant and ignored. Legal discourse now becomes a carrier for the illegal discourse, much like a host for a self-replicating virus. This is perhaps the farthest-reaching contradiction of late twentieth century capitalism.
CCJ: HOW DOES THIS RELATE TO TELEVISED MEDIA?
AK: The whole approach to the text we call television has been drastically altered. There is an active search involved. People now discard one part of the discourse in order to find that which it unwittingly contains. While some commercial television is still popular, the main desire to watch comes from the lure of forbidden knowledge. This causes vast problems for capitalists because their message is irrelevant, but the medium they use is not.
CCJ: DOESN'T THIS DESTROY THEIR CAPITALIST BASE, AS THEY ARE DEPENDENT ON ADVERTISING REVENUE?
AK: Yes, they are now dependent upon those outside to supply production. They must distribute whatever is given to them. Also as their

medium is appropriated their source of funds is also appropriated. They now encounter another contradiction; on the one hand they have to air irrelevant discourse that is ignored—especially with the War Against Violence and Porn, and then they have advertising that gives them revenue but is unpopular with the viewers. Then they have programming which no one has control of, but which is necessary because it provides a captive audience for the first two. This puts them in a bind, and leads to an unstoppable urge to appropriate the uncontrolled and illegal programming for their own ends.

CCJ: LET ME GET THIS STRAIGHT. THIS NEED TO CONTROL THE UNDERGROUND PROGRAMMING LEADS TO ATTEMPTS BY THE OVERGROUND TO CREATE ITS OWN UNDERGROUND PROGRAMMING.

AK: Exactly. The Overground—in all discourse—must attack the subversive influence of the underground, but the Overground's own need for the underground remains inadmissible in their discourse. This leads to the famous dual conscience in which the discourse's need for continuity threatens its own being . . .

CCJ: SO TV'S SURVIVAL DEPENDS ON ACTIONS WHICH THREATEN AND MAY POTENTIALLY DESTROY IT?

AK: Correct. The television media is bound by discursive rules that no longer allow the media its old options. In the CCC scandal, we see media's attempt to wrest control of the discourse defeated by itself.

CCJ: THESE NEW DISCURSIVE RULES HAVEN'T COMPLETELY REVERSED THE NINETIES TREND TOWARDS MAINSTREAM MEDIA HIP.

AK: I disagree, somewhat. There was fairly severe interruption in 1997 and 1998 that seems to be reversing itself now. In general, it's true that the nineties have been defined by corporate media capitalism's sponsorship of—and spon-

that are controlled by S&B and luminated 1s. All four of these encrypted BBSes are riddled with our agents, digital puppets, and baiters. Predictably, some of the baiters responded positively to the request, as did some of the puppets. The authors seem to be sanguine, and are calmly awaiting completed "articles" from these sources, most of them promised within three weeks. At appropriate points we are prepared to reroute exchanges to and from baiters to our agents, and hold the authors in check for as long as necessary.

Our strategy revolves around forcing the authors to turn the book in for publication in its present incomplete form.

You may well ask, Lloyd, why we don't ask you to simply terminate the book -- or, in fact, why we don't simply terminate the authors? The answer is threefold. Firstly, there is a buzz about the book, and your refusal to publish it could lead to suspicion and unnecessary controversy. Secondly, if we let the book go to press in its current form, it will effectively discredit the authors, insuring that we need not worry that they will be able to shift or extend activities around these themes into other arenas. Thirdly, it is useful for us to see the responses of the baiters to these calls for information. We can still learn something from these people, as well as ABOUT them.

What you can do, Lloyd, is have Karl Turringer over at the Random House Family turn up the heat on Ms Hyatt to get a finished manuscript for this book. He need not know why. Have him threaten to demand the return of their book advance. Hyatt will pass this demand on to the authors.

The writers, it appears, are barely surviving. Ken is homeless, staying with friends, and has recently applied for a job at Burger King. We're seeing that he gets the job, so that he has even less time for the book. Judith is not much better off -- she's living by the kindness of her housemates. The threat of a demand to return the advance will get the authors to rush the existing manuscript to print in something approaching its current form.

I appreciate your assistance in this trivial matter, and look forward to seeing you up at the Grove this summer, if not sooner.

always,
James

```
##############
#  /==$=\     #  <- From the High-Tech Fully
# /))-00(\   #     Electronic Desk of
# ((( -)))   #     R. U. Sirius
# )))\ /(((  #  -> rusirius@well.com
##############
```

Date: June 8, 1999
To: ralph.X@panthers.org
Subject: I'M DESPERATE

Ralph, puh-leeeeeeze. You've got to understand. I can't pay you up front. I'm working in FUCKING BURGER KING for christ's sakes. I told you, 20% of my royalties from this book. Jesus guy, that could be alot of money.

Have mercy. I just can't put a book out about a bunch of white people taking over the world. I mean, we already HAVE the world, at least from a certain perspective. If we put the Panthers in the vanguard of the book, we justify the book and we give you guys a very hip cachet and a good propaganda op.

Come on man. 20%. All I ask is twenty entries of about 300 words each. It's a good book. It makes fun of the honky libertarians . . . COME ON . . . puh-leeeeeeze.

Date: June 9, 1999
From: ralph.X@panthers.org
To: rusirius@cryptonet.zone3
Subject:

$3500 advance or no go. Lookit, r.u. I'm very honored that you want me to be your token nigga and alleviate your white guilt and all, and I can appreciate your dilemma from a standpoint of artistic legitimacy more than you might imagine, but look at it from MY perspective. I'm letting YOU capture ME in your trip, ya know? The Panthers ain't fiction. I mean, did Huey Newton write himself into *Still Life With Woodpecker?* No. $3500 or no go. And frankly, I hope you can't raise the money.

(I DO thank you for that taste of opiophoriu. That's some BAD shit) . . .

Later, whiteboy

sorship by—alternativeness. There's an odd attraction there that seems to go beyond merely the popularity of the subcultural products. It's the kind of late-night backslapping that you'll do with a disturbed and disturbing relative just before bedtime. You're hoping he or she will remain calm so that you can have a peaceful night's sleep. The media's appropriation of the

Never forget the profound ambivalence of the average American. People don't approve of those things that entertain and tittilate them, and those things that they do approve of fail to give them enjoyment.

Hip backfired though, since it gave impetus to reactionary forces and limited media's strategic moves for maintaining audience interest and excitement. Never forget the profound ambivalence of the average American. People don't approve of those things that entertain and tittilate them, and those things that they do approve of fail to give them enjoyment. Media got away with pimping outre, scandalous and semi-subversive aesthetics to the middle brow as entertainment for some time. This is nothing new. Actors and prostitutes once blurred together into the notion of courtesan. The HADL really hurt the capitalist media far more that the pirates ever could. Late capitalism and the anarchist rebels share a common interest in the transgression of boundaries. In that sense, the CCC scandal shouldn't surprise.

CCJ: WELL THANK YOU VERY MUCH FOR YOUR TIME. CAN YOU TELL US WHAT YOU'VE BEEN WORKING ON LATELY?

AK: I am looking forward to the publication of *Meditations upon a Toilet Seat: Sanitary Appliances [bathroom fixture?] and their Role in a critical-psychological post-postmodern discourse* by Princeton University Press, and I am also considering going back there in the spring.

The Boho Manifesto   June 5, 1999   BlackNet Issue #22

by St. Jude

Things fall apart ... the center cannot hold. Cool.

All this cultural misery we've been living through is the pain of metamorphosis ... Don't be superstitious, though -- the coming of the millennium
is just a coincidence. We can't afford to be sentimental about arbitrary
zeroes on the odometer. Five hundred years is the count we should notice.
It's taken five hundred years for the emergence of the middle class, the
triumph of the Bourgeois Paradigm, and its fall. In these its last years,
the Bourgeois Paradigm no longer works for us. Paradigm failure is
painful. Pain? Agony! We are experiencing the senescence and death of our
culture! Craziness, anomie, suicide/murder, apathy/accedia ... Help!
Everything's melting away -- hold on tighter! -- Religion! Country! Family! Too late. Too late. Clasp the corpse and its limbs fall off, its guts
spill worms....

The Bourgeois Paradigm is done. What is next?

Current French theorists are looking backwards for clues -- nomadology,
pre-bourgeois alternatives ... but devolution is not a real option. Evolution proceeds. There *will* be an evolutionary succession. In fact, the
inheriting paradigm has been emerging over the last two centuries ...
The chrysalis is splitting apart ... The imago emerges, wet and trem-
bling, shaking out its wings ... And ...

it's us! Glowing and starkers we stand in the morning sun!

We cast such long shadows because we stand in the first moments of dawn
... Our sun is rising.

But who the hell are we?
A new form is all but invisible. One way to tell if something is truly
new is that it's so very hard to *focus*. A new thing under the sun is
just a blur. Our peculiar class, our distinctive paradigm currently
eludes the vision of most of the culture. We are known as bohemians,
punks, hackers, slackers. These labels are not definitive. Who are we?
To start, let's examine the history of the species....

CLASS HISTORY IN A BOX:

PARADIGM	PASSIONS	VALOR	IDENTITY	ETHOS
pre-bourgeois	sex, drink, combat, dogs, horses, gambling, music, magic	physical prowess, wiliness, wealth, lineage	tribe, clan, land, lineage	athleticism
bourgeois	family, religion, possessions, production & exchange of goods	wealth, religiosity, cleanliness, reliability, patriotism	class, religion, country, ethnicity	socialization
boho	friendship, art/techne, innovation, leisure, production & exchange of artifacts, "the hack"	originality, skill, knowledge, personal charm	self, culture, species, planet	"hipness"

We've got the new paradigm. We've got the viable alternatives. They're dying off, and we'll just handily supplant them.... WRONG.

We must parasitize and destroy them. We must pirate, detourne, seize the media! Seize the CULTURE!

Mutate the world and take it over! Armed evolution!

MUTATE NOW!

= =
Date: June 5, 1999
From: rusirius@well.com
To: stjude@gods.com
Subject: how? why?

I liked your thing on the Blacknet. Mind you, I don't know how you keep going on with this whole thing of actually BELIEVING in any-thing. And why? But I admire it and wrote a song about it . . .

but why?

===

Date: June 9, 1999
From: stjude@gods.com
To: rusirius@well.com
Subject: the primate mind loves the us-and-them . . .

this hot-head young revolutioneer at the party last night -- somebody who wants to do physical actions -- was telling me that the
only unbustable affinity group is one with a shared ethnicity. Get a
grip. Blood ties, ethnicity, religion . . . these are what's killing
us, literally . . . that's what we should be mounting affinity groups
AGAINST. The persistence of these old forms of association is the
major obstacle to mutation . . . If you choose your group by fixed un-
alterable criteria -- by blood, by ethnicity, by place of birth --
how do you kid yrself you're mutating outa the oldstyle? Your actions should demonstrate your principles, no separations of ends and
means . . . We need more abstraction, please -- affinity by love of
football, affinity by hairstyle! Free affinity! Free association!

aaaaagggghhhhhhhhh
civilization, what a concept.
you might define the level of civilization by how abstract its associations are.
me and mate and kids
me and mate and kids and cousins and uncles . . .

and clan

and city state etc etc

as primates, in every category we're struggling up the fucking abstraction ladder . . . up from blood ties to nations and beyond . . .
up from battle to critical argument, up from cruel and stupid to em-
pathic and smart.

(Note: UPWARD. The physical metaphor of ascension is a powerful hy-
postasis for both holiness and intellectual abstraction . . .) The
original judeos of the judeochristian tradition loved to think of
themselves as ascending . . . sure of their own righteousness. They
were consciously becoming less savage than their neighbors by ab-
stracting -- making it into the high places of the spirit, after
shunning their neighbors' hilltop shindigs. They successfully abstracted themselves out of ritually killing their firstborn -- a

regional requirement -- by substituting a symbolic bloodletting, circumcision; they successfully moved up from subgods & demons to one big overLord, etc etc. . . The intellectual force was with them. They were ascending.

but most religions got stuck on the abstraction ladder . . . weighted down by scripture . . . no ascending nowadays. this religion kills that one, and all of them tend to kill intellectual inquiry. John Calvin roasted a scientist, his theological rival, over a slow fire in a public square in Geneva, to make him confess his methodological errors. (think about that when someone talks about putting their opponent's feet to the fire, or grilling them -- now it's a metaphor, a METAPHOR! tell me we've not ascended, a little . . .) murder is still the business of primates everywhere . . . but the process of abstraction IS proceeding. climb, little primates! scurry up, exfuckingcelsior . . . and now we're making a wonderful abstraction of association -- the Net. Nobody kills anybody on the Net. The Net is the next rung up . . . beyond ethnicity, nationality, religion, beyond blood being shared or blood being spilled thereby.

okay, it's a rant, but i believe it. it makes sense.
= =
VuD Virtual **u**nderground **D**igest
——————————> **as of 22:14 AM EST 14 Nov 1999**
• **verify timestamp!** • **verify timestamp!** • **verify timestamp!** •
Timestamp: AAG0IFN0IEp1ZGUgTWlsaG9uIDxzdGp1
VuD Virtual underground Digest 22:14:56 AM EST 14 Nov 1999

ATM Card Specs
by Sgt. Joe Friday
"Just the facts . . ."

The magnetic strip on the back of your ATM card has 3 tracks on it.

The first track can store 210 BPI (Bytes per inch), the second track stores 75 BPI, and the third stores 210 BPI.

Track 1:
Start Data Character
Field-Control Character: This character tells the ATM what type of account(s) the user has.
Data Field Separator Character
Account Number: The account number of the card's primary account.
Data Field Separator Character
Cardholder Name: Last name / First name, separated by a slash.

Stop Data Character
CRC-type Check Digit

Track 2:
Start Data Character
Account Number: The account number of the card's primary account.
Data Field Separator Character
Expiration Date: Month/Year the card expires.
Data Field Separator Character
Process Identification Number: NOT the user's password. This is a number used to verify the transaction between the ATM and the Main Computer.
Data Field Separator Character
Discriminate Data: Bank Identification Data: Bank Account Type (savings, checking, money market) and Usage Rating.
This code tells the ATM if you tend to have a lot of money in your account, or if you habitually overdraw your account, or if you hardly ever use your account.
Stop Data Character
CRC-type Check Digit

Track 3:
Start Data Character
Account Number: The account number of the card's primary account.
Data Field Separator Character
Expiration Date: Month/Year the card expires.
Data Field Separator Character
Encryption Digit: When the transaction request is sent to the main computer, it's encrypted. This digit tells which encryption key is used.
Discriminate Data: A duplicate of the discriminate data stored on Track 2.
Stop Data Character.
CRC-type Check Digit

When the card is being processed, the ATM verifies the account number, expiration date and name stored on each track. Once the information on the tracks are confirmed to match, the ATM compares them to the embossed information on the front-side. Only if the information matches will the transaction proceed. If the data doesn't match, then the card is considered damaged and the ATM will keep the card.
Copying the magnetic strip is easy. To do this, place a blank strip of magnetic tape on top of the valid magnetic strip. Using an iron set on low heat, gently rub the iron across the two strips for a few seconds. Lastly, peel the new strip apart from the valid one and you've got a copy of all the data from the valid ATM-card.

Please note that doing this would result in copying a legitimate card, which may indicate intent to defraud. Keep it in mind.

brain candy

Skate Busters

Skate Busters is a zine put together by a couple of young Skateboard Patrol officers from Ann Arbor. The editors relate some of their favorite busts (such as giving a "curb job" to a kid going down a hill at twice the skateboard speed limit), list tips on how to apprehend skating scofflaws ("black clothesline strung across the sidewalk at ankle height will stop 'em dead, plus it's fun to catch on video for watching at parties."), and even throw in a comic section. Patrol-hating skaters should get this zine so they can see how the minds of these cops work. ($4.50, 32 pages, black & white)

Forget It!

I paid 30 bucks for this plastic bottle of 12 tablets. The label, with a big yellow question mark, was intriguing. The brochure from the health food store said that Forget It! is made from a South American herb that grows only in a one-acre area in a certain rain forest. (The location is their secret.) I went home and took a couple of the capsules, which were filled with dark purple powder. It took about fifteen minutes to kick in, and I felt my worries starting to fade away. It was weird – I couldn't remember who my friend was when he called, but I just played along. After I hung up the phone, I noticed the bottle of pills, and read the brochure. Sounds cool, I thought, so I took a couple. After about fifteen minutes, I suddenly realized that I couldn't read the magazines on the coffee table. Whoa! Then my friend came over (at the time, I didn't know who he was) and he said, "What are these?" pointing to the bottle. "I don't know," I said. Let's try some and see what happens. We did, and in about fifteen minutes I couldn't talk and the other guy panicked and ran out of the house, screaming "I got the fear!" I fell asleep and woke up the next morning with a bad headache.

(Forget It! $29.95 per bottle of 12)

Rosebug

You can't buy these pets, or even legally own them, but you can find one if you ask around. They are sort of the late '90s answer to the Vietnamese pot belly pig. Except these little fellas never get larger than three inches. They're some type of beetle, from Indonesia, with a shiny metallic green shell and bright red legs. The main reason people are buying the rosebug, though, is because its head looks amazingly like Axl Rose's, before he got his hair transplant. It even has little red whiskers!

I ran into a guy selling rosebugs on Market Street and he was also selling accessories for the Rosebug, like tiny bandannas and baseball caps. The bugs were $10 each, so I asked for two. He told me that if I want them both to survive, I shouldn't take a boy and a girl. He explained that the male insect will attempt to devour the female if they are together for more than a couple of months. So I bought just one, along with an orange-colored wig that the guy adhered to the bug's head with a drop of Super Glue ("Won't hurt 'em," he explained.). I love my little Rosebug, and keep it in a bamboo cage. Every once in a while, it'll start chirping and swaying its body from side to side, then suddenly tear apart one of its little toys, but other than that, it's a very low maintenance pet. **(Rosebug $5-$15)**

neurotica

The Food and Drug Enforcement Administration made another successful haul when they raided the Springfield, Illinois home of Gertrude Schmidt, age 93. Ms. Schmidt, a widow, was smoking tobacco in her home, when some children who were shooting birds with a BB gun in an adjacent vacant lot smelled smoke coming from her open window. Doing as they were taught in a "citizen responsibility" class at school, the youngsters lined up in front of Schmidt's house and loudly chanted "Tobacco Violation!" while one of them ran home to call the FDEA's toll-free reward hotline. Officers arrived on the scene in minutes and used a special vehicle equipped with an explosive battering ram to gain entry into Schmidt's home. When Schmidt, who was sitting in a rocking chair, refused to drop the tobacco cigarette, she was shot thirteen times with hypodermic darts containing a memory-impairment drug (similar to the popular over-the-counter supplement "Forget It!"). Schmidt was arrested and charged with smoking tobacco in public. Schmidt is now undergoing treatment at NuRikers, a federal drug offender's boot camp managed under government contract by the NuFood corporation. Schmidt's home was confiscated. As required by law, the money from the sale of Schmidt's home will be deposited in a fund to purchase 10,000 additional "SqueakyCleen" mobile urine testing stations to be used in the nationwide neighborhood sweeps.

Tommy Daniels won't soon forget his recent trip to the AmeriMall shopping complex in Durango, Colorado. Tommy, age 17, had gone to AmeriMall to buy a pair of sports shoes, and brought along his pet manimal, Snoop Hoggy Hogg, to keep him company. "I wanted some of those Nikes that sound like uzi machine guns going off when you walk," explained Tommy, a fishing guide and ski patrol volunteer. "When I got to the shoe store, Snoop started talking! He was saying all sorts of nasty stuff to people, and I was getting some mean stares from other shoppers."

Tommy's manimal is a genetically altered pig that contains human DNA. The hybrid pets, which became popular last year, are required by law to contain not more than 5% human DNA. "Snoop was telling people they were too fat, or had bad taste in accessories, and I was extremely embarrassed," said Tommy. When Tommy returned home and explained what happened, his parents called a lawyer, who hired scientists to examine the manimal, and discovered that it possessed over 50% human DNA, giving it full rights as a U.S. citizen. The Daniels family filed suit against ManiMakers, the breeder of Hogg, for $100 million dollars. When scientists later learned that the human DNA used to make Snoop Hoggy Hogg came from a woman with Tourette's Syndrome, they increased the lawsuit to $200 million. Mr. Hogg now lives in Hollywood, California, and was recently wed to former model Anna Nicole Smith. Hogg will begin hosting a late-night talk show on Faux this fall.

```
= = = = = = = = = = = = = = = = = = = = = = = = = = = = = = = = = = = = = = = = = = = = = = = = = = = =
```
Date: Jan 3, 2000
From: judith.milhon@simulacra.net
To: Sophia@pen.com
Subject: The Rossmoor Virtuality

It's very late here. Just back from another Extropian hot-tub party
in Siliconia. Nothing makes me gloomier than the optimism of futurists. Especially their contingency plans to avert er . . . nonliv-
ing. They're mostly engineers, so they need to have solutions ready
for all possible problems -- and what problem is more urgent than
mortality?

Aside from the head-freezing, which I refuse to describe -- they describe it with *sound effects* -- the most optimistic project is the
Personality Upload. The idea is that your mind, your personality, all
that makes the "you" of you . . . is simply complex software, running
on your meat machine. Given the mushroomic expansion of computers, at
some future time there will be enough computing power for you to upload your personal software -- your consciousness -- which IS you,
they say -- into the Net. And so you can play in virtual reality forever, rappeling down through the planetary Web, after your body blows
away like a husk.

There in the Net "you" will conduct your extended life in an upscale
playground, where virtual bodies gorgeously morph, where the terrain
is freeform and the minds are too . . .

But to me it sounds static and horrible. It sounds like a hightech
retirement scheme: The Rossmoor Virtuality. It's a maintenance situation. Custodial. True, you are watched over by machines of loving
grace, which are less entropy-wracked than meat. But any maintenance situation is dangerously entropic. Out there in the natural
world we happily left behind, there are natural catastrophes. And
there's the simple wear and tear of Time, which will ravel even a
world-wide Web. Nonmeat machines have their limits, too. Machine-
based systems, even Net-distributed systems with redundancy, with
cleverness to spare . . . can they maintain themselves, and you,
forever? Hah.

And if we avoid a static situation, if we let our machines mutate,
who knows what they might mutate INTO? Heh heh heheheh.

But first and most important -- is that ME in there? I'm certainly
happy for my upload, my happy clone having adventures forever, but it
ain't ME, babe. Gah.

I appreciate the engineers springing eternal, but current survival
schemes seem as bad as The Alternative.

cheers, i'm sure, and love to the ascended uncle
jude

ps: had to take this out on you? no, i didn't. but i do love you, and
you are not american, and sometimes i want out of here.

===
Date: Jan 4, 2000
From: Sophia@pen.com
To: judith.milhon@simulacra.net
Subject: The Gold Bird Variations

Now, I am old enough to feel uneasy that my software runs only on
meat, true enough. I'm sympathetic to these hapless Extropians, and
I'm reminded of one of my favorite poems. You might quote this to the
next engineer who makes waves in your hot-tub:

Consume my heart away; sick with desire
And fastened to a dying animal
It knows not what it is; and gather me
Into the artifice of eternity.

Once out of nature I shall never take
My bodily form from any natural thing,
But such a form as Grecian goldsmiths make
Of hammered gold and gold enameling
To keep a drowsy emperor awake;
Or set upon a golden bough to sing
To lords and ladies of Byzantium
Of what is past, or passing, or to come.
It's the end of "Sailing to Byzantium."

cheers, indeed, my dear,

Sophia

===

Films

FUCK!
Ballantine Films
Director: Mark Dippé
Performers: CyberPiss Goddess, R. U. Sirius, Scrappi DüChamp, Jerry Seinfeld, Christy Canyon, Mr. Ballard, St. Jude, Missy Latimer, Reverend Lawrence Lindstrong, Bob Dylan

What the *FUCK*!?
       by
           Wagner James Au

Obsessively demented, cheerfully vertiginous, *fuck!* (Ballantine Films, 2000) is the sort of cinematic experience that allows no ambiguity of response. You leave the theater wholly convinced that someone, anyone, connected to its production must be taken and brutally assaulted to within an inch of their lives.

Sure, we're all happy that media is loosening up again, even to the point where this movie can be released. But let's not let that minimize the notion of violent sanction on Mondo Vanilli, all of whom have long been candidates for a Singapore Spanking or some other form of institutionalized brutality.

What to say about watching the band members bribe a security guard, enter a cemetery with picks, shovels, and electronic apparatus—and reappear later in the film marching behind the tottering figure of a decaying corpse mounted within a hydraulic exoskeleton with rhinestone-cape fluttering from its shoulder blades? It's not funny. It's not scary. It's not dramatic. It doesn't say anything. It *is* disgusting. No sale ... (The several reassurances in the press package—that the Exo-Elvis appearing onstage with Vanilli throughout the film is, in fact, a mere simulacrum—aren't particularly consoling.)

Fuck! covers the 1999 Mondo Vanilli tour. The band members (or rather corporate stock holders) clearly decided that the Nice juggernaut was—so to speak—ir*resist*ible. Rather than waving the flag for the First Amendment, the megamedia gang attempted a bit of pop jujitsu: when pushed, they pulled. Reconstructing themselves in the image and likeness of HADL doctrine, Mondo Vanilli began a circuit of performances bereft of any offense, implicit or explicit, to anyone, whatever their sexual, cultural or political politics. Nicknamed the Mondo Vanilla Tour by former fans and followers, this was Vanilli without mondo, and it didn't do much for their already sagging popularity.

The strategy is conveyed in a vivid montage that opens the film. A crowd seethes outside of the Chicago Amphitheater, a confused, barely controlled roiling between black-clad fans, HADL protestors, newfound HADL-type *fans*, and the local constabulary. PoMo pontificator Jean-Jacques Silencer comments to an MTV camera crew about the "confusion of signals." Meanwhile, backstage, the members of Mondo go through a startling, unnerving metamorphosis.

In stark black and white, Mondo Vanilli takes on the semblance of decency. As *Breakfast by the Sea*, a bit of Muzak from the new album, ambulates, piercings of all sizes are removed from the most improbable bodily appendages and dropped at the pretty feet of the CPG in a hundred flashes of steel and pewter. R. U. Sirius' roly-poly hirsute body is stripped, covered entirely in Nair, shaved bare and encased in a form-fitting shell of lifelike polyurethane. The scene has the obsessive rhythm of daydreaming, and you feel yourself watching with a kind of benevolent stupor, as Mondo Vanilli transforms itself into the Platonic Form of Feel Happy musicians, the Carpenters carved in crystalline.

That bravura scene is punctuated, reels later, by a horrific corollary image. Having assumed their new, country-club friendly personae, we follow them on tour through the Midwest where—in a few cases—they are actually *greeted* with glowing praise from church and civic leaders—while those hardcore fans who get the joke snicker up their sleeves. And the band is pursued by pink-faced groupies with *Charlie's Angels* haircuts, whom they serenade with ballads like *All the Love (I Have I Have for You)* from the new album, *Ease Of Living*.

Publicly melded into the humanoid forms of well-behaved and socially conscious artists, plasticine lips pursed in permanent concern, Mondo Vanilli members CPG and R. U. Sirius—and a couple of very seedy-looking men who are never identified—spend their downtime, backstage and at the hotel, plugged into a webwork of assorted biochemical and electronic IV's. In one breathtaking scene, we see four bodies encased in full body casts, IV's dangling into various body parts. We see various fluids leaking, and hear a peculiar bubbling sound. When the IV's and body casing are removed, we see things roll off R.U. Sirius' body . . . and begin to crawl away.

All in all, it's the usual Mondo Vanilli *"aren't we clever?"* schtick. By revealing the strategy behind the vanilla Vanilli period, MV gets to hang on to its hip cachet. But it's all a game, folks. The recent unofficial loosening of media restrictions allowed them to return to the popular transgression game. But if Wagonhead, Beastkit, Monk's Cunt, and Somerset MauMau hadn't all tested the waters of free expression several months ago and gotten away with it, you can bet this film would be in a secret vault somewhere and Mondo Vanilli would still be serving up treacle.

Fuck! is the sort of film you watch to confirm your suspicion that our slide into the wasted playground of apocalypse was not merely *completed* long ago—it is destined to be *repeated* in an endless loop, Nietszche's theory of eternal recurrence as high-tech gommorah. And we keep brushing the slime from our Toughskins, and dashing back into it. This may be a valid statement. But the way it's made here, and by whom, makes one wish to revive the hallowed Roman tradition of killing the messenger.

==

Date: Feb 9, 2000
From: stjude@vnli.com
To: rusirius@vnli.com
Subject: FUCK! that reviewer

You know, it's very nice of you to give all your friends jobs, and to shelter us here in the new vanilli compound. Yes, I'm pleased to be back and it beats hell outa Idaho in January. But I must say that being stuck in Bunker C with Connie, Lydia, and Thomasita is like living in a posh suburb of Hell. I will NOT play bridge on LSD. I don't LIKE spider venom in my iced tea. I HATE psychedelic art-deco. Look, I may be pathetically clean-living nowadays but i know i'd be happier up in the goth-tech citadel with y'all. Are all the rumors true? I hope.

Anyway, you'll be happy to know that the review by Au in *Details, Details!* contains several fatal errors. The most egregious: there's no
"hallowed Roman Tradition" of killing the messenger. In fact, the
Greeks and Romans hallowed the messenger . . . he's sacred, dude, no
killing allowed . . . which preserved freedom of information in the
ancient world. This reviewer's a moron -- forget him. Listen, you got
any room in the harem? I'd be happy to help out; as, maybe -- hall
monitor?

===
Date: 3, March 2000
From: rusirius
To: stjude
Subject: day of the 3 stooges

Where the hell were you yesterday when all the bad religious vibes
converged and got medeivil on my ass? or tried to? Security got two
of the three stooges on video tape . . . but missed the third entirely. Go ahead and ask Nolan to show it to you. In the early afternoon, when I woke up, there were three faxes on my secret faxline.
First there was a picture of one of those spiky throwing-star-of-
Davids . . . remember? The ones that were affixed to our doors last
year? And then, the second fax . . . a poem . . . "josephine has found
her/she's found her dog/ star shining/dogstar shining/she's found her
tarnished star/she's loved her tarnished star/she's killed her tarnished star/found him/felt him/killed him/nevertobeforgetten him/to-
day/today, shocking man/today." And a third fax . . . "namu myoho
renge kyo."

Security was put on full alert, and sure enough there was Josephine
creeping around the back end of building b, over by your place jude,
holding an old fashion colt 45, and there was Schwartzendruber slink-
ing along behind the scaffolding on the left side of building b, and
sure enough like in a situation comedy, they round the corner at the
same time and butt heads!!! and Josie's gun goes off right into
Nchiren's groin, i kid you not. Nichiren folds up like a deck chair.
While he moans, Josie accused him of harassing us . . . her and me.
"We're in love." Security gets them. Puts them both in lockup. No
doors, no windows, solid steel triple-bolted door a yard thick. And
Josephine fucking disappears. She fucking disappears. Like she was
some kind of phantom the whole time. 'Cept Nchiren still has the bullet in his dick. He's still down there in the cell. I don't know what
the hell we're gonna do with him really.

So it's 10 pm, and I'm expecting Sister Sarah, Christy and Karmela in
my room for the nightly festivities. They're half-an-hour late and
I'm drinking my third vodka on the rocks when this dude dressed in
black robes and a blue turban with one of those throwing star-of-
davids pinned on the front crashes into my room through the heat
vent. We look at each other. He bares his teeth at me. I stutter --
"Uh . . . am I overdrawn?" He's not amused. He opens his black robes
revealing a long scythe and a luger. He draws the gun. He's going to
chop my head off, but it's some kind of ritual. I'm made to take off
my clothes. He douses me in some kind of aromatic oil. He gets me
to my knees. He stands above me and raises the scythe. My life
tries to flash before my eyes, except I'm having trouble remembering any of it. And he starts to recite something in yiddish when
Sarah, Christy and Karmela burst through the door, laughing and
naked to the waist. "Oooooh kinky" Karmela squeels and all three
come running over to us, still laughing. My executioner threatens
with his luger but the ladies see only sex toys and before you
could count backwards from 10 the perplexed but erect religious
fanatic is on the floor next to me fucking Karmela and calling
her unclean. I whisper urgently to Christy, who reaches under
my bed for the handcuffs. The rest is herstory jude. His name is
Lee and he's in cell number three, just in case Josephine
reincorporates in cell two. I always knew the dungeon would come in
handy . . .

==
Welcome to Grrrlove Mailing List 2000

Grrrlove Mailing List, APRIL 2000
Date: April 1, 2000
From: smokeasy@flexi.org
To: GRRRLs
Subject: hi

hey chickens, I'm mirbane -- here posting a message fer my bosswoman,
madam x. she doesn't like to use the net much these days. sorry fer the
lower case letters, got tendonitis from rolling cigarettes all week.

First a little history:

Madam X had the foresight to start a private tobacco smoking club way
back in 1997. Dubbed the Smokeasy, and decorated in a nudge-nudge, wink-
wink Art Deco motif, the club morphed easily into an illegal underground

coldbed of culture when tobacco was made a Controlled Substance by the FDA in 1998.

Anyway, we been lurking a bit and i think the madam likes yr list, even tho she pretends to hate the net. i like it, too, tho haven't had the time to jump in the fray what with thugs or fedz or someone laying waste to our solar panels across town, and how do you expect to grow tobacco in the old BART tunnels without fucking electricity? sorry the tangent, i got customers gotta run.
--mirbane

Grrrlove Mailing
List, APRIL 2000
Date: April 5, 2000
From smokeasy@
flexi.org
To: GRRRLs
Subject: hi

```
#######################################################
#########        • Trudy B. Hyatt •           #########
#########       • Editorial Assistant •        #########
#########    • Hyatt@Ballantine.Books.com •    #########
#######################################################
```
Date: Nov. 20, 1998
To: stjude@scoobie.doobie.doo, rusirius@scoobie.doobie.doo
Subject: NOT grrrrls again!

About this next inclusion . . . I thought the riot grrrrl thing was already TIRED back in '95

Hey-YO, mirbane! Nell here. Welcome ...

Gris wants to know if anybody caught the broadcast patch-in stunt that, uh, SOME-BODY (by the goddess' left ineffable tit, I wonder who that might have been? innocent look, whistle ...) dropped on Our Fair Newschannel the other night during the reportage of the Mayor's Civic Awards. They were handing the gold medallion and award scroll to those prune-assed whiter-than-white Caring League when the patch went through. Heh. Pretty damn cool, and Gris figures that the safer sex info and latex availability info and the hotline numbers for the underground abortion havens will finally hit a demographic sorely in need of them. Not to mention the assfucking video, which probably improved a few evenings out there in television land.

That was Nixon's voice that got audiomorphed, by the way. For the groans and the begging. And the face grafted onto the domme was Tipper Somebody, if you remember her. Tipper? Skipper. Something like that.

Gris keeps calling 'em the Cringe League.

So did anybody SEE it?????

Grrrlove Mailing List, APRIL 2000
Date: April 5, 2000
From: Chrone2
Subject: Kool place

Been to the smokeasy myself. Kool place. Lotsa Goth revivalists hang out there, smoking of the clove (ugh) and looking like Death herself ... or like her brother, Dream.

Grrrlove Mailing List, APRIL 2000
Date: April 5, 2000
From: smokeasy@flexi.org
To: GRRRLs
Subject: madam x

I LOVE madam. She's kinda grumpy and groovy and has a past, like miss kitty, a Wild West madam of a cheesy whorehouse. she's always ordering people around and puffing on fat handrolled organic cigarettes and has a devoted following of young punks/beatniks/junkies/hackers: cigarette-people, in other words. Rumour has it she was part of the infamous IRS crack of

```
##############
#___/==$=\    #  <- From the High-Tech Fully Electronic Desk
# /))-00(\    #     of R. U. Sirius
# ((( -)))    #
# )))\ /(((   #  -> rusirius@well.com
##############
```

Date: Nov 22, 1998
To: Hyatt@Ballantine.Books.com, stjude
Subject: that marina, she really tries to kills me . . .

grrrrrrrrl . . . tired wired tired wired le's call duh hole thing off . . .

The way it works with words these days is as soon as people start using them, the hippest people declare themselves sick of the word and tell us that it's uncool to use it. This happens INSTANTLY now. So that if I call you a zyzabalunatic twice in the same sentence, introducing it to you for the first time, you would post an editorial note next to the second usage saying "I'm really sick of this trendy new word."

Meaning, content, context, or whether it helps or hinders communication is irrelevant here. It's a simple matter of, if you've heard the word several times over, you declare it unhip to use it again, and the tyranny of hip starts to work its magic . . . So I think grrrrl is like cyberpunk. People declared it uncool years ago, but nothing better comes along to replace it, and it actually DOES describe a sort of political aesthetic, push come to shove . . .

Also, Marina is Josephine, it turns out, who has stalked me in the plot, and has turned out to be real. She's now stalking me for real, even as we speak!!! She's crossed over! And if I go down to the corner store, there she'll be. So maybe out of all of this, the only spawn to make a perturbation is nutty Marina.

1997, but she now refuses to touch computers, maintaining that she doesn't understand the damned things.

Grrrlove Mailing List, APRIL 2000
Date: April 5, 2000
From: Amanda
Subject: help?

•¿¿¿•From the Electron-Chocked Desk of Jude Milhon•¿¿¿•
•¿¿¿¿¿¿¿¿¿¿¿¿•   •aka StJude•   •¿¿¿¿¿¿¿¿¿¿¿¿•
•¿¿¿¿¿¿¿¿¿¿¿¿•   •stjude@well.com•   •¿¿¿¿¿¿¿¿¿¿¿¿•
Date: Dec 2, 1998
To: rusirius
Subject: yr new grlfrnd's crazier

than usual, even. That wasn't exactly a fun party last night. 0, it was fun watching that guy get his faced pierced by 23 needles, watching him bleed into the elaborate goblet, watching your girlfriend give him head and then drain the jism out of him like a MacJobber drawing a syntheshake. It was fun watching her sip the gloopy red mess. But then she hadda go and chant some gibberish over the chalice and pass it around . . . Sorry I left without saying good night, but I'm the designated atheist.

I got to talk with yr ladylove beforehead . . . sort of -- "YiiiYiiiiYiiiiYiiii!" Quite the conversationalist. No problem -- I was distracted by her noserod. Holy shit, NObody in our species has ever had a nose piercing like that . . . ampallang through the root of her nose, between her eyes -- that's startling (I'd worry about brain abscess, no joke) . . . the rubies capping the ends of the bar touch her inner canthi -- so beautiful . . . more extreme than ballerina's makeup . . . the tiny complicated chains hanging down either side of her nose . . . the tiny rubies in them -- they are rubies -- I asked. I was hypnotized by her . . . for a while. Then I started to wake up: Uh oh. THIS is the contact for the ultimate hackerly ELEET? I've been a little edgy lately . . . some of the contacts I've made on these UberNets ring my paranoia bells.

I have a bad feeling about yr paramour. While yr fronts are engaged, watch yr back.

Hello All,

My name is Amanda and I'm writing a paper on women in the Middle East for school, and I was hoping you could help me with it. I need to talk about, you know, Islam, and the culture, and that kind of stuff.
Love Amanda

Grrrlove Mailing List, APRIL 2000
Date: April 7, 2000
From: diana
Subject: whitegirls

Amanda, DEAR

. . . ooh I am just so SICK of this white BULLSHIT getting on and entering other womens lives in your lame search for multiculturalism, it is racist BULLSHIT and I'm just so angry I'm gonna SPIT . . .

... and why aren't there more women of color on this damn list??? am I
the only one???

{{{{{{DIANA}}}}}}}

Grrrlove Mailing List, APRIL 2000
Date: April 7, 2000
From: Amanda
Subject: help? HELP?!?!?

Dear Diana,

I'm sorry. I'm a lit-
tle hurt and confused
by your post. I just
need some help with a
paper, and how will I
find out about other
cultures unless I
ask? I don't think
I'm a racist, I re-
ally don't mean to
be.
Love Amanda

Grrrlove Mailing
List, APRIL 2000
Date: April 7, 2000
From: skeezix
Subject: help?

Yo, babes!

Skeezix here. The
hell is this about
color? You are what
color your monitor
is. Last I heard,
wasn't any net check-
ing the ancestry of
your little one-and-
zero pulses through
the machine-mind.

```
##############
#   /==$=\      #  <- From the High-Tech Fully Electronic Desk
# /))-00(\     #       of R. U. Sirius
# ((( -)))     #
# )))\ /(((   #  -> rusirius@well.com
##############
```

Date: Dec 2, 1998
To: stjude
Subject: psycho bitch headquarters right here

PsychoStār is whacked, but fun. Look. What are you worried about? Star
has groupied the world's biggest heads. She's fucked up in such a big way
that it's transcendent. And so she's been allowed into the most exclusive
of human company. Makes sense to me.

It's fuckin' cut and dried. These people turn in the informative articles we need to complete Mutate. If the info is bogus, YOU'll know. But it
won't be. You'll be chuffed. You'll see.

```
###########################################################
########          • Trudy B. Hyatt •           ########
########          • Editorial Assistant •           ########
########     • Hyatt@Ballantine.Books.com •     ########
###########################################################
```
Date: Dec 3, 1998
To: rusirius@well.com,   stjude@well.com
Subject: TURN IT IN!!!

I've got some hard news. My bosses want their money back. That's right,
they're demanding you return their advance. I got them to hold off. We
only have a few days. Organize the material you have and turn it in!!!

What makes you think we're all the lilly-whitecrowd of your fears,
Diana?

Skeezix

skeezix@weasel.winnitech.edu


```
##############
#___/==$=\___  #  <- From the High-Tech Fully Electronic Desk
# /))-00(\   #     of R. U. Sirius
# ((( -)))   #
# )))\ /(((  # -> rusirius@well.com
##############
```

Date: Dec 3, 1998
From: the desk of rusirius
To: Hyatt@Ballantine.Books.com,   stjude@well.com
Subject: NO!!!!

We HAVE to wait until jude gets the responses from the 3LITE boards . . .
the UberNets. It'll only be two or three weeks. Pretend that you can't find
us!!!!

```
•¿¿¿•From the Electron-Chocked Desk of Jude Milhon•¿¿¿•
•¿¿¿¿¿¿¿¿¿¿¿¿•       •aka StJude•        •¿¿¿¿¿¿¿¿¿¿¿¿•
•¿¿¿¿¿¿¿¿¿¿¿¿•     •stjude@well.com•      •¿¿¿¿¿¿¿¿¿¿¿¿•
```
Date: Dec 7, 1998
To: rusirius, Hyatt@Ballantine.Books.com
Subject: about those cookbook delicacies . . .

every single haqr on the UberNet is asking for yet more time. Every fucking one of them! Also, chez.e.chez and monkee.c, the only two guyz i
have any rapport with at all, are being very weird and coy with me --
don't i think it's worth waiting for their ultrasecret recipes, huh, giggle,
huh??????
This shit's getting very strange, not unlike yr PsychoStär, who I remind
you, led me over there.

Fuck the coyboys. I say we wrap.

dear cunts:

so here you are be-
coming MultiCultral.
kOOl.

it *is* mostly white-
bread here, don't you
get it?

only white girls got
the money that this
game requires ...

marina

Oh Christ. She's
baaaaaak!

From: sliceolife
Subject: cuntcuntcuntcuntcuntcunt big fucking deal

Shit. Time to crank up the old bozofilter!

Grrrlove Mailing List, APRIL 2000
Date: April 11, 2000
From: Amanda
Subject: cuntcunt-
cuntcuntcuntcunt big
fucking deal

Oh, well. The more
things mutate the
more they stay the
same ...

Grrrlove Mailing
List, APRIL 2000
Date: April 15, 2000
From: smokeasy@
bigcur.flexi.org
Subject: shut the
bitch UP

hey marina, yer atti-
tude's heck ov cute.
What-say you do some-
thing usefuyl with
it? We've got chycks
here running the
fucking airwaves, me
and Madam we may be
running a small oper-
ation but fuck it we

```
##########################################################
########            • Trudy B. Hyatt •         ##########
########         • Editorial Assistant •       ##########
########     • Hyatt@Ballantine.Books.com •    ##########
##########################################################
```
Date: Dec 7, 1998
To: stjude@well.com, rusirius@well.com
Subject: YES!!!

!!!

```
 ##############
 #__/==$=\__     #  <— From the High-Tech Fully Electronic Desk
 # /))-00(\   #        of R. U. Sirius
 # ((( -)))   #
 # )))\ /(((  #  -> rusirius@well.com
 ##############
```
Date: Dec 7, 1998
To: stjude, Hyatt@Ballantine.Books.com
Subject: NO!!!

Give it another couple of weeks.

This is a do-it-yourself revolutionary handbook, RIGHT???????

REMEMBER??????

are doing our best you know? so shut yer trap and come dig a ditch
with me.

yer prolley some WHITE SUBURBAN POSEUR or like an fbi agent and yer only
here to throw a wrench in. to fuck up the grrrls 'cos you know like
everybody knows that grrrls can't stick together

who cares what color you are i sure don't. i'm brown, so give me a medal
right?

marginalize THIS, bytch.

--your friend the cunt who finally ran out of patience okay.
    mirbane

Grrrlove Mailing List, APRIL 2000
Date: April 19, 2000
From: LittleNell
Subject: ticklish?

Hey, did anybody else's system get tickled in the early morning today? Damn
bell-pager woke me up screamin' about somebody knocking on one of the doors.
I watched, and I have a pretty good idea of who it is, but since they did no
harm, as the hypocritical oaf said, I'm not gonna blow the whistle.

Nell.

```
##############
#   /==$=\   #   <- From the High-Tech Fully Electronic Desk
# /))-00(\   #      of R. U. Sirius
# ((( -)))   #
# )))\ /(((  #   -> rusirius@well.com
##############
```
Date: Dec 11, 1998
To: stjude
Subject: spies?

There's been a City Waterworks van parked outside my house the last
three nights in a row. There's two people just sitting inside at night, apparently a man and a woman. When I go out and try to see who's there,
they move so that I can't see their faces. Tonight they both started taking off and putting on coats while I stood on my porch pretending to
smoke a cigarette. They both wear black all the time.

Also, the weird bag lady's still down by the corner store in her tattered
robes and crown. She won't quite look me in the eye, but she's muttering
this bizarro poetry under her breath whenever I go by.

Grrrlove Mailing
List, APRIL 2000
Date: April 23, 2000
From: Skeezix
Subject: kill the
"bitch"

>Date: March 15, 2000
>From: Joan of Ark
>Subject: kill the
 "bitch"
>why can't you email
 bomb him or some-
 thing, really
>tell me who he is
 and let's all get
 him
Well, well, well.
Pretty feisty little
girlie, aren't we,
miss joan of arc? Or
should I say Agent
Albert Parsons?

266

Skeezix here. Yah, Nell, I was your crawler. Nice flypaper you got
there. The rest of you might want to check your machine logs from 01:17
to somewhere around 05:30. *And* improve security a little bit, too. If
you want a full list of your holes and weak spots, I took the liberty of
compiling them; email me for my hourly rates as security consultant.

So ... joan of arc is Agent Al. I found the quote above of particular
interest. Can you say "incitement", Agent Al? Thinking that it would
look pretty good on your record to have busted a ring of "e-terrorist"
chyx?

Let's see, you would have called us "threat to national security" and
the nooozetabloids would have screamed about lezzie right-to-knife
e-terrorists, right?

I found out a few other interesting things on my way through the neigh-
borhoodz, but most of them can stay buried for the moment.
Though I did think it particularly poignant that ... well, you tell me what *you* think. Watch the next message.

skeezix@weasel.
winnitech.edu

Grrrlove Mailing
List, APRIL 2000
Date: April 24, 2000
From: skeezix
Subject: well ...
lookie here!

(region copied)

Insurer: Silver Val-
ley Consolidated
HMO Group No:
14487-H-GV-2284

•¿¿¿¿• From the Electron-Rife Desk of Jude Milhon •¿¿¿¿•
•¿¿¿¿¿¿¿¿¿¿¿•   •aka StJude•   •¿¿¿¿¿¿¿¿¿¿¿•
•¿¿¿¿¿¿¿¿¿¿¿•   •stjude@well.com•   •¿¿¿¿¿¿¿¿¿¿¿•

Date: Dec 12, 1998
From: stjude
To: rusirius@well.com
Subject: persons in black

There's something similar happening here. So cliché. Why couldn't they
wear matching white polo shirts with stripes on the sleeves . . . Maybe
they're the Ballantine goon squad. They've got that bookgeek chic . . .
Shit. They're gonna beat us up for not giving back their $$ . . . and not
making delivery. Or maybe just to keep in practice. it's been a rough year.

```
#############
#   /==$=\    #  <— From the High-Tech Fully Electronic Desk
# /))-00(\   #     of R. U. Sirius
# ((( -)))   #
# )))\ /(((  #  —> rusirius@well.com
#############
```
Date: Dec 12, 1998
To: stjude
Subject: literary goons in black?

Don't be silly. This must be a sign that we're getting close to the Big Secrets!

Date: Dec 12, 1998
From: stjude@darqside.org
To: rusirius@well.com
Subject: CLOSER

. . . you mean, to the big secret that there are no secrets? yeah, right, you think there's a huge goblinment plot at work here? and it's gonna gitchoo because we're dangerous haquers about to dish dangerous data???? pah, it is to laugh. never underestimate yr paranoia, comrade. we're tiny tiny fingerling fish in this hyah pond . . . splish

```
##############
#___/==$=\_   #  <- From the High-Tech Fully Electronic Desk
# /))-00(\    #     of R. U. Sirius
# ((( -)))    #
# )))\ /(((   # -> rusirius@well.com
##############
```

Date: Dec 29, 1998
To: stjude@well.com,   hyatt@ballantine.books.com
Subject: Lucky to be alive

I'm in intensive care at San Francisco General Hospital. Concussion, several broken ribs, black eye, lost three teeth, which they're going to regrow for me, I hope.

The whole day built up to the incident. As Jude knows, there's been two humans in black parked right outside my house for the last three weeks, every night. Yesterday, they were even there in the morning. Three houses up the street, a very suspicious looking hippie vw van with two more humans-in-black, with headphones on. They started bopping their heads up and down like they were grooving to the music when they noticed I was looking at them, NOT before. There is also a queenly bag lady who seems permanently ensconced outside the corner store. She softly chants poetry whenever I go by. Sometimes she mentions the dogstar. Lately her poetry has seemed to comment on something specifically occurring in my life in that moment. The last line yesterday afternoon was "ain't no sense in rushing/when you arrive/you will not in" I got home and realized I'd locked my house keys inside. The whole day was like that.

The cop cars crept slowly past. When Psycho finally got home and let me in, there was this strange chain email letter waiting for me that threatened not bad luck but direct violence if I ignored it. I threw it out and my machine froze. I had to reboot.

PsychoStär wasn't herself either. I mean that quite literally. Hell,

Type: Spouse
Coverage Plan: full extended
Limit: extended
Patient: Worthington, Marina Lee

[snip]

Authorization: Worthington, David Blake

Address: 17 Westbriar Terrace
Argentum Astra Enclave
Silver Valley, California

[snip]

Occupation: Quality Assurance, Division Chief, Spanden Avionics

[snip]

Well, well, well, as I said before. From the paperwork I grabbed, looks like Marina's hubby is ... you guessed it: middle management. I'd laugh, but the rest of the story looks too painful. I rooted around in the files a bit. Davy Blake had you committed after the miscarriage, didn't he, Marina? Depression is a convenient diagnosis, and resisting the meds wasn't smart, not after the ordinances about unmedicated persons and liability. And you signed that enclave agreement, didn't you?

Grrls, Marina is currently incarcerated ... Or, we should say, under treatment at Loving Hands Care Facility in Silver Valley, Colorado. It's one of the christian women's organization facilities that got built when privatization of the public loony bins went all the way. Usually well-meaning, ineffectual white ladies on the administrative team, you know the type.

Hell, look back over Marina's posts and you'd get a pretty good idea of what the target of her anger looks like.

she's schizy as all fuck, but yesterday was like having sex with a CIA dude or something . . . hard to explain.

Finally, in the early evening, I went for a walk because sitting around the house and peeking out the window at the two vans with the humans in black was driving me nuts.

So, I was huffing and puffing uphill on Ambersand Street when the strangest sight did appear before mine eyes . . . Six blonde ladies . . . and I EMPHASIZE the word LADIES, walking towards me. Attractive middle-aged gals, expensive-but-modest ankle length dresses, heavy dollface makeup, sprayed hair, very fifties looking. But all wearing PINK LEATHER JACKETS! and on the leather jacket, right over their hearts, a day glo painting of a bleeding heart wrapped in barbed wire with a small yellow double helix just to the right.

I started giggling. But then I noticed they were surrounding me. Well, to make for an abrupt end to this story, they stomped the living shit out of me. They were calling me a prick, a dirtbag and an asshole, your basic hostile buttstomping shit, except one of them, who looked and sounded terribly familiar. She kept repeating the lines; "My roses feel silly. My words feel silly. My fish feel silly." Weirder still, Psycho drove by five minutes later, while I was still trying to find my feet, and took me to the hospital. She didn't talk to me. She was flirting and cooing with somebody on the cellular the whole way there, as if nothing important was happening. I thought I saw a light flicker on the inside of her nose ring, and then I passed out.

My suggestion, in case any of you get a notion to go bounding off into the blue, or Silver Valley, to stage a rescue mission or something, is to plan it on a medium other than this list. Agent Al and his buds would *love* to have health-care terrorists to play with too, I bet. And crossing state lines.

'N since I've been so kind as to incriminate myself as far as file pilferage goes, this persona will self-destruct in ten seconds following the post of this message. "Skeezix" will go back under, which won't be hard, because one dumb indian looks like another to you wasitchu.

bye, marina. You fucked up. But I won't. But I wish you luck, in that pastel-painted hole where they're keeping you, drifted to the gills with the latest designer tranq/moodlifter cocktail. Good thing there's the net-access program for the institutionalized, hey, babe?

Damn shame. I will remember you. And the rest of you on this list.

Grrrlove Mailing List, APRIL 2000
Date: April 26, 2000
From: satanspawn@smokeasy.gov
Subject: agents?

i dunno who's more fulla shit here, this "agent" or this disappearing skeezix act, or marina hirself. i mean, marina should shut the fuck up regardless of whether she's in a hospital or has a husband or whatever, but this skeezix superhero stuff stinks like the bottom of embarcadero station ... who is she, our fairy fucking godmother?

•¿¿¿ • From the Electron-Rife Desk of Jude Milhon• ¿¿¿•
•¿¿¿¿¿¿¿¿¿¿¿¿•   •aka StJude•   •¿¿¿¿¿¿¿¿¿¿¿¿•
•¿¿¿¿¿¿¿¿¿¿¿¿•   •stjude@well.com•   •¿¿¿¿¿¿¿¿¿¿¿¿•
Date: Dec 29, 1998
To: Hyatt@Ballantine.Books.com, rusirius@well.com
Subject: Re: Lucky to be alive

I'm fairly boggled right now. I just got home after visiting Ken in SF General. They released him from the ICU, after wrapping him completely with plastic (that's what they do nowadays, and I guess it prevents infections, but gah, it's horrible to visit a mummy.) He could hardly talk because his mouth was swollen and stuffed with toothgrowing stuff . . . but he can use the laptop, not that he has a lap.

Next to his bed there was a huge horrible postmodern bouquet -- carnivorous flora, and fungus and thorny branches -- and, o my god, it was from Ballantine! But I was not frightened, not me. I fed it a fly.

Trudy, no joke. Could Ken have been done by book company goons?

joan of arc, if yer really an agent then you already *know* everything i'm saying. hardly any secret. and if the disappearing skeezix is still reading this list, i don't care who fucking knows it, all of this isn't some big mystery. maybe marina's a lunatic, maybe skeezix really is a cracker to respect.

i just think all this paranoia's fucking stupid. i mean we should all know by now that any of us could be anybuddy,

maybe these are all just messages you're writing in your sleep, to yourself, hacking sendmail in your sleep so you wake up and you got all these messages from the Grrrls all over the world. but you wrote 'em yerself. see what i'm saying? so fuck the paranoia.

i mean, take the Smokeasy. we are just trying to make a place where people can hang out and smoke whatever they want and grow their own food and smokes, and considering the little army we've had to build up to create something THIS SIMPLE. i don't know why they wanted to make us stop in the first place, we weren't hurting anybody!

so if this is the way things iz, then everything is fucked, i mean EVERYTHING and wondering about feds and stupid bytches in LA and whether they're lying is a waste of time. if there are agents on this list, they can byte me. anyone wants to talk, you can email me privately. this list is going to shit and fast.
--mirbane

ps: Madam sez the only time women should think about computers is when we're blowing them up.

Grrrlove Mailing List, MAY 2000
Date: May 9, 2000
From: chrone2
Subject: SMOKEASY BUSTED!!!!
o my god, i was there last night when they busted

```
###################################################
######### • Trudy B. Hyatt •           #########
######### • Editorial Assistant •      #########
######### • Hyatt@Ballantine.Books.com • #########
###################################################
```
Dec 29, 1998
To: rusirius@well.com stjude@well.com
Subject: Re: Lucky to be alive

Ken, I was shocked to hear about your injuries. *I* had Ballantine send you the flowers. (Were they really menacing? Maybe Flowers by Wire has its local dialects -- I suggested something perky, to cheer you up.)

Jude, not a chance. Come ON. I like to think that the book publishing industry is one of the last bastions of gentility. No way.

hmmm. I'll try to check around . . .

```
###################################################
######### • Trudy B. Hyatt •           #########
######### • Editorial Assistant •      #########
######### • Hyatt@Ballantine.Books.com • #########
###################################################
```
Dec 30, 1998
To: rusirius@well.com stjude@well.com
Subject: Re: Lucky to be alive

I think I can assure you confidently that Ballantine Books does NOT have a Goon Squad. That's a really strange idea, when you think about it -- a Ballantine goon squad?? I wonder if all this religious stuff is not just getting on your nerves generally. Ken, I know you didn't beat YOURSELF up, but are you sure about the details? I'm told that if you have a concussion you can have a retrograde amnesia or a distorted memory of what happened just before your injury. But don't worry about that. Just get well.

Trudy
ps: of course, the Random House Family is a very large company. but REALLY -- no, impossible.

out the smokeasy ... it was around 2 am, and everybody was
groovin' on their particular mixes, n suddenly something hits
the outer door like a quake, shakes the whole place, and this loud-
speaker blasts through: OPEN UP. WE HAVE A WARRANT. NOBODY
ATTEMPT TO LEAVE. and immediately, no pause at all, baLAMMALAM,
the door is flat on the floor and a SWAT team jams in, cool with
their military moves, little machine pistols, gasmasks and
goggles ... and they say, so help me: UP AGAINST THE WALL, and
in the door they fix this enormous fan, and this typhoon sucks
all the smoke out ... And then they turn off the heavy ordnance
and do a doff-gasmask parade-rest thing, and then this big dude
starts reading:

"Under the authority of this and that ..." and we're all standing there
listening, and I notice the insignia. They're CDC, this outfit. This is
hard core. We're fucked -- it's the tac force -- the SWAT team of the
Centers for Disease Control.

A little kid who looked like the real Tank Girl threw a beermug at the
reading dude and maybe broke something on him, and there was instant
shit. During the mess
a couple of us threw
smokebombs, and some
of us got out. I'm
gone, goner than
ever. Maybe I'll
never see any of you
f2f again.

•¿¿¿¿• From the Electron-Rife Desk of Jude Milhon •¿¿¿¿•
•¿¿¿¿¿¿¿¿¿¿¿¿•   •aka StJude•   •¿¿¿¿¿¿¿¿¿¿¿¿•
•¿¿¿¿¿¿¿¿¿¿¿¿•   •stjude@well.com•   •¿¿¿¿¿¿¿¿¿¿¿¿•
Date: Dec 30, 1998
To: rusirius@well.com
Subject: Re: Lucky to be alive

Your teeth sprouting yet? I agree they're not giving you enough drugs.
How COULD they? Have you had email from many different groups claiming credit for yr stomping? From your description of the ladies who
fucked you up, i doubt they're religious. Although the barbwire heart and
the double helix sounds like . . . Catholic terrorist right-to-lifers -- Sacred
Heart faction? But all the dirty-talking . . . well, it could just be misanthropy -- you are, yes, a penised person. Maybe they're a Marianist Feminist splinter group? Only I'd think they'd be wearing VirginMary-BLUE
leather jackets. . . .

Damn, it's hard to focus yr paranoia when you have as many enemies as
we do.

Don't it make you proud?

Outlive the fuckers.
Mutate and ... you
know....

Grrrlove Mailing
List, JULY 2000
Date: July 1, 2000
From: speakeasy!mir-
bane@roving.edu
Subject: fuck the CDC!

I'm in one of the
holding camps. FUCK!

I'm talking to you via their online library, btw. thanks, MELVYL, hee hee -- learn yer haqr skills babys, you never know when they might come in necessary!!!!!

Looking back, i'm surprised madam let me gak around the Smokeasy, much less help with the farms. see i'd only been on the scene like a coupla weeks, not a junkie or nothing just this little, stupid fucking 14yr-old with no divination at all, you know? i just liked to play chess with the old hippie type guys and do stuph on the public terminals on the ground floor, vacuum down some espresso, play hangrope with the punks and stuff. and then i'd say the magick word and the vator would take me down to the store-room, and i was just doing cloves and nitrous oxide, you know, nothing to worry about. And madame makes me her right hand 'man'.

so here i am this idiot chyck thinking the holding camps are

**From the Electronic Desk of the Honorable Bruce Sterling,
United States Senator from the State of Texas
Date: April 15, 2000
To: stjude
Subject: again, paranoid praxis**

Here's another tidbit for your delectation.

btw, did you receive your invitation to Vice Pres Barlow's MayDay bash at the Lincoln Memorial? This is not to be missed, Jude. It'll be historical, at least . . .
————————-
**Date: Jan 8, 1999
From the electronic desk of
James P. Davenport**

**NSA.3lit3.soc.eng.
S&B, *****, luminated 1s, masonic order, #2, System Control, EFF Control, Cypherpunk Control, P.Dot.Aleph, White Temple, O.T.O-Ji-had, A:A:, Semblance of Order, >>><<<, Rapid Response.**

**To: psystär
O.T.O.-Jihad, >>><<<, Rapid Response, White Ladies Lounge #606**

(my roses feel silly, my words feel silly, my fish feel silly, m.b.x. ex.L!)

COMMAND:

Ok, beautiful. I accept your explanation. I will find out who at the White Ladies' Lounge gave you the false override, but the damage is done. And if you say that subject Sirius will cooperate if we make him feel wanted and give him a title and a few bucks, let's get on with it. I'll send special agent Johnson there to talk to him. I'll make sure that Sirius is not released from the hospital until Johnson sees him.

You'll like Johnson. He fucks like a stallion.

I'd like to have you with ME in a couple of weeks. Johanna is on one of her little "separate vacation" larks. I've already reserved the old lodge in Tibet. We will hunt down the last snow leopard, drink Russian Schnapps, I will wrap you in furs from half-a-dozen endangered species, and fuck your guts in.

273

Date: Jan 9, 1999
From: PsyStär
O.T.O.-Jihad, >>><<<, Rapid Response, White Ladies Lounge #606

To: James P. Davenport   NSA.3lit3.soc.eng.
S&B, *****, luminated 1s, masonic order, #2, System Control, EFF
Control, Cypher Control P.Dot.Aleph, White Temple, O.T.O-Jihad,
A:A:, Semblance of Order, >>>
<<<, Rapid Response

(my roses feel silly, my words feel silly, my fish feel silly, m.b.x. ex.L!)

That's my Jimmy! ;=)

I feel really badly about the fuck up. Who could have wanted this loser
stomped? Oh well . . . So when does my Johnson get here, Jimmy? This
metaslut is reduced to football players and rock stars. YiiiiYiiiiiYiiiiiYiiiii

this paranoid liberal
delusion, and the
bust goes down just
like chrone2 said ...
they busted my arm
after i threw a glass
at somebody special.

they really do have
those camps in north-
ern california, if i
get out i'll show you
my scars. if yer under
eighteen, they send
you straight there.
because you're an ad-
dict, according to the
CDC, just by virtue of
smoking a fucking

clove cigarette in the wrong place at the wrong time. and if you're a kid
and a junkie, even just a nicjunkie, you gotta go through strict deprogram-
ming, FOR YOUR OWN GOOD -- stricter than they have for the 'dults and full
of eight year old miracle crack babies and kids whose parents did too much
PCP when they were in the womb, and even kids stupider than me who talk astonished that they got caught when they were tricking and selling bad data
on the streetcorners and all kinds of obvious shit. not recommended.

Anyway, sisters ... pull it tighter underground and always wear yer
paranoia condom ...

New York Daily News   July 16, 2000

Quant Couple Breaks the Bank

by John Markdown

Infamous Wall Street quants and tech gurus
Gracie and Zarkov are walking off today with
more capital than the yearly budget of the government of the United States of America. Using
a test model of a Sun Microsystem nanocom-
puter that is not yet commercially available, and
an "Investment Virus," the couple is now in pos-
session of more wealth than anybody in the history of the world.

The "Investment Virus" allowed the couple to
create a massive capital flow that moved, within
nanoseconds, from national currency to national

currency and from speculation to speculation. Apparently, the nano-computer was able to plan, create and exploit wild market fluctuations, sometimes in less than a second's time.

While the couple's success has produced the highest overnight stock market boom in its history, the market system itself has been shaken to its roots. President Gore has joined international leaders in calling for "an international state of emergency" and asked for cooperation among nations in creating a "one-world monetary system that can prevent future disasters of this nature." The president blamed the Republican congress for creating a climate of "isolationism" that has led to "a lack of cooperation" among nations and "wild arbitrage discrepancies" in the monetary and market systems. The President also blamed the recent actions of the Government of China, which has passed a law encouraging a "second economy," legitimizing the black market barter in a

cont pg. 4

Date: Jan 21, 1999
From: Magickal Lexington Johnson, esq.
NSA.Op.H37
*****, luminated 1s, masonic order, #2 P.Dot.Aleph, A:A:, Semblance of Order, >>><<<

Stanford, 1966
System Control 1970 - Present
PsyOps: 1980 - 1985
NLP/CLP/AIF/MC 1969 - Present
Private Defense Holding Corporation: 1992 - Present
(indicate file encrypted)

To: James P. Davenport NSA.3lit3.soc.eng.
S&B, *****, luminated 1s, masonic order, #2, System Control, EFF Control, Cypherpunk
Control, P.Dot.Aleph, White Temple, O.T.O-Jihad, A:A:, Semblance of Order, >>><<<, Rapid Response.

(my roses feel silly, my words feel silly, my fish feel silly, m.b.x. ex.L!)

Let One's Talk

This "R. U. Sirius" dude is one fuckin' out there nutter. Admittedly, he's in the hospital under heavy sedation. But I couldn't get him to understand what I was offering him. He seems to see everything as some kind of art project or entertainment industry thing. Here I am, pretending to offer him a Top Secret position in the NSA, and he keeps on telling me that I have to call his agent, and that he wants 15%!!! I tried three times. I can terminate him or I can just leave.

btw, PsychoStär was even better than expected. MAN! Made my stay worthwhile.

Date: Dec 12, 2000
From the electronic desk of James P. Davenport NSA.3lit3.soc.eng.
S&B, *****, luminated 1s, masonic order, #2, System Control, EFF
Control, Cypherpunk Control, P.Dot.Aleph, White Temple, O.T.O-Ji-
had, A:A:, Semblance of Order, >>><<<, Rapid Response.

Yale 1958
Pentagon 1963–1966
Central Intelligence Agency 1967–1968
System Consultant, Office of the President 1968 - 1976, 1980 - 1992
System Control 1969 - Present
PsyOps 1969 - Present
NLP/CLP/AIF/MC 1969 - Present
Private Defense Holding Corporation 1992 - Present
(indicate encrypted file)

To: PsyStar
O.T.O.-Jihad, >>><<<, Rapid Response, White Ladies Lounge #606

(my roses feel silly, my words feel silly, my fish feel silly, m.b.x. ex.L!)
Let One's Talk

Command:

Yes, the assignment has long been pointless, it's true. But I thought you
were enjoying keeping an eye on S.F. for us. The Mitchell Brother Theater
is NOT that obscure, baby. It's a power point. One can smell the dark currents of sweat, menses, jealousy, semen, cunt juice, fratricide. Powerful
magick, my dear.

Anyway. Sure. We can get you an assignment in L.A., not a problem.
Enough of this Sirius. Terminate the fucker midnight, at the turning of
the Winter Solstice, December 21.

San Francisco Chronicle
September 10, 2000

DEBATE DEBACLE DETOURS SIRIUS CAMPAIGN

"There's a small nuclear device in my left sportscoat pocket!" Presidential frontrunner R. U. Sirius shouted at Republican candidate Newt Gingrich. Before he could get the entire sentence out, a grotesque reddish-green boil sprouted on his right cheek. While the local audience in Scranton Civic Auditorium in Scranton PA and over four million television viewers watched in astonishment, the boil grew to the size of a small balloon. Gingrich, seated to Sirius' right, walked briskly away and backstage. Armed Secret Service Agents, protecting President Gore, quickly surrounded candidate Sirius. An on-the-spot search uncovered nothing but a wallet and a bottle of the smart drug Vasopressin. As Sirius was led off by the Secret Service agents, President Gore quipped, "I feel his pain," to audience laughter and applause.

It was easily the strangest turn of events in any Presidential campaign in US history, surpassing even the incident on October 23, 1996 when independent Candidate Ross Perot

cont. pg 6

```
===================================================
```
DATE: 15 September 2000
FROM: security@mondovan.com
TO: rusirius@mondovan.com
SUBJECT: INTERCEPT

Sir,
The security server intercepted the following e-mail message. What
action do you want taken?

FROM : justpat@mondovan.com
> To: mgant@gm.com
> SUBJECT: Hi, Melissa!!!
>
> Hey, Miss! What's up? Congratulations about your
> promotion!!! Regional manager, all right!!!! I'm sorry I
> haven't written in
> a while, but things
> have been so hectic   ##############
> around here I don't   #__/==$=_   # <- From the **High-Tech** Fully **Electronic Desk**
> know which way is   # /))-00(\   #   **of R. U. Sirius**
> up. Busy, busy,   # (((-)))   #
> busy!   #)))\ /(((# -> **rusirius@well.com**
>   ##############
> Things are really   **Date: Dec 14, 2000**
> chaotic here since   **To: StJude**
> R. U. freaked out.   **Subject: THE MESS**
> Did you see that,
> by the way? Unbe-   So . . . here we are, in minimalist implosive times exploding in public.
> lievable. Anyway,   What will they say? They will say, "It's a mess." That's what they always
> the Vanilli Com-   say. My room is a mess. My hair is a mess. The world is a mess. And peo-
> pound is like a   ple want TIDY. Fuck 'em. Any critic wants to MESS with me gets fragged.
> fortress now. There   And that's that!
> are rumors that no
> one is allowed in or out. I've been so busy that I haven't had the
> chance to leave, and quite frankly, I don't want to test things and
> find out. There's a long history of people following a charismatic
> leader and winding up dead. Jim Jones, David Koresh, those people
> in Switzerland and Idaho; I don't even want to think about it.
> Don't tell anyone, but I think R.U. is really starting to take this
> stuff about himself seriously.
>
> Every night I hear screaming from R.U.'s end of the compound. Of

•¿¿¿• From the Electron-Rife Desk of Jude Milhon •¿¿¿•
•¿¿¿¿¿¿¿¿¿¿¿¿•   •aka StJude•   •¿¿¿¿¿¿¿¿¿¿¿¿•
•¿¿¿¿¿¿¿¿¿¿¿¿•   •stjude@well.com•   •¿¿¿¿¿¿¿¿¿¿¿¿•

Date: Dec 14, 2000
To: rusirius
Subject: An essay on the post-novel

Hey, I've just figured out what happened to the "novel." And why we are now, you and I, forced to valorize this THING we're working on as a "post-novel."

The post-novel is a hack, of course. And we're honorary hackers, subverting the longterm stalemate between writer and publisher, career and function, text and product. In the process of getting this book published, that process has become horribly clear.

Consider novels written today, however pomo. Mid-second chapter in a Don Delillo novel I say to myself: this is the *best* thing I've EVER READ in my *LIFE*. And at the end, I go hm, or eh? Now substitute the name of almost any current novelist who has a real NY Reviewer reputation . . . What's happening here? Why, wake up, darling! It's the same thing that's happening everywhere in late capitalism: the novel has become entirely market-driven.

What is a novel? Whatever it may be to you, your novel is a marketing concept to your agent, or (if you're already in the club) to your publisher: it's just two chapters and an outline. To make an agent AND a publisher care *enough*, you gotta pitch 'em hard and fast. You slam 'em with your wizzy, diabolical, irresistible chapters, one-TWO . . . and an outline.

Those two chapters are hard work, baby -- months and months of rethink and rewrite and polish, polish, while the novel pullulates in your mind. And then you sign the publisher's contract . . . and then you get the advance. And then . . . you notice that you have to produce the whole rest of it in eight months.

You're slogging around hip-deep in new ideas after an intriguing plot shift right in the middle, when WHOOPS! it's the 1st draft deadline, where's the *stuff*? You gotta *deliver*. You temporize, so you can space out and rethink the whole middle development, and YOW! it's your agent, the rotten turncoat, beating on you for the overdue text, text, text . . . The din from the publisher-agent axis continues day after night. So in terrible despair you forget the new ideas, eliminate a subplot, cheat on a key

> course, that end is
> off limits to the
> rest of us now. St.
> Jude sends us video
> mail every day try-
> ing to reassure us
> that nothing is
> wrong, but I can
> tell she's faking it.
>
> I gotta tell you, I
> think the unthink-
> able has happened.
> R.U., the prankster
> extraordinaire, the
> guy who never took
> anything seriously,
> is now starting to
> seriously think he
> has been "pro-
> grammed" to lead
> mankind. He's
> turned into a liv-
> ing example of the
> phrase "power cor-
> rupts".
>
> I realize that I've
> probably scared you
> with what I've
> written. I don't
> mean to. I'm fine. I
> can take care of
> myself.
>
> Anyway, tell Mom I
> said Hi and I'm
> fine. If you see Dad
> tell him I said the
> same. And tell our
> brother to hurry up
> and get e-mail,
> willya?? What's he

> waiting for? I want to write to him directly!!! :-) See ya!
>
> Love, Patrick

===============
FROM : rusirius@
mondovan.com
TO: security@
mondovan.com
SUBJECT: RE:
INTERCEPT

Send the first and
last paragraphs un-
changed. Disable this
guy's outgoing mail.
I think it's time for
disciplinary action.

event sequence, mock up an ending and ship them the 1st draft -- a
sewn-together frankensteined mockery of your creation . . . And when
the editorial changes come back you can hardly bear to look at them . . .
you just want to FINISH . . . you want this nightmare to be OVER . . .

This is the novel today. It used to be not so odd to spend 15 years writing
a novel, polishing, enriching, perfecting. Now you got 15 months, tops.
The contract you signed so ecstatically locks you into this frame, and
you're a gone goose whose foie will become gras or else. It's like producing your next album if you're a musician -- you get out the product in fifteen months or your career's, as they say, in the toilet. See?

R. U. baby, (at the risk of sounding like I got a Lucky stuck onto my
lower lip) -- you gotta resist the process. If you want to forget the POST-
NOVEL and be a real NOVELIST you gotta concentrate on getting just two
things. The first thing you need is a rich, giving lover who believes in you
all the way. And the second is a rent-paid room remote from same. As my
Brit friend sings:

Information's independent,
Always Longing to be Free.
But *Art*'s always been a *rent-boy* --
Highest-bidder, bought-and-spent boy --
Needing sweet plu-tog-am-ee . . .

ps: Is that too erudite for americans? A rent-boy is a hooker, and pluto-
gamy = coupling with the rich.
pps: To get yet MORE erudite: Ars dura, vita brevis.
    (Life is short, Art is hard-ass.) Hee hee.

Date: Sept. 16, 2000
From: stjude
To: rusirius@well.com
<PGPencrypt>
Subject: The Rolling Spin wants YOU

. . . they want you so bad.
They've been calling me all day: want to interview me NOW . . . so I
assume they're trying to nail you on these rumors. I'm stalling them
off. What's the strategy, Kenneth? You know me: I'm in this all the
way. But shit, it's not helping my work any.

Uh oh. Oh shit. Too far off balance . . . I think I'm gonna

So I'm cruising in the nutrient bath, sluggish but irritable, sucking, sucking . . .
Things just aint
the same for me
nowadays. Seems like
all I do is suck,
and it's doin me no
good. Makes me feel
crazy, like I need
something else, need
it bad . . . And then
I see HER.

•¿¿¿ • **From the Electron-Rife Desk of Jude Milhon** • ¿¿¿•
•¿¿¿¿¿¿¿¿¿¿¿¿•   •aka StJude•   •¿¿¿¿¿¿¿¿¿¿¿¿•
•¿¿¿¿¿¿¿¿¿¿¿¿•   •stjude@well.com•   •¿¿¿¿¿¿¿¿¿¿¿¿•
Date: Dec 16, 2000
To: hyatt@ballantine.books.com
Subject: You say we still need an Ending??? Nonsense.

Absurd. We need three or four.

Since the Novel's gotten so effete that most of them close with a mere
nano-resolution -- the merest glint of closure -- our Post-Novel should
pile on climax after climax, each separate level of reference in the text
knotting itself up in spasms.

We will exhaust our readers with climaxes. Our readers will be left fucked
out, their sense of closure SO overloaded that they're in a closure *refrac-
tory period* for WEEKS . . . Call this the Terminator trope. Oh no HERE IT
COMES AGAIN.

Heh heh heh.

>st guido<

She's beautiful.
Plasmids are slip-
ping around under
her skin like neck-
laces—she's super-F!
She's long and lean
-- a rod, of course.
And I know she's
not my species but
she's so exciting,
so F-able. My male
plasmid is SHAKIN'
in me. She's rotat-
ing in the slow cur-
rent. Glycoproteins

in her skin flash when she moves, like the ember scum on lava.
Now my maleness pulses, bursting, think I gotta . . . I'm
gonna . . . AHHH! Penises shoot like fireworks outa me! Two, three
of 'em!

My middle dick shoots all the way over to her: it curls and snakes
around her waist. Its tip starts to tickle her; it's rooting and bur-
rowing . . . She's shakin too now; she rotates slow, dragging my snake
tight around her . . . now I'm trying to put it into her, rooting between her glycoprotein petals. Now it's almost . . . Yeah. I'm in . . .
and I'm squelching it into her, going deep, deeper, feeling her plasmids part around me, right into her center. I drag her towards me,
reel her in to me, feeling crazier the closer she gets . . . Oh yeah
oh yeah . . .

She's here, she's
right here, we're
pulled tight to-
gether, it's like
everything is her,
and I'm right
inside her chromo-
some ring, and her
ring is circling
around me like a
star halo, and I
feel this explosion
in my center, and
I know that my
own ring is rup-
tured . . . it's an
open strand of beads
now, and it's push-
ing into my dick,
bead after bead . . .

•¿¿¿•From the Electron-Stuffed Desk of Jude Milhon•¿¿¿•
•¿¿¿¿¿¿¿¿¿¿¿•   •aka StJude•   •¿¿¿¿¿¿¿¿¿¿¿•
•¿¿¿¿¿¿¿¿¿¿¿• •stjude@well.com• •¿¿¿¿¿¿¿¿¿¿¿•
Date: Dec 17, 2000
To: rusirius@well.com
Subject: Re: Trudy's letter

>>They're pressuring me horribly to get you to sign off on the current
>>draft. They want to make the final decision right now, accept or reject.

christ on a bike! they want to cut us off!

the manuscript's a horrid farrago right now. they see it in its present
form, they'll cut our throats. you got YOUR advance ready to give back to
them, EH??? we are doomed, o fuck o dear.

okay, okay, i shall summon the Master -- watch this, ward, and pray. . . .

baby let me push it to you, get it in you, gotta get it all in
you . . . i can feel the stars pulsing out of my dick like a
roman candle, and she whirls . . . and it's okay baby if I give
it all, it's okay if I die behind it, baby, cause i gotta give it
up, give it ALL, give it to you, give it to you give it to you
give it

oh

sorry.
o christ

That was INTENSE.

I think I went all the way -- splooged out all my DNA and died.

•¿¿¿•From the Electron-Stuffed Desk of Jude Milhon•¿¿¿•
•¿¿¿¿¿¿¿¿¿¿¿¿•   •aka StJude•   •¿¿¿¿¿¿¿¿¿¿¿¿•
•¿¿¿¿¿¿¿¿¿¿¿¿•   •stjude@well.com•   •¿¿¿¿¿¿¿¿¿¿¿¿•
Date: Dec 17, 2000
To: hyatt@ballantine.books.com
Subject: Re: They're pressuring me horribly
bcc: rusirius

Dear Trudy,

They want to call the sixth draft the finished manuscript???? And accept or reject it as it is NOW???? It is beyond absurd.

They might suggest that it is complete because they can't see the patterns still to emerge. The text is richer, and more austere, than they can now believe. Some of the nexi of its themes are barely schematic . . . some are suspended contraposed -- like Gaudi's cathedral, held inverted so that gravity itself creates the arches which will, when set upright, resist its power. Henry James, in speaking of the structure of *The Wings of the Dove*, recalled regretfully his architectural vision of the work before and during its construction -- those cyclopean walls, the vaults, the flying buttresses! -- and how he was forced to view it post-pub -- as scrim, lath and wallpaper. This must not happen to us!

The editors may look back from the completed work to this fertile chaos, and trace it in the schema that prefigured its solid arches . . . perhaps. But they can't see today what it truly is, until its full becoming.

Please accept my petition in this matter, and grant us another deadline a month hence, if it please the honorable Vice-Director of Marketing.

As ever, your obsequious etc,

Judith Milhon, Beatified
<st jude>

Sorry. Christ. Can't talk now. Gotta sleep. Talk tomorrow.
<Sorry>

>jude<

= = = = = = = = = = = = = = =
Date: Sept. 17, 2000
From: StJude
To: rusirius
<PGPencrypt>
Subject: done and done

Well, i feel really different about everything this morning.

i feel like we should maybe call it quits. I hate to bring this up, but you're starting to buy your own fuhrer shtick, and i'm beginning to mumble heil.

i just had an insanity counterattack, sort of. after last night i'm done, in more ways than one. take this as my letter of resignation. you could try to talk me out of leaving,

you might try to prevent me, but we both know there's little point to
it. i'm certainly not going to blow your cover. that would be like
murder. for my sake,
i just want to stop
doing what we're do-
ing. for your sake, i
wish you'd stop too.

you know, you've done
everything you wanted
to do. i did too. how
about shutting it all
down?

i've sorta seen god,
atheist style. and
when that happens,
like Rilke said: you
must change your
life.

now, as epiphanies
go, this was fairly
Ed Wood. And just
imagine: after a
life of celestial
sex and challenging
drugs and hyper-
haut-technology, the
ultimate experience
-- the full cos-
mopsycho-tantric
blowout -- is
a microbial blue
movie?????
(I think it was
E.Coli, btw.
I seem to remember
things from school
about F+ and Endo-
gutso Coli?)
anyway: a microbe. a
germ. . . . ah!

```
##############
#___/==$=\____   # <- From the High-Tech Fully Electronic Desk
# /))-00(\      #    of R. U. Sirius
# ((( -)))      #
# )))\ /(((     # -> rusirius@well.com
##############
```
Date: Dec 21, 2000
To: hyatt@ ballantine.books.com
Subject: hey czyck

Trudy-0
this is Jude, signing onto R.U.'s account. He's not around, so I thought
I'd tidy up his dot.mailrc for him.

There's been a little problem. We've been set back a week. R.U.'s run into
yet another extreme situation. Extreme situations are normal for him,
right, but this is . . . *more* extreme.

Got your enote. Yes, we do know we're over the latest deadline by 3
months, but after six years I think we have to face it: missed deadlines
are NOT unusual. And this time, lovey, we're talking FINAL DELIVERY.

REALLY: FINAL DELIVERY.

You see, R. U. was just getting ready to give the manuscript the last
once-over. He had it with him, in fact, when the horrible thing happened. He'd gone to pick up his girlfriend Psycho Stār after work, at the
Mitchell Brother Theater (legend has it that once there were *two* Brothers
Mitchell . . .) R. U. and Psycho S were just inside the front doors, in the
little lobby there, chatting with another dancer, Tiffany, getting ready to
leave, when it happened.

The doors bash open, there's a shout, and everybody turns to the
doors just in time to see -- oh shit, it's Josephine, and she's got an automatic rifle cradled against her big baglady bosom, and she's screaming
"TIME TO GO TO HELL, SIRIUS."

It's so unreal that nobody moves . . . no diving for the floor, no nothing:
they just stand there and look, while Josephine, this nut who's been
stalking R. U. since 1997, recites a poem. R. U. hates poetry, but he's just
standing there while Josephine rants in blank verse, jogging the gun up

and down with the fucking iambic, until she gets to the end . . . many many feet later, you bet. It's something about how she and he will be united forever in the Ether, or maybe it was in thee, either . . . something . . . She has a weird accent. Then she sort of nods her head, like "okay, that's that," raises the gun and blasts four shots point blank.

One shot nicked the top off R. U.'s right ear: he says it was like somebody slapping him on the side of the head. Two rounds hit nothing.

The fourth went straight into Psycho's mid-brain. Dead center forehead hit . . . right in her third-eye tattoo: heh: it was a 3rd *bulls*eye. hee-heeheeeee

R. U. says it was such a perfect hit that Psycho's head just sort of opened up like a hatch, and her brain flopped onto the floor like a peeled cantaloupe. Josephine drops the rifle, looks at Sirius and says, "Jesus, you ARE a lucky sod."

Josephine sits down heavily on the floor, away from the little brooklet of blood now babbling down toward the doors, and starts going through her bags, muttering that she has something apropos to this whole thing that she'd like to read, she wrote it some time ago . . . it's right here somewhere . . . R. U. looks at Psycho twitching and sort of smiling on the floor, looks at Josephine, looks up at the ceiling, and starts humming to himself . . . THEN Tiffany flips -- begins to scream and scream, and people rush out from backstage, and it's complete bedlam.

In the chaos Sirius walks over to Josephine and tells her that he'd like to invite her out for a drink to talk things over, but she'll have to wait around for the police, and he's gotta finish the final reading of this book he's working on for Ballantine, so ciao.

Psycho died fairly soon -- sooner than you'd think, given her history -- smiling a sweet sweet smile the whole time. Funny thing. R. U.'s been trying to figure out how to ditch Psycho Stār for the last few months and several times he was muttering about finding a hitman. You might wonder why he didn't just break up with her. You don't know Psycho. She wouldn't go away.

Anyway, he went home that night and did the final proof on about half the book, didn't even call me. The following afternoon he called, and for ten minutes he just raved about how great the book was, before telling me, "something sorta weird happened last night." As he described the

hmmmm

maybe i HAVE splooged out all my germinal stuff, because i feel i've done it all. i've finished with my life. i want to re-tire to some neohip-pie TAZ and spend the rest of it drooling on tie-dyes.

well, you know what i mean.

always, nonetheless, your friend and comrade

jude

ps: just got confirmed -- it's really gonna happen. you can mail my pen-sion checks c/o rave.new. world@maui. zowie.int
= = = = = = = = = = = = = = =
Date: Sept. 17, 2000
FROM: rusirius @mondovan.com
To: stjude @mondovan.com
SUBJECT: RE: done and done

get a grip!

i've sent the doc down to see you.

RUS

==

Date: Sept. 17, 2000
FROM: stjude@
mondovan.com
TO: rusirius@
mondovan.com
SUBJECT: RE: done and
done

oh yeah, nothing's
wrong with me. i just
got the post-E.Coli-
tal triste.

doc gave me this di-
agnosis -- well, ac-
tually he muttered
about post-traumatic
hallucinatory doo-dah
doo-dah -- doc's
humor-impaired -- and
he kept trying to
shoot me up with
valium.

he did give me some
blue pills, some yel-
low pills, AND some
GREEN pills. he said
i could call him at
ANY time, day or
night, and then he
hinted at a mercy
fuck. so kind.

when i told him i was
cutting out, he also
hinted you'd given
the order to have me
confined to quarters.

incident he couldn't stop laughing. R. U. always sees the humor in accidents . . . it's what I love about him. Anyway, he said that he was going
to read the rest of the book (this was yesterday) and send it off to you
the next day (Today!). "What the hell," I thought. Never cared much for
Stär. R. U. and his hysterical femmes. Sheesh. But then at midnight I got
a call from his drinking buddy, Dave Vigliano. R. U. had had a few drinks
and then broke out the Forget It! He said R. U. got this strange look on
his face and popped six caps all at once. Then he looked even stranger
and just tipped the whole bottle down his throat. Sluiced it all down with
great glugs of scotch straight from the bottle. Goddess, that's disgusting:
what a pig he can be. You know how I hate alcohol. Anyway, Vig wasn't
too alarmed at that -- R. U.'s got such a monster tolerance for Forget It!
that a usual dose won't even make him absent-minded . . . He can take
six and still find his KEYS.

Anyway, he's sitting there in Vigliano's apartment looking (yes) bemused -- and then he starts picking up lamps and matchbooks and doilies
and asking, "What's this? What's this here?" Vig is about to flip -- This is
idiotic even for R. U., and he's thinking about Emergency Rooms, and
suddenly R. U. lurches out of his chair, points out the door and shouts,
"What's THAT?" And he was gone.

So he's around somewhere, having an out-of-brain experience. Vig
says the last time he did a whole bottle of Forget It, he snapped out of it
in five days. That would be nice. But just in case, I've got his personality
loaded into an expert system that I can crank up. It can finish reading the
book and sign off on it *for* him. If the bastard doesn't get his brain up
and running within the week, I'll run cyb-R. U. for you, and you've got
your final delivery, no problem. In fact, if he STAYS encrypted this time,
we could strap him down and go for a total replacement. . . .

Hey. That means he'd become his image for real: R. U. SIRIUS!!!
crazed Chairman-Mao King-Hip Poster Boy of the new anarcho-wanko-
dada, doo-dah doo-dah . . . Starting out with a clean set of megalomemories, instead of the horrible lowlife past that must haunt his every
thought as is (except when he's on Forget It!, of course). Hmmm, now
that I think about it, maybe I'd be doing the poor bastard a favor. I could
do it anyway. Just terminate the fucker -- replace him with his fantasy
self. R. U. SIRIUSLY. What do you think? I'll leave it up to you. Save us a
few days at the very least. And I sure could use the 17K!

•¿¿¿•From the Electron-Stuffed Desk of Jude Milhon•¿¿¿•
•¿¿¿¿¿¿¿¿¿¿¿¿•   •aka StJude•   •¿¿¿¿¿¿¿¿¿¿¿¿•
•¿¿¿¿¿¿¿¿¿¿¿¿• •stjude@well.com•   •¿¿¿¿¿¿¿¿¿¿¿¿•

Date: Dec 24, 2000
To: Hyatt@Ballantine.books.com,
Subject: we've done it

Listen, Trudy. RU is apparently out of the loop -- maybe he'll FORGET IT for keeps, and in the meantime I'm not waiting for no 3L1T3 supersecret insider info, no. This book needs no hacker's cookbook -- we don't want it.

Consider: a Book of Rules goes out of date immediately, as identified holes in the fabric get patched . . . What's important is to spread the word that when any hole is patched we can find NEW holes. We're the little vermin in this war, varmints -- mice and rats and bugs and viruses -- we're everywhere. The guardians of security haven't a chance. We have the discovery, the exploration . . . they can only stand and try to maintain.

It's misleading to include a rulebook. It implies there's a sort of holy writ. Forget it -- the important word is there's no word. (The rules are . . . NO RULES -- to quote a fine old anarchist bumpersticker.) The game's afoot, now and forever. It scampers on little feet, very fast. The game changes weekly, as new ideas, new widgets get invented and immediately shared. Any newbie to the game can find *up-to-the-minute* instruction online . . . and the online, and the virtual underground, is as immanent as god used to be.

We may already have won . . .

We've built ourselves a virtual country, a permanent TAZ, those of us who have faced the American clampdown. Our Subterrania exists, a supranational nation. Anyone who wants to join can find a way in. Govt agents and counterintelligence people can get in as easily -- but what'll they gain compared to what they may lose? There's no organization to bust in here. There are no leaders -- everyone's a leader. There's a net of minds only loosely connected to identities, physical OR virtual. Breaking up the American underground is like trying to bust the planetary Net . . . they tried that, and they failed. And the govt infiltrators, what danger they're in! Immersed in the siblinghood of an entirely imaginary underground, many of them will listen and understand . . . and slip their leashes and join the struggle for real, because an anarchist counterforce that checks and balances the central government is as American as apple macturnovers . . .

(for my own good.)
i'm outa here.

we have met the enemy
and they are us.

you got stuff to send
me, do it c/o Hack-
tic in Amsterdam.

in the meantime, you
should take 200 of
those pills and call
me if you feel bet-
ter. actually, call
me only if you want
ANOTHER revolution,
you sorry sellout
motherfucker

>jude<

ps: i expect you to
rescind my do-not-
pass at the gate-
house. if not, you
may lose a couple of
your baby SS-niks.
I'M armed. I'M fe-
male. i'm GONE.
= = = = = = = = = = = = = = = =
Date: Feb.5, 2001
From: justpat@
mondovan.com
To: rusirius@
mondovan.com
Subject: K. Eric
Drexler Interview

I really hope this was
some kind of a fucking
R.U. Sirius joke,
man!!!!!!!! I am so

mad I can't fucking type!!!! This morning, following your instructions, the crew and I drove to the Institute to do the K. Eric Drexler interview you arranged. When we got there, we asked to see Dr. Drexler, and the receptionist got all nervous and said there was no Dr. Drexler at the Institute. After we caused a stink with the cameras and the boom mike, the director of the Institute came down and took us aside. This director, Dr. Hazelton, said that due to Dr. Drexler's "condition" the video interview was out of the question. I asked what Drexler's condition was. Hazelton said he couldn't show me unless I promised not to use it. I said I'd think about it.

Hazelton brought us into one of the labs and showed us a little terrarium made out of a fish tank. There was a little house and little bonsai trees in it, like a picturesque village in a model train set. The label at the top said "ERIC Drexler". I looked into the terrarium and there he was!!!! THE FUCKING GUY IS ONLY ONE INCH TALL!!!!!!!!!! I mean, what the fuck is this? I'm expecting to interview a normal, full sized guy-type guy, and instead I'm talking to a fucking sea monkey. The first thing I thought of was, we can't use the lavaliere mic on this guy; the fucking tie clip is bigger than he is!!! Did you know Eric Drexler was only one inch tall, and you didn't fucking tell me?????

Bruce Sterling used to say that hacker activities will always fail, because hackers always rat each other out. Didn't work out like that, did it? Turning in your friends and co-conspirators isn't likely if you can't find out who and where they are. Humans do need friends, yes . . . and your truly best friend may be a pseudonym emanating from singapore . . . or from down the street, who knows? No matter: you can share your ideas and your emotions with each other as few humans dare to do face2face. The online is an intimate medium. And if you need to boast about your exploits—humans sometimes need to strut and crow -- your fifth pseudonym can mouth off to an entire planet about its spectacular, time-stamped, digitally-signed Deed.

There's safety in true independence. You can engage in a discourse with the best minds of the planet without ever needing to know who they "really" are. In fact, they are their ideas, more than they are a physical identity . . . so you can abstract your associations completely, have complete freedom of association at last. This is how a still un-upgraded version 1.0 species can triumphantly transcend race, gender, nation, credential, status. A stellar pseudonym might belong to a highschool student in Peoria. . . . or a professor at Princeton . . . and can the govt bust a pseudonym? If a handle could be linked to a body, would the govt dare bring charges, knowing that a public arrest and trial will motivate thousands of highschool students -- and professors -- to take the place of their martyr to freedom?

We, and the virtual underground, have won. The book is finished. We need only to publish it to announce the victory.

Anyway, the next three hours were a fucking disaster. Couldn't fit the boom mic into the terrarium. We just hung the lavaliere from one of his fake bonsai trees and he talked into that. Sandy ransacked the van and found some XCU macro lenses, the kind used for filming nature specials. We captured a firefly in a jar and used that for the indirect lighting. Fucking disaster left and right. The gist of it is, Drexler said in his squeaky voice that he felt he was the natural "guinea pig" when it came to human trials for his nanotech experiments. About three weeks ago he took a capsule that contained a couple of billion nanomechs that were supposed to remove fat from his muscles and convert it to compact muscle protein, sort of like an instant hunk pill. It worked fine (he was totally rip in three days), but the nanobugs didn't shut off. They kept compacting his muscle tissue, and he kept getting smaller and smaller, until eventually the other researchers had to put him in a glass dollhouse. He says they're working day and night for the cure.

Anyway, the whole thing's on the Avid. Scan it and tell me if it's worth editing, or do we just dump the fucker???

= =
Date: Sep 20, 2001
From: rusirius@vnli.com
To: stjude@well.com
Subject: we won, i guess

Listen, I don't know how the news is playing over in Europe, but while i've been holed-up indulging my psychotic-paranoid drug-induced imitation of a post-punk Jim Jones, "we" have apparently won the war. Check the internet! No . . . not cryptonet. I mean, the straight, out-in-the-open, formerly niceNet . . . Or turn on the tv. Try Sex Ed for Kids with Pee Wee Herman on NBC this afternoon at 2 pm. No shit, jude. This has been apparently going on for the last week and a half. Outrider called. There's several million naked and semi-naked people surging through the streets of Washington D.C. in a bachanalian orgy, many of them displaying previously verboten images on electronic-media-wearables. And Gore apparently told the media that there's no popular support for stopping it, and he and the Tipster are going to go light up a doobie and head down to catch the Dead, who are playing a free show at the Washington Monument. Christ, pathetic fucking boomers. I hear Phil Lesh can't even move his hands, what with the arthritis and all. Maybe he'll just creak his joints.

Anyway, I suppose this is something to celebrate . . . except I've seen
too much bad weirdness go down and everybody over at building b is
still acting like it's all still serious business. Christ, I walked
over there to see if anything was happening that would reflect this
sudden seachange in the body politic and the place was crawling with
lawyers, all gearing up to defend Scrappi in his copyright violation
case next week. Lawyers, accountants . . . nothing's changed . . .

Maybe I should split. But I'm just too paranoid to move. What if
there's something bogus about all of this? Listen. why don'tcha visit
America and let me know what's up . . .

email me . . . i'll be anxiously awaiting . . .
= =
Date: 23 Sep 2001
From: stjude@well.com
To: rusirius@vnli.com
Subject: It's happened!

Indeed. I'm in Cleveland where things are pretty ordinary -- as compared to the endless orgy in Washington DC. But the news is that people
are saying and thinking what they want, nanotech is ubiquitous and
everyone seems to be able to get whatever they want for next to nothing
. . . it's like the most absurd hippy daydream you ever had.

So listen . . . time to leave, guy! Word on the streets is that you're
being totally controlled by the corporate managers there. People tell
me that their email messages aren't getting through to you. You're
NOT in control. Connie is running the show and she's even more paranoid than you are.

Why don't you come out and join the dance? Will you, won't you, will
you, won't you . . . won't you join the dance?
= =
Date: 23 Sep 2001
From: spydergrrrl@vnli.com
To: stjude@well.com
Subject: try again

Jude, I'm sure that r.u. will be very hurt when he doesn't get return
email from you, and your last note certainly will not be passed on to
him. So why not send him a nice little reassuring note about how people are looking forward to the TV special, and how much you liked the

piece on him in Newsweek. Don't cross me, Jude. We have friends in
Cleveland . . . Why don't you come home. We miss your sly ways with
bridge.

I can write the enote for you if you like.

> Your friend always,
>   Mondo Connie

==

stjude's diary
Dec. 31, 2001

I figure I owed r.u. big time for pushing me out of the vanilli compound . . . considering what's
up in the country. In fact, the first world has been liberated. Liberated from want. Liberated from
repression. It's very nice, but those of us who got the guerrilla spirit are . . . well maybe we're already a bit bored. So we were talking one night about poor crazy r.u. and the vnli compound and
how they're the last paranoids on earth. And how my old partner in crime is a prisoner of his
own cult and his habits and all. So . . . what with nothing left to hack, we decided . . . let's do an
INTERVENTION!

So . . . it's 0600 hours when we hit the Mondo Vanilli enclave—right on time. Marin county's
knobby hills screen us from the gatehouse until the last 30 meters; then it's a doublelane
straightaway up to the steelmesh razorwired gates. The lights are all on, but the gates are full
open—jesus: slacker losers. Riding point we got a Jeep Cherokee in full battle rig, then me and
mine in the 1972 Valiant fourdoor, and the hovercraft covers our tail. I give the signal to pull up
and I revise the op. We chinese firedrill among the vehicles, and I pile into the hovercraft with the
hitwomen and the ninja anesthetist. We slide silently up to the gates. Little Nell lets go with the
baby flashbomb, and the guards wake up and come running out waving some gnarly-looking
sidearms. Nell hits 'em with the knockout smokebomb, and they go down like dominos. The
whole thing was almost noiseless, and the gate is ours. Nothing else moves in camp, dead silence
except for the spooky Marin nightnoises. Oh it's sweet. Simcere and I crawl out and look the casualties over.

They're kids! RU, you perverted swine. Three of 'em look like blonde angeleno runaways, and the
fourth is Asiamerican. None of 'em older than thirteen, I bet. Too bad, baby sisters. Nell steps up
and administers the coup-de-grace. She's stylin: her mirrorshades flash as she aims down along
her arm, hits easy and then swaggers over to the next crumpled crumpet. Nell's got her piece
chrome-plated, crazy bitch. She lights up some kind of foul tobacco thing, and strikes a pose
looking over the bodies (I guess that's what she's doing—impossible to tell with mirrorshades).

Sim and I drag 'em inside the gates, over behind the gatehouse. Lay 'em out side by side on the
tan California grass. In the spotlights their camo gear looks like jammies, and they're smiling. Angels. Got yr sugarplums for hours, babies, that's our Nell—love those ketamine darts.

Pile back into the hovercraft, take it up to only 10 inches. (Lower means quieter.) Slide down the funway past bunker c, me old home, another 30 meters to RU's bunker. It's dark. We don't have to break the door because it's not locked. I push it open all the way . . .

The room is dark but there's a single candle guttering on a long table next to a half-eaten lobster tail in sauce bernaise and a spilled bottle of scotch, and all these bags with powders and weird plant cuttings, syringes, hookahs, all kinds of crap spilling around, and it reeks like someone freshly dead . . .

He's alone, supine on a big platform in the middle of the room, like a corpse on a catafalque. He's not moving, but he's breathing—we can hear him breathe, and it sounds like we're just in time, indeed. We creep over . . . Fool's wearing . . . fur pajamas? Feels like it. Somehow I'm glad I can't see his face. Nell's in the bathroom setting the charge. When she's done, Sim throws in the bags and crap from the table and slams the door . . . Meanwhile the ninja slips a black silk hood over RU's head—damn, he doesn't even twitch—breaks an ampoule and dribbles it over the pro-trusion that is his nose, and we're off. We hump him out to the hovercraft, dump him onto the sideflaps and bind him there like a dead moose. Furry enough: he's wearing a mink jumpsuit with zippers all over it. Fucker's gained more weight: the hover's lopsided and drags the ground. Sim has to pump it up to 16 inches, and moments later we're out through the gates, down the road, around the hill. We all grab him and hump him onto the gurney on the floor of the Cherokee. The ninja hooks him up to the lifesupports. As I open the door to the front seat I see the treetops flash yellow: there's the explosion. That means the RU Sirius memorial medicine cabinet is now just scattered molecules. Exactly which molecules I don't want to know. I hop in and we rabbit back along Lucas Valley Road to the freeway while the hover and the Valiant split towards the coast.

Just as we hit the 101 onramp we see the helicopters coming over us— six of them in a close for-mation, heading toward the Mondo Vanilli Moonwalker Ranch. And yeah, just as we expected, they're not DEA or FBI: they're sporting the colors of that other branch of the government. Makes me shudder to look at them. If we'd been a quarter-hour later we'd have met them, and we'd have been theirs. They were gonna reel him in at last. And they'd have busted the whole MV camp if they found what everybody knew they'd find.

As we make it onto the freeway I breathe deep . . . Nobody EVER wants to tangle with those motherfuckers. CDC's hardball regardless. But the Centers for Disease Control TAC Squad. . . . Shit! If they decide you need "help" (their motto is FOR YOUR OWN GOOD) . . . you're truly SCREWED.

The lifesupps in the backseat area just keep on chugging over RU's mink-suited body. Still can't see his face, thank Goddess—because of all the tech going into it. His fur's all thrashed where they had to slash it to poke tubes in, all over him . . . so he just looks like an ICU-case teddybear. Asshole asshole asshole.

He's going to get well in spite of himself. He's going to become healthy over his own dead body, dumbass male figpucker. Never say StJude doesn't pay off her obligations . . . If it takes a WHOLE BODY transplant, we're going to bring him around. We've got the technology, and with these guys medical science is not an oxymoron. When we finish with him, he'll be as good as new.

No, actually that won't do . . . when you're dealing with RU Sirius, the only good outcome is BETTER than new. LOTS better. Filthy fucking male pigdog.

We need him.

R. U.'s Diary
Going into ChatMode With Remakable (Wo)Men
Jan. 2002

Uh . . . As we were saying, remember(?) back on pg. 4, back at the beginning of this book . . . "Since this revolution has no time to look back, we've scraped this together. We've picked what we can from the debris we've collected. This is as close to *Ten Days that Shook the World* as it's gonna get."

Indeed. Things got a little crazy for us in those later years. I suppose I plumb forgot to keep much of a diary. Got hella paranoid one day 'round Christmas and dumped all of my email exchanges after the year 1996 too. Thought Jude would piece it together, but heck, when she got back from visiting with Justpat in Cleveland—where she got caught up in the outbreak of the pink goo—she claimed that her data'd gotten more corrupted 'n an immigration agent in San Diego and—for instance, my long email exchange with her about the final victory, wherein we arrived at the understanding that the big icon of the two of us that now appears on all user's screens when they log on to NanoNet isn't REALLY a tribute, it's a JOKE. Like in highschool, when they elect the class clown for President, they're making fun. But (in singsong voice) making fun is a VERY GOOD THING, and pay no attention to that data construct behind the gif file and there's no place like home.planet.com. Anyway, the whole exchange looked more or less like this: suleikfi 93jfl, slll slll slll slll slll slll slll slll. And so forth.

And stjude'd gotten all the backups soaked in pink pheremones, manymany boyhoods back. And all the potato-fed pregnant midwestern girls are drifting out to sea, fed, sheltered, watched over by the nanobots of loving grace so what me worry?

No, I refuse to worry. Because it's all here, dear reader. The great decrypting software is in your head. And if we've blathered, boasted and bumbled in Fear and Loathing down so-called data highway 1010101, if our ReBootheels went a-wandering far past the twisted reach of ascii sorrow, if we lost our heads when they weren't attached and if in fact we're torturing you with bullshit even NOW, as we speak, don't judge us too harshly. We were, like you, beginners, newbies, arrivistas on the planet of the exploded post-novel cum advice-book on how to mutate and take over the world, wandering the unmapped territories without basic supplies, in search of the mutants, hoping against hope to go into ChatMode with remakeable (wo)men and to return to you, our dear $24.00(?) paying reader, with ALL of the answers, only to realize, dear [your name here], that the remakable (wo)man we came out to meet is YOU!

You know the plot. You know the characters. You know the terrain a little bit better, day by day. There are networks to construct, cd roms to create, movies to make, sequels, prequels, parties, and proposals. Revolutions. Hey, YOU. Mutate & Take Over the World!

Let's go into ChatMode:
rusirius@well.com or rusirius1@aol.com or R. U. Sirius c/o Ballantine Books, 201 E. 50th St., New York, NY 10022
stjude@well.com or StJude@aol.com or St. Jude c/o Ballantine Books, 201 E. 50th St., New York NY 10022

In the beginning was the word. Too many words perhaps. The Gutenberg past, its long, slow Faulknerian days of mint juleps, mosquitos, primal passions and armed poetics nipped at us though we were newbieborne to a whirl long deconstructed and impatiently awaiting a comprehensible user's manual. Ah well. Other horrible workers will follow. "Enough then of this long and pretentious wind," she whispers. "Blow it off. Leave this to thine editors, surely they will cut with blue pen and furrowed brow. So log off. Leave behind that ghostworld where the disembodied cacophony of reason's last speedfreek natterings call you away from this paradisical moment, and O that awful deepdown torrent O and the sea the sea crimson sometimes like fire and the glorious sunsets and the figure in the Alameda gardens yes and all the queer little houses and pink and blue and yellow houses and the rosegardens and the jessamine and the geraniums and the cactuses and Gibraltar as a girl where I was flower of the mountain yes when I put the rose in my hair yes like the Andalusian girls used or shall I wear a red yes and how he kissed me under the Moorish wall and I thought well as well him as another and then I asked him with my eyes to ask again yes and then he asked me would I yes to say yes my mountain flower and first I put my arms around him yes and drew him down to me so he could feel my breasts all perfume yes and his heart was going like mad and yes I said yes I will Yes.

But just one second. I must do but one more thing. I must . . . Press Control-E to Exit This Program.

Are You Sure You Want to Exit This Program? Press Control-E to Exit This Program. Are You Sure You Want to Exit This Program? Press Control-E to Exit This Program. Are You Sure You Want to Exit This Program? Press Control-E to Exit This Program. Are You Sure You Want to Exit This Program? Press Control-E to Exit This Program. Are You Sure You Want to Exit This Program? Press Control-E to Exit This Program. Are You Sure You Want to Exit This Program? Press Control-E to Exit This Program. Are You Sure You Want to Exit This Program? Press Control-E to Exit This Program. Are You Sure You Want to Exit This Program? Press Control-E to Exit This Program. Are You Sure You Want to Exit This Program? Press Control-E to Exit This Program. Are You Sure You Want to Exit This Program? Press Control-E to Exit This Program. Are You Sure You Want to Exit This Program? Press Control-E to Exit This Program. Are You Sure You Want to Exit This Program? Press Control-E to Exit This Program. Are You Sure You Want to Exit This Program? Press Control-E to Exit This Program. Are You Sure You Want to Exit This Program? Press Control-E to Exit This Program. Are You Sure You Want to Exit This Program? Press Control-E to Exit This Program. Are You Sure You

Want to Exit This Program? Press Control-E to Exit This Program. Are You Sure You Want to Exit This Program? Press Control-E to Exit This Program. Are You Sure You Want to Exit This Program? Press Control-E to Exit This Program. Are You Sure You Want to Exit This Program? Press Control-E to Exit This Program. Are You Sure You Want to Exit This Program? Press Control-E to Exit This Program. Are You Sure You Want to Exit This Program? Press Control-E to Exit This Program. Are You Sure You Want to Exit This Program? Press Control-E to Exit This Program. Are You Sure You Want to Exit This Program? Press Control-E to Exit This Program. Are You Sure You Want to Exit This Program? Press Control-E to Exit This Program. Are You Sure You Want to Exit This Program? Press Control-E to Exit This Program. Are You Sure You Want to Exit This Program?

David Fremont

PART THREE

KEY
LIME
TIME

SEGMENT FOUR:
AFTERTHOUGHT, WORLD ENDS

IN WHICH WE CEDE TO THE HUMOROUS DEFLATION, OR WHEN EVEN DADA FAILS, SMILE SADLY AND CLAIM TO BE PART OF THE PATHETIC ART MOVEMENT

3 Mar 2002
Brattleboro VT (UPS)

Small Explosion in Brattleboro

A small explosion in the Mrs. Sarah Fields Dessert Research Facility rattled windows in its immediate area yesterday, alarming residents but causing no damage. General Fields spokesperson Mary Albet announced today that the 3:14 PM blast was related to an innovative food manufacturing process still in its testing phase, details of which were blanketed by non-disclosure. Ms. Albet expressed GF's sincerest apologies to town residents for the inconvenience. She emphasized that the facility's containment vessel appears to be intact.

17 Mar 2002
NY Times Online (Reuter)

Green Skies Over Greenland?

In what appears to be a St. Patrick's Day spoof, two airmen based at Thule, Greenland, reported sighting a high-altitude "bright Kelly green" cloud formation over the north Atlantic in a routine training flight early this morning. Pilot Gerald Stope and his co-pilot Sandra Gore spotted

18 Mar 2002
The Daily Planet

Green Rain Falls on Georgia Islands
"Alien Test Fallout," Noted Scientist Explains

18 March 2002
The Daily Pirate [an online Underground daily]:
The 5th Column:
Takes Another Corporate Leak

Somebody calling himself Simple Simon just tipped the 5th Columnist to what may be the leak of the decade. Simon says he's working info-security for General Sarah Fields, and managed to intercept a top-secret legal dept memo which dealt with a Mrs. Sarah Fields facility in Vermont—the lab that's developing top-secret nano-manufacture techniques for desserts. The memo stated that "severe legal consequences" might follow a March 12 incident, when something went critical [hah?] and blew out a couple of ventilators, breaching containment, and spewing SOMETHING into the atmosphere. Two days of rummaging through top-secret corporate data got Simon what the something was: just "super-finely-divided particles of pie filling in an activated self-replicating form." Company lawyers are sweating they may have to pay major damages if air currents deploy the shit. And to add insult to injury, Simon says, the flavor was Key Lime. Gaak: would you darkside lawyers out there call that a fruit tort?

StJude's Diary
May 20, 2002:

The moon is bright enough to bring up the yellow phosphorescent sparks in the waves of this green world. Out all the windows we see nothing but green on all sides. No Jersey cliffs, no Atlantic. The smell is amazing, if I allow myself to notice it. The green goo has reached 6 or 7 stories below us here in the Empire State Building—and the people holed up in the rightmost World Trade Center tower are getting Rapture of the Green: they wanna jump. They say. Since the freak storm wiped out the survivalists on that nameless high Rocky, the only moodlightener we got here is chatting shortwave with the guys in the WTC. But they're boring as hell—gummint workers. Even the Pres is boring. Let 'em eat pie.

The Extropians down the hall are still partying. I'm glad THEY'RE doomed, at least. Goddam nanotechies even got their wish for an End of The World Party—and without time travel, too. Welcome to your future, punks. They get in my face, I say: O, go freeze your head. Heh heh heh heh.

The rise of the self-replicating green goo is visibly accelerating. I figure we have at most two days before this outpost—which I must consider to be the last holdout of our species, all other holdouts considered—will be overwhelmed at last, and we'll sink under the all-obliterating waves of well-salted Key Lime pie.

So, as we're waiting we're sitting around on the beige exec-suite wall-to-wall, on the highest habitable floor, me and my remaining co-conspirators, Bart and Eric and Tresca and Efrem . . . and we're going through some old clippings and scrapbooks and diskettes from the early days, back in the mid-nineties, when the future seemed likely to arrive, at least . . .

more than that—the future seemed to be teasing us, rubbing against us, frotting us irresistibly . . . The future blew into our ears and whispered to us we could do everything . . . we could map the primate wired-in stuff and REWIRE it—we could mutate ourselves smarter and kinder. We could mutate . . . and solve all our problems, personal and scientific. We could

No more. Our future is here.

Oh, Trudy, how I love you. You are so beautiful as you weep; the tears flow over your sweet cheeks as you tell us again how brilliant the MUTATE manuscript is, how tragic that it will never now see print. This is true. This book is a love letter to imagination and hope.

The green moonlight streams around us. Ken looks out over the green sea. It's been a couple of days since I slept, and I think I am reaching a crossover point. That which I imagine simply comes to be. We must keep the vigil here. Our world here is ending in a sweet sticky singularity, and that vigil is worth keeping. On the other hand . . .

I can stay awake no longer. I will sleep now. This will end.

ABOUT OUR CONTRIBUTORS

Aldo Alvarez received a master of fine arts in creative writing from Columbia University and currently pursues a doctorate in English at Binghamton University. His short fiction has been nominated for the Pushcart Prize and published in *The NRG Anthology*, *Psychotrain/Brownbag Press*, *ARK/Angel*, *Colume*, and *Christopher Street*.

Wagner James Au (wjamesau@well.com) has written in praise of gratuitous sex for *Penthouse Forum*, and in praise of gratuitous violence for *Harper's Magazine*.

Thomas Bell is a psychologist in private practice in Nashville. He is married and has two children. Under the pseudonym of Bada Shanren he is, like his namesake, sometimes crazy or sometimes pretends to be crazy. He is also a poet. In the past he has been a librarian and an editor. Tomorrow he will be five years old.

Ross Bender teaches a course in Comparative Hells on the IndraNet.

bOING bOING: Mark Frauenfelder (mark@well.com) became addicted to herbal sleeping pills after moving to an apartment ½ block away from the Viper Room and the Whisky A Go Go. When not tossing and turning in bed, he's an editor at *Wired* and *bOING bOING*. His book, *The Happy Mutant Handbook*, was published by Riverhead/Putnam-Berkley in November 1995. **Carla Sinclair** is master slave to *bOING bOING*. When she can sneak away from bOING's lair she freelances for *Wired* magazine and writes stuff like *Net Chick* (Holt) and *The Happy Mutant Handbook* (Riverhead).

Stephanie Brail is a writer who lives in Los Angeles with her significant other and cat. She cofounded a computer consulting business, Digital Amazon, designed to empower women through technology. When not Internet surfing and playing with various operating systems (including UNIX and both Mac and Windows), Stephanie creates FIMO jewelry and hangs out at the beach. She is perpetually writing her first novel.

Tiffany Lee Brown is the assistant editor of the *FringeWare Review* and resources editor for *Northwest Gardens*. She lives, writes, and plays music in PDX, Oregon, where her published ascii pops up under the moniker "Dyna Girl." She's also that cool babe on the cover of RU and Jude's *other* book. Heh.

Craig Brozefsky is a product of American White Trash culture whose sole project is fitting his life story into the forty-word limit of this complimentary advertising spot and conversation piece. He has not had much luck. email: nesta@mcs.net. "I regret that I have but six orifices to give you" —Nesta Stubbs

Patrick DiJusto is an adorable, anal, Aries, articulate, bearded, capricious, caustic, concupiscent, creative, cuddly, discerning, encyclopedic, honest, intelligent, Italian, kissable, maladroit, open-handed, petulant, right-brained, sentimental, sweet, sensitive, thoughtful, underemployed, un-married thirty-one-year-old writer/programmer from New York.

Scrappi DüChamp is a multipurpose human art factory and media personality. He writes and performs much of the music for MV inc. (formerly Mondo Vanilli), and coengineered and copro-duced the album *IOU Babe*. His musical productions have appeared on PBS television and NPR ra-dio. He has a degree in fine arts from the San Francisco Art Institute and has been exhibiting and publishing his painting and illustrative work since 1983. Scrappi has played a variety of instru-ments and lent his compositional support on numerous record albums and soundtracks, most re-cently the debut album for Dingle on SST Records.

Evan Gourvitz (Evan Godless) has been, at various times, a political science graduate student, a radical activist, an assistant at Ballantine Books, a Harvard Divinity School dropout, a Web devel-oper, and a member of Mondo Vanilli's (currently MV inc.) entourage. He is currently studying law.

Carmen Hermosillo de la Vega is a fourth-generation Latin American anarchist who holds de-grees in creative art and music history. A member of the editorial board of *FringeWare Review*, she is also one of the thirty-six immortal poison pens of cyberspace. Ms. Hermosillo asks that her work in this book be considered a memorial to her friend Tom Mandel. *Et lux perpetua luceat eis.*

Andrew Hultkrans is a writer and self-admitted dilettante whose hemming and hawing about media, advertising, pop culture, and the occasional lunatic has appeared in *ARTFORUM Interna-tional, MONDO 2000, FringeWare Review, IO,* and *bOING bOING's Happy Mutant Handbook.* He does his loose living in San Francisco.

Jamie Lawrence, SWM, working to make himself redundant in the workforce, ISO hot, aggres-sive, genius S?F. Must hate cats, jogging, and planning for a better future. Be into yourself, clothes, and sullenly chic Sartre geeks.

Jon Lebkowsky is a writer, editor, and publisher *(FringeWare Review, Unshaved Truths)* from Austin, Texas. He's also CEO for FringeWare, Inc., and has a day job as gonzo technologist. He may be the first cyberpunk to become a grandfather.

Elise Matthesen? Mechanical ears; body wrapped in silk, leather, linen, metal. Gender interrog-ative. Eats words, root, and branch. Rune-bearer, beloved of Freya and of three mortals. Lifelong midwest prairie priestess; the lightning that instructs, the rain that blesses.

Tim May was trained as a physicist and worked for twelve years at Intel. He discovered that al-pha particles and cosmic rays were the main cause of errors in memory chips, also known as "bit rot." He retired to the beaches of Santa Cruz and became interested in cryptography and anonymous communications systems. He helped to found the Cypherpunks group in 1992 and has been active in the public debate over Clipper and other government restrictions on crypto.

Brock N. Meeks is the Washington Bureau Chief for *Interactive Week*, a newsmagazine covering the digital media industry. He also is the editor/publisher of CyberWire Dispatch, a Net-based news service. In addition, he is a contributing writer for *Wired* magazine and writes the Muckraker column for *HotWired*.

Anders Mikkelsen will say nothing, as he refuses to lend his distinguished name, brilliant mind, and biting wit to this sordid enterprise of self-promotion. His fine education was not completed so he could sell out for millions like a high-class whore. *Alles Klar*.

Steve O'Keefe is the former editorial director for Loompanics Unlimited. He now works in the pork products industry, helping clog the arterials of the Information Superhighway with a steady stream of Spam.

scribe.waterfish@sfnet.com is the online identity of **Gregory J. Pleshaw**, chairman of the International Conspiracy to Combat Conventional Wisdom. Pleshaw, age twenty-five, is currently living somewhere between the deserts of New Mexico and the rain forests of Humboldt County, hard at work on his first novel. He has contributed to *Wired*, *Nucity*, and the *Daily Lobo*. He's single and regularly enjoys double espresso on ice.

Bob Soloman is an independent video designer/director in New York City specializing in computer graphics and animation.

Alan Sondheim moderates Fiction-of-Philosophy and Cybermind out of jefferson.village. virginia.edu. He is editing *Cybermind: Being On-Line* for Lusitania, and his Internet Text is available on the Web. His *Disorders of the Real* is available from Station Hill, and his films are distributed through Canyon Cinema (San Francisco). He teaches at Film/Video Arts and the New School for Social Research, both in New York.

Simone Third Arm, performance director, vocalist for MV inc (formerly Mondo Vanilli), and vocalist for Exterminating Angel is widely known in the San Francisco Bay Area as a performance artist. She's performed with Don Novello (i.e. Father Guido Sarducci) and Timothy Leary. She dances with Harupin-Ha, the S.F.-based Japanese Butoh troupe. She's also a skilled trapeze artist and contortionist. She's managed two successful boundary-breaking theaters, Submit Theater and Hangar 18. Her comic book, *Colonic Comics*, is available through Last Gasp. She is the cyberpiss goddess of annihilating feces.

In the 1980s **Nolan Void** was often seen frequenting the after-hours clubs of New York—often in the company of Coy Luvdahl and the fabulous Pillowcase Girl. Since 1990 he has been wandering the far reaches of cyberspace, sometimes in the company of his beloved

Dr. Arachidi, but always with a bottle of Absynthe at hand. He doesn't really work, but rather waits . . .

rosie x is a writer, video maker, radio producer, and electronic publisher. She started *geekgirl*, the world's first cyberfeminist 'zine in digital and hard copy format, in 1994. *geekgirl* is a thoroughly wicked read and its success must be attributed to the team, robj and lisa pears. she lives with geekboy robj and her cat, thumper, in sydney, australia. http://www.next.com.au/spyfood/ geekgirl spyfood@next.com.au

This book is sarcastic towards several public friends, but the authors would like to point out that we have also made assholes of *our selves*, so no apologies. *We do* however wish to express love and respect for the very gracious Dr. Timothy Leary.

Additionally: The information regarding the Phil Zimmerman Defense Fund on page 26 is true. We encourage your contribution.

ABOUT THE AUTHORS

R. U. Sirius is cofounder and former editor-in-chief of the legendary cyberculture magazine *Mondo 2000*. He was coeditor of *MONDO 2000: A User's Guide to the New Edge* and cowriter of *Cyberpunk Handbook: The Real Cyberpunk Fakebook*. He is also a contributing writer with *Wired*, an associate editor with *bOING bOING* magazine, and a regular columnist for *Artforum International* and *Japan Esquire*. His band, MV inc. (formerly Mondo Vanilli) has been confusing record labels for several years. He appears as himself in the films *Virtual Love* and *Twists of the Wire*, and introduced the Australian television special *Fear and Loathing on the Information Highway*. He frequently lectures and comments in the media on subjects ranging from cyberspace to sexuality.

St. Jude, a culture-hacker, polygamist, and anarcho-terrorist, was a member of the founding gang and a senior editor for the legendary cyberculture magazine *Mondo 2000*. She was a contributing writer/editor for *MONDO 2000: A User's Guide to the New Edge* and cowriter of *Cyberpunk Handbook: The Real Cyberpunk Fakebook*. She is a contributing writer for *Wired* magazine. She's been a lifelong troublemaker and UNIX programmer, the first identified female hacker (in Steven Levy's seminal book *Hackers*), and the inventor of the term "cypherpunk." She appeared as herself in the Australian television special *Fear and Loathing on the Information Highway*, as a smartdrugs SM witch in *Ruby Wax's Spiritual Quest* for the BBC, and was interviewed in rosie x's Australian radio series on women on the Net. She writes The Fifth Column for *The Net* magazine, and comments to the media whenever they'll listen. She's working on her next book, *Girls Need Modems*.